AWASH IN COLOR:

Homer, Sargent, and the Great American Watercolor

AWASH IN COLOR:

Homer, Sargent, and the Great American Watercolor

By SUE WELSH REED *and* CAROL TROYEN

With contributions by ROY PERKINSON *and* ANNETTE MANICK

Museum of Fine Arts, Boston

in association with

Bulfinch Press · Little, Brown and Company

Boston · Toronto · London

This exhibition was organized by the Museum of Fine Arts, Boston, and is made possible by a generous grant from *The Boston Globe.*

This catalogue was supported in part by grants from the Andrew W. Mellon Foundation Publication Fund and from the National Endowment for the Arts, a Federal agency.

Copyright © 1993 by the Museum of Fine Arts, Boston, Massachusetts

Library of Congress Catalogue card No. 92-063335
ISBN 0-87846-367-4 (paper)
ISBN 0-8212-2020-9 (cloth)

Edited by Cynthia M. Purvis
Designed by Carl Zahn
Typeset in Monotype Bell (semibold) by Carl Zahn and Acme Printing Co.
Printed in U.S.A. by Acme Printing Co. Wilmington, Massachusetts
Bound by Acme Bookbinding Co., Charlestown, Massachusetts

Cover and jacket:
Front: Winslow Homer (1836-1910), *The Blue Boat*, 1892 (detail)
Back: Winslow Homer, *Sponge Diver*, 1898 (detail)
Frontispiece:
John Singer Sargent (1856-1925) *Simplon Pass: The Lesson*, 1911 (detail)

All color photographs by the Department of Photographic Services, Museum of Fine Arts, Boston, except fig. 12, page xxxiv, courtesy of the Metropolitan Museum of Art, New York.

First Edition

Bulfinch Press is an imprint and trademark of Little, Brown and Company (Inc.)
Published simultaneously in Canada by Little, Brown & Company (Canada) Limited

Exhibition dates:
Museum of Fine Arts, Boston
April 28 – August 15, 1993

CONTENTS

FOREWORD

IN 1899, the Museum of Fine Arts bought four watercolors by Winslow Homer, including the spectacular *Leaping Trout* (cat. 56). These were the first of forty-five watercolors by Homer to come to the Museum, and the first works in the medium to be purchased for the collection. Thirteen years later the Museum purchased a group of forty-five watercolors by John Singer Sargent. These groups, by the greatest American masters of the medium, form the basis of an outstanding, comprehensive collection of American watercolors that has grown steadily over the years. Among our most recent acquisitions of watercolors is a group of superb modernist paintings, including the Stuart Davis and the Jacob Lawrence in this exhibition, presented by Mr. and Mrs. William H. Lane in 1990, and *Yosemite Falls* by William Zorach, donated by Claire and Richard Morse in 1992. Their gifts, as well as the contributions of such distinguished benefactors of the past as Maxim Karolik, John Taylor Spaulding, Denman Waldo Ross, and William Sturgis Bigelow (complemented by astute purchases by the Museum's staff), have built for this institution a collection of American watercolors that is unsurpassed in its range and quality. Yet, owing to the fragility of these works and their extreme sensitivity to light, even the greatest masterpieces among them are rarely seen by the public. Thus it is an especially great pleasure to present "Awash in Color: Homer, Sargent, and the Great American Watercolor," drawn entirely from the Museum's outstanding collection.

Bostonians seem to have always had a special affection for watercolor, and both the collections and the exhibition programs of this institution reflect their continuing enthusiasm for the medium. We are fortunate to possess masterworks by such artists of international reputation as Winslow Homer, John Singer Sargent, and Edward Hopper, and to house preeminent collections of watercolors by the American Pre-Raphaelite painters, by the American Impressionists (among them Childe Hassam and Maurice Prendergast), and by such modern masters as Charles Demuth, Charles Burchfield, and John Marin. In the past twenty years, we have dedicated exhibitions to Winslow Homer's works on paper (1977), drawings and watercolors presented to the Museum of Fine Arts by Maxim Karolik (1979), and Boston watercolor painters of the 1970s (1976). In addition, our collections have been a rich resource for several recent exhibitions organized elsewhere celebrating American masters of the medium. However, this is the first comprehensive exhibition of the treasures of this collection; it both demonstrates our strengths and constitutes a historical survey of the medium in America. The accompanying book is the first publication since our 1949 checklist to document these important works of art.

The exhibition was organized by Sue Welsh Reed of the Department of Prints, Drawings, and Photographs and by Carol Troyen of the Department of Paintings. It is part of a series of exhibitions presented at the Museum in recent years in celebration of the permanent collection, and the collaboration among members of several curatorial departments here as in the previous shows has resulted in an illuminating diversity of points of view. This project has benefited greatly from the advice of Clifford S. Ackley, Curator of Prints, Drawings, and Photographs, and Theodore E. Stebbins, Jr., John

Moors Cabot Curator of American Paintings. We owe special thanks to Carl Zahn and Cynthia Purvis for designing and shaping the catalogue for this exhibition, which will serve as a scholarly record of our superb collection for many years to come. This book was supported in part by grants from The Andrew W. Mellon Foundation Publication Fund and from the National Endowment for the Arts, for which we are most grateful. And finally, the timely and generous support of *The Boston Globe* has enabled us to share with a wide audience one of the greatest treasures of the Museum of Fine Arts, its collection of American watercolors.

ALAN SHESTACK, *Director*
Museum of Fine Arts, Boston

INTRODUCTION

"This is the age of water-colour." So began the lead article of *International Studio*'s September 1921 issue, in response to a superb exhibition of American watercolors presented at the Art Institute of Chicago that fall. The same might be said of our own era, for since 1987, no fewer than five institutions with major collections of American watercolors – the Worcester Art Museum (1987), the Wadsworth Atheneum (1988), the Yale University Art Gallery (1990), the Metropolitan Museum of Art (1991), and now the Museum of Fine Arts – have organized exhibitions and produced scholarly commentaries on their holdings. Several other exhibitions have focused on a master's or a school's watercolor production: *Winslow Homer Watercolors* by Helen A. Cooper (Yale University Art Gallery, 1986) was perhaps the most spectacular of these; exhibitions dedicated to the work of Maurice Prendergast, John La Farge, John Singer Sargent, and the American Pre-Raphaelites, among others, also have had major sections devoted to watercolor.

The scholarly attention paid to watercolor in recent years has also been notable. In 1977, Theodore E. Stebbins, Jr., published *American Master Drawings and Watercolors*, a comprehensive volume that aimed "to survey the whole field of American drawings and watercolors from the late sixteenth century depictions of Indian life by John White and Jacques Le Moyne to the rich and eclectic products of our own day" (p. xi). It remains the standard work in the field, and has sparked a number of thoughtful dissertations. Of these, Kathleen Adair Foster's "Makers of the American Watercolor Movement 1860-1890" (Yale University, 1982) is a particularly rich resource, providing a thorough history of the medium in the second half of the nineteenth century as well as insightful interpretations of the work of the major painters, including John La Farge, Winslow Homer, and Thomas Eakins. Several institutions – among them the Museum of Art, Carnegie Institute; the Corcoran Gallery of Art; and the Brooklyn Museum – have produced catalogues of their watercolor collections – a documentary effort usually reserved for oils. Finally, important attention has been paid to watercolor technique, most significantly the exhibition catalogue *Wash and Gouache: A Study of the Development of the Materials of Watercolor* (Fogg Art Museum, 1977) by Marjorie Cohn. Cohn's analysis of the tools, materials, and methods of watercolor, addressed to the historian and connoisseur, contains many illuminating examples drawn from Harvard's rich collections. Equally informative is "Observations on the Watercolor Techniques of Homer and Sargent" by Judith C. Walsh, in *American Traditions in Watercolor: The Worcester Art Museum Collection* (1987).

It wasn't always so. Although the first works of art in the western tradition to be produced in this country were watercolors – Jacques Le Moyne's views of Florida and the Carolinas, produced during an expedition of 1564 – until the middle of the nineteenth century, watercolor was more a medium for outsiders than for the arts establishment. Itinerant painters such as Henry Walton and the elusive J.H. Davis, topographers like William Guy Wall and Edwin Whitefield, and John James Audubon and other naturalists used the medium with great skill. Profiting from its portability, its ability to render atmosphere and simulate textural effects, and its suitability for recording landscape, these artists generally used watercolor in preparation for commercial projects – handsome sets of prints illustrating scenic views of the North American landscape, or its fauna.

Books providing technical instruction in watercolor were readily available in America from the early nineteenth century. The first manual published in this country to include information about painting in watercolor was *Elements of the Graphic Arts* (1802) by the Scottish-born landscape painter Archibald Robertson; it was followed by *The Art of Colouring and Painting Landscapes in Watercolor* (Baltimore, 1815) by Fielding Lucas, Jr. At mid-century the American Art-Union published "The Art of Landscape Painting in Water Color" in its *Bulletin* of 1851. This series of articles advised the Art-Union's vast subscribership on the use of the medium, and reinforced Lucas's view of the appropriateness of watercolor for landscape painting. John Ruskin's *Elements of Drawing* (London, 1857) enjoyed wide circulation in America; many young artists followed his prescriptions religiously and produced precisely rendered drawings and watercolors based on the instruction in his book. Inspired by Ruskin's advocacy of the watercolor medium, several of his American followers, including John William Hill, established the first professional watercolor society in America.

The Society for the Promotion of Painting in Water Colors was formed in New York in 1850 to elevate the status of watercolor and to give it greater prominence. The Society organized only one exhibition before disbanding in 1855, to be succeeded by the equally short-lived New York Water Color Society. But by the next decade, interest in watercolor had increased, and in 1866, a more permanent institution was founded: the American Society of Painters in Water Colors (later the American Watercolor Society). In its first decades, the Society organized exhibitions that competed in size and importance with the annual shows of oil paintings held at the National Academy of Design and other arts institutions. The Society included among its members such masters as William Trost Richards, Jasper Cropsey, Winslow Homer, and John La Farge. The activity of these watercolorists attracted the attention of major patrons of American art: Thomas B. Clarke, William T. Evans, and Charles Lang Freer all collected watercolors.

Scholarly consideration of the American watercolor lagged behind public appreciation of the medium. There was no equivalent for watercolor painters to the artists' profiles found in Henry T. Tuckerman's *Book of the Artists* (1867) until 1921, when A.E. Gallatin's *American Water-Colourists* appeared. That book codified the pantheon of American watercolorists – Homer, Sargent, La Farge – and anointed their successors – Demuth, Marin, Burchfield – with brief, perceptive discussions of each master's style. The 1920s and '30s witnessed a dramatic increase in the number of exhibitions organized by American museums featuring watercolors. This activity culminated in two comprehensive surveys of American watercolor. Sherman Lee's 1941 doctoral dissertation, "A Critical Survey of American Watercolor Painting" (Western Reserve University) was the first scholarly investigation of the field. The following year, the Whitney Museum of American Art organized "A History of American Watercolor Painting" with a thoughtful catalogue introduction by Alan Burroughs. While saluting the late nineteenth-century masters of watercolor, the exhibition began with a survey of earlier developments in the medium; in so doing, it encompassed the amateur, the academic, and the avant-garde. Not until the Museum of Fine Arts circulated exhibitions of watercolors from the Karolik Collection in the 1970s was such an inclusive, democratic understanding of the medium again promoted. In 1966, the centennial of the American Watercolor Society was celebrated with an exhibition at the Metropolitan Museum, which coincided with the publication of Albert Ten Eyck Gardner's *History of Water Color Painting in America*. The exhibition reflected the society's membership; the book's brief text recapitulated and brought up to the present the history outlined in Burroughs's essay.

It is fitting that another investigation of the medium be organized in Boston, a famously watercolor-minded city, for the Museum of Fine Arts possesses the preeminent collection of American watercolors in the country. It is rich in works by both the great masters of the medium – Homer and Sargent, La Farge and Prendergast, Marin and Demuth, Burchfield and Hopper – and by such fascinating, if obscure, practitioners as Walter Paris and Mary Chapin, who are virtually unrepresented elsewhere. (It is regrettable that, while the Museum possesses fine examples by individual contemporary watercolorists of note – Philip Pearlstein, Richard Yarde, Robert Cumming – its holdings in the field of recent watercolor are limited. Therefore we have decided, however reluctantly, to end this exhibition with painters who came to prominence during World War II, with the hope that the Museum of Fine Arts will someday be able to organize from its own holdings an equally rich survey of American watercolors from the second half of the twentieth century.)

The Museum of Fine Arts was one of the first institutions to publish its watercolor collection, in 1949 producing a *Catalogue of Paintings and Drawings in Water Color* that included the basic data for nearly 700 watercolors (American and European) and illustrated every one. In 1962 the Museum published *The M. & M. Karolik Collection of American Water Colors & Drawings, 1800-1875;* this was the first scholarly catalogue in the field, providing biographies of some 350 artists and cataloging data (often with incisive discussions of individual objects) for more than 1400 drawings and watercolors. In keeping with the respect given to little-known artists in the Karolik catalogue, this book treats the William Hardings and the Winslow Homers with equal concern: each work received a careful technical examination as well as art-historical analysis, the results of which are published in the catalogue entries.

The proliferation of general surveys of American watercolors in recent exhibition catalogues (of these, Donelson Hoopes's essay, "The Emergence of an American Medium" in the Worcester Art Museum's catalogue, is perhaps the most serviceable short history readily available) and in the commercial press (among them, Christopher Finch's *American Watercolors*) obviated the inclusion of yet another complete history of the medium here. Rather, we have chosen to focus on less frequently studied aspects of watercolor's history in America. The role of the medium in advancing the cause of American modernism, and the interest of Bostonians in amassing an extraordinary collection of American watercolors, are detailed in the essays that follow.

ACKNOWLEDGMENTS

THIS EXHIBITION, drawn entirely from the collection of the Department of Prints, Drawings, and Photographs, is one in a series of shows organized in recent years to celebrate the permanent collections of the Museum of Fine Arts. For his inauguration of such a program, and for his continuing enthusiasm and encouragement of this project, we are especially grateful to director Alan Shestack. Equally important in bringing this exhibition to fruition has been the support of *The Boston Globe*, whose generous grant has enabled us to mount this show, and in so doing has underwritten the necessary conservation treatment and reframing of many of the works in the exhibition – a contribution whose benefits will be appreciated long after the exhibition has closed. We are also grateful to the National Endowment for the Arts for its grant in support of this book.

From the beginning, the idea of featuring the Museum's unsurpassed collection of American watercolors in a special exhibition received the enthusiastic endorsement of our respective department heads. Clifford S. Ackley, Curator of Prints, Drawings, and Photographs, spent many hours discussing with us the selection of works in the exhibition and patiently reviewing the entire text of this catalogue; Theodore E. Stebbins, Jr., John Moors Cabot Curator of American Paintings, was especially helpful as we refined the list of works to be exhibited, and made instructive comments on portions of the manuscript as well. Troy Moss's editorial advice during the formative stages of the project was invaluable, and we greatly appreciate her time and thoughtful guidance. Others who have read and discussed sections of the catalogue with us include Avis Berman; Priscilla Diamond; Trevor J. Fairbrother, Robert L. Beal, Enid L. and Bruce A. Beal Curator of Contemporary Art; Erica Hirshler, Stephanie Stepanek, and Deborah Weisgall; for their many helpful observations we are most grateful.

Our deep gratitude goes to our closest colleagues in this project, conservators Roy Perkinson and Annette Manick, who examined every watercolor in the show with us, patiently educating us about the subtleties of watercolor materials and methods. Many of their ideas about styles and techniques have been incorporated here. Their careful attention to the condition of each watercolor in the show and Gail English's sensitivity in matters of matting and framing has ensured that the objects look their best.

We are especially indebted to the research assistant for this project, Amy Werbel, who shouldered many diverse tasks with enthusiasm and good humor. Our catalogue has benefitted greatly from her research skills, and we are pleased that she was able to contribute several entries to the catalogue. Special thanks are due to Regina Rudser of the Department of Paintings, who cheerfully typed large portions of the manuscript. We also appreciate the support of our colleagues who shouldered an increased portion of day-to-day curatorial responsibilities while we were away from our desks preparing the catalogue: in the Department of Prints, Drawings, and Photographs, John Chvostal, Anne Havinga, Shelley Langdale, and Barbara Shapiro; in the Department of Paintings, Priscilla Diamond, Erica Hirshler, Charlotte Emans Moore, and Karen Quinn.

Many of our colleagues in other departments have contributed their expertise to make this exhibition worthy of the collection it celebrates. We greatly appreciate the efforts of Désirée Caldwell, Assistant Director, Exhibitions; Joshua Basseches, Manager of Exhibition Projects; Robert Mitchell, Director of Public Relations and Marketing; Patricia Loiko, Associate Registrar; Martha Reynolds, Grants Officer; and René Beaudette, Systems Support Analyst in Management Information Systems. We are indebted to Judith Downes, Museum Designer, for the handsome installation of the exhibition. For planning the interesting and diverse programs that accompany this exhibition we would like to thank William Burback, Joan Harlowe, Barbara Martin, and Gilian Wohlauer of the Department of Education; Gilian also lent her expertise to the preparation of the brochure, wall texts, and other educational materials that so enhanced our presentation of the show. For graciously meeting our many requests we are grateful to Nancy Allen and the staff of the William Morris Hunt Memorial Library at the Museum of Fine Arts; Maureen Melton was enormously helpful in securing information from the Museum Archives, and Karin Lanzoni deserves our special thanks for her tireless efforts in securing interlibrary loans. Because every object in this exhibition is drawn from the permanent collection, demands on the museum's photographers were especially heavy, and we appreciate the talents and efforts of Gary Ruuska and Tom Lang on our behalf, as we do the helpful participation of Janice Sorkow, Director, Department of Photographic Services. Among our colleagues in curatorial and conservation departments, Jonathan Fairbanks, Jeannine Falino, Edmund Barry Gaither, John Herrmann, Anne Morse, Jeffrey Munger, Richard Newman, Anne Poulet, Nicola Shilliam, Jean Woodward, and Eric Zafran lent their special knowledge to various phases of the preparation of the book and exhibition, and we are grateful for the information they supplied.

Our most heartfelt thanks go to Carl Zahn, whose unsurpassed talents as a designer are readily apparent in this handsome book, and to Cynthia Purvis, whose editorial skills are surpassed only by her patience and good cheer. Their special efforts, and their untiring support of this project, have served us well, and we are deeply grateful.

We would also like to express our thanks to the three institutions that lent supplemental materials to the exhibition. The Fogg Art Museum has graciously allowed us to borrow John Singer Sargent's watercolor pigments and brushes, and we appreciate the assistance of James Cuno, Director; Craigen Weston Bowen, Conservator; and Jane Montgomery, Registrar. The Portland Art Museum and the Bowdoin College Museum of Art have made available to us Winslow Homer's watercolor boxes and some of his painting tools; our thanks go to Barbara Shissler Nosanow, Director; Jessica F. Nicoll, Curator of American Art; and Michele Butterfield, Registrar at Portland, and Katherine J. Watson, Director; and Mattie Kelley, Registrar at Bowdoin.

In the course of preparing *Awash in Color*, we have drawn upon the hospitality and expertise of many colleagues and friends around the country. For their gracious assistance we would like to thank: Gerald Ackerman, Jeannette Bloom, Kathleen Burnside, Lawrence Campbell, Barbara Christen, Carol Clark, Christina Cohen, Marjorie Cohn, Donald Cresswell, Britt Crews, Anne d'Harnoncourt, Paul D'Ambrosio, Susan Danly, Odile Duff, Anita Duquette, Ross Farrar, Susan Faxon, Paula Feid, Stuart Feld, Richard Field, Ruth Fine, Cynthia Fleming, Ella Foshay, Carter Foster, Kathleen A. Foster, Patricia Fowler, Kristen Froehlich, Abigail Booth Gerdts, Lila Green, Sophia Hewryk, Anne and Edgar Hubert, Penley Knipe, John Kosa, John Krill, Barbara Krulik, Jacob Lawrence, Nancy Mowll Mathews, Robert Moorhead, James O'Gorman, Sally Pierce, Betty Ring, Charles Ritchie, William Robinson, Warren A. Seamans, Innis H. Shoemaker, Marc Simpson, Catharina Slautterback, Megan Smith, Peter Spang, Miriam Stewart, Richard Stomberg, Susan Strickler, Captain Al Swanson, Ruth Szalasny, Jeanette Toohey, Ulla Volk, Susan Vrotsos, Nancy Weekly, Jeffrey Wieand, Gretchen Worden, and James Yarnall.

Fig. 1. Photograph of Winslow Homer watercolors in the home of John T. Spaulding, Boston, 1920s. Museum of Fine Arts, Boston.

WATERCOLOR, A MEDIUM FOR BOSTON

Sue Welsh Reed

THE MUSEUM OF FINE ARTS, BOSTON, has long been recognized for its outstanding American watercolors. In the course of preparing this book it became evident that the Museum's collection of nearly two thousand watercolors is not only the largest and most representative of any, but also the finest. The reasons for the Museum's preeminence in this field are to be discovered in its own history and the history of collecting in Boston. They involve the institution, its trustees and staff, and the donors of works of art and funds for purchases. These donors were by and large Boston collectors. Just as this is the first time that a selection from the Museum's entire range of American watercolors has been featured in an exhibition and publication, so it is the first time that the history of the watercolor collection has been explored.[1]

From its beginnings the Museum signaled its recognition of works of art on paper through acquisition and exhibition. By showing its support of both contemporary American art and works of art on paper, the Museum led the way to collecting American watercolors. The original building in Copley Square opened on July 3, 1876, and in the same month the Museum accepted its first gift of drawings and watercolors by the French painter Jean-François Millet. The many exhibitions organized for the nation's Centennial celebration helped focus attention on American art. In the following years the Museum held several loan exhibitions of American art that included drawings, and mounted exhibitions of English watercolors.[2] The first American watercolors entered the permanent collection in 1888, given by the artist, Edward Darley Boit. Two years later, the building had been enlarged, and a room was designated as the Water-Color Gallery (although there was not yet much to put in it).[3]

Soon, in addition to borrowing watercolors for exhibition and accepting them as gifts, the Museum began to purchase them. As it did for any purchase, it often had to raise funds by taking up a subscription among friends and supporters. Around the turn of the century, however, several individuals donated funds specifically designated for the purchase of modern or American pictures. Among the first of these was the William Wilkins Warren Fund, established in 1895 with $50,000 for the acquisition of modern pictures. Winslow Homer's four watercolors – *Ouananiche Fishing*, *Indian Camp*, *Trout Fishing*, and *Leaping Trout* (cat. 56) – were purchased from that fund in 1899, as was his oil, *The Lookout – All's Well*. Such commitments encouraged subsequent gifts of art, including thirty-six watercolors by Homer, nine by Sargent, and dozens by John La Farge, and forecast the development of one of the Museum's great collections.

Watercolor was a familiar medium to nineteenth-century Bostonians. Like much of Boston's culture, watercolor painting was imported from England and it was viewed as an accomplishment of cultivated men and women. Early in the century it was taught privately by such artists as English-born John Rubens Smith (see cat. 4). Before long watercolor took the place of embroidery as a leisure occupation for women (see cat. 8). They were particularly fond of painting floral subjects – both botanical and decorative – and, like many of their male counterparts, used the compact and portable medium on their holidays and travels.[4]

In the 1870s the Boston Art Club held large democratic exhibitions that brought together watercolors by both amateurs and professionals. Soon, specialized groups were organized. The Boston Water Color Society (for men only) was founded in 1885, followed two years later by the Boston Water Color Club (initially for women, but by the mid-nineties for artists of both sexes). Despite the fact that most Boston art schools did not offer classes in watercolor, it was practiced widely in the city and instruction from capable artists seems always to have been available. A Boston writer on art could, in 1896, refer to that city's "army of water-colorists."[5]

By the early 1880s contemporary American watercolors were deemed worthy of collecting, and Bostonians began to acquire them.[6] Collectors of paintings in Boston had developed a particular taste that undoubtedly encouraged the purchase of watercolors. They preferred peasant subjects by Millet and small sketchy landscapes by Jean Baptiste Camille Corot and other painters of the Barbizon School. (In contrast, New York collectors were buying academic French salon pictures and showy Hudson River school paintings by such artists as Frederic Church.)

Boston painters William Morris Hunt (1824–1879) and Joseph Foxcroft Cole (1837–1892) advised a number of Boston collectors, and their influence is apparent in shaping local taste. Hunt and Cole had studied in France, and maintained connections there; they were among the first Americans to embrace the Barbizon style. Hunt was one of John La Farge's first teachers. Cole began his career at Bufford's lithographic business in Boston at the same time as Winslow Homer, and the two artists remained lifelong friends. It is likely that Hunt and Cole (a watercolorist himself) promoted the drawings and watercolors of Homer and La Farge, who were among the first major artists to find a good market for their watercolors in Boston. Bostonians' characteristic reticence and distaste for ostentation may also have played a role in their liking for watercolors, which were certainly perceived as more modest works of art.

Numerous Boston women collected watercolors. In a list of more than two hundred previous owners and donors of watercolors now owned by the Museum, approximately half are women.[7] Some can be identified as important art collectors; others appear to have possessed only a few works. Unfortunately, just as not enough is known of many women artists, too little information is available about many women collectors.

Throughout much of the nineteenth century Boston was a small city whose educational and cultural institutions were closely linked. Many of Boston's leading citizens were not only trustees of several such institutions, but were related to each other, had attended Harvard together, and were members of the same social clubs. They often shared the same tastes in art. Fortunately for this Museum, it was the only institution acquiring contemporary art for its permanent collection. (Harvard's Fogg Museum did not welcome contemporary art until the 1940s. Its directors and staff leaned heavily toward the old masters, English Pre-Raphaelites, and the work of John Ruskin.) Trustees and patrons could give or direct gifts of American watercolors to the Museum of Fine Arts without conflict. Boston collectors, with their shared interests, built the Museum's world-renowned collection of paintings by Millet and the Barbizon school, as well as by Monet and the Impressionists. Many of the same collectors shared a taste for certain American watercolors. After the First World War, a handful of Boston collectors dared to buy more avant-garde, modernist watercolors (though few oils). In the late 1940s, a Russian emigrant, Maxim Karolik, would begin to form the Museum's unique collection of American art on paper created before 1870. A look at some watercolor collectors in Boston during the past century reveals certain patterns of taste that have shaped the permanent collection of the Museum.[8]

BOSTON COLLECTORS OF HOMER AND LA FARGE WATERCOLORS

By 1880 established Boston collectors had begun to purchase watercolors by both Winslow Homer and John La Farge, each of whom would find a steady market for his watercolors in Boston. The two artists had become friends in New York, where for more than a decade after 1872 they occupied the same Tenth Street Studio Building. Despite their differences in subject, works by the two artists were often found together in the same Boston collections. Homer's humble English fisherfolk, Adirondacks scenery, or game fish were found alongside La Farge's exotic Samoans, South Pacific island views, stained-glass saints, or waterlilies.

In the spring of 1878 Homer held his first one-man exhibition and auction of watercolors and drawings in Boston. (Homer was making an effort to be independent as a painter, and an auction was a means to obtain cash readily.) Thereafter, his works on paper continued to find purchasers in Boston, largely through the gallery of Doll & Richards. Although Homer lived in New York during the 1860s and 70s, he maintained friends, family, and artistic connections in Boston, and it was this city that supplied his material needs after he moved to Maine in the mid 1880s.

La Farge was also closely connected to Boston, where he had relatives and friends. He stayed there frequently in 1876-77 while working on his murals for Trinity Church, commissioned by its architect, his friend Henry Hobson Richardson (1838-1886). Diagonally across Copley Square was the new Museum of Fine Arts. La Farge helped organize its art school and lectured there in 1879-80. He too, held auctions in Boston to raise money: one sale of oils in late 1878 and another containing drawings and watercolors in December 1879.[9] Like Homer's, La Farge's work was subsequently carried by Doll & Richards.

Much of what we know about Boston collections of La Farge and Homer comes from the two memorial exhibitions the Museum held in the early months of 1911.[10] To the John La Farge Memorial Exhibition, held from January 1 to 31, thirty-six private collectors contributed some 125 watercolors. Among the most generous lenders were Henry Lee Higginson, with twenty-two watercolors; William Sturgis Bigelow, nineteen; Edward W. Hooper's heirs, twelve; Sarah Choate Sears, four; and Susan Cornelia Warren, two.

The Winslow Homer Memorial Exhibition, which took place from February 8 to March 8, contained fewer objects, though its fifty-two watercolors covered all major phases of Homer's career from 1878 to 1907. Some thirty collectors were represented. The estate and heirs of Edward W. Hooper lent fifteen works, William Sturgis Bigelow and Horace D. Chapin each lent two.

Lloyd Goodrich, America's leading Homer scholar, later wrote about Boston collectors of Homer's watercolors, many of whom owned La Farge watercolors as well:

> In [Homer's] native city in the 1890s he attained a popularity such as Boston reserves for only a few favorites. Bostonians have always been great collectors of watercolors, for some occult reason, perhaps connected with thrift; and in buying his watercolors they also showed that other characteristic Boston trait, discrimination. From every exhibition at Doll & Richards a good part of the watercolors were sold, and the best. On the other hand, only four of his mature oils found their way into Boston collections during his life time. His chief patron in the city was Edward W. Hooper, treasurer of Harvard College and a trustee of the Museum, who beginning as early as 1880 bought over twenty water colors and drawings, and the oil, *Huntsman and Dogs*. Among other owners were many who made social and intellectual Boston what it was – Thomas G. Appleton, Martin Brimmer, Thomas Wigglesworth, Dr. Henry C. Angell, Dr. William Sturgis Bigelow, Henry Adams, Brooks Adams, John T. Morse, Jr., Mrs. Samuel D. Warren, Mrs. Sarah Wyman Whitman. And since Bostonians have a way of keeping what they like, many of his finest watercolors can still be found in the old houses on Beacon Hill.[11]

The collectors Brimmer, Wigglesworth, and Angell are known mainly for their paintings by Millet and other French artists of the Barbizon school. Dr. Henry C. Angell had begun to collect Barbizon paintings in the mid-1860s and continued to refine his collection until after 1900. He also bought American paintings by such artists as Hunt, Theodore Robinson, and Frank Duveneck, as well as peasant subjects in watercolor by Dutch artists of the Hague School (some of which came to the Museum). Angell favored sketches and small, unfinished paintings, and this taste is reflected in his five Homer drawings, the earliest works by the artist traceable to a Boston collection. These included three drawings dated 1864: two studies of boys playing and a powerful image of two Civil War soldiers, *Our Zouaves*. A fourth, *Cabin Interior*, appears to be a watercolor, perhaps from Homer's Virginia trip of 1875.[12] Henry Sayles, another noted Barbizon collector, lent a Homer "sketch" dated 1878 to the 1911 exhibition.

Martin Brimmer (1829-1896), who had briefly studied painting in France in the early 1850s, was a founder and the first president of the Museum, serving from 1870 to 1896. Brimmer promoted the work of Millet and in 1876 gave the Museum its first drawings by the artist, including several freshly observed landscape watercolors. Like Angell, he favored the Barbizon school, and he, too, owned modern American paintings. These included important works by Hunt and Elihu Vedder, many of which came to the Museum. Brimmer lent two of Homer's Bahamas subjects from the mid 1880s, *Sponge Fisherman, Nassau* and *Negress with a Basket of Fruit*, to a loan exhibition of watercolors held at the St. Botolph Club in 1891; these were the only Homers from a private collection in that exhibition.

Other collectors were more eclectic in their tastes. Thomas Wigglesworth, who had one of Boston's largest collections, owned academic French pictures as well as Barbizon works and American paintings.[13] He purchased Homer's major watercolor, *An Afterglow* (cat. 54), from Doll & Richards in 1883, the year it was painted. It was subsequently sold and eventually acquired by Bostonian William P. Blake, who left it to the Museum in 1922.

Susan Cornelia Clarke Warren (1825-1902), was the wife of Museum trustee and paper company owner Samuel Dennis Warren, Sr., and the mother of two sons with close ties to the Museum. Her husband encouraged her collecting interests and provided funds generously. She began with decorative objects, and soon became a discriminating collector of paintings. Bernard Berenson sometimes served as her advisor in the field of old masters, as he did for Isabella Stewart Gardner. Mrs. Warren's collection reached nearly 150 old master and modern paintings, and her home included a picture gallery where she instructively juxtaposed her paintings by Ingres and Daumier. Mrs. Warren gave the Museum its first major Millet, *Young Shepherdess*, and J.-L. Gérôme's *Eminence Grise*, one of the few French academic paintings in the collection. At her death in 1902 she left the Museum $60,000 to purchase what it desired from her collection when it was auctioned at the American Art Galleries in New York the following year. Mrs. Warren owned twelve watercolors by La Farge and one by Homer (*In the Adirondacks*); her four children must have elected to keep all but the six La Farge watercolors that appeared in her 1903 auction.[14]

Henry Lee Higginson (1834-1919), founder of the Boston Symphony Orchestra in 1881, and his wife, Ida Agassiz, were important Museum supporters.[15] Higginson was one of La Farge's steadiest patrons, and collected oils, drawings, and watercolors by the artist both for himself and for the Museum. In 1893 he purchased some thirty-five South Seas subjects directly from La Farge, paying $25,000 in installments. Higginson later wrote to Mabel Hooper La Farge, the artist's daughter-in-law, that he and La Farge "always had friendly & agreeable relations – & he gave me the first chance at his Samoan sketches."[16] Some of these works seem to have been shared with Edward Hooper and William Sturgis Bigelow. In 1911-12 Higginson gave the Museum forty-three La Farge watercolors as well as many drawings. By and large these are studies for decorative projects – glass and murals – and range in date from the 1870s to the 1900s. Like the Museum's own purchases, these too may have been acquired from the artist's estate.[17] As late as 1935 Higginson's La Farges were still coming to the Museum; in that year Mrs. Higginson made a bequest of three early landscape oils and three watercolors that included *Apple Blossoms*.

Lloyd Goodrich singled out Edward W. Hooper (1839-1901) as Boston's single most important Homer collector.[18] Hooper had a particular fondness for works on paper. He owned several major etchings by Rembrandt, and he was the first American to collect

William Blake's work; he eventually had nearly thirty drawings, as well as illuminated books by that English visionary poet. Hooper also admired the color and verve of Delacroix, and owned several oil sketches by the artist. While in London in 1890, Hooper had J.A.M. Whistler paint his daughter Ellen's portrait, and the next year he urged Whistler to compete for the commission for the Boston Public Library murals. He owned several marine watercolors by Whistler which he lent to Boston exhibitions.[19] Hooper also possessed at least twenty oils and as many watercolors by La Farge. Not surprisingly, Hooper was a Harvard classmate and friend of architect Henry Hobson Richardson, first cousin (and Beacon Hill neighbor) of William Sturgis Bigelow, brother-in-law of Henry Adams, and friend of John La Farge. During the 1890s he traveled in Europe at various times with one or another of them. In 1898, Hooper's relationship to La Farge was further strengthened when his daughter Mabel married the artist's son Bancel.

Treasurer of Harvard (1876-1898) and devoted Museum trustee (1878-1901), Hooper was not only treasurer of the building committee and of the Museum's art school, but also served on the Committee on the Museum, which was responsible for decisions on the acquisition of works of art. Tributes paid to Hooper at the time of his death emphasize equally his conscientious management of funds (both as treasurer of institutions and trustee for individuals) and his love of art. A friend wrote, "Before a great work of art, his was not the attitude of cultivated admiration, but of soul answering to soul. One of the greatest of our painters (La Farge) told me that he had thought no one loved art more, or more immediately, than himself, but that in Edward Hooper he recognized one who left him behind."[20]

Over his lifetime, Hooper amassed a comprehensive collection of Homer's watercolors. The subjects range from the country children of 1879 to the powerful Adirondacks scenes of the 1890s, and include English subjects (among them the spectacular *Wreck of the Iron Crown*) and Caribbean landscapes. As a member, along with Bigelow, of the Committee on the Museum, he almost certainly backed the 1899 purchase of one oil and four watercolors by Homer. One of these, *Leaping Trout* (cat. 56), with its veils of wash and jewel-like colors, is unusually close to works by La Farge. Hooper's enthusiasm for Homer's work probably influenced other collectors whose gifts over the years have greatly enriched the Museum's collection.

Hooper's bachelor cousin William Sturgis Bigelow (1850-1926) also acquired watercolors by both Homer and La Farge. A Museum trustee for forty-five years, Bigelow was an enormously generous donor in many areas, most notably those of Chinese and Japanese art. Independently wealthy, he abandoned his career as a physician to devote himself to collecting. Between 1882 and 1889 he lived in Japan in order to study Buddhism; there he entertained visitors, among them Isabella and Jack Gardner, Phillips Brooks, Henry Adams, and John La Farge (see cat. 44).

After his return to Boston, Bigelow continued to collect Asian art and also acquired watercolors by La Farge and Homer. One satisfied his refined aesthetic, the other his spirit of adventure. Bigelow's fine old Beacon Street townhouse had blue silk window draperies and a blue ceiling painted with gold stars in its sitting room.[21] The same elegance and sensitivity to color is reflected in the many exquisite watercolors by La Farge that Bigelow owned. He gave twelve to the Museum, mostly his favorite Japanese and South Seas subjects (including cats. 44 and 46), which he bought from La Farge (or from Higginson) and from Doll & Richards in the early nineties.

Another facet of Bigelow's personality is revealed by his rustic summer cottage on Tuckernuck Island, off Nantucket. Tuckernuck was an all-male retreat, "where he indulged in the taste for luxurious discomfort (or primitive conditions at disproportionate expense) that has long been typical of Bostonians on islands and in other remote family summer enclaves."[22] He is also said to have been a good shot with the pistol hunting plover along the shore. In keeping with this outdoorsy side of Bigelow's personality are the five Homers he left to the Museum: *Breaking Wave* and four Adirondacks subjects, including *The Blue Boat* (cat. 57).

Another collector who favored Homer was Horace D. Chapin (1850-1937), Bigelow's Harvard classmate and financial secretary, and Hooper's brother-in-law. Chapin lent three drawings and two watercolors to the Homer memorial exhibition, including *Returning Fishing Boats* (1883, Fogg Art Museum, Harvard University Art Museums). He continued to purchase Homer watercolors from later years. Chapin, who never married, left them to his sister Margaret (Mrs. Robert B. Osgood), who wrote to a Museum curator: "My [new] house has not as much wall space as [my old] although the Homers look well on the walls. How I do enjoy them as household companions & they also give great pleasure to others as well."[23] In 1939 Mrs. Osgood gave to the Museum four Florida and Bahamas subjects, including *Sponge Diver* (cat. 61) and donated seven others to Harvard's Fogg Art Museum. She herself purchased *Street in Santiago de Cuba*, which one of her descendants gave to the Museum in the late 1970s. It is the only one of Homer's relatively rare Cuban subjects in the collection.

A TASTE FOR MONET AND MACKNIGHT

WATERCOLORIST Dodge Macknight wrote to Isabella Stewart Gardner in 1909: "The other day you spoke of the Monet-Japanesque quality of my work. . . . That is exactly what I'm after . . . Picturesqueness of design together with brilliant color."[24] Keenly aware of Boston taste – and with the advantage of hindsight – Macknight linked his name with that of Boston's other favorite painter.

By the 1890s a new generation began to buy Impressionist paintings; Claude Monet's works were promoted by local or influential painters.[25] Many of the same collectors who were acquiring Monets were also enthusiastically buying watercolors by Dodge Macknight. Macknight lived in France between 1883 and the late 1890s. Beginning in 1888, he sent his watercolors almost annually to Doll & Richards. These one-man shows were enormously successful, continuing for more than two decades after 1900, when the artist settled permanently in Sandwich, Massachusetts. In Boston Macknight became

Fig. 2. Photograph of Dodge Macknight watercolors (at left) in the gallery of Desmond FitzGerald's home in Brookline, about 1920. From FitzGerald sales catalogue, American Art Galleries, New York, 1927.

friendly with Sargent and with a number of important collectors including Isabella Stewart Gardner, Desmond FitzGerald, and Denman Ross. Mrs. Gardner, who never purchased a painting by Monet – although she considered doing so – did acquire eleven Macknight watercolors. She exhibited them at Fenway Court in the Macknight Room, opened in 1915, together with her other American watercolors, including works by La Farge, Sargent, and George Hallowell.

Desmond FitzGerald (1846-1926), a successful engineer educated at MIT, was an amateur painter and watercolorist, and a Museum trustee.[26] He was not only an avid collector of Monet, but through exhibitions and lectures he encouraged many fellow Bostonians to buy Monet's work. FitzGerald owned dozens of Macknight watercolors, which he arranged in tiers opposite his Monets in the densely hung gallery he had added onto his Brookline house in 1913 (fig. 2).

Denman Waldo Ross (1853-1935) also collected both Monet and Macknight. He studied with Henry Adams at Harvard and earned his Ph.D. in history, but chose to devote himself to art. Ross was a painter, collected widely, and taught art theory at Harvard. He was a Museum trustee from 1895 and an important and generous donor. Like his Harvard colleagues Charles Eliot Norton and Charles Herbert Moore, Ross bought English and American Pre-Raphaelite watercolors, including H. R. Newman's *Wildflowers* (cat. 27); his interests, however, were more wide-ranging than theirs. Ross collected Asian and European art of all varieties. Most important for the growth of the Museum's collection were Ross's numerous Indian and Near Eastern textiles, paintings, and sculpture. He was the first to give the Museum paintings by Monet (three in 1906). He also gave two evocative Degas landscapes that are executed in pastel over monotype, and a Whistler painting. Ross owned many Macknight watercolors, giving more than thirty to Harvard and ten to the Museum.

Clara Bertram Kimball, the wife of David P. Kimball, a prominent lawyer, owned two Monets and several watercolors by Macknight. She also owned a Venetian watercolor by Prendergast, *The Clock Tower* (location unknown).[27] At her death in 1923 her husband gave the Museum several gifts in her memory, including the Monets, a Macknight (cat. 67), and two works by Homer – *Twilight at Leeds, New York* (oil, 1876) and *Girls on a Cliff* (cat. 51).

Other Monet and Macknight collectors included Dr. Arthur Tracy Cabot (1852-1912), brother of artist Lilla Cabot Perry (and himself an amateur watercolorist), who gave the Museum three Macknights and a Homer. Purchasing in the first two decades of this century were Robert J. Edwards and his sisters, Hannah Marcy Edwards and Grace M. Edwards. By 1939 they had given to the Museum ten Monet paintings (acquired under the advice of FitzGerald) and eleven Dodge Macknight watercolors. Edward Jackson Holmes served the Museum between 1910 and his death in 1950 both as a trustee and for a period of time, as director. Holmes saw to it that the Museum received not only his two Monet paintings, but also some twenty Macknight watercolors, including cat. 68.

WOMEN ARTISTS AS COLLECTORS

WILLIAM MORRIS HUNT conveyed his taste for sketchiness, naturalism, and poetry in art to his many women students, some of whom also had the means to collect art.[28] They found those qualities Hunt admired in the watercolors of his former student, John La Farge, especially the flower subjects. "Ownership of a La Farge floral watercolor came to be regarded as a veritable status symbol. Not surprisingly La Farge's friends and colleagues in Boston purchased many of the pictures directly from him before the artist could offer them for public sale."[29]

Sarah Wyman (Mrs. Henry) Whitman (1843-1904) was one of Hunt's most successful pupils. She promoted art education, serving on the committee to the Museum School for many years, and was instrumental in founding the "Harvard Annex" for women, which would become Radcliffe College. Whitman founded Lily Glass Works in Boston in the 1890s, and was a founder of the Society of Arts and Crafts. She was friendly with many intellectual leaders and painted portraits of such prominent Bostonians as Oliver Wendell Holmes, Phillips Brooks, and Martin Brimmer.[30] Her accomplished flower paintings were similar in subject to La Farge's work. Like him, she designed and manufactured stained glass; she executed memorial windows for Brimmer and Brooks at Memorial Hall, Harvard, and at Trinity Church, respectively. She also designed book covers. Whitman's personal collection is not well recorded; however, at her death she left the Museum Homer's bold black and white wash drawing, *Mussel Gatherers*, and three La Farge figural watercolors, including *The Fisherman and the Djinn*, which she had purchased from the 1903 auction of works owned by Susan Cornelia Warren.

Another student of Hunt, Elizabeth Howard Bartol (1842-1927), was a friend and contemporary of Sarah Wyman Whitman. Bartol was a strong portraitist whose exhibited work was noted favorably by the critics in the 1880s; ill health prevented her from painting much after 1895. She was the only child of Cyrus Bartol, the independently wealthy Unitarian minister of West Church, Boston. (His wife commissioned a watercolor view of the church from Maurice Prendergast in about 1900; see cat. 88).

Elizabeth Bartol was one of five women who gave the Museum in 1916 its first watercolor by a woman, Margaret Jordan Patterson.[31] Although her most important gift to the Museum was the European furniture collected by her Swan family ancestors, Bartol's bequest included oils by Hunt and La Farge, and three La Farge watercolors, among them the beautiful *Wild Roses in an Antique Chinese Bowl* (cat. 42).

Sarah Choate Sears (1858-1935), painter and photographer, was married to J. Montgomery Sears, one of the richest men in Boston. She was highly visible as the social rival of Isabella Stewart Gardner. However, unlike Susan Cornelia Warren, Sears preferred contemporary art to Mrs. Gardner's old masters.[32] Sears's activities as an artist led her to keep up with the times and she acquired watercolors that reached from La Farges of the 1880s to modernist works by Charles Demuth and John Marin of the 1920s.

Sears met John La Farge in 1877 while attending the Museum School. After her marriage in 1878, she continued to study painting privately with members of its faculty and at Cowles Art School with Dennis Bunker. Ross Turner instructed her in watercolors (see cat. 71). Sears began to exhibit her own watercolors at the Boston Art Club in 1883 and was a founding member of the Water Color Club in 1887. Taking up photography in the early 1890s, she made portraits of her children and her friends (including John Singer Sargent) and exhibited with prominent photographers working in the pictorialist style. Around 1915 Sears renewed her watercolor activity continuing to produce floral subjects until shortly before her death in 1935.

Sears commissioned portraits from her Boston School teachers and from Sargent – for whose attention she vied with Isabella Stewart Gardner. (Each provided a studio for him to use and each asked him to be a houseguest. Diplomatically, Sargent would choose to paint at one house and stay at the other.) Sears was friendly with Mary Cassatt and owned ten very fine pastels by the artist; through Cassatt she purchased pastels by Edgar Degas and Edouard Manet's *The Street Singer*, which was left to the Museum. Her interest in Impressionism also led her to buy the watercolors of Dodge Macknight. Sears owned at least six La Farge watercolors, including a handsome *Water Lilies* and one of several versions of *Fayaway*, the vivid image of a Polynesian woman standing in a canoe with her loin cloth held out as a sail. Sears lent La Farge watercolors to the 1891 St. Botolph Club exhibition and to the 1911 La Farge Memorial Exhibition. While none of them came to the Museum, her most elegant La Farge, *Roses in a Pi-tong* (see cat. 42), ultimately returned to the area, for it was was acquired by Harvard graduate Grenville H. Winthrop of New York, who bequeathed it to the Fogg Art Museum in 1943.[33]

Sarah Choate Sears was one of a number of Bostonians, largely women, who bought Maurice Prendergast's work.[34] In the mid-nineties she began to purchase watercolors and monotypes from the artist, eventually owning at least ten. She is also believed to have financed Prendergast's 1898-99 trip to Italy.

Shortly after the turn of the century, Sears's photographic activity led her to make the acquaintance of New York photographer and art dealer, Alfred Stieglitz. Although she ceased to make photographs after about 1905, she kept in contact with him, purchasing from his gallery a landscape watercolor by John Marin and Charles Demuth's *Zinnias and Daisies* of 1925 (cat. 101), which was bought by the museum after her death. One of a very few Bostonians to appreciate modernism at its beginnings, Sears owned drawings by Henri Matisse. Her taste for the colorful, free-flowing, two-dimensional aspects of modernist watercolors may have been further strengthened by her enthusiasm for Asian art, in particular Persian pottery, which she collected extensively.[35]

THE MUSEUM IN THE TWENTIETH CENTURY

THE MUSEUM reaffirmed its commitment to watercolorists linked with Boston in its new building on Huntington Avenue, which opened in 1909. The collection of watercolors grew, and after the opening of the Robert Dawson Evans Memorial Wing in 1915 significantly more gallery space was provided for pictures. The years 1911 and 1912 were important ones for the growth of the collection. "The Museum has been happily able to secure [twelve] watercolors and [ten] drawings by John La Farge, studies for mural paintings, for windows, etc. . . . These studies had remained in his studio up to the time when the Museum purchased them," noted the curator of paintings, Jean Guiffrey, in the Museum's annual report for 1912. The Special Picture Fund employed for this purchase may have been raised by Henry L. Higginson, who personally gave many similar works by La Farge at the same time.

In 1909, the Museum missed an opportunity to buy a group of Sargent watercolors exhibited at Knoedler's, New York; they went instead to the Brooklyn Museum. Three years later, the Museum succeeded in purchasing another group of forty-five watercolors directly from the artist (see cats. 72-83). These works, Guiffrey stated, "show the painter in the most attractive, the most varied, the happiest and at the same time the most just light. . . . They are truly works of a master who has taken pleasure in painting and in expressing by the brush in the enthusiasm of his travels in Italy, in Greece and elsewhere, all the picturesqueness and beauty which presented itself to his sight."

At Knoedler's in 1909 and again in 1912 Sargent shared the galleries with watercolorist Edward Darley Boit (1840-1915). Boit and his wife were wealthy Bostonians who lived much of the time in Europe; they were friends of Sargent and such other expatriots as Henry James. Boit had given Sargent one of his first major commissions, which resulted in the large and striking group portrait of the four Boit daughters, painted in Paris in 1882. Boit traveled widely, painting watercolors wherever he visited, and by the 1880s had a well-established style of his own, long before Sargent began to work extensively in

Fig. 3. Edward Darley Boit (1840-1915), *Paris, Place du Carrousel*, 1911. Watercolor on paper. Museum of Fine Arts, Boston. Picture Fund, 1912.

watercolor. Boit's watercolors were favorably received whenever they were shown in Boston (beginning in the late eighties), but they did not appeal to the New York critics, who preferred Sargent. Neither did they sell in New York. The thirty-eight watercolor views of Italy, England, France, and America purchased by the Museum in 1912 (from 103 exhibited by Boit) remain the only significant body of his work in a public collection (fig. 3).[36]

Purchase funds given around the turn of the century enabled the Museum to more readily make purchases of watercolors. The William Wilkins Warren Fund had been used for Homers in 1899. In 1904, Charles Henry Hayden, an amateur watercolorist, gave the Museum $100,000 for the purchase of pictures by American artists. While the Hayden Fund was used to purchase a number of oils, it quite appropriately became the principal fund from which important watercolors were purchased for many decades. This fund enabled the Museum to buy all forty-five Sargents. It also made possible the acquisition of thirteen additional works featured in this book, including two by Charles Demuth, two by John Marin, and four by Maurice Prendergast.

COLLECTORS IN THE TWENTIETH CENTURY

JOHN T. SPAULDING (1870-1948), the unmarried heir to the Revere sugar refinery fortune, collected voraciously. While sharing such well-established Boston tastes as that for Impressionism, his more daring acquisitions included Post-Impressionist works and twentieth-century American art.

Together with his brother William, John Spaulding began by collecting Japanese prints. (Architect Frank Lloyd Wright sometimes acted as their agent in Japan.) The Spauldings gave some 6,000 prints to the Museum between 1909 and 1921. This taste is consistent with the delicately designed watercolors of birds by Charles Emile Heil that John Spaulding owned (see cat. 70). He also owned eight fine watercolors by Winslow Homer (including cats. 51, 53 and 62), most of which he purchased as a group from Knoedler's in the twenties, and placed in a pleasing arrangement over a fireplace in his Boston home (fig. 1).[37]

Spaulding was a boyhood friend of Charles Hovey Pepper (1864-1950), a watercolorist and member of the "Boston Five," who campaigned to bring modernism to Boston. For many years Spaulding and Pepper served on the exhibition committee for the Boston Art Club. Together they traveled to meet artists in New York, Philadelphia, and Washington, bringing back for exhibition works by George Luks, Robert Henri, George Bellows, Rockwell Kent, and Leon Kroll. Spaulding bought many oils and a few watercolors by these and other American contemporaries, as well as work by Charles Demuth (see cat. 100). He owned a strong group of nine watercolors by Edward Hopper, four of them purchased from the artist's first one-man exhibition in New York; three are included here (cats. 111-113). Spaulding was one of Boston's few important collectors of contemporary art between the wars, albeit his choices were always representational and never abstract. Although he refused invitations to become a trustee, he maintained close associations with the Museum throughout his life and at his death he gave it virtually all the art works he owned.

A few Boston collectors were more daring in their choices of modernist watercolors. Ananda K. Coomaraswamy (1877-1947), a brilliant scholar from Ceylon, became curator of Indian art at the Museum in 1917. Like Sarah Sears, Coomaraswamy was also a pictorialist photographer and a friend of Alfred Stieglitz. (In 1924 Coomaraswamy persuaded the trustees to accept Stieglitz's gift of his own photographs and thus established the Museum's photography collection.) Coomaraswamy owned work by Arthur B. Davies; he gave the Museum one watercolor by Maurice Sterne and three by Abraham Walkowitz. These were virtually the only modernist pictures owned by the Museum until 1940, when it purchased a Demuth watercolor, followed by one by John Marin in 1946.

THE M. AND M. KAROLIK COLLECTION

MAXIM KAROLIK (1893-1963) fled to the United States from his native Russian Rumania in 1922. Trained as a concert tenor, this Jewish emigrant would become one of the Museum's most important donors of early American watercolors. Between 1948 and 1962, Karolik worked closely with curator Henry P. Rossiter, a Canadian-born journalist who had become a scholar of old master prints. This unlikely pair amassed more than 3,000 works of art that chronicle artistic activity on paper in the United States between 1800 and 1875.

The M. and M. Karolik Collection of American Water Colors and Drawings was the logical outgrowth of the M. and M. Karolik Collection of American Paintings and a continuation of its goals. When Maxim Karolik formally presented the latter collection to the Museum, he wrote to its director, Harold Edgell, "My wife and I are ready to offer the collection to the people through the Museum of Fine Arts. It was made for one purpose only: To show what happened in this country in the art of painting in the period of half a century – from 1815 to 1865 – and to show the beginning and the growth of American landscape and genre painting. The aim was to make a collection not of 'Americana' for the antiquarian, but of American art for the nation."[38]

By the time of that presentation in December 1945 Karolik and Rossiter had sown the seeds of the next collection. They had worked together in the 1930s to select the prints that were included in the first Karolik collection of eighteenth-century American arts. The high-style furniture and silver in that collection reflected the taste of Karolik's wife, Martha Codman Karolik (1858-1948), a wealthy Boston Brahmin. Maxim Karolik himself was drawn to nineteenth-century works made for and by middle-class Americans. Many of the artists were self-taught painters, and many had been forgotten after their deaths. Karolik liked to call this "the barren period." Virtually single-handedly he revived the work of Fitz Hugh Lane and Martin Johnson Heade, recovered genre subjects by James Goodwyn Clonney, and validated anonymous folk paintings as suitable for the art museum.

Beginning in 1944, Maxim Karolik placed on loan to the Museum a small number of original and reproductive prints, as well as drawings, relating to artists in the Karolik paintings collection. In so doing, he hinted that nineteenth-century works of art on paper would be his next focus. By the time Martha Karolik died in April 1948, Maxim Karolik and Henry Rossiter were already working together to form such a collection. They began by seeking the assistance of well-known dealers in American art, some of whom had previously sold paintings to Karolik and prints to Rossiter. A rare exchange of letters between the two men reveals the status of the search. The melange of old-world courtesy, charm, bluntness, egoism, theatrics, and orthography are inimitably Karolik's:

Newport, Rhode Island
July 21st, 1948

Dear Mr. Rossiter:
Here is my cheque for $4063.50 – to pay Knoedler, Kennedy, McIntyre, Spark, Newmann and Allison & Co. . . .I hope I am not embarrasing the Museum authorities with my system of doing the business part of our plan. . . .We are doing it with a definite purpose: to show the dealers that Karolik is not the only "golden angel" your Museum has to help you make a new collection of Prints, Drawings and Watercolors. As I said to you before, we must win over Mr. Edgell to our daring plan. After that, we will let him run the show. You stand behind him; I will stand behind you. He must first realize the importance of our plan and what is our aim. Having him on our side, we will be able to put on a little

pressure on the wavering trustees who are too refined, and therefore afraid to start something that appears to them *as news*. . . So far, we are on the right track, and moving fast. We must move fast, otherwise, we will invite competitors, who will try to grab the things before Karolik does. I speak from experience. Hope to hear from you soon. . . .

Maxim Karolik [39]

After thanking Karolik for the check, Mr. Rossiter responded:

Boston
July 23, 1948

Dear Mr. Karolik:
Early next week I will have a talk with Mr. Edgell and do my best to impress him with the importance and desirability of your collection of drawings and watercolors. I do not believe there will be any difficulty. You already have enough fine things to open the eyes of even the most wavering. I am sure that equally important items will continue to be offered. . . . [Knoedler's, Kennedy, and other New York dealers] are combing their stocks for other material to show me. I agree with you that now is the time to strike and strike hard before the prices stiffen. . .

Henry P. Rossiter

Karolik and Rossiter succeeded in convincing the director to propose the third collaboration to the Trustees. By February 1949 seven hundred works of art on paper were on loan to the Museum from Karolik; Rossiter placed 230 of them on view, in order to assist the Trustees in their decision. He defined the structure and scope of the collection in the accompanying mimeographed checklist: "To be offered by Mr. Maxim Karolik: American Drawings and Prints 1800-1875. Categories: Academic, Primitives, Prints, Amateurs and Semi-Primitives, Foreign Artists working in America, Historical and Topographical Drawings, Fracturs." The trustees accepted the offer and during the summer Rossiter closed two print exhibition galleries in order to store and begin to catalogue the collection. Although the two-volume *M. & M. Karolik Collection of American Water Colors & Drawings 1800-1875* would not see print until 1962, the collection was essentially formed in the late forties and early fifties.

Many prominent dealers in American paintings, antiques, and Americana assisted in the search. Rossiter wrote to one of them: "There were a number of items I returned with the greatest reluctance, but the truth is I have to think of space and relative merit. Also I still have to add at least one example each by about two hundred of the academic painters. I hope you will let me know if you acquire other items in this field. We want this collection of American drawings as fine as possible."[40]

In 1948, at the beginning of the campaign, Karolik purchased many significant drawings by artists who were already represented in the Museum's Karolik painting collection, among them James Goodwyn Clonney, George Inness, Martin Johnson Heade, and William Sidney Mount. The watercolors from the 1830s by Alvan Fisher and J.R.

Smith (cats. 3, 4) were acquired at this time, as were many depictions of the American landscape and drawings of the Civil War. During his summer travels Karolik bought a quantity of folk art from shops in New England resort areas. He continued to buy from such urban sources as Edith Halpert's Downtown Gallery. Among the superb examples acquired in 1948 were those by Eunice Pinney and Mary Chapin (cats. 7, 8).

The following year was another very good one in which Karolik purchased hundreds of objects. Among these were the distinctive watercolors by George Harvey, Fitz Hugh Lane, Antonio Zeno Shindler, J.W. Hill, and Samuel Colman (cats. 6, 12, 14, 21, and 31). Whatever was purchased had to please Karolik and Rossiter alike. They had strong personalities, but each respected the other's opinion. Written records, however, indicate that the ultimate choice was the curator's. "The Darley drawing did not ring the bell," Mr. Rossiter wrote to a dealer. "I decided against it before Mr. Karolik saw it. Had he been enthusiastic I might have had an argument with him but he was not even luke warm." On another occasion he stated, "I think I will return the two Edwards sketch books. They do not *enthuse* me and I have promised Mr. K. not to buy anything which does not *enthuse* me."[41]

By the early fifties the project was so well known that many unfamiliar dealers and individuals brought objects to the Museum to be considered for purchase by Mr. Karolik. Every now and then an artist's descendant would unexpectedly produce a treasure trove; the watercolors by Edwin Whitefield, Jasper Francis Cropsey, William Trost Richards, and James Wells Champney were acquired in this fashion (cats. 13, 23, 24, 34, 35, 39-41). In an unusual instance, Mr. Karolik acquired J.H. Hill's charming house portrait, *Sunnyside* (cat. 22), directly from a Newport auction.

Although the pace of acquisitions had slowed by the late fifties and the catalogue manuscript was nearing completion, it was not too late for a sparkling addition. Hamilton's colorful *Sunset on the Jersey Flats* (cat. 17) was purchased in 1961, while the final acquisitions to be included in the published catalogue were eight splendid wash drawings by Clonney, bought in February 1962 at an average cost of just over $1,000 apiece. These prices indicate the impact Karolik's collecting had had on the market; they are a far cry from the $20 Karolik had paid for a Clonney wash drawing in 1948.

The pioneering Karolik Collection provided thirty-three of the earliest watercolors included in this book. They greatly broaden our knowledge of American art in what can no longer be considered "the barren period."

MODERN ART COLLECTORS

GIFTS in recent decades have continued to strengthen the Museum's collection of twentieth-century watercolors. In 1966, Nathaniel Saltonstall, a founder of the Institute of Contemporary Art, bequeathed three watercolors by Demuth; another, *In the Province* (cat. 99) was a gift in his memory from John and Betty McAndrew. McAndrew taught art history at Wellesley College for many years. At his wife's death in 1986 the Museum received several important abstract European works of art on paper (including a drawing by Piet Mondrian and a watercolor by Robert Delaunay), as well as Stuart Davis's watercolor, *Pad* (1955). In 1990, William and Saundra Lane's gifts of pastels by Georgia O'Keeffe, Arthur Dove, and Joseph Stella, temperas by Charles Sheeler, and two early watercolors by Stuart Davis (*Boat Landing* and cat. 106) – along with many paintings – significantly strengthened the Museum's modernist holdings.

THE combined efforts, interest, and dedication of a large number of collectors, supporters, and staff of the Museum have created the world's finest group of American watercolors. The 127 outstanding examples included in this book – some forty purchases and eighty gifts – represent more than a century of collecting, but can only suggest Boston's abiding romance with the great American watercolor.

1. Whereas a large collection of prints ensured the establishment of a department with its own curator in 1887, drawings and watercolors, along with paintings, were under the Department of Western Art. In 1911 they became the responsibility of the newly created Department of Paintings, and in 1945 were transferred to the Department of Prints, Drawings, and Photographs, which has since cared for all western works of art on paper.

2. The Museum showed contemporary works on paper at its William Morris Hunt memorial exhibition in 1879 and at the William Rimmer memorial exhibition in 1880. It held a loan exhibition of watercolors by William Blake in 1880 and the same year showed Professor Charles Eliot Norton's drawings and watercolors by John Ruskin. In 1885 it presented 453 English watercolors in a loan exhibition.

3. In 1890 the Museum's watercolor holdings consisted of thirty-three by William Blake, purchased by subscription in that year, five Millets from Martin Brimmer, and six miscellaneous watercolors. The only American works were the two Boits. The Water-Color Gallery contained largely oils; see Walter Muir Whitehill, *Museum of Fine Arts, Boston, A Centennial History* (Cambridge, Massachusetts: The Belknap Press of Harvard University Press, 1970), pp. 48-49. From 1876 to 1892 the Boston Athenaeum placed on loan to the Museum fifty-two watercolors made between 1806 and 1820 by British artists, originally owned by Thomas Dowse, a Cambridge leather dresser who won them in a lottery. These meticulously executed, miniature versions of

important old-master paintings from British collections, had been made as models for engravers. In Boston, they were probably regarded as stand-ins for the old master paintings the Museum lacked, rather than as examples of English watercolors. See Harry L. Katz, "The Thomas Dowse Collection of Watercolors," in Jonathan P. Harding, *The Boston Athenaeum Collection: Pre-Twentieth Century American and European Painting and Sculpture* (Boston: The Boston Athenaeum, 1984), pp. 93-109.

4. An album in the Boston Athenaeum illustrates the kind of watercolors made by women in Boston in the early 1870s. Compiled by Emily M. Eliot (1857-1925) later Mrs. John H. Morison, mother of historian Samuel Eliot Morison, the album contains thirty-two watercolors and drawings. Eighteen watercolors are by women: eleven are landscapes (New England seashores predominate, but two by Mrs. E. Cunningham depict towns in China); six are flowers; and one is a bird. As a whole the works in the album convey the modest nature and limited subject matter of the enthusiastic amateur. Among the recognized names of professionals are Christopher Cranch, Theodore O. Langerfeldt, Ellen Day Hale, and Sarah Wyman Whitman.

5. William Howe Downes, "Boston Art and Artists," *Discussions on American Art and Artists* (Boston: American Art League, 1896), p. 279. The Museum School did not offer watercolor classes, although the medium was used in design classes, including those taught in the 1880s and 90s by watercolorists Joseph Lindon Smith and C.H. Walker. Frank Benson made

his watercolors during periods when he did not teach at the school. Mercy A. Bailey taught watercolor at Cowles Art School in the mid 1880s. Among the Boston artists who advertised private instruction in watercolor were Thomas Edwards in the 1820s, Ross Turner and Robert David Wilkie in the 1880s, and S.P.R. Triscott and Charles Herbert Woodbury in the 1890s.

6. For a full discussion of the rise of the American watercolor movement, which was centered in New York City, see Kathleen Adair Foster, "Makers of the American Watercolor Movement: 1860-1890," (Ph.D. diss. Yale University, 1982).

7. Ninety women are listed among the 210 donors and former owners of watercolors in the Museum's *Catalogue of Paintings and Drawings in Water Color* (Boston: Museum of Fine Arts, 1949), pp. 301-305. Relatively few objects in the collection can be traced back to the point of purchase.

8. Information about many of the collectors has been gathered from essays relating to the Museum's collection of paintings. These include: Alexandra R. Murphy, "French Paintings in Boston: 1800-1900," in *Corot to Braque* (Boston: Museum of Fine Arts, 1979); Carol Troyen, "The Boston Tradition: Painters and Patrons in Boston 1720-1920," in *The Boston Tradition, American Paintings from the Museum of Fine Arts, Boston* (New York: The American Federation of Arts, 1980); Susan Fleming, "The Boston Patrons of Jean-François Millet," in Alexandra R. Murphy, *Jean-François Millet* (Boston: Museum of Fine Arts, 1984); Carol Troyen and Pamela S. Tabbaa, *The Great Boston Collectors: Paintings from the Museum of Fine Arts* (Boston: Museum of Fine Arts, 1984); and Trevor J. Fairbrother, "Painting in Boston 1870-1930," in Fairbrother, *The Bostonians: Painters of an Elegant Age, 1870-1930* (Boston: Museum of Fine Arts, 1986), as well as Erica E. Hirshler's artists' biographies in that book. In addition, several colleagues in the Department of Paintings have generously shared unpublished papers, lectures, and research files on collectors: Carol Troyen on the Karoliks; Peter Sutton on Thomas Dowse; Eric Zafran on Monet; and Erica Hirshler on Hooper, Whitman, and Sears.

9. It was in 1879 that George Loring Brown also held an auction of his work in Boston. It contained numerous watercolors never before put on the market; see cat. 15.

10. No catalogues were prepared for either the Homer or La Farge exhibition. Their contents must be derived from Museum records, including loan cards for individual objects and lists of lenders published in the Museum's annual reports for 1910 and 1911. William Howe Downes lists his recollections of the contents of the Homer exhibition in *The Life and Works of Winslow Homer* (Boston: Houghton Mifflin, 1911), pp. 288-290.

11. Lloyd Goodrich, *Winslow Homer* (New York: The Macmillan Company, 1945), pp. 127-128.

12. These four, plus an undated *Boys Playing Marbles*, were on deposit at the Museum between 1911 and 1915 and their appearances are recorded by small photographs. While no records of Homer's 1878 auction survive, the early dates of Angell's drawings suggest he may have bought them from that sale.

13. *Elms in Summer* by George Inness was a gift to the Museum in 1941 from Wigglesworth's great nephew, Edward Jackson Holmes.

14. See Erica E. Hirshler, "Mrs. Gardner's Rival: Susan Cornelia Warren and her Art Collection," *Fenway Court 1988* (Boston: Isabella Stewart Gardner Museum, 1989), pp. 44-55.

15. They purchased one of America's greatest old master paintings, Rogier van der Weyden's *Saint Luke Painting the Virgin* and gave it to the Museum in 1893. Ida Higginson's sister was married to the great Millet collector, Quincy Adams Shaw. The Higginson-Agassiz-Shaw circle was outspoken in its dislike of Impressionism; see Whitehill, *Museum of Fine Arts, Boston*, p. 335.

16. James L. Yarnall, "John La Farge and Henry Adams in the South Seas," *American Art Journal* 20 (summer 1988), p. 99 and note 231.

17. In 1912 the Museum acquired a number of La Farge drawings and watercolors from the artist's estate, using a "special picture fund" for the purpose. Given Higginson's close connections with the artist, he may very well have been the moving force behind this acquisition.

18. Hooper's collection was that most extensively represented in the Museum's memorial exhibition to Winslow Homer in 1911. Ten of Hooper's watercolors were identified as being from his estate; the remaining five were lent by his daughters Mrs. Greely S. Curtis and Mrs. Roger Warner; the oil, *Huntsman and Dogs* (1891, Philadelphia Museum of Art,) was lent by his daughter Mrs. Bancel La Farge. Hooper's five daughters, who include Mrs. Ward Thoron and Mrs. John Briggs Potter (wife of the Museum's keeper of paintings from 1902-1935), would lend the works they inherited from their father to subsequent Homer and La Farge exhibitions.

19. Four were lent to the 1897 Boston Art Students Association exhibition of watercolors and pastels.

20. John Chipman Gray, typescript annotated "Boston Transcript July 3, 1901," in a folder on Edward W. Hooper (HUG 300), Harvard University Archives.

21. Bigelow's interior decoration was still in place in the 1970s when the house was occupied by his relatives Mr. and Mr. Francis B. Lothrop.

22. Whitehill, *Museum of Fine Arts, Boston*, p. 106.

23. Undated letter to W.G. Constable, curator of paintings, in object files, Department of Prints, Drawings, and Photographs, Museum of Fine Arts, Boston.

24. Quoted in Karen M. Haas, "Dodge Macknight – *painting the town red and violet. . .," Fenway Court 1982* (Boston: Isabella Stewart Gardner Museum, 1983), p. 47.

25. These included John Singer Sargent, Lilla Cabot Perry (sister-in-law of John La Farge), and Homer's old friend Joseph Foxcroft Cole.

26. Fitzgerald exhibited a watercolor at the Boston Art Club's twenty-fourth exhibition in 1881.

27. See Carol Clark, Nancy Mowll Mathews, Gwendolyn Owens, *Maurice Brazil Prendergast, Charles Prendergast, A Catalogue Raisonné* (Williamstown, Massachusetts: Williams College Museum of Art, 1990), no. 1808, last known in Kimball collection in 1901. This may be the same as no. 687, *St. Mark's Square, Venice (The Clock Tower)*, the only other watercolor of the subject catalogued, now in the William A. Farnsworth Library and Art Museum, Rockland, Maine, that was formerly owned by Sarah Choate Sears of Boston.

28. Much helpful information about Hunt's students can be found in Martha J. Hoppin, "Women Artists in Boston, 1870-1900: The Pupils of William Morris Hunt," *American Art Journal* 13 (winter 1981), pp. 17-46.

29. James L. Yarnall, *John La Farge: Watercolors and Drawings* (Yonkers, New York: The Hudson River Museum of Westchester, 1990), p. 35.

30. Some of the information on Whitman is derived from unpublished biographical notes compiled by Betty S. Smith.

31. The other donors were Mrs. A. F. Wadsworth, Miss A. E. Wadsworth, Miss M. F. Hooper, and Mrs. Arthur Cunningham Wheelwright. Mrs. Wheelwright was also a patron of Lilian Westcott Hale. She lent three watercolors and two oils by La Farge to the Museum's 1911 memorial exhibition; her daughter Mary C. Wheelwright lent La Farge watercolors in the 1930s and 40s, and gave the Museum cat. 43.

32. See Stephanie Mary Buck, "Sarah Choate Sears: Artist, Photographer, and Art Patron" (M.F.A. thesis, Syracuse University, 1985).

33. Sears's collection was left to her only surviving child, Helen (Mrs. J. D. Cameron Bradley), who over the years sold some objects and left the rest to her three children.

34. See Gwendolyn Owens, "Maurice Prendergast Among His Patrons," in Clark et al., *Prendergast*, pp. 48-50.

35. The influence of Persian miniatures and Chinese paintings on Sears's floral watercolors was noted in a February 1920 review, source unknown, quoted in Buck, "Sarah Choate Sears," p. 88.

36. In the same year that they were purchased, Boit placed Sargent's spectacular painting of his daughters on permanent loan to the Museum; the daughters gave it in his memory in 1919. For more on Boit, see Kent Ahrens, *Oils and Watercolors by Edward D. Boit* (Scranton, Pennsylvania: Everhart Museum, 1990).

37. The two small images of palm trees are no longer accepted as authentic works by Homer.

38. Whitehill, *Museum of Fine Arts, Boston*, p. 520. The catalogue of the Karolik paintings was published in 1948, and the paintings placed on exhibition (in new galleries) in 1951.

39. Both letters are in departmental files, Department of Prints, Drawings, and Photographs. The dealers mentioned, who were among those pursuing works for Karolik and the Museum, are William Collins of Knoedler's, Rudolf Wunderlich of Kennedy & Co., Robert McIntyre of William Macbeth, Harry Shaw Newman of the Old Print Shop, and Victor Spark.

40. H. P. Rossiter to Rudolf Wunderlich, December 1, 1948; departmental files, Department of Prints, Drawings, and Photographs.

41. H. P. Rossiter to Victor Spark, August 30 and May 23, 1949, respectively; departmental files, Department of Prints, Drawings, and Photographs.

Georgia O'Keeffe (1887-1986), *Seated Nude
XI*, 1917. Watercolor on paper.
The Metropolitan Museum of Art. Purchase,
Mr. and Mrs. Milton Petrie Gift, 1981.

A WAR WAGED ON PAPER: WATERCOLOR AND MODERN ART IN AMERICA

Carol Troyen

"We are beating the world in watercolors, just now."
— Henry McBride, *The Dial*, May 1921

McBRIDE'S CLAIM reflects a critical link between the interests of the avant-garde and painting in watercolor, for among the leaders of the modernist movement in America were several artists who chose watercolor as their primary medium. This in itself was noteworthy: despite the activities of the American Watercolor Society and the various art clubs across the country, watercolor was still considered "lighter fare," not the medium on which an artistic revolution could be built. Yet John Marin and Charles Demuth and with them Georgia O'Keeffe (who worked prolifically — and brilliantly — in watercolor between 1916 and 1918) were among the chief proponents of modernism in America in the teens, and the medium through which they raised its banner was watercolor. In the 1920s, equally innovative developments in imagery and technique were introduced by Charles Burchfield and Edward Hopper, who worked extensively in watercolor during that decade. The work of artists such as these not only elevated the status of the medium, but also established watercolor as a vehicle for the introduction of new styles. In their hands, watercolor contributed significantly to the advancement of progressive art in the twentieth century.

If much of the battle for modern art in America was waged on paper, the reasons these artists gravitated toward watercolor rather than oil are quite varied, and reside in their personalities. Demuth's health was delicate (he wrote to Alfred Stieglitz that painting in oils required too prolonged an effort),[1] while Marin's robust, athletic nature drove him to paint out of doors, often in rough, inaccessible places — much easier with a small box of watercolors than with cumbersome oil painting equipment. Hopper concentrated on watercolor in response to a favorable market: he had been unable to sell any work until he began painting watercolors in the twenties. O'Keeffe's rigorous self-discipline led her to work through one medium at a time, first charcoal, then watercolor, and then oil, while Burchfield's impatience in the late teens — his mind was "teeming with ideas," he said, and pictures were spewing forth[2] — meant that oil was too time-consuming, so he grafted oil painting techniques onto watercolor.

The efforts of Marin, Demuth, Burchfield, and the others were acknowledged in a historic show organized by the Brooklyn Museum of Art in 1921. "A Group Exhibition of Water Color Paintings by American Artists" was the first major display of recent achievements in the medium. The next year, collector and critic A.E. Gallatin published *American Water-colourists*, the first serious survey of American watercolor painting. These events demonstrated, in Gallatin's modest words, that "during recent years a number of America's most talented artists have made a serious study of water-colour drawing, with admirable results." Noting that no "American school of water-colourists has actually been established," Gallatin saw the best of these painters as united by "the spirit of modernity,"[3] and celebrated the differences in their techniques, from Demuth's essentially classic, transparent wash style and Marin's expressive, gestural manner to Burchfield's scumbled layers. Others, too, had been working actively, and inventively, in watercolor in the teens, among them Abraham Walkowitz, Marguerite and William Zorach, and Max Weber. For all these painters, intent on forging a new style, making watercolor a major vehicle was in itself an act of rebellion.

Watercolor was not taught in art schools. It was not a particularly visible medium in the museums or galleries: dealers often scheduled watercolor displays as end-of-season shows,[4] and the Metropolitan Museum of Art routinely waited until late spring or summer to bring out its American watercolors. The medium typically lent itself to small-scale, delicate works and was often used for sketches and preparatory studies. As such, it ran counter to the desire that had governed American artists from Washington Allston and Thomas Cole to Winslow Homer: to make works of epic scale and meaning. Yet its very ranking as a minor medium made it appealing to those attempting to forge an American artistic identity. It had no inhibiting academic constraints. It was perceived as a democratic medium, based on inexpensive, readily available, and easily transported materials, and on spontaneous and essentially instinctive techniques. It had distinguished American forebears – John Singer Sargent, John La Farge, and especially Homer – but, despite the accomplishments of J.M.W. Turner and others, no daunting European tradition. Watercolor was an area in which American artists could hope to make dramatic, innovative statements and to define an indigenous art.

WATERCOLOR AND THE AVANT-GARDE

THE STORY of American modernist watercolors begins, as does the story of American modernism generally, with Stieglitz on the one hand, and Paul Cézanne on the other. In June of 1907, the Galerie Bernheim-Jeune in Paris mounted an exhibition of Cézanne's watercolors; this was followed in October by a large retrospective, also including watercolors, at the Salon d'Automne. Many American artists (among them Maurice Prendergast, Edward Steichen, Max Weber, John Marin, Alfred Maurer, Abraham Walkowitz, and Walter Pach) were in Paris at the time, and presumably visited the exhibitions. The American notion of watercolor practice was dramatically altered by what they saw: whole areas of the sheet left bare, ephemeral washes, areas of color breaking free of underdrawing, forms suggested rather than defined (see fig. 1). Until that time, most painters had aimed to produce watercolors that were carefully detailed and highly finished. The Cézanne exhibitions influenced artists to try a new stylistic vocabulary in a variety of forms and media. Watercolor, ever malleable, was well suited to the modernist enterprise.

Perhaps the most important American gallery-goers in Paris that summer were the watercolorist Maurice Prendergast and the painter and photographer Edward Steichen. Prendergast was overwhelmed by Cézanne. After seeing the show at Bernheim-Jeune, he wrote his patron Mrs. Oliver Williams of Boston that Cézanne "had a watercolor exhibition late in the spring which was to me perfectly marvelous. He left everything to the

Fig. 1. Paul Cézanne (1839-1906), *Trees and Rocks*, about 1890. Graphite and watercolor on paper. Philadelphia Museum of Art. Samuel S. White III and Vera White Collection.

Fig. 2. Henri Matisse (1869-1954), *Nude*, about 1905. Watercolor on paper. The Metropolitan Museum of Art. The Alfred Stieglitz Collection, 1949.

imagination; they were great for their sympathy and suggestive qualities" – and predicted the impact the French master would have on his style.[5] Prendergast's innovations in turn influenced others, as did the enthusiasm for Cézanne he communicated to his friends. "The influence of Maurice B. Prendergast is not alone to be measured in terms of his beautiful vision and his color: one needs to hear what the continual references to Cézanne in his conversation meant to the Americans who knew him abroad and, later, at home."[6]

Steichen, working as Alfred Stieglitz's agent, was also an enthusiastic visitor to the Cézanne exhibitions, and counseled Stieglitz (who was himself in Paris for part of that summer) to present a show of the watercolors at the latter's gallery, 291, in New York. Stieglitz was reluctant for a while[7] but gradually came around to Steichen's view, and in March of 1911 he mounted the first exhibition of Cézanne's works ever to be seen in America. His skepticism had turned to enthusiasm, and the show had a marked effect on young painters and critics.[8]

Stieglitz had already arranged the New York debuts of several of the most exciting modern European masters. In 1908 and 1910 he put on shows of watercolors and drawings by Rodin and Matisse. Following the Cézanne exhibition in 1911, he hung eighty-three drawings and watercolors by Picasso, made between 1905 and 1910, and showed Francis Picabia's New York studies (most of which were watercolors) in 1913. That Stieglitz (often prompted by Steichen) was the first to bring these artists to America is well known; it should be noted, however, that all of these shows featured works on paper, primarily watercolors, and as such gave a special status to that medium among the young artists eager to consider themselves avant-garde. The Rodins and Matisses (see fig. 2), with their sinuous lines and graceful splashes of color, reinforced the American watercolorists' determination to simplify. The Picassos introduced a new formal vocabulary. And the Picabias – in whose seeming outrageousness the press reveled – gave a European imprimatur to their own highly abstracted and personal renderings of the urban scene. Practical considerations no doubt influenced Stieglitz's preference for watercolor shows – works on paper, being smaller and generally lower in monetary value than oils, were easier and cheaper to import, and were more suitable in their scale to the tiny spaces of 291. However, Stieglitz claimed that his special affinity for watercolor, and for the so-called secondary media generally, was based on egalitarian sentiments: "[I do] not see why photography, water colors, oils, sculptures, drawings, prints. . . are not of equal potential value. I cannot see why one should differentiate between so-called 'major' and 'minor' media. I have refused so to differentiate in all the exhibitions that I have ever held."[9]

Among Stieglitz's first exhibitions of works by American artists was a show of watercolors by John Marin (hung with oil sketches by Alfred Maurer), which opened in March of 1909. He presented Marin's watercolors and pastels – the travel sketches Marin made in Europe the year before – again in 1910, gave him another show in 1911, another in 1913, and thereafter showed his works almost annually, providing Marin with continuous support and promotion second only to those afforded Georgia O'Keeffe. And Marin repaid Stieglitz handsomely: his works always sold well, he was an eloquent and charming defender of modernism, he enjoyed consistent critical support (despite the derision occasionally heaped on Stieglitz and other 291 artists), and the compelling presence of his watercolors demonstrated to his fellow artists that works of consequence could be made in a medium often previously considered minor.

Marin's Tyrolean watercolors, shown at 291 in 1911 and celebrated the next year in Stieglitz's journal, *Camera Work*, were daring examples of the wet-on-wet technique, with blended and stained and blotted color producing atmospheric, visionary landscapes (see fig. 3). Though these works have recognizable motifs, they are more evocative than descriptive, and mark a significant change from the attractive tourist watercolors he showed at 291 the year before. Some writers attributed Marin's development to the influence of Cézanne (critic, caricaturist, and sometime gallery director Marius de Zayas claimed that "the exhibitions at '291' of Cézanne and Picasso watercolors and the talks in the gallery stimulated [Marin] to open up to the suggestion of abstraction as a motive").[10] Others found the source of Marin's abstraction in the work of Whistler. Noted critic Charles Caffin, for example, said that Marin was "the first modern to attempt this abstract use of form," and left those "beautiful evasions" [the Nocturnes] "to be carried further by others who would view the facts of appearances in clear open daylight and yet discover how to render their abstraction."[11] But neither artist's example fully explains the monumentality of these works. In them, Marin uses the transparency and delicacy of watercolor, thought to disqualify the medium from real seriousness of purpose, to create heroic images.

Stieglitz was not alone in promoting American achievements in watercolor in the teens. The Carroll Galleries showed Cubist watercolors in 1914, and in 1915 exhibited watercolors by Prendergast and Derain. Charles Daniel showed Demuth's watercolors from 1914 and, after 291 closed in 1917, Daniel put on several group exhibitions of watercolors. In 1920, Daniel mounted a ten-year retrospective of Marin's work, orchestrated by Stieglitz. Watercolors and drawings were the subject of Stuart Davis's first solo show at the Sheridan Square Galleries in 1917. In addition, New York's most prominent galleries were paying significant attention to the "old masters" of the medium: Sargent, Whistler, Homer, and Eakins all had shows of their watercolors in this decade.[12]

The principal alternative to the shows at 291 and the other small galleries was the annual exhibition of the American Watercolor Society in New York. The American Watercolor Society was founded in 1866 by a group of artists (many of whom were primarily oil painters) who wished to elevate the status of the medium (for watercolor was considered the domain of amateurs and women). They arranged shows that paralleled the oil painting annuals at the National Academy of Design, and these exhibitions soon became a regular and popular feature of the New York exhibition season. Following the lead of their colleagues in New York, professional painters in Boston, Philadelphia, and other cities also founded watercolor clubs and arranged annual displays. Such figures as Winslow Homer, Thomas Eakins, and William Trost Richards were members and showed in the annuals. But by the turn of the century, the hardwon status as a main-

Fig. 3. John Marin (1870-1953), *Tyrol Series No. 3*, 1910. Waterolor on paper. Philadelphia Museum of Art. The Alfred Stieglitz Collection.

stream medium, once sought as a blessing, had become a curse. The Society's annuals had long since become the forum for the most hidebound painters, while the great practitioners of the medium maintained only a token presence there.

John Marin actually showed with the American Watercolor Society just as he was beginning to work with Stieglitz: he submitted four works to the 43rd annual, held in the late spring of 1910. Although none of these watercolors can be identified today, their titles suggest that they were like the European views he had showed earlier at 291 – tame compared to the Tyrolean works, but, with their free-flowing washes and liberal use of the white paper, far more radical than anything else in the annual.

To be sure, that show was a strong, handsome gathering. It contained some 550 works, and included, as was the Society's usual practice, pastels and drawings (among the latter, Sargent's masterly portrait of William Butler Yeats, lent by John Quinn) as well as watercolors. The selection encompassed the subjects traditionally treated by watercolorists. There were conventionally composed landscapes by such artists as Charles Gruppe, W. M. Hunt, and James Smillie.[13] There were quite a few floral still lifes. There were boisterous urban scenes by William Glackens and illustrations by John Sloan, and several heroic marine subjects clearly inspired by Homer.[14] There were many watercolors with a strong narrative or illustrational aspect, and numerous travel "sketches," such as Alice Schille's *A Market in Dalmatia* and William H. Lippincott's highly finished *Courtyard, Cuernavacca*. Predictably, the prices asked for these watercolors favored the established, conventional painters: Marin's pictures, priced at $9 and $22, were among the cheapest, while the most expensive works in the show were works like Taos painter E. Irving Couse's *Magic Flute*, priced at $1000. The William T. Evans prize for the most distinguished watercolor was awarded to R.M. Shurtleff for *June*, an intimate view of a stream in the forest composed in the Barbizon manner. Like most of the works in the show, it was highly proficient technically, deliberately crafted, and appealing, if not challenging. These watercolors, many encased in gold mats and heavy gold frames, were presented as the equivalent of oils – massive, dignified, and finished. Marin's watercolors, on the other hand, asserted the primacy of the medium by emphasizing the qualities that were not like oil: spontaneity, transparency, and, above all, the freedom to leave large areas of the paper blank.[15]

Watercolors were also included in the two big surveys of modern art mounted in the teens, the International Exhibition of Modern Art, or Armory Show, which opened in New York on February 17, 1913, and the Forum Exhibition of Modern American Painters of 1916. The Armory Show, which included nearly 1300 works of art, was an attempt to present the new art on a scale and in a forum comparable to that of the big academy exhibitions. Although the watercolors in the Armory Show were hardly discussed at all, they comprised about ten percent of the works on view. As was standard practice in international exhibitions of this sort, they were grouped with drawings and segregated by nationality. The show presented the opportunity to see more watercolors by Rodin, Cézanne, and Picasso, as well as several by Gauguin. A sizeable group of watercolors by Signac demonstrated the medium's suitability to a sparkling Post-Impressionist style. Among the Americans showing watercolors, a number, including J. Alden Weir, Charles Hovey Pepper, and Dodge Macknight, worked in a traditional manner (which by this time meant an Impressionist style, sometimes with moody Whistlerean overtones).[16] Several progressive painters, including Marin, of course, but also Stuart Davis, chose to be represented only by watercolors. Both new figures on the scene, for example, Oscar Bluemner, and such familiar, yet consistently innovative, painters as Prendergast, showed oils and watercolors in equal numbers, asserting the value they placed on the medium.

The impact of the Armory Show – especially of the European paintings on view there – has been well documented.[17] However, it should be noted that, as exhilarating as the presence of the European moderns must have been for the American painters, the attention paid to Duchamp, Picasso, Matisse, Cézanne and the others at their expense must have been somewhat disheartening. Although twice as many American as European works were displayed, the native art was far less important in the minds of most critics. And whereas the audience for Stieglitz's modernist shows at 291 tended to be quite small and generally predisposed to the new art he was promoting, the Armory Show, grand in scale and in the ruckus it generated, spawned a whole new public for modern art. That public may not have been overly sympathetic to what it saw, but it came away from the show aware that an artistic revolution had taken place. Suddenly a preponderance of New Yorkers knew who Cézanne and Duchamp were, and as a result, the French painters' prices began to rise. It would be at least a dozen years before Marin and the other Americans would be so well known. As stimulating as the Europeans' stylistic innovations must have been, they were at the same time daunting competition for a group struggling to establish an aesthetic identity and claim their market share.

In the celebrated Forum Exhibition, organized in 1916 by Robert Henri, Alfred Stieglitz, the critic Willard Huntington Wright, and three others, watercolor played a somewhat larger role. The show was designed "to present for the first time a comprehensive, critical selection of the serious painting now being shown in isolated groups; to turn public attention. . . from European art and concentrate it on the excellent work done in America; and to bring serious, deserving painters in direct contact with the public without a commercial intermediary." Sixteen artists were chosen to demonstrate "the very best examples of the more modern American art"; the works selected were, in the organizers' view, "the best paintings of each artist, regardless of medium."[18] Marin showed only watercolors (although he was producing oils in those years), and a number of other painters, including Charles Sheeler, Alfred Maurer, and Man Ray, chose to be represented by works in both media. For perhaps the first time outside of Stieglitz's walls, oils and watercolors were shown together as expressive equals.

The Forum Exhibition was not just an effort to continue to put progressive American art before a public suddenly much more conscious of European developments than ever before. It was also designed, as the organizers asserted, to create a market for such painting. By the time of the show, the work of such American realists as Luks, Bellows,

Fig. 4. Charles Demuth (1883–1935), *In Vaudeville: The Green Dancer*, 1916. Watercolor and graphite on paper. The Philadelphia Museum of Art. Samuel S. White III and Vera White Collection.

and Henri (which had come to be perceived as quite acceptable) had begun to sell; the market for French painting, both nineteenth- and twentieth-century, was growing stronger. But American modernists commanded very low prices – when they could sell at all – and watercolors traditionally sold for much less than oils.[19] Ferdinand Howald, the great Columbus, Ohio, patron of the new American art, paid only $20 for his first Demuth watercolor in 1916, and $130 for his first Marin than same year.[20] Despite the Forum Exhibition's ambitions, it did little to improve the market, and Marin's 1911 strategy of exhibiting his watercolors in both traditional and avant-garde arenas to maximize his exposure was employed by other artists through the teens. Charles Demuth, for example, showed his watercolors almost every year at Charles Daniel's gallery beginning in 1914, but he also participated in the annual Philadelphia watercolor exhibitions held at the Pennsylvania Academy.

DEMUTH, MARIN, AND O'KEEFFE

FROM the first appearance of his work in New York, Demuth was compared to Marin. Henry McBride, the prescient critic for the *New York Sun*, wondered, "Is he sufficiently different from Marin?" even while praising the twenty-five Provincetown landscape watercolors presented at the Daniel Gallery that fall.[21] A few years later, Hamilton Easter Field, editor and publisher of *The Arts*, contrasted Marin's rough, vigorous treatment with Demuth's more refined approach.[22] Despite Demuth's continuing affection for Marin and admiration for his work,[23] there was some rivalry between them, generated in part by the differences in their personal and pictorial styles, and by the consistently healthier market enjoyed by the older artist. However, in the teens, Marin's watercolors were a direct inspiration to Demuth, whose previous works had been in an impressionist style. The landscapes Demuth showed at Daniel's in 1914 were emulations of Marin's spontaneous, wet-on-wet technique. In fact, Demuth painted a *Landscape after Marin* (1914, private collection) in homage to the Tyrolean paintings he had seen at 291 and again in the Armory Show. The same liquid style, but now with Demuth's darker, cosmopolitan sensibility more in evidence, was exhibited in a group of floral still-lifes that Demuth displayed at Daniel's the next year. McBride's reservations gave way to unabashed enthusiasm in his discussion of the second show, in which he offered a perceptive description of Demuth's technique: "Mr. Demuth uses thin drawing paper and he allows his colors to run generously. . . . There is almost no attempt at realization, yet the stir and breeze of nature flow over his brilliant lines. Mr. Demuth has gained as an artist. His work has more breath and vitality, and always his drawings are decorative."[24]

The breezy, decorative, and yet slightly decadent aspect of much of Demuth's art in this period distinguishes it from Marin's, as does the figurative subject matter Demuth took up beginning about 1912 and developed extensively over the next six or seven years (see fig. 4). Various European precedents – very different from the antecedents detected in Marin – have been suggested for these watercolors. Demuth's images of the fashionable haunts and bohemian entertainments of the *haut-monde* were seen to contain "much that is Matisse, more that is Picasso, and a great deal that is Toulouse-Lautrec" when a group of the vaudeville pictures premiered at the Daniel Gallery in 1916.[25] There was also precedent for Demuth's subject matter in recent American art. Maurice Prendergast had painted a few cabaret scenes in Paris, and Shinn and Glackens had produced music hall subjects at the turn of the century. The simple, idiosyncratic, and seemingly casual style of Demuth's paintings has been related to Rodin's watercolors of nudes, which were shown at 291 in 1910 and again at the Armory Show; their *fleurs-du-mal* quality has been linked to Aubrey Beardsley's decorative approach to illustration.[26] And the drawings for stories by Zola, Wedekind, James, and others were in part a reflection of Demuth's student years in Philadelphia, where the illustrator tradition was strong, and where the *fin-de-siècle* sensibility, so evident in his work, had permeated more traditional illustrations.[27] Yet Demuth's ambitious compositions and inventive techniques surpassed Rodin's simple exercises; compared to Beardsley's mannered languor, Demuth's frenzied rhythms and nervous yet graceful lines electrify.

Demuth's technique in these watercolors was novel for an era that still placed such emphasis on careful finish. They were painted on very thin paper – some of it, bearing the watermark "Irish Linen," was undoubtedly writing paper. The poor quality of the paper (along with the raciness of several of the images) has led some to suggest that the watercolors were not made for public display, but rather for private consumption only,[28] or at least that, at this time Demuth was not very particular about his materials. In fact, he deliberately chose a paper that buckled frantically when wet, causing his color to puddle and pool. This property yielded a host of patterns, sometimes speckled, sometimes moiré, that are ornamental while suggesting textures. Similarly rich effects resulted from his choice of pigment, which was most likely thinned-down gouache, and which produced a mottled look in some areas and a smoky opacity elsewhere.[29] These scribbled caricatures are miracles of control, from the supple, interlocking areas of wash, so liquid yet so carefully contained, to the witty uses of paper reserves for such details as the ends of cigarettes or the whites of the eyes of his cabaret performers.

The stories Demuth chose to illustrate reflect his own taste for Symboliste literature; the nightclubs he depicted were the ones he frequented, and he more than once included in them portraits of himself and his friends. The confessional aspect continued in Demuth's watercolors of the late teens and twenties, if somewhat less overtly. They recorded his holiday travels – to Gloucester, Provincetown, Bermuda – and the architecture of his beloved Lancaster (often given cryptically personal titles, such as "from the garden of the chateau"). Even his still lifes, seemingly so restrained and objective, were sometimes invested with an anthropomorphic message, as was revealed in his note to Stieglitz concerning *Eggplant and Peppers* (1922, Fisk University, Nashville, Alfred Stieglitz Collection; see cat. 100) in which he compared the eggplant to "a heart – maybe mine."[30] The technique of these later watercolors seems cooler, more classical, less passionate than the illustrations, but they are in their own way equally mercurial, equally

Fig. 5. Charles Demuth (1883-1935), *Red Chimneys*, 1918. Watercolor on paper. The Phillips Collection, Washington, D.C.

Fig. 6. Paul Strand (1890-1976), *John Marin, Taos, New Mexico*, 1930. Gelatin silver print. The J. Paul Getty Museum. Copyright 1971, Aperture Foundation, Inc., Paul Strand Archive.

evasive. In *Red Chimneys* (fig. 5), for example, Demuth turned to conventional watercolor paper and used the inherent granularity of the opaque pigments he favored to imitate the texture of the mottled, sun-bleached rooftops. These watercolors are far less liquid than the illustrations, and techniques such as blotting and lifting, used rather spontaneously before, are now employed in a manner that is deliberate, structural, architectonic; in some of his works, Demuth even seems to have used square pieces of blotting paper to create a faceted, cubified effect. But what remains constant is Demuth's use of the white paper to dematerialize his image. His pictures – both the architectural subjects and the still lives – are built of simple forms whose solidity he deliberately undercuts; edges are taut in one place while blurred and diffuse in others, fading into the paper. The rooftops, the pears, the leaves on a branch consolidate and then dissolve, much as Demuth himself would burst into town for an explosion of revelry, and then disappear to Lancaster to recover, and to paint.

The personal nature of Demuth's watercolors undoubtedly enhanced their appeal for the romantic Stieglitz, who valued intuition over intellect, personal expression over analytic thought, and spiritual interpretation over realistic description. On the other hand, Demuth's cosmopolitan manner and the *fin-de-siècle* cynicism expressed in his art was out of sync with the wholesome naturalism and American innocence Stieglitz required of his artists. Stieglitz was not insensitive to Demuth's essential shyness and self-doubt, as their correspondence attests (his New Year's greeting to Demuth in 1916 was typical of his terse, but affectionate, support: "I see by the 'Sun' that the watercolors are on exhibition. They are really fine to me"[31]). But the artist's seeming worldliness – Stieglitz found his work too refined, too French – and the competition he may have feared Demuth's exquisite watercolors would offer to the work of his favorites, Marin and O'Keeffe, may have convinced Stieglitz to keep him at arm's length. Despite Demuth's frequent pleas to join Stieglitz's group of artists, he did not exhibit under Stieglitz's banner until 1925.[32]

Stieglitz's affection for artists whom he could promote as "naturals" (that is, as essentially unaffected by European developments and academic strictures, and as such, truly American) explains, in part, his life-long devotion to Marin. Marin's work was described in *Camera Work* as "characterized by a playful spontaneity that has something of the infectious charm of the natural, unconscious movements of children whose naive simplicity it approaches more nearly than any work being produced today deserving to be called adult art."[33] Despite the clear debt of his work to Whistler, Cézanne, and cubism, Marin obligingly claimed to have spent little time in art museums or with other artists during his five years in Europe. Throughout his life he endeavored to "maintain and project a sense of his naïveté."[34] And the extreme physicality of Marin's technique and subject matter could be promoted as something quintessentially American (see fig. 6). "The work is local," wrote Stieglitz's friend, the critic Paul Rosenfeld in 1922. "None but one American-born could have rubbed this pigment and made it into the peculiarly tempered colour it is. The nervousness of Marin's pictures is deeply American, deeply

Yankee. . . . There is something Walt Whitmanish, a little crude and rough in its essence."[35]

Whether representing New York, New Mexico, or Maine, Marin's watercolors tend to be small in scale but monumental in feeling. His passion for the act of painting is evident in the materials he used: his papers were often handmade and richly textured; he frequently presented them in silver mats and frames of his own design. Not only did he use charcoal and opaque pigments along with traditional transparent washes, but also incorporated paper cutouts, pieces of string, and other collage elements into his pictures. He drew in the paint with the end of his brush, and "erased" areas of pigment to suggest the rising spray of his beloved Maine coast. In addition to using a variety of brushes, he applied paint with his fingers, with matchsticks, and with surgical syringes. His techniques – scraping, blotting, lifting – are equally varied and innovatively used, but are handled with such bravura as to seem effortless. The images that resulted in the teens and twenties (fig. 7) were complex, audacious, and dynamic, and were seen as "fast in the American life of the hour as a fibrous, tough little apple-tree is lodged and rooted in the ground."[36]

Stieglitz's insistence on the elemental strength and originality of the American painters he supported was an attempt to define an American artistic identity. It was furthermore a defense against the prevailing view that contemporary American art was merely a satellite of European developments.[37] It explains his affection for watercolor, a "natural" medium without a strong European tradition. It also explains some of the odder inclusions in 291's exhibitions programs: Gelett Burgess, a sophisticated humorist and an amateur painter, whose watercolors were exhibited in 1911 as "personal expressions," and the 1916 show of drawings and watercolors by Georgia Engelhard (Stieglitz's niece), who was billed as "a child ten years old . . . unguided and untaught." And it was one of the factors explaining Stieglitz's immediate and total enthusiasm for the work of Georgia O'Keeffe, beginning in 1916, when he received a group of her drawings from O'Keeffe's college friend, Anita Pollitzer.

Stieglitz defined O'Keeffe as a natural almost from the beginning. Upon receiving the charcoals that he would show at 291 in the late spring of 1916, he noted "A young girl [O'Keeffe was thirty years old at the time] of unusual sensibility has done some really personal abstractions."[38] He cast her in the role of the untutored, unique American genius – sometimes, as has recently been noted, to her detriment.[39] Nonetheless, like Marin, she concurred with this characterization, not going to Europe until she was sixty-six years old and often saying of herself, "I am one of the intuitive ones."[40]

O'Keeffe would address this theme repeatedly, denying, as did Marin, the relevance of foreign influences and minimizing the importance of her artistic education.[41] "It was in the fall of 1915," she wrote, "that I first had the idea that what I had been taught was of little value to me. . . . I said to myself, 'I have things in my head that are not like what anyone has taught me – shapes and ideas so near to me – so natural to my way of being and thinking that it hasn't occurred to me to put them down.' . . . There was no one

Fig. 7. John Marin (1870-1953), *Seascape*, 1914. Watercolor over graphite on heavy white wove paper. Harvard University Art Museums. Gift of James N. Rosenberg.

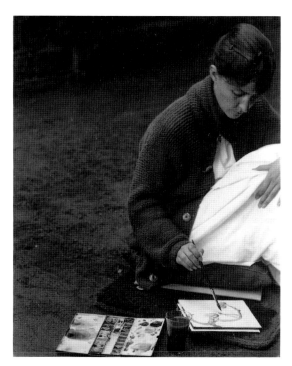

Fig. 8. Alfred Stieglitz (1864–1946), *Georgia O'Keeffe: A Portrait - with Watercolor Box*, 1918. Gelatin silver print. National Gallery of Art, Washington, D.C. Alfred Stieglitz Collection.

around to look at what I was doing – no one interested – no one to say anything about it one way or another. I was alone and singularly free, working into my own, unknown – no one to satisfy but myself."[42]

O'Keeffe prided herself on her creative independence, staking her claim on the artistic frontier: "I grew up pretty much as everybody else grows up and one day seven years ago found myself saying to myself – I can't live where I want to – I can't go where I want to – I can't do what I want to – I can't even say what I want to – . School and things that painters have taught me even keep me from painting as I want to. . . . I decided I was a stupid fool not to at least paint as I wanted to and say what I wanted when I painted."[43] She published this statement in the catalogue of her exhibition of 100 oils, watercolors, pastels, and drawings organized by Stieglitz and shown at the Anderson Galleries in New York in 1923. In the same catalogue, her friend Marsden Hartley described her intuitive genius, and her valiant struggle to express her beliefs, in the language of the American West: "She had seen hell. . . . She looks as if she had ridden the millions of miles of her every known imaginary horizon, and has left all her horses lying dead in their tracks."[44] O'Keeffe as the natural, as the plain, self-created, independent-minded American, was an image soon taken up in the press. Reporting an extraordinary price Stieglitz claimed to have obtained for a 1927 oil of a calla lily, the *New York Evening Graphic* proclaimed, "Not a rouged, cigarette-smoking, bob-haired, orange-smocked Bohemian, but a prim ex-country schoolmistress who actually does her hair up in a knot is the art sensation of 1928!"[45]

Although the romantic myth of O'Keeffe as an untutored American primitive is only partially true – she was extremely well-read, profited greatly from her education at several art academies and with such inspiring teachers as William Merritt Chase and Arthur Wesley Dow, and was keenly aware of artistic developments at home and abroad – the work she created leading up to her 1923 exhibition at the Anderson Galleries was in fact the result of a tremendous effort of self discipline and spiritual isolation. About 1915, O'Keeffe began working almost exclusively in charcoal, making the drawings sent to Stieglitz. She gradually reintroduced color into her work in the middle of the next year, but continued to restrict herself to making works on paper, most of which – despite the extraordinary expansiveness of her statements – were very small in scale. Her method was monastic. Rather than working at an easel, she sat on the floor, with the paper on the ground in front of her (see fig. 8). It was a very physical, concentrated way of working, and one of distillation rather than reaction, as she described to Polltizer: "Did you ever have something to say and feel as if the whole side of the wall wouldn't be big enough to say it on and then sit down on the floor and try to get it onto a sheet of charcoal paper? . . . I've been crawling around on the floor till I have cramps in my feet."[46]

O'Keeffe's watercolor method was practiced, yet spontaneous. Many of the watercolors she produced between 1916 and 1918 were executed in series – a mode of working she shared with Marin and Demuth. Her process was much more obsessive than theirs, however, for she would attempt a pictorial idea endlessly, until it satisfied her.[47] Some of the watercolors from 1916, for example, *Train at Night in the Desert* (Museum of Modern Art, New York) have the barest of graphite underpinnings. Some – such as the celebrated *Blue Lines* (1916, Metropolitan Museum of Art, New York) – have counterparts in charcoal, while still others seem to develop themes first essayed in black and white (e.g., *Red and Black* [1916, art market], which probably reflects *Blanket Drawing*, a 1916 charcoal).[48] Yet most of O'Keeffe's watercolors from this period have no linear scaffolding. She tended to work wet-on-wet, with her fluid, transparent washes carefully controlled so that colors bleed into one another, creating contours and producing subtle tonal variations. Counteracting the fluidity of her washes, O'Keeffe used paper reserves as linear elements – as with the horizon in the famous "Light Coming onto the Plains" series of 1917 (see fig. 9) – and to keep color areas at bay. Her technique and her self-discipline were ideal for series work: again and again she was able to find an evocative motif, a convincing gesture, which she repeated numerous times, letting the watercolor medium's natural accidental qualities affect the variant expressions. Most of the paintings produced during this period were based on observed forms, but the freedom afforded by the medium contributes to their unprecedented combination of description and suggestiveness.

As O'Keeffe's thematic groups of watercolors are known today, they seem to spell out an organic sequence. The celebrated "Blue" watercolors of 1916, for example, develop from detail to simplicity, from a design that fills the sheet completely and that resembles an art-nouveau textile design, to the most abbreviated and powerful graphic statement (see figs. 10 and 11). Similarly, the seven paintings that make up the *Evening Star* group of 1917 seem to evolve from an image of a gathering nova – an atmospheric, primordial shape – to a vibrant, powerful orb and then to dissolve again. It is likely that O'Keeffe imposed these arrangements on the watercolors after they were painted (rather than numbering them to document the sequence of creation), and so their ordering was clearly a part of the creative process. Unlike Marin's sequences (which gather together variations on a theme), or Demuth's (which set out a narrative), O'Keeffe's are a metaphor for evolution, distillation, and spiritual potency. As such, they validate Stieglitz's presentation of O'Keeffe as a natural.

Most of her watercolors were made in Canyon, Texas, far from art galleries and museums (but with *Camera Work*, and its reproductions of the latest European and American works, near at hand). The watercolors were not unaffected by other works of art [49] – and the sequence of sixteen watercolors of nudes made in 1917 and 1918 (see fig. 12) has often been attributed to the influence of Rodin's drawings, which O'Keeffe did see at 291. However, her method differed markedly from Rodin's. Though both were made from the model, Rodin worked by a kind of automatic writing technique, proceeding first with pencil (but never taking his eyes off the model until the drawing was done) and filling in with color washes afterward. O'Keeffe used no underdrawing to define the body; rather, she manipulated washes to define its contours. As did Rodin (and as Demuth did, in his Rodin-inspired nudes of 1913), O'Keeffe left much of the paper blank, and used no props

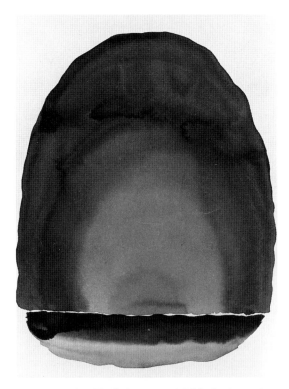

Fig. 9. Georgia O'Keeffe (1887-1986), *Light Coming on the Plains* III, 1917. Watercolor on paper. Courtesy Amon Carter Museum, Fort Worth, Texas.

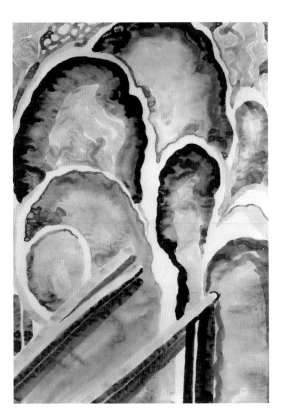

Fig. 10. Georgia O'Keeffe (1887-1986), *Blue #1*, 1916. Watercolor on tissue paper. The Brooklyn Museum. Bequest of Mary I. Cockcroft.

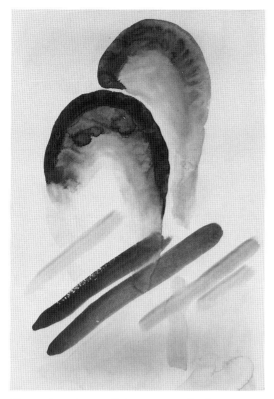

Fig. 11. Georgia O'Keeffe (1887-1986), *Blue #3*, 1916. Watercolor on tissue paper. The Brooklyn Museum. Dick S. Ramsay Fund.

Fig. 12. Georgia O'Keeffe (1887-1986), *Seated Nude XI*, 1917. Watercolor on paper. The Metropolitan Museum of Art. Purchase, Mr. and Mrs. Milton Petrie Gift, 1981.

or backdrop to create a sense of context for her figures. Her colors were sometimes naturalistic but more often arbitrary. This and her direct application of wash produced compositions that were far more abstract than the French master's. His work may have provided justification for the radical simplification of forms, but the evocative quality, the sense of figure emerging from amorphous shape, is hers.

In 1918, when the nudes were completed, O'Keeffe resumed making oils. The few watercolors from that year – such as *The Flag* and *Trees and Picket Fence* – tend to be more descriptive than the earlier paintings. Stieglitz noted that the medium had become a struggle for O'Keeffe. "Georgia has been having an awful time with the watercolors," he wrote to Arthur Dove. "She has done a few things, oils, which are worthy to be added to her good things of last year. . . . She claims to be having a hellish time getting her mind clarified," but that the oils were "very much more under control and full of quality."[50] Thereafter, O'Keeffe would make watercolors only occasionally – the best known of these are probably the paintings of cannas made about 1919-1920[51] – but some of the forms she devised during her intense period of involvement with the medium recur in her later oils.[52]

Stieglitz seems to have exhibited O'Keeffe's watercolors only once before the important Anderson Galleries show of 1923. In April 1917, Stieglitz displayed "watercolors, drawings in charcoal, oils, and a piece of statuary." This would be the last show at 291; it included, among other pictures, *Blue Lines*, the "Blue" series, and the very early *Tent Door at Night* (about 1913, University Art Museum, The University of New Mexico, Albuquerque). It resulted in a fair amount of critical enthusiasm[53] and at least one noteworthy sale. The watercolor *Train Coming into the Station* (1916; possibly *Train Coming into Canyon*, the painting now at the Amarillo [Texas] Art Center) reportedly sold to Stieglitz's friend Jacob Dewald for $400 – a remarkable price for an unknown artist.[54] The sale makes clear Stieglitz's determination from the outset to establish the highest market value for O'Keeffe's art.

O'Keeffe was not included in the Brooklyn Museum's "Group Exhibition of Water Color Paintings by American Artists" of 1921, an omission for which Paul Strand, writing for *The Arts*, took the organizers to task in his otherwise appreciative review of the show.[55] Hailed as "the best collection of American watercolors that has ever been seen . . . a service to art, artists, and the country,"[56] the exhibition was a survey of the medium from Homer and Sargent to Marin and Demuth. Coming on the heels of a controversial modern French painting show, the watercolor exhibition was seen as part of Brooklyn's continuing adventurousness in the arts, and asserted watercolor's promotion from establishment status to the ranks of the avant-garde. The Brooklyn show wrested the medium from the hands of the amateurs and conservatives, and inaugurated a decade of intense interest and activity in watercolor on the part of painters, critics, collectors, art galleries, and museums.

The "Group Exhibition of Water Color Paintings" in fact coincided with an exhibition of the mainstream tradition in American watercolor, for across the bridge in Manhattan, the New York Water Color Club and the American Watercolor Society opened their joint show in December. Critics found the display too large and the works too clever (that is, too concerned with virtuosity).[57] There was surprisingly little overlap in participants in the two shows, the Society's being dominated by such established painters as Jane Peterson, Luis Mora, Joseph Pennell, Gifford Beal, and a host of now-forgotten artists, while the Brooklyn show, though not excluding some of the above-named painters, was introduced by a gallery devoted to Homer and Sargent. It featured strong representations by La Farge and Prendergast, and included several popular Impressionist-inspired painters, such as Dodge Macknight and C.H. Woodbury, but placed its main emphasis on the moderns. Marin was represented by fourteen watercolors; Demuth by seven; Marguerite Zorach by six and her husband, William, by five. By prefacing the show with works by the great turn-of-the-century masters of watercolor, Homer, Sargent, and La Farge, the exhibition's organizers identified the younger watercolorists as heirs to a great legacy. By including large numbers of the moderns' works (rather than only one or two examples, as was the general rule in the society's annuals), the organizers were able to show the evolution of their styles, and to give the visitor a real understanding of their art. And by excluding the pastels, drawings, colored lithographs, and works in other media that customarily infiltrated Society shows, the Brooklyn exhibition made explicit the innovative nature of American watercolor.

In his review, Strand argued that Brooklyn should have been even more adventurous, and objected to the absence of Max Weber, Abraham Walkowitz, Charles Sheeler, Stanton Macdonald-Wright, and Thomas Hart Benton. He found virtue in those who used the medium unaffectedly, admiring Arthur B. Davies especially for "his fresher and translucent handling of the medium – white paper used instead of Chinese white." On the other hand, he criticized the "oil-like opacity" in the work of Macknight, Sargent, and others, and condemned Prendergast as "effete" – code, perhaps, for what the Stieglitz camp might have viewed as too redolent of French influence.[58]

Strand singled out Homer, Demuth, and Marin for special praise. As one of Stieglitz's surrogate voices in these years, he found their work "a challenge and a realization. . . an affirmation that a truly indigenous expression is as possible in America as in Europe." For perhaps the first time, Marin was cited as Homer's heir: "Marin is . . . moving with all Homer's virility and [directness] into the American scene. His work attests frankly to a conscious recognition on his part that he is rooted in this American continent." Once again, Marin and Demuth were compared. Both were lauded for developing watercolor's inherent characteristics, with Marin besting the younger artist in the American traits of manliness and native directness: Demuth "is a very sensitive rather than a robust talent." He "has yet to disentangle himself from the sophistication of contemporary French influence," while Marin's art is "America and nowhere else . . . a true embracement of this everyday American world . . . one of the few contemporary workers in any medium who is contributing to what may truthfully be called an American culture."[59]

The Brooklyn exhibition was the first major forum to associate the moderns with the established American masters of the medium. From this point, not only would the younger generation be elevated by the comparison, but their stature would also be measured by the degree to which they were perceived as continuing the direct, natural American style of Winslow Homer. The next year, in *American Water-colourists*, Gallatin juxtaposed Homer and Sargent, and Demuth and Marin, prompting Henry McBride, in a jaunty column entitled "American Art is 'Looking Up'," to remark, "to place Marin, Demuth and Burchfield firmly beside the fixed star, Winslow Homer, in a serious critical estimate is, to say the least, going some. It will not only be sure to affect the ideas of collectors but will put heart into the entire younger school."[60]

HOMER AND SARGENT

THE ATTEMPT to identify an American style also affected the reputations of Homer and Sargent, even as the popularity of their watercolors enhanced the reputations (and market) of the modernists. The watercolors of Homer and Sargent began to be exhibited and discussed with increased frequency just at the time Stieglitz began showing Marin's work. In February 1909, Sargent and his friend the Boston painter Edward Darley Boit had a large show of their watercolors at Knoedler's Gallery in New York. Though there were numerous inquiries about individual works, Sargent insisted on selling the watercolors as a group, and only to an important museum, so the pictures would continue to be shown together. The Brooklyn Museum took the lead in the pursuit of American watercolors; it bought eighty-three of the eighty-six Sargents exhibited for $20,000, or about $240 each. The bulk of the purchase price was contributed by the president of the museum, and the rest was raised by public subscription – a testimony to Sargent's popularity.[61] Three years later, Sargent allowed the Museum of Fine Arts, Boston (which had tried to get the 1909 group) to buy forty-five watercolors made in Italy between 1908 and 1911; the Metropolitan bought a group of ten in 1915. Two years later, the Worcester Art Museum bought eleven, painted in 1917 at Ormond Beach and Villa Vizcaya in Florida, for $2750, or $250 each. That Sargent insisted on selling the watercolors *en bloc* so that thematic groups would remain united, even though he would have made more money by selling the pictures individually, indicates the importance of the medium to him. At the same time, he created an extraordinary demand for his watercolors by dramatically holding out for a big sale[62] – a theatrical manipulation of the market that Stieglitz would employ a decade later. And, as Stieglitz would realize and turn to his advantage, "the widespread publicity attached to (these sales) had considerable influence in stimulating an interest in watercolor painting."[63]

After Homer's death in 1910, the marketing of his work was handled by his brother Charles, and by Knoedler's. The Metropolitan Museum bought twelve Homer watercolors from the group displayed at the memorial exhibition it mounted in 1910; Brooklyn bought twelve through Charles Homer in 1911; and Worcester acquired fourteen from

Knoedler's between 1908 and 1917, for prices ranging from $540 to $2200 (the latter for the 1904 work, *Turkey Buzzard*). Like the Brooklyn, Boston, New York, and Worcester Sargents, these groups, as well as the superb collection of Homer watercolors put together by Chicago patron Martin Ryerson (the bulk of which is now owned by the Art Institute of Chicago), would be the nuclei of the many Homer and Sargent watercolor exhibitions mounted in museums across the country over the next decade.[64]

Homer's and Sargent's watercolors (though not their oils) were exhibited together on several occasions – in Boston, in Paris, and most notably in a 1917-18 show that circulated to seven museums. There was rarely an attempt to claim that they were at all alike: they were simply recognized as the best. Indeed, they were portrayed as defining opposite poles of the American watercolor style: Homer's "virility and love of nature" were contrasted with Sargent's refinement, his "wonderful mastery, tact, and elegance."[65] When these exhibitions began, in about 1909-10, no superior merit was claimed for either artist. Sargent's sophistication, as well as the audacious compositions, lack of finish, and anti-purist approach to technique that characterized his watercolors, were compatible with the international interests and the vogue for sketchy finish and abstraction in progressive American art circles.[66] But by the 1920s, when critical responses to works of art were marked by a more insistent nationalism, Sargent's work began to be seen as facile and vaguely insincere. His reputation was eclipsed by Homer's, whose work became the touchstone for contemporary achievements in watercolor.

Homer in 1921 was widely hailed as "America's master in watercolor," as an artist who "never seemed interested in his own virtuosity" but (unlike many modern painters) was "a humble lover of nature, of truth, of life."[67] When a group of forty-nine watercolors were shown at the Carnegie Institute in 1923, they were admired as having "the freshness of a world far removed from that of our eighteenth-century academic beginnings. At [the] core [of his work] is a fund of that personality which in American art is the proud substitute for convention." Homer was, in other words, a natural, an intuitive and self-taught interpreter of the watercolor medium (the catalogue elsewhere describes him as taking a long time "to conquer the stubborn character of oil paint") whose "directness," whose "blunt naturalism," and whose "crisp spontaneity are intensely American."[68]

Sargent's 1924 retrospective at the Grand Central Art Galleries in New York was, compared to Homer's 1923 show in Pittsburgh, a highly publicized and controversial affair. It included seventy-two works, among them twelve watercolors. The show was enormously popular – some 60,000 people attended – and critical opinion was divided.[69] The catalogue contained paeans by such long-time Sargent advocates as Charles Caffin, Christian Brinton, and John Van Dyke, written between 1902 and 1919. But as if with one voice, modernist critics decried what they saw as Sargent's lack of depth and connectedness with American life; their tepid acknowledgment of his remarkable technical facility made it clear that it was viewed as a dubious asset.[70] Increasingly, only the most loyal of Sargent's followers would side with conservative critic Royal Cortissoz in regarding Sargent as "the great modern virtuoso of the medium, a Paganini of the brush."[71]

After Sargent's death in 1925, the Museum of Fine Arts, Boston, put on a large memorial exhibition and the Metropolitan Museum subsequently hung a somewhat smaller show. In both, watercolors (contributed by Worcester, Brooklyn, Boston, and the Metropolitan, as usual) played a significant role – they accounted for about half the works shown. After this, while adulation for Homer could be measured in the dozens of watercolor shows presented in museums and major art galleries, especially during the 1936 centennial year, no significant critical study of Sargent's work would appear and no major exhibition of his watercolors or oils would be mounted until his centenary in 1956.[72]

WATERCOLOR IN BOSTON AND PHILADELPHIA

ONLY IN Boston did Sargent's popularity remain constant. There, paradoxically, cosmopolitanism was a matter of civic pride, while attitudes toward the avant-garde, both European and American, were, at best, equivocal. In general, in the twentieth century the city's critics and collectors were more sympathetic to progressive art on paper than in the oil medium, perhaps because such distinguished watercolorists as Homer, Sargent, La Farge, and later Prendergast had connections to the city, and also because buying an adventurous watercolor was less of a risk, aesthetically and financially, than buying a radical oil. Around the time of the Armory Show, which traveled to Boston in abbreviated form (all American works were omitted), exhibitions of works on paper by several avant-garde artists appeared there for the first time.

In 1909, forty-six Rodin drawings were shown in Boston (as well as in Philadelphia); they were deemed "quite meaningless to the average viewer."[73] In 1911, the 23rd Annual Exhibition of the Boston Society of Water Color Painters featured a group of Matisse drawings (lent by Sarah Choate Sears, a watercolorist and broad-ranging collector). In 1925, the Boston Art Club showed Marin, and in 1926 the St. Botolph Club presented Hopper watercolors. And in September 1928, the Boston Art Club mounted a Picasso drawings show. Yet paralleling these events were equally momentous reactionary occurrences. In 1911, Edward Forbes, the director of the Fogg Art Museum, issued a statement detailing that institution's policy on contemporary art: "The difficulty is, first, that all modern art is not good, and we wish to maintain a high standard. In having exhibitions of the work of living men we may subject ourselves to various embarrassments," and therefore, no contemporary art was to be shown at the Fogg.[74] This philosophy persisted for several decades, and Boston institutions and organizations followed suit. After the Picasso show at the Boston Art Club in 1928, protests were so vehement that all but one member of the club's art committee were forced to resign, and under the leadership of a new, more conservative chairman, H. Dudley Murphy, the club issued a public statement claiming that it had "purged itself of modernism."[75]

The Boston Art Club and the city's two watercolor clubs had long been intertwined. The Boston Society of Water Color Painters was founded in 1885, with Sargent, Hassam, Boit, and Ross Turner among the members. The Boston Water Color Club, founded in 1887, was for women only (in response to the all-male Society); it was led by such painters as Sarah Choate Sears, the miniaturist Laura Coombs Hills, and Marcia Oakes Woodbury. In 1896, men were admitted, and exhibitions were held every February at the Boston Art Club. The Society showed at various commercial galleries in town; however, the two groups sometimes held combined shows. There was a great deal of overlap in the memberships of the two associations (although the Society remained all male), and with the Boston Art Club as well, the head of whose art committee, H. Dudley Murphy, served as vice-president of the Water Color Society through the 1920s.

The annuals of these two organizations tended to be self-congratulatory ("Boston prides itself on being the 'water color capital' of the nation") rather than experimental. In their preference for a pure watercolor technique (that is, one based on transparent washes in the English tradition rather than on extensive use of opaque pigments), they were bound up with the local tendency to anglophilia.[76] Through the twenties, these shows were dominated by a group of painters who worked extensively or exclusively in watercolor, among them C.H. Woodbury, Frank Benson (see fig. 13), H. Dudley Murphy, Charles Hopkinson, and the somewhat younger John Whorf. Most were second-generation Boston School painters, gravitating toward the masculine, outdoor subjects of Winslow Homer, executed in a light-filled, dashing style derived from Sargent, yielding works that were lively, popular, and not especially challenging. At the same time, a rebel faction was active – this was the group that had encouraged the 1928 Picasso show, and that was purged from the Boston Art Club thereafter. The "Boston Five" (Charles Hovey Pepper [see fig. 14], Harley Perkins, Marion Monks Chase, Charles Hopkinson, and Carl Cutler) was dedicated to bringing modernism to Boston, and whereas their brightly colored, decorative manner was tame compared to the radical abstractions of Marin or O'Keeffe, it was far more vigorous than the fare offered by the Boston Society of Water Color Painters. Even so, some of the Boston Five exhibited with the Society from time to time; they also showed as a group in New York, generally at the Montross Gallery.

One of the most important exhibitions of the work of the Boston Five was put on by the Harvard Society of Contemporary Art in February of 1930, to inaugurate that group's second season. The Harvard Society, founded by three precocious undergraduates (Lincoln Kirstein, Edward Warburg, and John Walker), was pledged to introducing to Cambridge the kind of contemporary art the Fogg would not display, and in the late twenties and early thirties it put on an astonishing series of shows that would become the basis for the initial exhibition programs of the Museum of Modern Art. Although the Boston Five was less advanced than the Society's pioneering founders (in 1930, they hosted the first Bauhaus show in America, for example), the Harvard exhibition was a gesture of solidarity with those artists who championed modernism in Boston against an increasingly old-fashioned artistic establishment.

A measure of Boston's conservatism in the arena of modern watercolor in the teens and twenties is the attention the city paid to Dodge Macknight, while largely ignoring a major figure of twentieth-century watercolor, Maurice Prendergast. Macknight was one

Fig. 13. Frank W. Benson (1862–1951), *Old Tom*, 1923. Watercolor on paper. Museum of Fine Arts, Boston. Bequest of Mrs. Edward Jackson Holmes, Edward Jackson Holmes Collection.

Fig. 14. Charles Hovey Pepper (1864–1950), *The Statesman*,
about 1936. Watercolor on paper. Museum of Fine Arts,
Boston. Charles Henry Hayden Fund.

of three watercolorists heralded in a large exhibition mounted by the Copley Society in
1921. Held in the rooms of the Boston Art Club, this popular show presented forty-six
watercolors by Homer, forty-eight Sargents, and an equal representation – forty-five – by
Macknight. Macknight's reputation, though now rather eclipsed, was at its peak in the
1920s, as is made clear by the lenders to that show. All the Macknights were supplied by
the city's cultural leaders. The list of lenders – including G. Peabody Gardner, Edward
Jackson Holmes, Sarah Choate Sears – comprised a "who's who" of Boston.

Macknight, although only four years younger than Sargent, was in many ways his
descendant. Like Sargent, he used watercolor to record his travels, making brightly colored, boldly composed sketches of such exotic locales as Mexico and the American
Southwest. (Unlike Sargent, however, his primary medium was not oil; rather, he worked
exclusively in watercolor.) The blue-brown palette that Sargent favored in his watercolors was heated up to purple and magenta in Macknight's hands; the same brilliant green
and yellow accents Sargent used were employed by Macknight as well. The two were
often compared; Macknight was also seen to have appropriated a sense of atmosphere
from another of Boston's artistic passions, French Impressionism.[77]

Although Macknight's support was not limited to Boston (A.E. Gallatin, in New
York, called him "one of the most significant of the American water-colourists" and discussed his work almost as extensively as he did that of Whistler, Sargent, and Homer),[78]
local collectors' enthusiasm meant that his work was rarely available elsewhere. The
openings of Macknight's annual shows at Doll & Richards Gallery in Boston were as
much theater as art – the gallery had to be barricaded till 10 AM on the day of the opening to keep purchasers at bay – and were reported with bold headlines in the press:
"MACKNIGHT SELLS 15 WATERCOLORS IN 11 MINUTES." "Record-Break-
ing Sale of Water Colors Amounts to Twenty-six Out of Thirty in Only Three Days."[79]
This extraordinary popularity persisted in Boston until about 1930, when the artist, then
seventy years old, seems to have retired from painting.[80]

In the same period, Maurice Prendergast, once Boston's most highly acclaimed resident watercolor painter, took his art in a direction few Bostonians could follow, and for
the last twenty years of his career he was generally neglected by local collectors and critics. Whereas in 1897, shortly after his triumphant debut at the Boston Art Club annual,
the Boston *Transcript* hailed him as "a brilliant and distinguished colorist," by 1913 he
was derided in the same paper as "mannered" and "incoherent." Even those once supportive found much that was puzzling in his later style, and he was associated with other
artists equally unfathomable to Bostonians: "Mr. Prendergast is becoming more impressionistic in his own whimsical and amusing way. He draws his figures almost as badly as
Matisse, and is fully as ingenious."[81]

Prendergast's early, much-beloved watercolors were themselves highly experimental and reflected the influence of adventurous European styles. They were decorative in a
manner paralleling art nouveau; their colorful palette, dotted with red accents, reflects a
Post-Impressionist aesthetic, as does the freedom from conventional perspective. Techni-

cally, Prendergast preceded Marin in his reliance on free-flowing, transparent washes and on pencil lines acting as independent graphic elements; another innovative component of his style was the active use of the white paper as a pictorial element.

By the turn of the century (after a sojourn to Italy probably subsidized by his first major Boston patron, Sarah Choate Sears), his works became even bolder compositionally – a modernist impulse Bostonians could accept because it was coupled with heightened attention to detail and a subdued palette, and because its Venetian subject matter appealed to a community attuned to Sargent and Henry James (see fig. 15). But subsequent trips abroad – most notably in 1907, when he was overwhelmed by Cézanne's work – ultimately resulted in a new, classicizing approach to subject matter and in a technical reliance on "wet, swirling brushstrokes enjoyed for themselves"[82] that emphasized the paper surface – developments that Bostonians found incomprehensible. Despite the fact that Prendergast exhibited frequently with the various art clubs in Boston through the teens and twenties, and also showed with his friends C.H. Pepper, Charles Hopkinson, and other popular watercolor painters, he made very few sales in Boston, and local institutions ignored him entirely for many years.[83]

Prendergast's later works were better received in New York. In the teens such noted champions of modern art as John Quinn and Lillie P. Bliss became devoted patrons.[84] They were especially enthusiastic about Prendergast's work in oil, which by the time of his 1915 show at the Carroll Gallery, had replaced watercolor as his major vehicle for stylistic experimentation. Yet the city's institutions were no more supportive than Boston's had been. The first museum exhibition of Prendergast's work was organized by the Whitney Museum in 1934, ten years after his death. The Metropolitan Museum didn't acquire a Prendergast, oil or watercolor, until the 1950s.[85]

Fig. 15. Maurice Prendergast (1858-1924), *The Grand Canal, Venice*. 1898-99. Watercolor and pencil on paper. Daniel J. Terra Collection. Courtesy, Terra Museum of American Art, Chicago.

WHEREAS Boston's only watercolor painter of the early twentieth century to play a significant role in the modernist revolution was Maurice Prendergast, Philadelphia could claim both Marin and Demuth as sometime citizens, and boasted of a rather larger number of collectors who were enthusiastic supporters of the American modernists. These included the painter Earl Horter, Samuel and Vera White (whose watercolors by Marin, Demuth, Walkowitz, and Horter were given to Philadelphia Museum), and the combative Albert Barnes (who in addition to acquiring superb Cézannes and Matisses would acquire some twenty Prendergasts – primarily oils – and about forty Demuth watercolors). Philadelphia had long been a center of watercolor painting, and in the mid-nineteenth century was home to such distinguished practitioners of the medium as James Hamilton, William Trost Richards, and Thomas Moran. By the turn of the century, the city could claim at least two artists' associations that sponsored regular watercolor exhibitions. The Art Club of Philadelphia, an all-male society founded in 1874, included among its members painters, sculptors, architects, artist-illustrators, and musicians. It presented the First Annual Exhibition of Watercolors and Pastels in the spring of 1891. Its earliest

Fig. 16. Earl Horter (1883-1940), *Toledo*, 1924. Watercolor on paper. Philadelphia Museum of Art. Samuel S. White III and Vera White Collection.

shows were much like those put on by New York's watercolor societies at the same time, dominated by very finished and highly detailed figurative and landscape subjects. Views of exotic locales were popular, as were romantic story-telling pictures, often featuring characters in historical costume. Most exhibitors seem to have handled their medium in a tight, highly controlled fashion, with much opaque pigment in evidence. Though the Art Club would show more freely painted works in the ensuing decades, it would remain the more conservative of the watercolor displays in Philadelphia.

The second group, the Philadelphia Water Color Club, held its annual exhibitions at the Pennsylvania Academy beginning in 1904. From the beginning, the club was led by established figures – Sargent, Edwin Austin Abbey, Joseph Pennell, and Cecilia Beaux were honorary members; the regular membership included Thomas Anshutz and Hugh Breckenridge (both on the Pennsylvania Academy faculty), Violet Oakley and Jessie Willcox Smith. Even in its first decade, more than half the members were women and, as is indicated by the presence of Oakley and Smith, the illustrator tradition was strong.

Yet the city's more innovative painters also exhibited with the Water Color Club: Arthur Carles (who worked in watercolor for only about a decade) showed his work in their annuals beginning in 1904; John Sloan, Everett Shinn, and other Ashcan School painters who began their careers in Philadelphia also exhibited wash drawings and pen-and-ink illustrations with the club in the early years, as did the young Stuart Davis. In the 1911 annual, the place of honor was given to fifteen watercolors by John Marin, a former student at the Pennsylvania Academy.[86] Marin would have an equally generous representation in the 1913 and 1914 annuals, but would participate only sporadically after that.

In the 1920s, one of the most talented local painters to participate in the Academy annuals was Earl Horter.[87] An eclectic artist who had no formal training in the fine arts, Horter experimented with numerous avant-garde styles, European and American, in the 1920s and '30s – styles he knew first-hand, for his great success as a commercial artist enabled him to build a superb collection of modern art, including seventeen Picassos, ten Braques, and important works by such fellow Pennsylvanians as Charles Demuth and Charles Sheeler. About 1915, Horter began showing his drawings at the Academy; he began exhibiting watercolors in the early 1920s. *Toledo* (fig. 16), shown at the twenty-second annual Philadelphia Water Color Club exhibition (1924) typified one manner in which he worked: it is rendered in very wet, transparent washes with a great deal of paper reserved for the whites. The piled up, blocky, cubic structures recall Cézanne and the Cubist painters Horter admired; his palette is equally Cézannesque. In other works, he painted quite opaquely, echoing the decorative manner of late Braque still lifes or the precise, rhythmic style of Sheeler's architectural drawings. In all of these works, his skill as a designer and draftsman is paramount; his sophisticated appreciation of any number of vanguard styles was anomalous in the Academy exhibitions.

While Horter was collecting French moderns, other progressive Philadelphia painters, Arthur Carles and Carroll Tyson among them, were organizing exhibitions housed at the Pennsylvania Academy that were designed to bring this art to a wider public. A series of shows mounted in the early 1920s juxtaposed "Representative Modern Masters" (all of them French) from Courbet to Braque with those American artists demonstrating "The Later Tendencies in Art," including Demuth, Marin, Weber, and William Zorach, all of whom exhibited watercolors.[88] By and large, however, the Academy's interest in modernism, demonstrated in shows like these, did not carry over to the watercolor annuals, and the catalogues of the shows mounted in the teens and twenties recorded the work of such home talents as Hugh Breckenridge and Henry McCarter. Out-of-towners, including a large group of Bostonians, were liberally represented. In general, these exhibitions seem to have been a comfortable and popular mix of the traditional and the experimental, with a wide range of approaches represented.

Among the moderns, Charles Demuth remained the most loyal to the Philadelphia Water Color Club, exhibiting half a dozen pictures or so almost every year through the teens and twenties. However, he was not recognized by the annual's jury of selection until 1926, by which time his early cubist manner had given way to a more realistic style: his *Roses* (1926, Museum of Fine Arts, Boston) won the Dana medal at the twenty-fourth annual. That same year, 1926, his *Plums* (fig. 17) was awarded a silver medal at the Philadelphia Sesquicentennial exhibition; the top prize went to the ever-popular Frank Benson. Demuth's reaction to all this attention was typically self-deprecating. He wrote to Stieglitz, "I must write you and tell you the news, – I don't think it is, as yet, given to the public. The Sesqui Exhibition gave me a silver meddle (sic) on my branch of plumbs (sic) that water colour you had last winter in my show. It seems funnier to be noticed than not to be."[89]

TRAINING IN WATERCOLOR

ALTHOUGH the Pennsylvania Academy sponsored watercolor exhibitions, and although several of the most talented watercolor painters of the modernist generation were trained there, it offered no instruction in watercolor. Neither did the School of the Museum of Fine Arts in Boston, nor the National Academy of Design in New York. At the Art Students League, watercolor classes were not a part of the regular curriculum, although classes in illustration may have touched on watercolor techniques. Only in the League's Saturday classes was instruction available in watercolor; most of the enrollees were women.[90] At most fine arts academies, in fact, watercolor remained a marginal field throughout the modernist period, and the establishment's neglect of the medium may well have contributed to its attraction for artists like Marin, O'Keeffe, and the others, intent on a new expression.

Watercolor, however, was an important part of the curriculum in schools dedicated to training students for useful industry rather than fine art. It was, as well, a required subject of study in most women's art schools in the twentieth century, as it had been a staple of instruction in nineteenth-century female academies. Watercolor was emphasized at both Moore College of Art in Philadelphia (see fig. 18) and the Cooper Union for the

Fig. 17. Charles Demuth (1883-1935), *Plums*, 1925. Watercolor and graphite on wove paper mounted on cardboard. Addison Gallery of American Art, Phillips Academy, Andover, Massachusetts.

Fig. 18. Photograph of watercolor class at the Philadelphia School of Design for Women (later Moore College of Art), from 1926-27 course catalogue. Moore College of Art and Design, Philadelphia.

Advancement of Science and Art in New York City, whose programs were inspired by the methods of the Art Training School, South Kensington, London. Moore (originally the Philadelphia School of Design for Women) was dedicated to the training of young women "in a knowledge of the principles and practice of the art of design." Beginning in 1880, it offered courses in watercolor as one of its principal subjects of instruction because it was viewed as the branch of art "most closely connected with practical industry." A course in watercolor painting was required of all Moore students in each of their four years of study. The medium soon became known as a specialty of the school.[91]

Although the men's art program at the Cooper Union included few courses in which watercolor might have been used (and in general, the term was avoided in the men's division's course listings), the Women's Art School offered classes in watercolor from 1903 on. Watercolor was emphasized as suitable for decorative design and for other work women might pursue: "the chief interest in a school designed to fit one for self-support lies, naturally, in the financial returns . . . the Portrait, the Illustration, the Designing, and the Miniature, Pastel and Water Color Classes, are the chief sources of revenue to the students."[92]

Through the early twentieth century, watercolor retained its reputation both as a medium suitable for commercial art and for women, and it also continued to be regarded as a medium for amateurs. Watercolor manuals proliferated at the turn of the century; many of these were written by women.[93] Most assumed that readers were beginners ("Play with each color as a child would"[94]) and took them, step by step, over the basic handling of tools and selection of materials, through elementary principles of composition and design, and especially of techniques: wet-on-wet, dry brush, and so on. Although for the most part these books advocated conventional procedures, by the 1930s and '40s, the eclectic practices and eccentric materials adopted by avant-garde watercolorists had begun to find their way into watercolor manuals. The draftsman and painter Adolf Dehn, whose popular instruction book appeared in 1945, noted the trend away from a purist viewpoint: "Many of our younger artists. . . use opaque white, black ink, pastel or crayon along with their watercolor, achieving new and exciting results." He also described, with amusement and admiration, how George Grosz made his own brushes by gluing shaving bristles, feathers, and toothbrush bristles onto handles.[95]

As is to be expected, these manuals reflect their authors' varying tastes in technique, ranging from an insistence on pure, transparent washes to a mixed-media approach, and from an oil-painting like degree of finish to a sketchy style. Eliot O'Hara, a talented painter working for the most part in transparent washes, put out a series of manuals in the 1930s advocating a pure painting approach, while Adolf Dehn, who began as a graphic artist, and only took up watercolor in the mid-1930s, counseled the aspiring painter to work as he did: making drawings out of doors to serve as the basis of watercolors produced in the studio. His style, and the style he described, are essentially graphic; his lyrical landscapes were as much drawn with the brush as freely washed, resulting in handsome pictorial patterns based on elements in nature. Dehn's method, along with his orientation toward drawing with watercolor, was typical of a host of painters (Reginald Marsh and George Grosz among them) working in watercolor in the 1930s and '40s. And Dehn's homely, folksy landscape style became the mainstay of amateur production for his generation (see fig. 19).

THE MARKET FOR WATERCOLORS

THE proliferation of watercolor manuals in the period between the wars and the activity of the commercial art schools are additional indicators of the heightened interest in watercolor from the early 1920s onward. The American Watercolor Society held joint exhibitions with the New York Water Color Club, beginning in 1921; that consolidated show included 464 pictures selected from 1300 works submitted. Entries to the Society's annuals would peak in 1929, when over 2500 works were submitted; membership would increase steadily during the decade; and attendance at the annuals would swell from about 2200 in 1924 to 5322 in 1928.[96]

During these years, sales were brisk at the annuals, and even vanguard artists were enjoying a healthy market. Their work was further sanctioned when several museums began buying modern watercolors in the 1920s. Brooklyn took the lead. Its 1921 exhibition of watercolors became a biennial display; increasingly, it was dedicated to the recognition of new talent, and the institution's astute purchases from these shows underscored its enthusiasm for watercolor. Among the paintings Brooklyn bought from its inaugural show was *February Thaw* by Charles Burchfield (fig. 20), whose New York debut at the Kevorkian Galleries the year before Henry McBride had anointed as among "the most interesting 'first appearances' of the winter."[97] Edward Hopper's sale of *The Mansard Roof* (fig. 21) to Brooklyn out of the 1923 Watercolor Biennial marked a change in his fortunes, for it was the first work in any medium he had been able to sell in ten years.

The Metropolitan Museum was far more progressive in its acquisitions of contemporary American works on paper than in the purchase of oils, thanks to its farsighted curator, William Ivins. In 1923, Charles Demuth wrote in astonishment to Stieglitz that "the Met did buy one of my old water-colours" (probably *Flowers*, 1918);[98] that institution would acquire its first Burchfield, *False Front* (1921) the next year. In 1928, the Wadsworth Atheneum in Hartford acquired two watercolors by Edward Hopper, one by Demuth, and one by Preston Dickinson. The Museum of Fine Arts, Boston, was busy acquiring the old masters of American watercolor (adding eleven Homers – four of them purchases – ten Sargents, and sixteen La Farges to its collection) in that decade; the Fogg, despite its reservations about exhibiting the work of living artists, had been quietly acquiring modern watercolors in the 1920s, so that by the end of the decade the museum owned four Marins, three Demuths, three Hoppers, and a Burchfield.[99] Prices were ascending rapidly, too: a Marin could command as much as $1500 in those years; Demuths were occasionally bringing $1000 or more.

But by far the most celebrated watercolor acquisition of the decade was the $6000

Fig. 19. Adolf Dehn (1895-1968), *Shower in Colorado*, 1940. Watercolor on paper. Museum of Fine Arts, Boston. Ellen Kelleran Gardner Fund.

Fig. 20. Charles Burchfield (1893-1967), *February Thaw*, 1920. Watercolor over pencil on paper. The Brooklyn Museum. John B. Woodward Memorial Fund.

Fig. 21. Edward Hopper (1882-1967), *The Mansard Roof*, 1923. Watercolor over pencil on paper. The Brooklyn Museum. Museum Collection Fund.

Fig. 22. John Marin (1870-1953), *Back of Bear Mountain*, 1925. Watercolor on paper. The Phillips Collection, Washington, D.C.

Marin bought by Duncan Phillips from Stieglitz in 1926. Although willing to pay extraordinarily high prices for French paintings for his gallery in Washington, Phillips was a bargain hunter when it came to American art.[100] In the spring of 1926, he bought two Marin watercolors from Stieglitz, and in December 1926, he purchased three more, for about $1600 each. But after reading an enthusiastic discussion of Marin's *Back of Bear Mountain* (fig. 22) in a review by Henry McBride, Phillips returned to Stieglitz's gallery and bought the watercolor for the unheard-of price of $6000 – at the same time receiving another Marin watercolor as a gift and being allowed to buy two others at deeply discounted prices. In Phillips's mind, he got four Marins for about $2000 each. In Stieglitz's mind, the $6000 sale was an opportunity to bolster the market of his favorite watercolor painter, and he "leaked" the story of the record price to the press, to Phillips's great annoyance.

Stieglitz argued that Marin's success would secure watercolor's stature as a medium for significant artistic expression while elevating the prestige and value of other American watercolors in a market long dominated by the French. Initially, the ploy served Stieglitz's end. *The New Yorker* commented, "The Rotarian can now admit he likes Marin because he has become successful. Last week Duncan Phillips . . . bought four Marins, the largest fetching $6000. [Previous to this] two or three hundred persons have felt that Marin was the greatest American [artist], now that a picture of his has brought $6,000, hundreds of thousands will know it."[101] But when the full story of the sale became known, "Field Marshal Stieglitz" was taken to task for manipulating the market, and for taking liberties with the delicate development of modern art in America: "A false inflation of the values of one artist is scarcely fair to modern art as a whole. . . . Marin is a fine artist and Mr. Stieglitz a very fine Field Marshal. But the modern art movement in this country is such a sincere and eager thing, that we, for one, dislike to see it rise into glory through propaganda that is even faintly dubious."[102]

This incident, though it tarnished Stieglitz's reputation somewhat, did have the desired effect of expanding Marin's public recognition and increasing the respect paid the watercolor medium in the marketplace. Commercial enthusiasm for American watercolor peaked during the next year (1927) at the auction of Bostonian Desmond FitzGerald's art collection at the American Art Association in New York. Primarily a collector of Impressionist painting (with an auxiliary interest in rather traditional American watercolors of his period), FitzGerald owned only one watercolor by Winslow Homer, *The Portage* (fig. 23). It was that work, and not the landscapes by Monet and Pissarro, that commanded the highest price at the sale. *The Portage* fetched $15,700, a record for American painting in the medium.

The strengthened market for American watercolors in the 1920s made art dealers willing to take on new painters. Thus Stieglitz introduced Oscar Bluemner with a watercolor show in 1928, the same year that Milton Avery made his debut at the Frank K.M. Rehn Galleries. Stuart Davis had his inaugural show at the Downtown Gallery, which included watercolors and temperas, in 1927. But the most important watercolor painters to emerge in this decade were Edward Hopper and Charles Burchfield, both of whom would eventually be represented by Frank Rehn. Though not normally associated with American modernism, their watercolor styles were innovative and influential; conversely, their rapid success as watercolor painters may in part be explained by the fact that shows of Demuth, Marin, and other moderns had already accustomed the public to seeing adventurous work in that medium.

HOPPER AND BURCHFIELD

HOPPER and Burchfield were friends and admirers of one another's work. Their watercolors were frequently shown together and, like Demuth and Marin, they were often compared. They came to prominence at the same time, Burchfield in a 1920 show at the Kevorkian Gallery of his watercolors of Salem, Ohio, houses, and Hopper in two exhibitions of watercolors at Frank Rehn's gallery. The first of these, in 1924, was hung in the gallery's back room while more prominent space was devoted to figure paintings by William Merritt Chase, Childe Hassam, Frank Duveneck, Leon Kroll, and others; to Hopper's surprise, all eleven watercolors on display, as well as five others, sold. Three years later Hopper showed four oils, a dozen watercolors and a group of etchings at Frank Rehn's gallery; this show was equally successful. In the three-year interval, prices for Hopper's watercolors doubled, from $150 to $300, and Hopper, who heretofore had been concentrating on oil painting but getting little recognition for it, began devoting more and more effort to watercolor. His enthusiasm for watercolor lasted about fifteen years, and culminated in a group of landscapes – made in the mid- and late thirties – that rival oil paintings in their size and ambition.

Hopper soon became widely admired as a watercolorist, particularly by those with progressive taste. Harley Perkins, one of the "Boston Five," solicited Hopper's work for a show for Boston in 1926; in 1928, the Wadsworth Atheneum's energetic director, A. Everett Austin, brought Hopper watercolors to Hartford, where the local museum public found them disturbingly modern in both style and subject.[103] The Museum of Modern Art gave Hopper a retrospective in 1933 in which the watercolors greatly outnumbered the oils. In 1935, Hopper won First Purchase Prize in watercolor, for his masterly *Yawl Riding a Swell* (fig. 24) at the Worcester Art Museum. By the end of the decade, Hopper also had been accepted by the conservatives: in 1939, the Art Institute of Chicago's Eighteenth Annual International Water Color Exhibition gave special retrospective displays to John Whorf, Henri Matisse, and Hopper. The twenty-six watercolors shown, primarily from the 1920s, provided a handsome survey of Hopper's work in the medium.

Unlike other acclaimed watercolor painters of his generation, Hopper was not a natural watercolorist, a technical virtuoso, or a flamboyant celebrator of the medium. As Lloyd Goodrich noted in 1927, "Technically, Hopper is one of the most accomplished of contemporary American painters, but his accomplishment has never taken the form of fireworks. He dislikes slippery, superficial brushwork as much as he dislikes sentimentali-

Fig. 23. Winslow Homer (1836-1910), *The Portage*, 1897. Watercolor on paper. Yale University Art Gallery. Bequest of Doris M. Brixey.

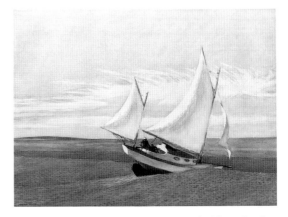

Fig. 24. Edward Hopper (1882-1967), *Yawl Riding a Swell*, 1935. Watercolor over graphite on off-white wove paper. Worcester Art Museum. Museum purchase.

ty, and while his painting is always capable, always under control, he never indulges in tricks."[104]

Hopper was not attracted to seductive hues, rare pigments, or exotic, interesting papers. His watercolors are carefully planned and structured, and painstakingly produced; he had little interest in exploiting the accidental effects of working wet-on-wet or of allowing colors to bleed into one another. And so he avoided painting "subway rushes or beaches with their multitudes of writhing people" – subjects involving the evocation of motion – and natural forms with "their voluptuous, decorative character," where improvisational techniques could be used to good effect.[105] He concentrated instead on urban landscapes and man-made forms, whose inherent geometries were well suited to his controlled, structured approach to watercolor. In many ways, Hopper's watercolor technique was traditional. He built the pictures of very thin, transparent washes carefully laid down in small, controlled strokes, then wiped out areas, applying more thin washes over top. The result was a patination of surface that was nonetheless inelegant – deliberately so. The surfaces of Hopper's watercolors are, like his subjects, labored, mute, even raw; his friend Burchfield called his pictures "provocative in their terseness" resulting from his "modest, unobstrusive – almost impersonal – way of putting on paint."[106]

At the same time, Hopper's meticulous layering of barely tinted washes generated a kind of luminosity and atmosphere that gave his watercolors life, while achieving a fascinating solidity and weight that was at odds with the "lightness" of the medium. His palette is not sensuous, but strong and clear, and is animated by judicious use of unexpected, brilliant accents: the orange chimneys in *Anderson's House* (cat. 112) for example, seem all the more audacious in contrast to the neighboring pale tints.

Hopper's deliberately plain, hardworking technique was perfectly suited to his stark, undecorative subject matter; his directness is his strength. Hopper's emergence on the New York art scene coincided with the revival of interest in Thomas Eakins, another controlled, deliberate watercolorist, and with renewed enthusiasm for Homer's watercolors.[107] Hopper's earliest admirers were also devotees of Homer's work. John Taylor Spaulding, a Boston collector with wide-ranging tastes and special enthusiasm for watercolors, owned nine Hoppers, four of them bought from Hopper's 1924 Frank K.M. Rehn Galleries show; he also owned eight Homer watercolors. Stephen C. Clark pursued both Homer and Hopper watercolors; so, to a lesser extent, did Sam Lewisohn, Duncan Phillips, and Abby Aldrich Rockefeller in the late twenties and early thirties.[108] In his "realistic, spare, almost Puritanical strain," Hopper was seen to be Homer's descendant, even as Marin, in his feeling for nature, was viewed as Homer's heir.[109]

Unlike Hopper, who worked comfortably in both media, Charles Burchfield worked almost entirely in watercolor, and frequently expressed dissatisfaction with his attempts at oil.[110] His watercolors were in their own way as deliberate as Hopper's, and often work against the natural properties of the medium to take on the characteristics of oil. At about the time he began to set aside his first subject matter, based on childhood recollections and nature fantasies, in favor of weightier themes – the "hardness of human lives"[111] as reflected in the misery of the small-town houses he painted repeatedly in the late teens – he started to develop a more assertive watercolor technique. He began working on large sheets; his forms became more aggressive. He moved away from the conventional method of painting transparent washes over pencil underdrawing (see *Sunlight*, cat. 107) and toward a manner and materials that he associated with oil: "My 1916 watercolors were meticulously done; everything was first carefully drawn and anchored in pencil, then the colors filled in. . . . I gradually abandoned the prepainting pencil work and . . . I virtually abandoned the pointed brush for the sable 'bright' oil brush, which allowed a more robust, firm stroke, similar indeed to the oil on canvas technique."[112]

Burchfield's aspirations for his watercolors led to further experiments with materials in the 1920s. According to the catalogue raisonné of his work, Burchfield's 1921 image *Noonday Heat* (private collection), which was once owned by George Bellows, is varnished watercolor; his 1924 *House of Mystery*, which won the Art Institute of Chicago's Blair Purchase Prize, is tempera with oil glaze.[113] As early as 1917 (see *Spring Patterns*, cat. 108) he was using charcoal (not pale graphite) for underdrawing as an oil painter might do; he also scumbled the charcoal with his pigment to produce gritty textures. An intuitive painter who altered his design as he proceeded, Burchfield frequently made changes in his watercolors that read like pentimenti: he scraped down and painted over rather than delicately lifting up and blotting.

By the 1920s he frequently abandoned the classic watercolor technique of working from light to dark; by gravitating toward opaque pigments Burchfield was able to approach the oil painter's practice of beginning with dark tones and adding highlights. He preferred smooth papers, and often used his brush to create texture. This is especially apparent in the watercolors of the 1930s, where brushstrokes are prominent and paint has been pushed around by the brush – an assertiveness of touch, of gesture, that was anathema to watercolor purists. In the late thirties and early forties, however, such painters as Ben Shahn and Jacob Lawrence found, as Burchfield had, that the emphatic power of this technique was especially appropriate to strong social commentary.[114]

Although he was extremely prolific – his catalogue raisonné records some 1,400 works produced over a fifty-year career – Burchfield was well known for taking years to finish pictures. He reworked his watercolors repeatedly, glazing colors over one another to achieve "a structure of deeply luminous, resonant tone on which the visible stroke is only the final accent."[115] In 1943, he returned to depicting childhood memories and fantasies and, while he was developing new compositions, he also began enlarging some of his early pictures that dealt with such subjects. *The Coming of Spring* (fig. 25) was apparently the first picture he treated in this way, affixing strips of paper to the top, bottom, and sides of an earlier watercolor. Its new monumentality suited Burchfield's quintessentially American theme, "the big epic power of nature."[116]

Burchfield, who spent most of his career in artistic isolation outside of Buffalo, is often characterized as a particularly American type in the mythic mode of Winslow Homer: the painter as hermit, as solitary, visionary, unworldly, pursuing his own muse.[117]

Fig. 25. Charles Burchfield (1893-1967), *The Coming of Spring*, 1917-1943. Watercolor on paper mounted on presswood. The Metropolitan Museum of Art. George A. Hearn Fund, 1943.

In fact, Burchfield was well trained, an articulate interpreter of his own art and that of others, and connected to the national art scene. By the time he was forty, his art was widely known and exhibited, and had attracted a sophisticated and enthusiastic following.

After his debut at the Kevorkian Gallery, Burchfield showed with the Montross Gallery for four years, between 1924 and 1928. He then joined Frank Rehn's gallery in 1929, which was the beginning of a life-long association. Rehn gave Burchfield exhibitions nearly every year; Burchfield also participated in contemporary art annuals – not only in the watercolor shows but also, as Adolf Dehn admiringly noted, in "the big oil painting exhibitions"[118] such as the Carnegie Internationals in Pittsburgh, the Corcoran Biennials in Washington, and the annual exhibition of paintings and sculpture at the Pennsylvania Academy in Philadelphia. There the power and scale of his watercolors enabled them to hold their own against the more "serious" media. His prices were solid – by 1930, he averaged about $650 per watercolor – and his work sold well. The Metropolitan Museum and the Brooklyn Museum bought Burchfield watercolors in the early 1920s, as has been noted. One of the first works in any medium to be acquired by the Museum of Modern Art shortly after it opened in 1929 was Burchfield's watercolor, *Railroad Gantry* (1920); when the Whitney opened as a museum in 1931, it owned four watercolors (and two oils) by Burchfield. And the painter attracted important private patrons as well: Stephen C. Clark, Duncan Phillips (who put on a show of early Burchfield watercolors at the Phillips Memorial Gallery in 1933), Edward W. Root (who owned at least twenty-one works, and was a close friend) and Abby Aldrich Rockefeller.

In 1935, Rockefeller gave six early Burchfield watercolors to the Museum of Modern Art. She had begun buying his work in the late 1920s. Her enthusiasm no doubt contributed to his inclusion in *Paintings by 19 Living Americans*,[119] the Museum's second exhibition, which opened in December 1929, and to the Museum's decision to show his early watercolors the following spring ("Charles Burchfield: Early Watercolors 1916-1918," was the first solo show mounted by the Museum). Rockefeller was a great champion of American art, and between 1925 and 1935 she built up an impressive collection of American modernism, often supporting struggling artists by hanging shows of their work in the top-floor gallery of her house. Her special enthusiasm was for works on paper. Of the 140 works of art she gave to the Museum of Modern Art in 1935, more than one hundred were watercolors and pastels. She especially admired Marin, Prendergast, Weber, Davies, George O. "Pop" Hart, and William and Marguerite Zorach. Demuth was a particular favorite: Rockefeller owned eighteen watercolors, ranging from the vaudeville subjects of the early teens to the late, elegant still lifes.[120] The Museum of Modern Art had been founded as a forum for European modernism; Rockefeller's gift, supplemented by exquisite Demuths and Marins donated over the next two decades by Philip Goodwin, the museum's architect,[121] made the Modern the country's major repository for twentieth-century American watercolor.

Rockefeller's taste was shaped by the influential dealer Edith Halpert of the Downtown Gallery (who is popularly given credit for kindling Rockefeller's interest in modern

American watercolor)[122] and possibly by a provocative exhibition mounted at the Newark (New Jersey) Museum in 1930 by Holger Cahill, future director of the WPA Federal Art Project. "Modern American Water Colors" was a large, democratic survey of contemporary watercolors by 107 artists, each represented by one painting. All the works were quite recent, although some – such as Charles Demuth's *Pears* (1929) – had by this time acquired a classic look. The overall taste exhibited would become Rockefeller's (and eventually the Museum of Modern Art's), with Weber, Hart, Burchfield, and Preston Dickinson in evidence. The brief catalogue essay, by Cahill, was decidedly boosterish in tone: "The water color is coming into its own," he claimed. "The medium has attracted some of our best artists," including Marin, William Zorach, and Demuth, who "have raised the water color art of America to new levels of distinction."[123]

THE MUSEUMS EMBRACE WATERCOLOR

IN THE 1930s, museums continued to promote American watercolor. Both the kind of overview of contemporary achievements in the medium at Newark, and the smaller show, focusing on the work of a limited number of artists on the model of the Museum of Modern Art's "19 Living Americans," became a standard component of exhibition programs, especially of smaller museums, during this decade. The Phillips Memorial Gallery in Washington, D.C., which had shown "16 Americans" in 1928, shortly after it dedicated itself to modern art, organized "An American Show of Oils and Water Colors" – some 123 works – in 1931. The Smith College Art Museum presented "Five Americans" in 1934. And for over a decade the Addison Gallery of American Art at Andover maintained an exhibition schedule that emphasized watercolor, often introducing (or reintroducing) the work of a painter given little recent exposure. In addition to group shows of contemporary American watercolorists mounted in 1933, 1935, and 1939, the Addison showed the work of C.H. Woodbury in 1935, Maurice and Charles Prendergast in 1938 and, in the same year, the late-nineteenth-century painter William Stanley Haseltine. These exhibitions featured, or focused exclusively on, the artist's work in watercolor.

Smaller museums may have gravitated toward watercolors in these years because such exhibitions were easier to arrange and less expensive to put on than comparable shows of oil paintings; it is also possible that smaller, less formal works on paper made the avant-garde and the unfamiliar easier to digest. The Addison's concentration on watercolor was also a reflection of New England's traditional predilection for the medium: the Museum of Fine Arts, Boston, consistently emphasized watercolor in its monographic exhibitions of nineteenth-century American artists.[124] The museum also provided several showcases for recent work in watercolor. The first of these, in 1929, was a conservative gathering, emphasizing the work of such New England watercolorists as Frank Benson, Dodge Macknight, and John Whorf. The same artists were seen again at the museum a decade later, in the Fiftieth Anniversary Exhibition of the Boston Watercolor Club. That show, drawn from the club's membership of New England-based painters, consisted essentially of handsome, if unexciting landscapes by local painters working in the manner of John Singer Sargent or Winslow Homer. At the same time, in April of 1939, the Museum originated a more forward-looking exhibition, "Ten American Watercolor Painters." It included works by Burchfield, Dehn, Arthur G. Dove, Hopper, Marin, and Reginald Marsh, among others, and was the source of a number of important watercolors that entered the Museum's collection.[125]

The most unusual inclusion in this exhibition was Arthur Dove, who, with the exception of the efforts of his dedicated patron, Duncan Phillips, was given little museum exposure in his lifetime.[126] Dove first used watercolor in his twenties when working as an illustrator for popular magazines. He began painting watercolors in earnest only about 1930, using the medium for sketches and preparatory studies for larger works in oil. By the time of the "Ten American Watercolor Painters" show, failing health had caused him to turn to the medium more frequently. Though still relatively little known, Dove's watercolors are a charming and profound part of his oeuvre, and are closer to the observed, natural world than are his oils.

Painting in watercolor came naturally to Dove. A small watercolor block seems to have been his constant companion; he used the medium for sketching out of doors and, later, to record scenes witnessed through the windshield of his car. Dove often painted quite wetly, using the texture of his paper (and the inevitable puddling and pooling of his washes) to generate textures analogous to natural effects. His watercolors give little evidence of lifting, scraping out, and other complex techniques; rather, they are quite freshly painted, in broad, simple strokes of strong color (sometimes augmented with pen and ink contours), a directness of approach that clearly aided the reduction of a scene in nature to an abstract, yet suggestive design. Despite the almost total lack of public recognition of his work, Dove's use of the medium was completely confident. He enjoyed and exploited its organic qualities to the extent that, as has been pointed out, such accidental effects as the bleeding of a gray wash into a tan one in *Gas Tank and Building 38* (fig. 26) was carefully replicated in *Tanks* (1938, Museum of Fine Arts, Boston), the oil painting that followed.[127]

In the 1930s, the newly organized Whitney Museum of American Art took the lead in displaying American watercolors. Even though the Whitney – first the Studio Club, then the Galleries, and finally the Museum – observed the traditional hierarchy of the media (ranking oil painting and sculpture as the major art forms, with prints, drawings, and watercolors considered secondary areas to be pursued less vigorously), the sheer volume of its activities in those years made its contributions to the history of American watercolor significant. That watercolor was considered an auxiliary medium is apparent in the structure of the Whitney annuals which, beginning in 1932, usually showed paintings one year and sculpture the next, with watercolors and prints tacked on to the sculpture show. Nonetheless, they attracted many visitors, elicited much critical debate, and were the largest regular displays of watercolor in New York.

The annuals (or, as they were called, "biennials," since works in each medium were shown every other year), were based on the system of "no jury, no prizes." Invited artists were given a voice in selecting the works (usually no more than two per artist) by which they would be represented. The First Biennial Exhibition of Contemporary American Sculptures, Watercolors and Prints was held in 1933; it was extremely varied and, like the biennials that followed it, was an exciting and highly visible forum for new talent and new stylistic developments. Andrew Wyeth first showed in the 1938 sculpture and water-color annual. Jacob Lawrence's strong paintings were seen in the 1943 biennial, not long after his riveting Harlem Series premiered at the Downtown Gallery. The flat, graphic, structured surfaces of Lawrence's work grew out of his innovative use of such matte media as tempera and casein, which artists were beginning to explore in the 1940s.

Fig. 26. Arthur G. Dove (1880-1946), *Gas Tank and Building 38*, 1938. Watercolor. Harvard University Art Museums. Gift of George Burton Cumming in memory of E. Louise Lucas.

Although the Whitney Museum maintained a policy of not giving solo shows for living artists, it took the lead in mounting retrospectives and memorial exhibitions for such celebrated watercolorists as Maurice Prendergast (1934) and Charles Demuth (1937). However, its group shows were eclectic to the point of eccentricity. Late in 1929, for example, shortly before the Whitney reorganized itself as a museum, the Studio Galleries opened an exhibition of watercolors by Stuart Davis, Mark Baum, Richard Lahey, and Paul Rohland, a show that has been aptly described as "a typically Whitney mixture that hung the accomplished with the promising and the experimental with the conventional."[128]

In his review of the show, critic Henry McBride singled out Stuart Davis from that gathering and praised him as "the best delver into the abstract we have."[129] As such, Davis was not the Whitney Studio Club's usual bill of fare, in either oil or watercolor. There was little modernist art in its collection, while the realist tradition was strongly represented. It owned numerous watercolors by Thomas Hart Benton, John Steuart Curry, Emil Ganso, George Luks, Jerome Myers, and Charles Sheeler (including what is perhaps his masterpiece in a water-based medium, *Bucks County Barns* [fig. 27]), but none by Marin, Demuth, Dove, or O'Keeffe and, oddly enough, given the institution's destiny as the repository of the artist's estate, none by Hopper. These omissions, accept-able in a private organization like the Studio Club, were inappropriate in a public institu-tion, and in anticipation of the opening of the Whitney as a museum in 1931, Juliana Force, the director and guiding spirit, set about to right the imbalance. In 1931, she bought two watercolors by Marin (for a total of $1,350), two by Demuth (as well as his masterpiece in oils, *My Egypt*), and four gouaches by Max Weber. She also spent $2,500 for three glorious Central Park watercolors by Maurice Prendergast.[130]

Fig. 27. Charles Sheeler (1883-1965), *Bucks County Barn*, 1923. Tempera and crayon on paper. Whitney Museum of American Art, New York.

The Whitney compensated for the disproportionate representation of realism and modernist abstraction in its permanent collection with a series of historic group shows in which watercolors played a significant part. "Abstract Painting in America," which opened in February 1935, traced the history of abstraction in American art from the Armory show to that date; it included watercolors by Demuth, Marin, Walkowitz and Weber, among others. Watercolors made up one-fifth of the exhibition, and were not segregated in the catalogue. Similarly, the 1946 exhibition "Pioneers of Modern Art in

America" documented the modern movement between 1908 and 1922 in oil, watercolor, and sculpture. It was a sweeping show that attempted to include painters of all stylistic persuasions, and so it embraced the likes of Maurice Sterne and John Marin, Bernard Karfiol and Stanton MacDonald-Wright. Many watercolors were included, and artists such as Burchfield and Marin, who were almost exclusively watercolorists, were particularly generously represented. The show also marked one of the only public appearances of watercolors by O'Keeffe since she had created them in the teens.

One of the most important exhibitions of American art to be mounted during the war years was the Whitney's "A History of American Watercolor Painting" of 1942. It was the first comprehensive survey of the subject ever presented, and contained 224 examples ranging in date from about 1800 to 1941. It honored the finest practitioners of the medium from John James Audubon and William Guy Wall to Burchfield, Hopper, and Demuth.[131] The exhibition asserted the importance of watercolor: "One of the chief points which the exhibition makes is that the medium, instead of being subservient to other processes – engraving and oil painting – today competes with them and takes an independent and respected place in contemporary art."[132]

The leading figures in the Whitney's exhibition were artists who are most admired for their watercolors today. Winslow Homer (represented by nine works) was considered the premier painter, whose watercolors demonstrate an unmatched technical skill and an "implacable respect for the solidity of things"; La Farge was hailed as the most intellectual of the painters; Eakins, as analytical and unsentimental; Prendergast, for perhaps the first time, was allied with modern watercolorists and was credited with achieving effects comparable to Cézanne's. Even Sargent, his reputation still in decline and his work assessed as technically brilliant but superficial, was represented by six watercolors.[133]

The show was quite even-handed in its treatment of twentieth-century painters, slanted neither toward the Whitney's roster of realists nor toward the modernists. Even the academic painters were well represented, as one reviewer noted: "The *fin-de-siècle* watercolorists, Henry Bacon, Frank Boggs, and H. Broadfield Warren, are here given the attention which they deserve. It is not always a demerit to be old fashioned in art."[134] Nonetheless (with the exception of O'Keeffe, who was not included), the artists who had done the most to advance watercolor in the twentieth century dominated the later portion of the show. There were ten Demuths, seven Hoppers, and seven Burchfields. The greatest praise was reserved for John Marin, who was hailed as being as frank and direct as Homer.

The adulation of Marin, and the association of his art with Homer's, climaxed in the exhibition, "American Watercolor and Winslow Homer," organized in 1945 for the Walker Art Center in Minneapolis by the Whitney's research curator Lloyd Goodrich. This show designated Homer as the artist who raised watercolor to the level of major expression; it canonized him as the greatest American watercolorist and identified the significant modern practitioners of the medium as those who continued his traditions.[135]

Accompanying the twenty-one Homers in the exhibition were a sampling of works by his predecessors and contemporaries, followed by greater concentrations of the work of five modern masters – Burchfield, Dehn, Hopper, Marin, and Marsh – whose style and outlook were seen as indebted to his. Hopper was credited with continuing the "naturalistic" style invented by Homer; Burchfield, with developing the brooding, reflective side of the master's nature; while Marsh and Dehn were the heirs to Homer's graphic talent. Of the five, the greatest was adjudged to be Marin, the most generously represented artist in the show after Homer. It was Marin who was singled out as approaching Homer in power, energy, and ability to communicate the physical sensations of nature. Repeatedly, he was lionized as the greatest contemporary painter.[136]

While "American Watercolor and Winslow Homer" toured the Midwest, a new generation appeared at the Whitney. The 1946 Whitney "Annual Exhibition of Contemporary Sculpture, Watercolor, and Drawings" was dominated by figurative painters, many of them working in an agitated linear style or exhibiting bizarre, even disturbing imagery rendered in a surrealist-influenced manner. At the same time, William Baziotes, Arshile Gorky, Adolph Gottlieb, Robert Motherwell, Mark Rothko, and others to be associated with the Abstract Expressionist movement exhibited their watercolors for the first time at the Whitney.

The physical approach and all-over composition that artists of the New York School would later adopt would not seem to be especially well suited to delicate, small-scale watercolor. But beginning in the mid 1940s, many of them would produce a fine, characteristic body of work in watercolor or other water-based media. The early, surrealist-inspired phase of Abstract Expressionism, with its fluid manner; its emphasis on automatic writing, random gestures, and exploitation of accidental effects; and its penchant for underwater organic forms was quite logically, and handsomely, developed in watercolor. *Baptismal Scene*, the watercolor Mark Rothko showed at the 1946 Whitney exhibition, for example (fig. 28), was based on watery, biomorphic imagery and on drawn forms floating free of washes of color that suggest atmosphere and indefinite space. As such, it expertly exploited the characteristic delicacy of watercolor and its ability to create luminous effects.

Many of the techniques these artists employed in their large, dramatic canvases from the late 1940s onward – dripping and staining, allowing color to bleed, using diluted oil paint in a manner that mimics the transparency of wash – have analogs in watercolor practice. Arshile Gorky pioneered this approach at the beginning of the decade. His oil paintings resemble watercolors in large scale, for they are thinly, even transparently painted, their line moves free of color areas, and large areas of canvas are left bare. The brawny style of such artists as Jackson Pollock and Clyfford Still carry on the athletic masculinity characteristic of Homer's and Marin's work in watercolor. Though the heroic canvases of the New York School have overshadowed their work in watercolor, the impact of the medium on their art is undeniable.[137]

As watercolor had contributed to the development of progressive art in America in the teens and twenties, so too the techniques and characteristics of the medium were employed to shape the work of the post-war avant-garde. In 1930 Holger Cahill noted, "the best American water colorists have no superiors in the world today."[138] By the time Abstract Expressionism was being touted as the first great American style, watercolor was proclaimed "the American medium."[139]

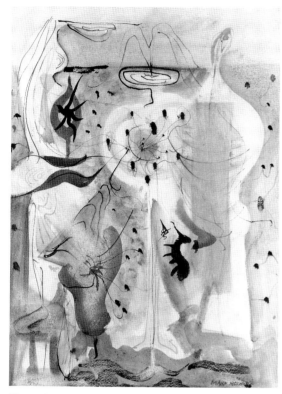

Fig. 28. Mark Rothko (1903-1970), *Baptismal Scene*, 1943. Watercolor on paper. Whitney Museum of American Art, New York.

1. "I've only painted in water-colour; the strain is greater, but, I don't have to return and fuss if it goes bad as one always does in oil or tempera." Charles Demuth to Alfred Stieglitz, September 4, 1923. Alfred Stieglitz Papers, Beinecke Rare Book and Manuscript Library, Yale University, New Haven, Connecticut. Forbes Watson, in his profile of Demuth, attributed the artist's choice of watercolor to his characteristic restraint: "Water color fits him like a glove. . . . Oil is a medium for an exuberant nature. And Demuth despises exuberance. He is far too selective for that." "Charles Demuth," *The Arts* 5 (January 1923), p. 78.

2. Charles Burchfield, quoted in Joseph S. Trovato, *Charles Burchfield: Catalogue of Paintings in Public and Private Collections* (Utica, New York: Museum of Art, Munson-Williams-Proctor Institute, 1970), p. 37.

3. A.E. Gallatin, *American Water-colourists* (New York: E.P. Dutton & Company, 1922), pp. 1, 2; vii.

4. Reviewing the Montross Gallery's April, 1926, watercolor show, the critic for *Art News* wrote: "In the spring a dealer's fancy lightly turns to acquarelles. Even as he throws off his fur coat and dark stuffy suit to appear on the Avenue arrayed as one of Solomon's lilies, so does he banish from view the solemn oils that have lent an air of funereal pomp to his Galleries during the winter months, to bring out his gay little water colors, flowers and birds and streams that babble and sing and perfume the air." *Art News* 24 (April 17, 1926), p. 7.

5. "I got what I came for a new impulse. I was somewhat bewildered when I first got here, but I think that Cézanne will influence me more than the others." Prendergast to Mrs. Oliver Williams, Paris, October 10, 1907. Archives of American Art, Prendergast Papers, Roll 917, fr. 192-240.

6. Walter Pach, *Ananias or The False Artist* (New York: Harper & Brothers, 1928), p. 190, quoted in John Rewald, *Cézanne and America. Dealers, Collectors, Artists and Critics 1891-1921* (Princeton, New Jersey: Princeton University Press, 1989), pp. 32-34.

7. According to legend, Stieglitz laughed at the first Cézanne he saw, and when told a single watercolor cost a thousand francs, he replied, "You mean a dozen. Why there's nothing there but empty paper with a few splashes of color here and there." Stieglitz, quoted in Dorothy Norman, "From the Writings and Conversations of Alfred Stieglitz," *Twice a Year* 1 (fall – winter 1938), pp. 80-81.

8. Man Ray's reaction was typical: "I was terrifically excited. . . . Just a few touches of color on a white paper. The watercolors looked unfinished, this is a quality I admired most as well as the use of the white of the paper as part of the painting. It was marvelous." Man Ray, interview with Arturo Schwartz, quoted in Rewald, *Cézanne and America*, p. 151.

9. Dorothy Norman, ed., "Writings and Conversations of Alfred Stieglitz," *Twice a Year* 14-15 (1947) quoted in Barbara Rose, *Readings in American Art since 1900: A Documentary Study* (New York: F.A. Praeger, 1968), p. 45.

10. Francis Naumann, "Marius de Zayas, 'How, When and Why Modern Art Came to New York'," *Arts Magazine* 54 (April 1980), p. 116. Other critics, however, found Marin more appealing than Cézanne: "The watercolors of Cézanne. . . are certainly a long drop from the inspired color clairvoyance of Marin." J.E. Chamberlin, "Cézanne Embryos," *New York Evening Mail*, March 8, 1911, quoted in Rewald, *Cézanne and America*, p. 146.

11. Charles H. Caffin, "A New Thought Which Is Old," *Camera Work* 31 (July 1910), p. 22. See also Henry McBride: "In the present Marin exhibition there are a dozen watercolors which, if they bore the butterfly signature, would be rated, even by museum directors, as ranking near the top of Whistler's achievement." McBride in the *New York Sun*, reprinted in "Some Critics on John Marin, 1910-1921" (New York: Montross Galleries, 1922), n.p.

12. For Homer's and Sargent's watercolor exhibitions in these years, see below, pp. xlix-li and n. 64. Whistler's watercolors were shown at the American Fine Arts Society in New York in 1912 and at

Knoedler's in 1914 (both shows included oils and pastels). Nine of Eakins's watercolors were included in the 1917-18 memorial exhibition at the Pennsylvania Academy; they figured more prominently in a 1923 Brummer Gallery show.

13. The show was not restricted to living artists; in fact, it served as a memorial exhibition for Smillie, who died in 1909 and who was represented by thirty-eight works – as opposed to the usual entry of one or two.

14. For example, such as G.W. Edwards's Fishermen (#29) a remake of Homer's oil, *The Fog Warning* (1886, Museum of Fine Arts, Boston). Homer himself sent two drawings to the show, untitled and priced at $40 and $75 – clearly a token contribution.

15. Reviews of the 1911 exhibition were mixed, and failed to mention the Marins. In years to come, however, Marin's shows would become the standard against which the American Watercolor Society annual was measured, and increasingly would be found lacking: "The annual combined exhibition of the American Water Color Society and the New York Water Color Club has been pushed ahead this year to an earlier date than ever before, making its opening coincident with the yearly exhibition by that arch watercolorist, John Marin, and thereby inviting disastrous comparisons. The water color cohorts. . . bring their usual skillful manipulation of the medium to graceful, often engaging, outcome . . . but giving small inkling of what can be done with a medium generally looked down upon as one fit for the dilettante or the less robustly minded practitioner. . . . not more than two dozen out of some five hundred examples of this special phase of painting have enough spark and crackle to make themselves felt above the general average gentility of the exhibition. . . . Taken solely on the score of what the medium is capable of at the hands of such a past master as Marin. . . or even such excellent men as Reginald Marsh . . . or Edward Hopper or Charles Hopkinson (at his best), the present exhibition is very much of a disappointment." Ralph Flint, "Watercolors Now Shown at Fine Arts Building," *The Art News* 29 (Saturday, November 1, 1930), p. 24.

16. Kermit S. Champa, "Some Observations on American Art, 1914-1919: 'The Wise or Foolish Virgin'," in *Over Here: Modernism, The First Exile 1914-1919* (Providence, Rhode Island: David Winton Bell Gallery, Brown University, 1989), p. 12.

17. The standard source is Milton Brown, *The Story of the Armory Show*, 2nd. ed. (New York: Abbeville Press, 1988).

18. *The Forum Exhibition of Modern American Painters* (New York: The Anderson Galleries, 1916), p. 5.

19. Champa, "Some Observations on American Art," p. 20.

20. E. P. Richardson, introduction, *American Paintings in the Ferdinand Howald Collection* (Columbus, Ohio: Columbus Gallery of Fine Arts, 1969), p. 4. In contrast, the pioneer collector John Quinn bought a Cézanne watercolor (*House on the Hill*, 1890-94, Philadelphia Museum of Art) from the Montross Gallery in 1916 for $1,200.

21. Henry McBride, "Demuth's First Exhibition," *New York Sun*, November 8, 1914, reprinted in Daniel Catton Rich, ed., *The Flow of Art: Essays and Criticisms of Henry McBride* (New York: Atheneum Publishers, 1975), p. 69.

22. Field, "Watercolor Exhibits at the Daniel Gallery," undated clipping, Archives of American Art, A.E. Gallatin Papers, Roll 508.

23. Demuth would eventually own five Marin watercolors himself, including the spectacular *Sunset* (1922, collection of Eleanor and Tom May), and in the 1920s would go to great lengths to persuade his patron Albert Barnes, to buy a Marin, as he recounted to Stieglitz, "I have written and talked to Barnes, I hope to some end, – but, God knows – about the Marins. – I think that he will be in. . . . I hope that he takes those sea things. They are the only really great marines since Courbet, – I think, – Homer's after all, were, – illustrations – of course, really good illustrations, but still only that." Charles Demuth to Alfred Stieglitz, March 12, 1923. Alfred Stieglitz Papers, Beinecke Rare Book and Manuscript Library, Yale University, New Haven, Connecticut.

24. Henry McBride, "What is Happening in the World of Art," *New York Sun*, October 31, 1915, sect. 3, p. 8.

25. Willard Huntington Wright, *International Studio* 59 (January 1917), p. xcviii.

26. Barbara Haskell, *Charles Demuth* (New York, Whitney Museum of American Art, 1987), pp. 19, 28. Demuth comes closest to Rodin in a group of watercolors of nudes executed about 1913.

27. See, for example, the illustrations of Philadelphians Henry McCarter, who worked in an art-nouveau mode at the turn of the century, and Jessie Willcox Smith, some of whose watercolors exhibit a nocturnal sensibility and penchant for decorative patterning not far from Demuth's own. One of Smith's most famous series of illustrations, for Charles Kingsley's *Water Babies*, was published in 1916, the year Demuth completed his first narrative series, the illustrations for Zola's *Nana*, and appeared, with watercolors by Demuth, at the Fifteenth Annual Philadelphia Watercolor Exhibition (1917).

28. See cat. 96. *In Vaudeville: The Green Dancer* (fig. 4) is painted on paper with the watermark, "Clover Linen Goldsmith Bros."

29. I am grateful to Roy Perkinson, Annette Manick, and Sue Welsh Reed for discussing these watercolors with me.

30. Demuth to Stieglitz, January 29, 1923. Alfred Stieglitz Papers, Beinecke Rare Book and Manuscript Library, Yale University, New Haven, Connecticut.

31. Stieglitz to Demuth, December 31, 1916. Alfred Stieglitz Papers, Beinecke Rare Book and Manuscript Library, Yale University, New Haven, Connecticut.

32. Stieglitz would write to Demuth, "For remember my fight for O'Keeffe and Marin is my fight for you as well. You may not understand but somehow or other I'm sure you must feel what I've said to be absolutely true." Stieglitz to Demuth, undated letter. Stieglitz papers, Beinecke Rare Book and Manuscript Library, Yale University, New Haven, Connecticut.

33. J. Nilsen Laurvik, "The Water-Colors of John Marin," *Camera Work* 39 (July 1912), p. 38. See also Paul Rosenfeld, another Stieglitz ally, who said of Marin, "The unconscious mind has selected Marin for his medium. . . . He applies his wash with the directness of impulse that is supposed to be discoverable only in the work of small children." "The Water-Colours of John Marin," *Vanity Fair* 18 (April 1922), p. 54.

34. Ruth E. Fine, *John Marin* (Washington, D.C., National Gallery of Art, 1990), p. 76. This sense of Marin has persisted through the years. Sherman Lee called him "the primitive of watercolor *painting* in this country." Lee, "Critical Survey of Watercolor Painting" (Ph.D. diss, Western Reserve University, Cleveland, 1941), p. 267.

35. Rosenfeld, "The Water-Colours of John Marin," p. 92.

36. Ibid., p. 48.

37. A celebrated exchange between the president of the board of the Metropolitan Museum of Art and one of his trustees the year of Marin's first show at 291 dramatizes the disdain with which contemporary American art was viewed early in the century. The trustee asked, "What do you mean by American art? Do you mean English or French or what? There is nothing American worth notice." Quoted in Avis Berman, *Rebels on Eighth Street: Juliana Force and the Whitney Museum of American Art* (New York: Atheneum, 1990), p. 5.

38. Stieglitz to Paul Haviland, April 19, 1916, quoted in Sarah Whitaker Peters, *Becoming O'Keeffe. The Early Years* (New York: Abbeville Press, 1991), p. 37.

39. See Anna Chave, "O'Keeffe and the Masculine Gaze," *Art in America* 78 (January 1990), pp. 115-24, 177-79.

40. See O'Keeffe to Waldo Frank, summer 1926, quoted in Jack Cowart, Juan Hamilton, and Sarah Greenough, *Georgia O'Keeffe. Art and Letters* (Washington, D.C.: National Gallery of Art, 1988), p. 184.

41. See Peters, *Becoming O'Keeffe*, pp. 40, 122.

42. Georgia O'Keeffe, *Georgia O'Keeffe* (New York: The Viking Press, 1976), unpaged.

43. O'Keeffe, in *Alfred Stieglitz Presents One Hundred Pictures, Oils Watercolors Pastels, Drawings by Georgia O'Keeffe American* (New York: Anderson Galleries, 1923), unpaged.

44. Hartley, in ibid.

45. Quoted in Hunter Drohojowska, "The Unknown O'Keeffe," *Art and Antiques* (September 1989), p. 84.

46. O'Keeffe to Pollitzer, December 13, 1915, in Anita Pollitzer, *A Woman on Paper: Georgia O'Keeffe* (New York: Simon and Schuster, 1988), p. 39.

47. She wrote to Pollitzer in 1915: "You see I took the cart before the horse – drawing with no idea of composition. If I ever get this darned watercolor anything like I want it – maybe I'll send it to you – Today's is the 10th edition of it – and there it stands saying – 'Am just deliciously ugly and unbalanced.'" Pollitzer, *A Woman on Paper*, p. 29.

48. I thank Elizabeth Glassman of the Georgia O'Keeffe Foundation for this suggestion.

49. Sarah Peters argues convincingly for the Symboliste antecendents of much of O'Keeffe's early work. Peters, *Becoming O'Keeffe*, especially pp. 43-79.

50. Stieglitz to Arthur Dove, September 18, 1919; and to Paul Strand, November 17, 1918; quoted in Peters, *Becoming O'Keeffe*, p. 227. Stieglitz wrote to Strand about the strength of the new oils, to Dove about her recent difficulties in producing watercolors.

51. These watercolors are now in the collections of the Yale University Art Gallery, Mr. and Mrs. James A. Fisher of Pittsburgh, and the Columbus Museum of Art.

52. See, for example, her *Flower Abstraction* of 1924 (Whitney Museum of American Art, New York), in which the ovals from the Blue watercolors of 1916 recur, converted to tones of salmon but still in their limpid haze.

53. See Henry Tyrrell, "New York Art Exhibition and Gallery Notes: Esoteric Art at '291'," *The Christian Science Monitor* (May 4, 1917), p. 10, and William Murrell Fisher, "The Georgia O'Keeffe Drawings and Paintings at '291'," *Camera Work* nos. 49-50 (June 1917), p. 5; both reprinted in Barbara Buhler Lynes, *O'Keeffe, Stieglitz and the Critics, 1916-1929* (Ann Arbor, Michigan: UMI Research Press, 1989), pp. 167-170.

54. Benita Eisler, *O'Keeffe and Stieglitz: An American Romance* (New York: Doubleday, 1991), p. 139.

55. Paul Strand, "American Water Colors at the Brooklyn Museum," *The Arts* 2 (January 1922), pp. 148-152.

56. Henry McBride, New York *Herald*, Nov. 13, 1921, quoted in Annette Blaugrund, "Introduction," *The Brooklyn Museum: American Watercolors Pastels Collages* (Brooklyn, The Brooklyn Museum, 1984), p. 11.

57. Hamilton Easter Field, "Comment on the Arts," *The Arts* 2 (January 1922), p. 176.

58. Strand, "American Watercolors at the Brooklyn Museum," pp. 149-150. Stieglitz in this period pledged to further art preserving "America without that damned French flavor." Stieglitz to Paul Rosenfeld, 1923, quoted in Sasha M. Newman, *Arthur Dove and Duncan Phillips: Artist and Patron* (Washington, D.C.: Phillips Collection, 1981), p. 31.

59. Demuth "has truly experimented with the technique of water color, with the free flow and interpenetration of translucent pigments suspended in water. He has revealed much of its unique charm and has enlarged . . . the scope of its expressiveness." Of Marin, Strand noted: "Flowing color, interpenetra-tions of pigment, dry color dragged across paper texture, white paper counting as color, all these without once intruding upon the medium of all, he has developed and holds amazingly under control." Ibid., pp. 151-152. Strand's views, and especially his contrast between the too-European Demuth and the natural American Marin, echo the opinions of Stieglitz in these years.

60. Henry McBride, "American Art is 'Looking Up'," *New York Herald*, October 15, 1922, in *Flow of Art*, pp. 165-166.)

61. Blaugrund, "Introduction," *The Brooklyn Museum: American Watercolors*, p. 8.

62. Trevor J. Fairbrother, *John Singer Sargent and America* (New York and London: Garland Publishing, Inc., 1986), pp. 328-329; Annette Blaugrund, "'Sunshine Captured': The Development and Dispersement of Sargent's Watercolors," in Patricia Hills, ed., *John Singer Sargent* (New York: Whitney Museum of American Art, 1987), pp. 230-233. Susan E. Strickler notes that Sargent's price was extremely low. ("American Watercolors at Worcester," in *American Traditions in Watercolor. The Worcester Art Museum Collection* [Worcester Art Museum, 1987], p. 16.) She compares Sargent's charges to Frank Benson's, who in 1913 (at the beginning of his career as a watercolorist), sold two watercolors to Worcester for $250 each.

63. Helen Appleton Read, "New York Season," *The Art Digest* 3 (February 1, 1929), p. 15.

64. The first of these, and the first major exhibition of Homer's watercolors after his death, was a show of some seventy works organized by the Brooklyn Museum in October of 1915. Beginning in 1916, there were almost annual installations of American watercolors in "Gallery 25" of the Metropolitan Museum, where one wall customarily was given over to Homers and Sargents. In 1917, Homer's friend John Beatty, director of the Carnegie Institute in Pittsburgh, organized the exhibition "Winslow Homer and John Singer Sargent: An Exhibition of Watercolors"; it was a prelude to a large Homer show, of forty-nine watercolors, presented in Pittsburgh in 1923.

65. "Paris," *Art News* 21 (June 9, 1923), p. 6.

66. Fairbrother, *John Singer Sargent and America*, p. 336.

67. Field, "Comment on the Arts," p. 176.

68. Royal Cortissoz, "Foreword," *An Exhibition of Watercolors by Winslow Homer* (Pittsburgh: Department of Fine Arts, Carnegie Institute, 1923), pp. 10-12.

69. Fairbrother, *John Singer Sargent and America*, p. 349.

70. Henry McBride said, "Sargent has been out of the public eye for such a long time that he seems like a new thing." But it was all surface: "The fabric he created for us still dazzles here and there, but in places it has been worn thin. . . . In the long run tricks tire and it is only the soul that counts." McBride, "A Sargent Retrospective," *The Dial* (April 1924), in *The Flow of Art*, p. 196. McBride's reservations were echoed by Forbes Watson, who said of the watercolors, "His manual dexterity is supreme. Only the vision to see his subject as a whole fails him." Watson, "John Singer Sargent," *The Arts* 5 (March 1924), p. 150.

71. Royal Cortissoz, "Introduction," *Exposition d'Art Américain* (Paris: Association Franco-Américaine d'Expositions de Peinture et de Sculpture, 1923), p. 16.

72. See H. Barbara Weinberg, "John Singer Sargent: Reputation Redivivus," *Arts Magazine* 54 (March 1980), pp. 104-109.

73. "Studio Talk," *International Studio* 37 (April 1909), p. 165, quoted in Nancy Mowll Mathews, "Maurice Prendergast and the Influence of European Modernism," *Maurice Brazil Prendergast and Charles Prendergast: A Catalogue Raisonné* (Williamstown, Massachusetts: Williams College Museum of Art, 1990), p. 41.

74. Edward Waldo Forbes, "The Relation of the Art Museum to the University," *Proceedings of the American Association of Museums* 5 (1911), p. 52, quoted in Nicholas Fox Weber, *Patron Saints: Five Rebels Who Opened America to a New Art, 1928-1943* (New York: Alfred A. Knopf, 1992), p. 4.

75. "For the past five or six years, we have had an explosion of modernist art at the club. You know what I mean, that crazy stuff. The committee in charge of exhibitions has been showing principally works of this kind. We believe the people are rather tired of this sort of thing." Henceforth, the club's audience could expect a move away from extreme modernism, to the safer realms of "sanity in art." H. Dudley Murphy, quoted in Albert Franz Cochrane, "Approaching Dawn of Boston's Important Art Season," *Boston Evening Transcript*, September 15, 1928.

76. "Boston's Own," *The Art Digest* 2 (March 1, 1928), p. 4. This was an often-sounded theme: "The art world of Boston, familiar through generations of collectors with the delicate and distinguished values of water coloring, maintains perhaps more than any other part of the New World a lively appreciation and understanding of this gentle art which, like so many of her valuable traditions, persists as a happy inheritance from Old England." Dodge Macknight artist files, Boston Public Library, unidentified newspaper clipping, November 21, 1923.

77. If Macknight "has caught something of the breadth and dexterity in Sargent's work he has learned something also from the art of the modern French Impressionists. His pictures are full of light and air." Cortissoz, "Introduction," *Exposition d'Art Américain*, p. 18.

78. Gallatin, *American Water-colourists*, pp. 10-12.

79. Artist files, Boston Public Library, unidentified clipping.

80. Macknight was teamed with Homer and Sargent on at least one other occasion in the 1920s. In 1923, the Association Franco-Américaine d'Expositions de Peinture et de Sculpture sent to Paris a show of 193 watercolors by the artists it considered "representative of the American genius in art" – Homer, Sargent, and Macknight. (The show also included a group of sculptures by Paul Manship.) That the association was headed by such prominent Bostonians as Morris Gray (the president of the Museum of Fine Arts), Edward Forbes (the director of the Fogg), and Sarah Choate Sears (an eminent collector and active watercolor painter), explains the inclusion of Macknight. The catalogue was written by Royal Cortissoz, who strained to demonstrate that each of the four artists was "a thoroughly American type, thoroughly modern." Curiously, Cortissoz also portrayed each of the painters as "detached from the academic tradition," intimating that watercolor, lacking portentous credentials, was a medium especially suited to the American penchant for directness and free expression. Cortissoz, "Introduction," *Exposition d'Art Américain*, pp. 6, 12.

81. See "Exhibition by Messrs. Brackett, Prendergast, Noyes, and Burdick," *Boston Weekly Transcript*, April 30, 1897, p. 2; "Four Boston Painters," *Boston Evening Transcript*, January 8, 1913, p. 25; and William Howe Downes, "Exhibition of the Watercolor Club," *Boston Evening Transcript*, February 16, 1911, p. 11.

82. Theodore E. Stebbins, Jr., *American Master Drawings and Watercolors* (New York: Harper & Row, 1976), p. 249.

83. The Museum of Fine Arts did not acquire a Prendergast until 1927, when it was given the watercolor *Bathing, Marblehead* (1897). It did not organize a monographic exhibition until 1960. The closest thing in Boston to a show in his lifetime was "Maurice Prendergast, 1861-1924: A Memorial Exhibition," presented by the Harvard Society of Contemporary Art in May of 1929.

84. Ferdinand Howald of Columbus, Edward Root of Utica, and Albert Barnes of Philadelphia were other supporters. Duncan Phillips, who bought quite a few Prendergasts for his gallery, published a memorial tribute in 1924 that was the first serious article about the artist.

85. The Cleveland Museum of Art was the first public institution to purchase a Prendergast watercolor, acquiring *May Day Central Park* from its 1926 memorial exhibition.

86. The hanging committee was praised for "its courage in placing Mr. Marin's work in so favorable a place – defying traditions and doing insidious violence to the timid powers and the commercially inclined." "Philadelphia," *American Art News*, November 25, 1911, p. 7.

87. For Horter, see Anne d'Harnoncourt, "Earl Horter," in *Philadelphia: Three Centuries of American Art* (Philadelphia: Philadelphia Museum of Art, 1976), pp. 523-524.

88. For a discussion of "Paintings and Drawings by Representative Modern Masters" (1920) and "Exhibition of Paintings Showing the Later Tendencies in Art" (1921), see Carolyn Diskant, "Modernism at the Pennsylvania Academy, 1910-1940," *In This Academy. The Pennsylvania Academy of the Fine Arts, 1805-1976* (Philadelphia: Pennsylvania Academy of the Fine Arts, 1976), pp. 206-207.

89. Demuth to Stieglitz, October 12, 1926. Alfred Stieglitz papers, Beinecke Rare Book and Manuscript Library, Yale University, New Haven, Connecticut.

90. Art Students League catalogue, 1911-12. Additional information about watercolor instruction at the Art Students' League was generously provided by Lawrence Campbell, noted critic and archivist at the Art Students League, who indicated that "watercolor classes were marginal, if they existed at all. Eakins, a first-class watercolorist, taught lecture

classes at the League, but only in anatomy and perspective." Personal correspondence, June 8, 1992.

91. Philadelphia School of Design for Women (later Moore Institute of Art, Design, and Industry), *Announcement for the School Year*, 1880-1940.

92. Cooper Union for the Advancement of Science and Art, *Annual Report* 1880-1940. A similar attitude was held at Boston's School of the Museum of Fine Arts, where instruction in watercolor was offered only in the Department of Decorative Design, whose purpose was to "equip the student for professional (i.e., commercial) work." In that department, whose enrollees were mostly women, a course was introduced in the 1890s on "the study of natural flowers in watercolor." The peripheral status of watercolor was reaffirmed in the late 1930s, when the Decorative Design division offered an optional watercolor course. See School of the Museum of Fine Arts, annual reports, 1894-1938.

93. For example, Grace Barton Allen, *Water Color Painting* (Boston: Lothrop, Lee & Shepard co., 1898); Gertrude Estabrooks, *Water Colors. Gertrude Estabrooks' Methods and Colors for Flowers, Heads, Landscapes* (Chicago: n.p., 1905); Cecilia Elwes, *Flower Painting in Watercolour* (New York: Pitman, 1932).

94. Adolf Dehn, *Water Color Painting* (New York and London: American Studio Books, 1945), p. 25.

95. Ibid., pp. 6, 47.

96. Ralph Fabri, *History of the American Watercolor Society* (New York: The American Watercolor Society, 1969), pp. 31-33.

97. Henry McBride, "Charles Burchfield," *The Dial* (August 1920) in *The Flow of Art*, p. 159.

98. Demuth to Stieglitz, April 21, 1923. Alfred Stieglitz Papers, Beinecke Rare Book and Manuscript Library, Yale University, New Haven, Connecticut.

99. In contrast, the Fogg owned only three Homer watercolors and one by Sargent by 1930.

100. Although he reportedly paid $30,000 for a Corot and $125,000 for Renoir's *Luncheon of the Boating Party* in 1923, Phillips bristled at being offered a Walkowitz watercolor for $600 and countered with $400; in 1925, he managed to secure an early Demuth masterpiece, *Red Chimneys* (fig. 5) for $200. This information, and the story of the "$6000 Marin," come from Timothy Robert Rodgers, "Alfred Stieglitz, Duncan Phillips, and the '$6000 Marin'," *Oxford Art Journal* 15 (no. 1, 1992), pp. 54-66.

101. *The New Yorker*, January 1, 1927, quoted in Rodgers, "The '$6000 Marin'," p. 63.

102. "Field Marshall Stieglitz," *The Art News* 25 (April 2, 1927), p. 8, quoted in ibid.

103. Weber, *Patron Saints*, p. 140.

104. Lloyd Goodrich, "The Paintings of Edward Hopper," *The Arts* 11 (March 1927), p.138.

105. Charles Burchfield, "Hopper: Career of Silent Poetry," *Art News* 49 (March 1950), p. 63.

106. Ibid, pp. 16-17.

107. One of Hopper's first champions (and good friend) was Lloyd Goodrich, who was also the first modern chronicler of Homer's and Eakins's work.

108. Regarding his introduction to Hopper's work, Duncan Phillips wrote to Frank Rehn, "Immediately after leaving your place that day, Mrs. Phillips and I had almost forgotten him [another painter whose work they were considering], Hopper effacing him so completely." Phillips to Rehn, November 1925, quoted in Garnett McCoy, "Charles Burchfield and Edward Hopper. Some Documentary Notes," *Archives of American Art Journal* 7 (July-October 1967), p. 12.

109. Goodrich, "Hopper," p. 137. Homer's watercolors, too, were characterized as possessing "a sturdy disregard for elegance." "Fine Art," *The Nation* 814 (February 3, 1881). pp. 80-81, quoted in Judith Walsh, "Observations on the Watercolor Techniques of Homer and Sargent," in Strickler, ed., *American Traditions in Watercolor*, p. 45. See also Burchfield, "Hopper," p. 15: "The art of Edward Hopper is destined to become a classic, like Homer's and Eakins' whose tradition he has so ably carried on."

110. This was a recurring theme. Concerning the oil *Grain Elevators* (1938, current location unknown) he wrote, "I have not given up the subject. Someday I expect to go at it again; this time in watercolor. In fact, it is the failure of this picture in oil that made me resolve to abandon the medium, although I cannot blame the medium for the failure of the picture!" *Charles Burchfield, His Golden Year* (Tucson: The University of Arizona Press, 1965), p. 50.

111. Burchfield, quoted in Trovato, *Charles Burchfield*, p. 73.

112. Burchfield, quoted in Trovato, *Charles Burchfield*, p. 37. The pointed brush is preferred by most watercolorists since it can provide a large reservoir for the wash while creating a small outlet for its release. See Marjorie B. Cohn, *Wash and Gouache: A Study of the Development of the Materials of Watercolor* (Cambridge, Massachusetts: The Center for Conservation and Technical Studies, Fogg Art Museum and The Foundation of the American Institute for Conservation, 1977), p. 30.

113. Trovato, *Charles Burchfield*, nos. 677 and 690.

114. Burchfield's experiments with atypical materials and techniques, which indicate his ambitions for his watercolors, were paralleled by the efforts of such painters as Joseph Stella, whose daring combinations of media were often prompted by a desire to achieve old-master stature for his work (see Joann Moser, *Visual Poetry: The Drawings of Joseph Stella* [Washington, D.C.: National Museum of American Art, Smithsonian Institution, 1990], pp. 8-9), and by Oscar Bluemner, whose elaborate recipes for pigments and complicated layering techniques were prompted by a desire to immortalize his work (see *Oscar Bluemner: American Colorist* [Cambridge, Massachusetts: Fogg Art Museum, 1967], unpaged).

115. E. P. Richardson, "Watercolor: The American Medium?" *Art News* 44 (April 15, 1945), p. 29.

116. E. P. Richardson, "Three American Painters: Sheeler-Hopper-Burchfield," *Perspectives USA* 16 (summer 1956), p. 117.

117. For example, Larry Curry describes him as a natural; that is, self-taught, innocent of international styles and trends: "Charles Burchfield stands alone in the history of American watercolor. He began to paint with no knowledge of contemporary trends and felt no need to discover them. . . . Burchfield enjoyed no artistic heritage. The basis of his art was almost entirely limited to the man himself, responding to his private world." *Ten Americans. Masters of Watercolor* (New York: Andrew Crispo Gallery, 1974, n.p.)

118. Dehn, *Water Color Painting*, p. 45.

119. That exhibition, which also featured works by Demuth, Preston Dickinson, "Pop" Hart, Kuhn, Marin, and Weber, among others, in general paralleled Rockefeller's taste.

120. For Rockefeller's collection, see Dorothy C. Miller, "Contemporary American Paintings in the Collection of Mrs. John D. Rockefeller, Jr.," *Art News: The 1938 Annual* 36 (March 26, 1938), pp. 104-116.

121. Goodwin was another collector with a special interest in watercolor. He gravitated toward Stieglitz's artists, especially Marin and Demuth, and divided his collection among the Museum of Modern Art, the Yale University Art Gallery, and the Wadsworth Atheneum.

122. Their first encounter was related by Aline Saarinen in *The Proud Possessors* (New York: Random House, 1958), p. 359: In 1928, Halpert put on an exhibition of American seascapes to which Rockefeller had loaned, anonymously, a Homer watercolor. When she visited the show, Rockefeller (whom Halpert had not yet met) expressed interest in the watercolors by Marin and William Zorach hung on either side of her Homer. Halpert told her they were not available except "to the idiot who owns the Homer and doesn't have the descendants to go with it." Rockefeller then announced, "I am the idiot," and was allowed to buy the Zorach for $750 and the Marin for $250. Halpert, one of the first to identify a historic connection between Homer and other painters of the nineteenth century and the moderns – Marin, Demuth, and so on – would represent many of these artists in the 1930s. In March 1931, she presented an exhibition of "Seven Masters of Watercolor," featuring the work of Demuth, Preston Dickinson, Hart, Marin, Sheeler, Walkowitz, and William Zorach, all of whom would be represented in depth in Rockefeller's collection.

123. Holger Cahill, introduction to *Modern American Water Colors* (Newark: The Newark Museum, 1930), pp. 7–8.

124. Its 1925 Sargent memorial exhibition, for example, included almost as many watercolors as oils, and its centennial exhibition of La Farge and Homer, mounted in 1936, was dedicated to the artists' work in watercolor.

125. These include, in the current exhibition, Edward Hopper's *First Branch of the White River* and Reginald Marsh's *Steel Structures*.

126. In December 1933, the Museum of Fine Arts in Springfield presented a "Selection of Watercolors by Arthur G. Dove." No catalogue or checklist survives for this show, so that its size and contents cannot be determined. Other than Springfield's exhibition, and the show of Dove's oils and watercolors mounted by Stieglitz at An American Place in 1937, the Museum of Fine Arts' display of eight Dove watercolors probably represented the largest public showing of his work in that medium up to that time.

127. Cohn, *Wash and Gouache*, p. 39.

128. Berman, *Rebels on Eighth Street*, p. 272.

129. Henry McBride, "Work of Four American Painters," *New York Sun*, November 30, 1929, quoted in ibid.

130. The absence of Stieglitz group artists from the Whitney's collection had less to do with Juliana Force's antipathy toward their style (in fact, she admired them greatly) than with the obstacles Stieglitz erected to her acquiring them. For a discussion of their relationship, see Berman, *Rebels on Eighth Street*, pp. 228, 301-304.

131. Although the exhibition claimed to represent activity in the medium up to the present time, it was not a showcase for new developments in watercolor; the annuals filled that function. The younger generation of painters – among them Lawrence and Wyeth but also Gottlieb, Baziotes, and others – was not represented. The most recent works in the show were from 1940 and 1941, but they were by Marsh (b. 1898) and Dehn (b. 1895), both well established as painters in watercolor.

132. Alan Burroughs, "Introduction," *A History of American Watercolor Painting* (New York: Whitney Museum of American Art, 1942), p. 14.

133. Ibid., pp. 9-14.

134. James W. Lane, 'Acquarellia Americana" *Art News* 41 (February 15-28, 1942), p. 12.

135. Lloyd Goodrich, *American Watercolor and Winslow Homer* (Minneapolis: Walker Art Center, 1945), p. 43. Goodrich asserted that Homer "revolutionized the vision and technique of watercolor. Colored drawings he transformed into painting. Literal representation he changed into an art built on pure visual sensation. A medium confined mostly to amateurs and specialists he turned into one in which a serious artist could express himself fully and richly. Almost every leading watercolorist since Homer, no matter how far each has developed from his simple naturalism, owes something to his achievement."

136. In reviewing this exhibition, E.P. Richardson proclaimed that "Marin has developed the capacities of watercolor for rapid spontaneity, for delicate and figurative exquisiteness, for nervous vitality, variety, and surprise, to the highest point reached in our time." "Watercolor: the American Medium?" p. 29. Three years later, Clement Greenberg would assert, "if it is not beyond all doubt that [Marin] is the best painter alive in America at this moment, he assuredly has to be taken into consideration when we ask who is." John O'Brian, ed., *Clement Greenberg: The Collected Essays and Criticism* (Chicago: University of Chicago Press, 1986), vol. 2, p. 268. A more popular forum, *Look* magazine in 1948 conducted a poll of critics, curators, and museum directors to determine who were the ten leading painters of the day. Marin, whose Yankee subject matter was seen as an even more significant measure of his achievement than his formal daring, was pronounced Number One. "Are These Men the Best Ten Painters in America Today?" *Look* (February 3, 1948), p. 44.

137. A lingering prejudice that the medium is insubstantial, and not suited to major statements may in part explain why abstract expressionist watercolors are still relatively little known today. As Adolph Gottlieb related, "A dealer, when I was very young, was considering giving me a show of my watercolors, and she turned me down. She said, 'Well, you know, the history of art was never made with watercolors anyway'." Gottlieb, quoted in Cohn, *Wash and Gouache*, p. 16. For an excellent study of works on paper from this period, see Jeffrey Wechsler, *Watercolors from the Abstract Expressionist Era* (Katonah, New York: The Katonah Museum of Art, 1990).

138. Cahill, *Modern American Water Colors*, p. 8.

139. See Richardson, "Watercolor – an American Medium," and Frederic Whitaker, "Watercolor, the American Medium," *American Artist* 26 (June 1962), pp. 64–75.

NOTES ON MEDIA AND PAPERS

Roy Perkinson and Annette Manick

JOHN SINGER SARGENT described painting in watercolor as "making the best of an emergency." In these few words he elegantly connected artistic conception with the medium of its expression: the freshness of an artist's vision is perfectly embodied by the watery medium of watercolor, which is both elemental in its simplicity yet subject to vagaries of the moment and the hand. Surely there is no other medium that, by its very nature, can so easily flow, spread, and dry as if governed by its own laws, rather than those of the artist. Watercolor often challenges the artist to be a risk-taker, but the reward is luminous color and a fresh, informal quality unmatched by other media.

From the artist's standpoint, the physical behavior of watercolor also carries with it another benefit that may not be apparent to the viewer: the remarkable capacity to produce an image through analogy between the physical behavior of watercolor and the visual characteristics of the subject. The atmospheric mood of Marin's *Clouds and Mountains at Kufstein* (cat. 92) arises so naturally from the way watercolor spreads and diffuses on wet paper that it is hard to imagine than any other medium could have been as successful. In *La Biancheria* (cat. 79), Sargent deftly applied a brushful of pale yellow color directly on damp washes of cool blue and allowed the colors to bleed into each other, thereby emulating modulations of light and shadow in the white linens. In Homer's *The Blue Boat* (cat. 57), the irregular puddling and sedimentation of green and red pigments form an expressive analogy for the texture and color of the foliage in the landscape.

Spontaneity of effect does not, however, preclude planning or changes, and anyone who has ever dared to put brush to paper is surprised to discover how much deliberation and forethought may be required to achieve the appearance of artless abandon. As mentioned above, Sargent was adept at exploiting the intrinsic fluidity of the medium, but success with watercolor depends on more than recognition that watercolor flows easily. A well-developed sense of the timing and stages of one's work is indispensable. One must anticipate the precise moment when a wash of color is neither too dry nor too wet to allow the next touch of the brush or blotting of color. Sargent captured sunlight flooding an airy arcade by allowing warm ochre tones to spread into freshly painted passages of sky blue in *Genoa: The University* (cat. 72). If the ochre color had been applied too soon, it might have spread too far, supplanting the blue and thereby flattening out the roundness of the columns. If too late, the ochre might simply lie on top of the blue, thus creating an unintended color; and perhaps, upon drying, a distinct boundary would have formed between ochre and blue, once again defeating the desired appearance of curvature. Sargent's ability to envision and plan the development of a picture is evident in *The Cashmere Shawl* (cat. 81). After a few initial washes of color had dried, he scribbled transparent, waxy crayon in some areas before applying the next washes. Watercolor was repelled by the crayon but absorbed elsewhere. The result is that the final layers of color are occasionally interrupted by transparent "windows" of scarcely visible wax through which one sees colors that were applied earlier. Through his planning, Sargent achieved complex effects of color which, though seemingly random and accidental, beautifully suggest the texture of fabric.

There is a common perception that watercolor is utterly unforgiving. This idea probably stems from the fear that a stroke of watercolor cannot be changed once applied; moreover, that all one's mistakes will be easily seen and cannot be concealed beneath subsequent layers, as in oil painting. There is considerable truth in this, for certain watercolor pigments behave almost like dyes and are not easibly removed from paper. But watercolor is not a straitjacket for masochistic artists. Armed with the right paper and with knowledge of how each color performs, a stroke of dried color can be rewetted and lifted off the surface or blotted to soften its intensity. The great English artist, J.M.W. Turner, is said to have repeatedly dunked his watercolor in a pail of water, washing off much of the previous color but contributing to the complex, luminous washes for which he is so highly regarded. The spiky foliage and undergrowth in Homer's *Palm Trees, Florida* (cat. 62) owes much of its success to the artist's skill in lifting and partially removing layers of watercolor. Sometimes he not only lifted color but scraped it away entirely in order to regain the brilliant white of the paper, or, in other instances, to prepare for the grainy effect created when a new wash of color is applied over the roughened paper (see *The Blue Boat*, cat. 57). Homer reworked and edited his watercolors to a surprising extent, although because of his great experience with the medium and his ability to convey the impression that the final effect was achieved immediately, his changes often go unnoticed except under the most deliberate scrutiny (see *An Afterglow*, cat. 54).

In offering helpful guidelines to amateurs, manuals on watercolors sometimes leave the impression that success with the medium depends entirely on observing inviolable laws, and that the penalty for ignoring them is utter failure. The evidence of the pictures in this book suggests that the medium is subject only to the limitations of one's imagination. Furthermore, creativity often refuses to be the slave of a particular medium. In the dynamic relationship between the artist's ideas and the physical materials chosen for their expression, it is generally the former that has the last word. Artists frequently upset protocol about what should or should not be done with a particular medium. Even though using the medium of oil paint, Cézanne envisioned Mte. Ste.-Victoire through the eyes of a watercolorist. The color field paintings of Morris Louis might leave a hidebound oil painter yearning for substance and impasto, yet make a watercolorist's pulse race. Perhaps it is fitting, therefore, that this survey should begin with a somewhat unexpected choice, a fluid and lively work by Benjamin West (cat. 1). He disregarded convention by combining pen and ink with washes of oil paint rather than watercolor, but he thereby created an image that so perfectly embodied a watercolorist's vision that it was catalogued as such for many years – until the spoilsport conservators arrived and found otherwise.

This project provided an unusual opportunity to become intimately familiar with the techniques of many masters of watercolor. Careful examination of the pictures was a pleasure, but it also enabled us to verify or revise prior information on the media, types of paper, and artists' methods. In recording information about media and papers, we were concerned to be both accurate and consistent. The following discussion of terminology and the materials of watercolor painting is necessarily brief, but it is intended to enhance the reader's enjoyment and understanding of the pictures.

MEDIA

WATERCOLOR basically consists of pigments mixed with a water-soluble vehicle such as gum arabic, which makes the paint more workable and helps secure it to the surface of the paper. Some pigments are made by pulverizing colored minerals; some are obtained from naturally occurring vegetable substances, while others are made from synthethic chemical compounds. Pigments are derived from diverse sources and thus vary considerably in their physical and chemical behavior: some can fade very quickly, but others are light fast; some are opaque, while others are nearly as transparent as glass. Artists become familiar with the individual characteristics of each color, learning that one will produce an indelible stain on the paper, another can be easily lifted or disturbed by a second application of paint, and still another appears rather opaque even when thinly applied.

Watercolor is commonly regarded as a transparent medium, but the artist's working method and selection of materials, in service to aesthetic intent, are ultimately more important than any theoretical notion of watercolor. Partisans of transparent effects insist that a picture must be painted in transparent – not opaque – washes if it is to be called a watercolor. On the other hand, English Pre-Raphaelite artists sought to make watercolors that looked like oil paintings, with opaque passages and complicated glazings. The pictures in this book represent many points within this spectrum.

Our task of describing the medium of each picture was complicated by the existence of the term "gouache," which refers to watercolor that is opaque and usually more thickly applied than ordinary watercolor. The characteristics of gouache arise from the use of inherently opaque pigments, the inclusion of white,[1] or the careful modification of the vehicle to allow application of paint in thicker layers. While one might argue that the distinction has as much to do with method as with materials, color merchants have for many years sold paints called "gouache." When one examines Sargent's *Carrara: Workmen* (cat. 83), the evidence of a thickly applied, commercially prepared gouache seems indisputable; therefore it is tempting to describe this picture as "watercolor and gouache." On the other hand, did Alfred Miller purchase *both* watercolor and gouache to paint *Snake Indian Pursuing a Crow Horse Thief* (cat. 16)? Without further evidence that ready-made gouache was available to him, one must assume that he simply used his understanding of the watercolor medium to achieve a range of transparent and opaque effects. Therefore, when a picture in this book is done primarily in transparent washes, it is described simply as "watercolor." If it is mainly opaque in effect, it is said to be done in "opaque watercolor." If the picture seems to be a hybrid of the two approaches, it becomes "transparent and opaque watercolor."

PAPER

THE ARTISTS represented here used a great range of paper or paper-like materials, including paper as thin as hotel stationery (see Charles Demuth's *Illustration No. 8 for Zola's Nana*, cat. 96), and as coarse and robust as paper intended for use beneath carpeting (W.T. Richards's *Near Paradise, Newport*, cat. 36). Ross Turner used a commercially prepared illustration board for *A Garden is a Sea of Flowers* (cat. 71), while Demuth employed ordinary construction board for *In the Province* (cat. 99). Clearly, almost any surface that does not repel water can be used as a painting support for watercolor. Nevertheless, most artists preferred to use paper made specifically to enhance and facilitate the application and manipulation of the medium.

Traditionally the best watercolor papers were made from carefully selected rags, beaten into pulp and formed by hand into sheets one at a time. The essential tool in this process was the paper mold, which consisted of a metal wire screen or mesh attached to a rectangular support. The papermaker dipped the mold into the vat of paper pulp, capturing a slurry of fibers on the sieve-like surface. After excess water drained through the wire screen, the wet pulp was transferred to felt blankets for pressing and drying.

Even then, one important step was needed. A sheet of paper at this stage would have been as absorbent as a blotter and would have thwarted the watercolorist's attempts to lay in a uniform wash of color: the color would have been drained from the brush almost as soon as it touched the surface. The remedy was to treat the surface of the paper with something that would make it less absorbent while remaining receptive. Each sheet of paper was dipped into a vat of dilute, gelatinous glue. After final drying, this thin layer of glue (called "sizing") provided the perfect surface for classic watercolor paper. Strokes of watercolor would remain on the surface long enough to permit further manipulation, if desired, or would dry in a transparently luminous layer without sinking dully into the paper.

The thickness and surface texture of paper are almost as important as its absorbency, and manufacturers have long sought to provide a range of papers to suit any technical or aesthetic requirement. The thinner the paper, the more likely it is that buckling will interfere with manipulation of the paint or prevent uniform drying. Nevertheless, out of preference or merely for reasons of economy, artists sometimes use thin paper and try to overcome the problem of buckling through special preparation prior to painting. The sheet is dampened, affixed to a rigid support, and allowed to dry.[2] When watercolor is applied, some cockling of the paper occurs but tends to disappear as the paint dries. Thicker papers, though more costly, not only resist buckling but also allow the artist easily to create a highlight by scratching through a layer of color – or even scraping away entire areas of color – without cutting through the sheet.

In England and America the thickness of watercolor paper is often designated by the weight of a ream (500 sheets) of a certain size (usually 22 x 30 inches). Thus "300 pound" paper is approximately twice the thickness of "140 pound." However, because many of the artists discussed here did not use traditional paper, we decided to devise our own categories of thickness (with the caveat that these judgments are necessarily somewhat subjective). Paper thinner than a page in this book is called "thin." "Moderately thick" paper ranges from about two pages almost up to a postcard. "Thick" and "very thick" complete the categories, with the latter referring to paper at least as thick as an ordinary plastic credit card.[3]

The texture of paper plays an important role in both the execution and final effect of a watercolor painting. The meticulous brushwork of Newman's *Wildflowers* (cat. 27) required a relatively smooth surface for realization of the artist's botanically precise vision. In contrast, much of the liveliness and energy of Marin's *Crotch Island, Maine, The Cove* (cat. 93) was achieved by the artist's effective use of rough paper. As his brush careened across the surface, it deposited color on the textural "hills" while leaving the "valleys" sparkling white. Traditionally, watercolor paper is available with three different textures (in order of increasing roughness they are "hot-pressed," "cold-pressed" and "rough"); but again, a number of the pictures in this book are on very nontraditional supports, and it was therefore necessary to devise descriptive categories. Comparison of the textures of 127 different sheets of paper was extraordinarily tedious, and the results are of course subjective. The scale adopted runs as follows, in order of increasing roughness: smooth, if notably smooth; undescribed, if neither particularly smooth nor with sufficient texture to warrant mention; slightly textured; moderately rough; and rough.

TECHNICAL TERMINOLOGY

Wet-on-wet is a technique that can produce wonderfully spontaneous effects, but success depends in part on the ability of the artist to judge the state of wetness or dryness of the paper. Watercolor applied to dry paper will usually dry with distinct boundaries; but watercolor applied to damp paper will tend to spread and diffuse outward into the wetted area, drying without a definite edge, and with more or less uniform gradations of intensity. This technique might be employed, for example, to record the subtle transitions from light to dark in a cloudless, blue sky. If color is applied to a wet wash of another color, the results can be more complex. Sometimes the new color will both push aside and blend with the previous wash so that after drying, the new color appears to have "grown" organically within or beside the first. Sargent used this method to represent the round shapes of the columns in *Genoa: The University* (cat. 72), which are illuminated on one side by blue light from the sky and on the other by the warm, yellowish sunlight reflected from the marble pavement. In Marin's *Clouds and Mountains at Kufstein* (cat. 92), the atmospheric blending of color was achieved by working wet-on-wet.

The *dry brush* technique – a term that seems almost oxymoronic – is frequently used by watercolorists. Obviously the brush cannot be completely dry, otherwise it would be impossible to apply paint to paper. When employing this method, the artist carefully controls the amount of watercolor in the brush so that there is scarcely enough to permit transfer of color to the paper. One can do this in many ways, for example, by loading the brush with very little color from the palette or color dish, by preparing one's color so that it has a fairly dry and viscous consistency, or by draining excess watercolor from the brush onto absorbent paper. When this "dry" brush is dragged across a somewhat rough sheet of paper, color will be deposited on the high points of the surface, skipping over the low points. This effect is apparent in the wispy branches of the trees at the upper left in Macknight's *Flags, Beacon Street, Boston* (cat. 68). Andrew Wyeth is well known as a practitioner of dry brush watercolor and used this technique in *Memorial Day* (cat. 127) to execute the rough texture of the wall surrounding the windows, some of the cracks in the ceiling, and details of the hanging lamp.

Scraping through a layer of watercolor with a sharp blade or other tool may be done to lighten or remove color. Because the sizing might also be scraped away, the artist must adjust his technique if reapplying watercolor to areas that have been scraped.

After a watercolor wash has dried, light areas can be *lifted* out by remoistening wherever desired with plain water (sometimes with gum arabic or sugar added), allowing the color to soften, then blotting it up.

Blotting is a basic, time-honored method of softening, lightening, or removing damp color and is done for many purposes, including editing part of a picture or creating visual textures (Charles Demuth's *Eggplant and Pears*, cat. 100).

Graphite is the correct term for the black material in ordinary writing pencils. As the catalogue entries demonstrate, this is the preferred drawing medium for preliminary sketching of the image prior to application of watercolor.

Resist is a waxy material like a colorless crayon. Strokes of resist protect the paper from subsequent washes of watercolor, creating unusual textural effects. Sargent is the only artist in the catalogue who used resist.

Laid paper, when viewed with light behind it, shows a regular pattern of closely spaced, parallel lines, crossed perpendicularly every inch or so by more widely spaced lines. This pattern is produced by the wire screen of the paper mold.

Wove paper does not have the distinct pattern of lines seen in laid paper. It is formed on a mold with a screen so finely woven that the paper pulp is more uniformly distributed than in laid paper.

A *watermark* is any design, letters, or numbers visible in a sheet of paper when it is held to the light. Traditionally, a watermark is created by attaching a filigree of wire to the top of the paper mold. When the sheet is formed, the raised wire design causes the paper to be thinner, and allows light to pass through more easily than the surrounding paper. In this catalogue, the watermark "J WHATMAN" occurs frequently. This is the mark of the English papermaking firm, whose watercolor papers became the standard for high quality throughout much of the nineteenth and twentieth centuries.

1. A special note is appropriate here about white pigments used in watercolor. Historically, white pigments that were satisfactory when used in oil painting generally had insufficient opacity, tended to darken, or had inadequate handling properties when blended with a gum arabic vehicle to make watercolor. In the early nineteenth century, color manufacturers finally succeeded in making a white watercolor with acceptable opacity from finely divided particles of zinc oxide. Because of its importance in the pantheon of watercolors, Winsor & Newton (the well-known English manufacturer of artists' materials) promoted it under a special name, "Chinese White."

2. Since the nineteenth century, watercolor papers have been available in "blocks" or pads whose outer edges have been glued together. Although less effective than stretching as a technique for eliminating buckling, this is a conveniently portable format for working in the field. Many of the watercolors by Homer and Sargent bear physical evidence of having been executed on a watercolor block.

3. For the reader who is familiar with the traditional terminology for thickness of watercolor paper, the three categories of moderately thick, thick, and very thick correspond respectively to 90, 140, and 260 pound (or thicker) papers.

CATALOGUE OF THE EXHIBITION

USE OF THE CATALOGUE

The watercolors are arranged chronologically by approximate date of execution, except in the case of multiple works by one artist, which have been kept together. A biography precedes each artist's work. See the index for an alphabetical listing of artists included in the catalogue.

CATALOGUE ENTRIES

Undated watercolors have been assigned dates based on stylistic or material evidence. Measurements are given for the complete sheet to the nearest sixteenth of an inch, and in millimeters. Watermarks are cited whenever visible. Inscriptions are noted if they appear to be in the artist's hand, or if they provide additional information on the work. The descriptive terms for materials – papers and pigments – and various techniques referred to in the text are defined in "Notes on Media and Papers." Whenever it is known, the earliest version of a title has been used.

AUTHORS

SWR	Sue Welsh Reed
CT	Carol Troyen
ABW	Amy B. Werbel

Benjamin West

Born Springfield, Pennsylvania, 1738;
died London, England, 1820

West's extraordinary rise from a provincial talent to the presidency of the Royal Academy in London and "Historical Painter to the King" is one of the most remarkable success stories in American art. And whereas many of the well-known legends of his life – that he made his first paints from herbs, roots, and his mother's indigo and his first brush from a cat's tail – may well be fiction, West's phenomenal success in England from the 1760s on made him a beacon for the many young American painters who followed him abroad.

West was an innkeeper's son from Chester County (near Philadelphia), Pennsylvania. He had little formal training, working mostly from instruction books and studying briefly with English-born William Williams and the Moravian preacher and painter John Valentine Haidt. While still in his teens, West produced his first professional works; these are ambitious, if technically unsophisticated paintings, and include portraits, landscapes, and a precocious *Death of Socrates* (about 1756, private collection) rendered in a fledgling neoclassical style.

In 1760, encouraged by the local intellectual circle of which he was a part, West went to Europe to study and improve his craft. He was the first American-born painter to do so. While in Italy (1760-63), he became part of an international community of artists, including Gavin Hamilton and Anton Raphael Mengs, that was forging the new neoclassical style. By mid-decade he was established as a portrait and history painter in London. Whereas many of his contemporaries there were still working within the baroque tradition, West advanced the genre of history painting with such works as *Agrippina Landing at Brundisium with the Ashes of Germanicus* (1768, Yale University Art Gallery, New Haven), a classical subject whose treatment in his hands was both archaeologically correct and politically relevant. He further revolutionized the genre in 1771 with *The Death of General Wolfe* (1770, National Gallery of Canada, Ottawa), in which he applied grand-manner treatment, formerly reserved for themes from ancient history, to a recent event. These innovations, and West's measured yet theatrical style, won him critical acclaim and important patrons, including King George III. Three decades of royal commissions followed, as did a long period of service as president of the Royal Academy of Arts (1792-1820). Although West never returned to the United States, his London studio, where John Singleton Copley, John Trumbull, Thomas Sully, and many others worked, became in effect the first American academy.

West was a prolific draftsman, though he rarely used drawing as an end in itself. He worked in a variety of media – chalk, graphite, pen and ink and wash – and he occasionally supplemented his ink drawings with watercolor. Most of his drawings are compositional studies for his works in oil but he also made figure studies, landscapes, and copies after antique statuary. Despite his position as one of the leading neoclassical painters in England, he never adopted the austere outline style characteristic of so much neoclassical drawing, nor was he affiliated with English landscape watercolorists. Rather, his best works on paper show his admiration for baroque drawing, principally Italian but also Dutch, which he would have had ample opportunity to study in royal collections.

Benjamin West
1. *Angels Announcing the Birth of Our Savior*, about 1790

Pen, brush and brown ink; transparent and opaque oil paint on moderately thick, cream laid paper, affixed at its edges to an original mount of medium thick laid paper
13⅝ x 9¼ in. (346 x 236 mm)
Inscribed on banner held by angels, in brown wash: Glory to God on High / on Earth, peace Good will toward men
Gift in memory of John Hubbard Sturgis by his daughters, Miss Frances C. Sturgis, Miss Mabel R. Sturgis, Mrs. William Haynes-Smith (Alice Maud Sturgis), and Miss Evelyn R. Sturgis. 45.599

Although West's long-standing relationship with his patron, King George III, would soon deteriorate, he still enjoyed his status as "Historical Painter to the King" when he began this sketch. *Angels Announcing the Birth of Our Savior* is a preliminary design for the eastern-most window of the south aisle of St. George's Chapel at Windsor, one of several commissions West undertook there. In 1778, the king had decided to renovate Windsor Castle and make it the principal royal residence;[1] about 1782, plans were drawn up to refurbish the interior of St. George's Chapel, a late-Gothic structure (built between 1477 and 1528). West was directed to submit designs for the windows, in order that the medieval stained glass could be replaced with windows decorated with the more modern "painted glass" technique.[2] This composition anticipated a modest-sized oil sketch (private collection), a full-scale cartoon (location unknown), and the window itself, which was in place in the chapel by 1792.[3]

The designs West produced for the chapel illustrated the Life of Christ. The great tripartite east window represented the Resurrection; the west window, the Crucifixion. Over the altar was a mammoth painting of the Last Supper (now in the Detroit Institute of Arts). The windows in the north and south aisles were dedicated to Nativity subjects; the window for which *The Angels Announcing Our Savior's Birth* is a study depicted the passage from Luke 2:8-14 in which the angel proclaims "tidings of great joy."[4] The final verse, "Glory to God in the highest, and on earth peace, good will towards men," is inscribed on the banner borne by the angel in the foreground.

Although not specifically classical, that figure is generally reminiscent of the Apollo Belvedere, which West was fond of quoting, and is somewhat more distantly related to such energetic baroque figures as Guido Reni's *St. Michael* (1635, Santa Maria della Concezione, Rome), of which West is believed to have owned a copy.[5] But whereas in the 1760s such allusions lent additional layers of meaning to West's grand narrative pictures, here they merely enrich his repertory of figure types. West used the pose of the angel on the right in many compositions of this period, both sacred and secular.[6]

Few of those, however, exhibit the freshness and animation of this drawing. West's vigorous pen line defines the lithe, long-limbed figures with generalized features and flamelike hair. The translucent washes not only provide color notes but determine spatial relationships and augment the diagonal movement of the figures.[7] The brown wash establishes a middle distance; the gray-green area into which the angels descend is perceived as deep space. West reserved the bright white of the paper for the foremost angel and his banner, a device that projects the figure forward and makes his proclamation all the more dramatic.

CT

1. Allen Staley notes that "Apart from portraits, all West's work for George III after 1778 was connected with Windsor." In addition to the decorations for St. George's Chapel, West painted eight pictures for the Audience Chamber at Windsor, produced designs for a ceiling in the Queen's Lodge, and crafted three large watercolors for celebrations at the castle in 1789. Another project, the decorations for the King's Chapel at Windsor Castle illustrating the progress of revealed religion, was begun in 1780 and was the most ambitious historical cycle to have been attempted in England in the eighteenth century; both West's slowness in completing the paintings and the king's deteriorating health led to the monarch's disenchantment with his painter. The cancellation of this commission in 1801 marked the end of West's royal patronage. See Helmut von Erffa and Allen Staley, *The Paintings of Benjamin West* (New Haven and London: Yale University Press, 1986), pp. 89-98 and Nancy L. Pressly, *Revealed Religion:*

Thomas Sully

Born Horncastle, Lincolnshire, England, 1783;
died Philadelphia, Pennsylvania, 1872

Benjamin West's Commissions for Windsor Castle and Fonthill Abbey (San Antonio: San Antonio Museum of Art, 1983).

2. For a description of this technique, and an account of the transfer of West's designs onto glass, see Jerry D. Meyer, "Benjamin West's Window Designs for St. George's Chapel, Windsor," *American Art Journal 2* (summer 1979), pp. 53-57.

3. West's windows for St. George's Chapel were removed in the mid-nineteenth century, and have disappeared. See Meyer, "Benjamin West's Window," p. 65.

4. Pressly, "Revealed Religion," pp. 51-52 and cat. 26, p. 53.

5. See Von Erffa and Staley, *Paintings of Benjamin West*, p. 395.

6. Among the many examples of this stock type are *Cupid Releasing Two Doves* (1798-1808, private collection) and the figure of John the Baptist in *The Baptism* (about 1794, Bob Jones University, Greenville, South Carolina).

7. These washes, long believed to be watercolor, have recently been identified as thinned oil paint. West handled the pigment as though it were watercolor to achieve a luminous effect. This effect was especially desirable since West produced this drawing for a stained glass window, also dependent on transparency.

Thomas Sully immigrated to the United States with his actor parents in 1792, and soon after began studying art with local masters in Charleston, South Carolina, and in Richmond and Norfolk, Virginia. He started his career in the late 1790s as a miniature painter, working in a meticulous watercolor technique until about 1802, when he produced his first oil painting. He traveled to New York in 1806, to Boston (where he met Gilbert Stuart) in 1807, and to Philadelphia in 1808. Generous patrons sent him to England in 1809, where he worked under the tutelage of Benjamin West and Thomas Lawrence, whose portrait style was especially influential. Upon his return, Sully settled in Philadelphia, and embarked upon a career as one of the country's most sought-after and prolific portraitists. Beginning in 1811, he exhibited almost annually at the Pennsylvania Academy of the Fine Arts; his work was also shown at the National Academy of Design in New York and at the Boston Athenaeum. His stylish, richly colored, pleasing portraits soon won him an international clientele: he had patrons from Charleston to Boston, and won further fame with portraits of Queen Victoria and with numerous likenesses of the British actress Fanny Kemble and other theatrical personalities.

As a mature artist, Sully turned often to watercolor to develop ideas for portraits, to flesh out sketches made in early sittings, and to indulge the more romantic side of his nature in landscapes and subject pictures. He recommended his method to the many students he attracted during the course of his long career. For their benefit, in 1851, he gathered notes of his practice and technical knowledge, which were eventually edited and published as *Hints to Young Painters* in 1873, the year after Sully's death.

During his lifetime, Sully's popularity waxed and waned with changing tastes, as is reflected in his register, a chronological record of his paintings and the prices charged for them. In this century, the height of his fame came in the 1920s, the era of the colonial revival, when a memorial exhibition was held at the Pennsylvania Academy (1922).

Thomas Sully
2. Sheet of Figure Studies, 1830s
Pen and brown ink and watercolor on moderately thick, beige, antique laid paper (recto and verso)
8¾ x 11½ in. (222 x 291 mm)
M. and M. Karolik Collection. 52.1634

Although Sully filled notebooks with picturesque landscape views and copies after European masters,[1] most of his sketches are studies for portraits and other figurative compositions. These include drawings of single figures submitted for the consideration of his patrons, and sheets of smaller sketches, often six or more to a page, that represent ideas for future subjects. Some of the vignettes can be linked directly to finished portraits in oils. Others have only a general relation to poses and groupings Sully would use later. Sully recommended his diligent method of preparation to aspiring artists, counseling them to experiment on paper before attempting a formal composition: "The first sitting may be short, as . . . sketches on paper, of different views of the person, will be sufficient to determine the position of the portrait."[2]

In the Museum of Fine Arts' two-sided sheet (see fig. 1), Sully employed a supple, flowing line augmented with colored washes. Though

Fig. 1. *Sheet of Figure Studies*, verso.

Fig. 2. *Mother and Son (Mrs. William H. W. Darley and Francis Thomas Sully Darley)*, 1840. Oil on canvas. Metropolitan Museum of Art, New York. Bequest of Francis T. S. Darley.

Fig. 3. *Figure Studies*, 1837-38. Pen and brown ink, gray wash and watercolor on paper. New York art market.

schematic, his figures have character, and are firmly grounded in space. There is no apparent thematic relation between the figures on the sheet; however, they do seem to have been produced in one sitting, with the watercolor touches the result of a second campaign.

This sheet probably dates from the late 1830s, for Sully used the sketch of a mother and child in the upper right (recto) for his 1840 portrait of his daughter Jane and her son, now at the Metropolitan Museum of Art (fig. 2).[3] Another, similar page of drawings most likely from the same sketchbook corroborates this dating. That sheet (fig. 3) contains designs later adapted for portraits produced between 1838 and 1840. At lower left is a figure similar in pose and setting to that in the portrait of Mary Mackall Bowie Johnson (1840, The Art Museum, Princeton University, Princeton, New Jersey). At upper center, Sully rehearses a pose he would use in his 1838 portrait of Queen Victoria (private collection); a variant of this pose also appears at the lower right on the verso of the Museum of Fine Arts' watercolor. Such vignettes and others on these sheets make clear the close link betwen Sully's portrait compositions and his subject pictures. The poses and settings tried out here – a young woman gazing soulfully out of an arched window, a matron arranging a floral bouquet, a mother assisting a child at prayer – evoke the kind of sentimental narrative Sully sought to suggest in both genres.

CT

1. See, for example, the notebook that Sully inscribed "Lessons in Landscape Painting. Copies after Varley and others" (begun 1814) in the Yale Center for British Art, New Haven, or the sketchbook produced between 1810 and 1819 in the collection of the Metropolitan Museum of Art, New York.

2. Sully, *Hints to Young Painters* (Philadelphia: J. M. Stoddart & Co., 1873), p. 15.

3. John Caldwell and Oswaldo Rodriguez Roque with contributions by Dale T. Johnson, *American Paintings in the Metropolitan Museum of Art* (New York: Metropolitan Museum of Art, forthcoming), vol. I, p. 249. According to the artist's register, the painting was begun in April of 1839 and completed in December of that year. However, the canvas is dated January 1840.

Alvan Fisher

Born Needham, Massachusetts, 1792;
died Dedham, Massachusetts, 1863

Alvan Fisher was one of America's first native-born landscape painters. About 1811 he left his job in a country store and became an apprentice to the Boston ornamental painter John Ritto Penniman, who most likely introduced him to watercolor. Ten sketchbooks in the Museum's collection, used between 1816 and 1837, demonstrate that by the late teens, Fisher was using both monochromatic washes and watercolor to paint landscapes and tree studies.

While most of Fisher's finished works were in oil, he used watercolor more extensively than either of his close friends, landscapist Thomas Doughty and portraitist Chester Harding. In retrospect, he seems to have found his habits old-fashioned, for in a letter published in *The Crayon* in 1856, Fisher refers to a younger group of artists "whose eminent success in studies from nature, in oil colors, make me regret that I so long confined myself to the lead pencil and watercolors." Fisher left many such self-critical records, including a note on a sketch, "Miserable, but from nature."

Fisher's art education was representative of his generation. He was taught materials and technique, but in order to acquire a personal style, he had to study prints and work diligently from nature. From Penniman, he later said, "I acquired a style which required years to shake off – I mean a mechanical ornamental touch, and manners of coloring." In 1814 Fisher began to paint portraits for a living, and soon added barnyard and stable scenes to his repertoire, depending on such precedents as works by the Englishman George Morland, and compositions by Dutch animal painters, familiar from print sources. In 1817 Fisher traveled around New England and along the Hudson River sketching from nature. Between 1822 and 1825 he maintained a studio in Hartford and visited the South, making portraits of race horses. He toured England, France, Italy, and Switzerland in 1825-26, copying paintings and sketching from nature; some of his landscapes were used to decorate pottery by the English firm of Enoch Wood & Sons. Returning to Boston he became a respected painter who exhibited widely in Boston, New York, Philadelphia, Charleston, and elsewhere.

John Rubens Smith

Born London, England, 1775;
died New York City, 1849

Alvan Fisher
3. *The Hunter, A Self-Portrait*, 1837
Watercolor over graphite on moderately thick, cream
wove paper
13 x 9¾ in. (331 x 248 mm)
Signed and dated lower right in red paint:
AFisher.1837
M. and M. Karolik Collection. 61.276

Alvan Fisher often combined fishing or hunting
with his sketching expeditions in New England.
Here, he appears in a rare self-portrait, not as a
painter but as a gentleman sportsman and successful deer hunter. The artist has portrayed himself
with rifle in hand, quarry at his feet, seated on a
rock covered with a red blanket or cloak whose
bright hue is picked up by his bow tie. The painting was almost certainly made in the studio to
recollect a particular occasion.[1]

The figure style is consistent with Fisher's
paintings of the 1830s, while the competently rendered face and the blunt-fingered hands find parallels in Fisher's oil, *Portrait of a Gentleman* (1835-
40, Museum of Fine Arts, Boston). The generalized landscape setting has led to some uncertainty
as to the actual location.[2] However, the original
mount of this watercolor, though no longer extant, reportedly was inscribed on the reverse: "the
artist at North Conway, New Hampshire," an area
Fisher first visited in 1834 and frequented in the
company of the painters Thomas Doughty and
Chester Harding.[3]

The watercolor technique of *The Hunter* is
knowledgeable and quite sophisticated, showing
Fisher's grasp of English practice, perhaps learned
during his stay in England in the mid 1820s. The
lightly clouded sky is confidently brushed in, very
like the sky in Fisher's *Bunker Hill Monument*
from his 1834-37 sketchbook (Museum of Fine
Arts, Boston). Dry brushstrokes enliven the texture of the fir trees at the upper left. The face was
painted with miniaturistic care, with particular attention to the transparent shadow cast by the hat
brim. The artist scraped with a knife to lighten
the brim and to suggest highlights on the water in
the foreground and define the grasses on the
banks. Fisher lifted pigment to create the pale
rhododendron bush at the left, opposing its values

to the darker leaves he brushed in at the right.

The whole is engagingly naive, with the perspective and the drawing – especially of the deer –
somewhat awkward. Yet the sitter's gentle direct
gaze and his honest self-presentation, both reti-
cent and proud, produce a memorable image.

SWR

1. The sitter's identity is confirmed by a bust-length
portrait of Fisher by James Frothingham (undated, private collection); see the cover of *The Connecticut Historical Society Bulletin* 27 (October 1962). The accompanying article by Robert C. Vose, Jr., served as the catalogue of an exhibition of Fisher's paintings held in
Hartford and at the Museum of Fine Arts, Boston, February 28-April 17, 1963, and remains one of the best
sources of information about Fisher.

2. Fred B. Adelson, "Alvan Fisher in Maine; His Early
Coastal Scenes," *The American Art Journal* 18 (1986), p.
65, suggests that *The Hunter, A Self-Portrait* was executed in Maine where Fisher's whereabouts are secured
by a drawing of Mount Desert from Franklin Bay, dated
August 27, 1837.

3. The information on sketching trips and on the inscription on the mount of the watercolor that was then
in the possession of the New York dealer Harry Stone
are from Alan Burroughs, "A Letter from Alvan Fisher,"
Art in America 32 (July 1944), p. 123.

John Rubens Smith was born into a family of
moderately successful British artists. His grandfather, Thomas Smith of Derby, was a landscape
painter; his father, John Raphael, worked as a
landscapist and engraver. As a young man, John
Rubens adopted the profession of his father and
grandfather. At fourteen, he became a student at
the Royal Academy in London. Ten years later he
was exhibiting regularly at the Academy, selling
large numbers of portraits and genre scenes in
watercolor, mezzotint, stipple engraving, oil and
pastel, and conducting his own courses in drawing
and perspective.

Smith made a brief visit to America in 1802,
and four years later immigrated to Boston, carrying enthusiastic letters of introduction from
Benjamin West (then President of the Royal
Academy) to Gilbert Stuart and Washington
Allston. Shortly after his arrival in the city, Smith
opened a drawing academy, which attracted many
wealthy Bostonians, including his future wife,
Elizabeth Sanger.

In 1814, Smith moved to New York and opened
a second drawing school across the street from the
American Academy of Fine Arts, where the artist
served as librarian and keeper of paintings and
casts. Smith clashed with John Vanderlyn over the
exhibition of nudes at the academy, in particular
Vanderlyn's *Ariadne Asleep on the Island of Naxos*
(1814, The Pennsylvania Academy of the Fine
Arts, Philadelphia), and, writing as "Neutral
Tint," further irritated his colleagues with newspaper articles addressing this and other academy
policies. These difficulties caused Smith to leave
New York first for Boston in 1827, and two years
later for Philadelphia, where he opened a third
drawing academy. In 1844, the artist returned to
New York, where he operated his final drawing
school.

Smith published an art instruction manual, *Picturesque Anatomy*, during his second period of residence in Boston; shortly thereafter he issued the
Art of Drawing the Human Figure, *Chromatology*,
and *Juvenile Drawing Book*. The artist was particularly renowned as a teacher of perspective, and
reportedly instructed Thomas Sully in that subject. Smith's pupils in Philadelphia also included
Peter Rothermel, Thomas Cummings and

Emanuel Leutze. While Smith is known principally as an instructor and art critic, he also created perceptive, skillful, and detailed watercolor portraits, town and country views, and numerous engravings after the work of other artists.

John Rubens Smith
4. *A Philadelphia Physician*, 1839
Watercolor over graphite on moderately thick, dark cream wove paper
17 x 13 1/16 in. (432 x 332 mm)
Signed lower right, in black ink: Painted by J. R. Smith/1839 Phila
M. and M. Karolik Collection. 60.437

In 1839, Smith painted this portrait of a well-dressed physician, one of many watercolor portraits he produced in Philadelphia during the late 1830s and early 1840s. His aptitude for watercolor is evident in his delicate handling of fluid and translucent wash areas, as in the background wall, and in his more robust treatment of such thickly textured details as the quill pen. The fine parallel marks used to describe the hands and face of the sitter point to Smith's experience as an engraver, and reflect as well a miniature painting technique. The precisely drawn desk, chair, and architecture of the room is evidence of the artist's work as a perspective instructor.

A preparatory study executed in pencil and wash (fig. 1) demonstrates Smith's original plan for the watercolor. The skeleton in the closet is larger in the study, and stares directly at the viewer with a ghoulish expression. The cabinet and closet doors are not cropped, and a second chair of a different style is shown clearly. In the finished watercolor, Smith eliminates extraneous detail, sacrificing the second chair and reducing the scale of the skeleton, while adding a painting on the back wall. The sitter now assumes a more formal pose. A small sketch at right in the drawing shows the sitter in reverse, which suggests that Smith may have contemplated making an engraving of the image.

The identity of the polished gentleman in this portrait has not yet been determined,[1] though elements in the watercolor provide clues to his pro-

Fig. 1. *Preparatory sketch for "A Philadelphia Physician,"* about 1839. Graphite and gray wash. Private collection. Photograph courtesy of The Philadelphia Print Shop, Ltd.

fession and affiliations. A painting hanging behind the sitter's head most likely shows Ely Hall at Thomas Jefferson Medical College, built in 1828. The inclusion of the building here suggests that the sitter was an alumnus or faculty member of the institution.[2] The skeleton indicates an interest in anatomy, while the numerous books seen at right, as well as the sitter's pose with a journal and letter, raise the possibility of an academic career.

The sophistication of this portrait was recognized in its own day, for it seems to have been exhibited twice within a few years of its completion. It was probably the "Physician" exhibited by Smith at the Pennsylvania Academy of the Fine Arts in 1840, and it may have been the painting exhibited at the National Academy of Design in 1844 as the property of a "Dr. Lewis."[3] The watercolor then seems to have disappeared from public view until it was acquired by Maxim Karolik in 1948.

ABW

1. It is tempting to identify the sitter as the Dr. Lewis who was the first recorded owner of this watercolor, though details of Lewis's biography remain elusive. See Kathleen Foster in *Philadelphia: Three Centuries of American Art* (Philadelphia: Philadelphia Museum of Art, 1976), p. 305. Examination of the portrait and engraving collections of the College of Physicians of Philadelphia revealed a close resemblance between the sitter and Dr. Joseph Carson, a Philadelphia obstetrician, pharmacologist, and medical historian. An album of Smith's drawings is thought to have descended in the Carson family, strengthening the putative connection between Carson and Smith. Unfortunately, other evidence contradicts this identification. Carson, an alumnus and professor of the University of Pennsylvania Medical School, wrote a history of that institution, Jefferson Medical College's rival for medical talent in Philadelphia, and so is unlikely to have been shown in front of a Jefferson building. Dr. Frederick Wagner, University Historian at Jefferson Medical College, confirmed that the sitter does not resemble any of Jefferson's faculty or administration from the period of Smith's portrait.

2. Ely Hall is depicted in Frederick B. Wagner, Jr., ed., *Thomas Jefferson University: Tradition and Heritage* (Philadelphia and London: Lea & Febiger, 1989), p. 30. Graduates of the college would have been proud of their affiliation with Jefferson; it ranked among the nation's finest medical schools at the time.

3. The watercolor is listed in the *National Academy of Design Exhibition Record* (New York: New York Historical Society, 1943), vol. II, p. 130, as number 320 in the 1844 exhibition, owned by a Dr. Lewis and titled "Portrait of a Physician." See Foster, *Philadelphia*, p. 305.

George Harvey

Born Tottenham, England, about 1800;
died Bantham, South Devon, England, 1878

Although George Harvey painted in oil, the majority of his works were watercolors, either portrait miniatures or landscapes. He is best known for what he called "atmospheric landscapes of North America," a series of forty images executed between 1835 and 1840. Harvey wanted to have his watercolors reproduced as high-quality, hand-colored aquatints, following numerous English models and a few American ones such as William Guy Wall's *Hudson River Portfolio* (1820-1825). However, both the American and English economies suffered setbacks in the mid-1840s and Harvey succeeded in publishing only one set of four prints, *Scenes of the Primitive Forest of America*, in 1841. The choice of watercolor for preparatory studies for hand-colored aquatints was traditional, although Harvey's fine miniaturistic brushstrokes were very different from the broader washes of most other artists.

Harvey was educated in England. Although little is known of his early life, he was probably the G. Harvey who showed a flower piece at the Royal Academy exhibition of 1819, since he later exhibited flower paintings with some frequency. Harvey lived in America for three decades. He returned to England occasionally for education or business and made it his permanent home after 1848. Arriving in New York about 1820 he spent several years sketching the scenery of the frontier areas of Ohio, Michigan, and Canada. In 1828 he was living in New York where he was made an associate of the National Academy of Design.

From 1829 to 1835 Harvey lived in Boston and exhibited regularly at the Boston Athenaeum. He claimed to have painted more than 400 miniatures during those six years. Several of these in the Museum of Fine Arts, Boston, attest to his grasp of character, meticulous technique, and sensitivity to color (see fig. 1). In 1835 he retired for a time to Hastings-on-Hudson, New York, where he designed and built himself a cottage and also used his architectural skills to renovate Washington Irving's home, Sunnyside (see cat. 22).

After *Scenes of the Primitive Forest of America* was published in 1841, Harvey spent a decade trying to fund the remainder of the series. He exhibited all forty watercolors in New York in 1843, and at the Boston Athenaeum in 1844. He went to

Fig. 1. *Portrait of a Woman*, 1835-40. Watercolor miniature. Museum of Fine Arts, Boston. Bequest of Mrs. Edward Jackson Holmes.

England in 1848 where he gave numerous lectures on North America, illustrated by sixteen-by-eighteen foot painted enlargements of his watercolors, but still failed to find subscribers. What little is known about the remainder of his life indicates similar patterns of transatlantic travel and hopes unfulfilled. Harvey painted watercolors of Florida (by 1857), of Bermuda, and of Newport, Rhode Island (advertised in a prospectus for thirteen chromolithographs, New York, 1871). He exhibited at the Royal Academy from Bolton in 1873 and for the last time from Bantham, South Devon, in 1878.

George Harvey
5. *Winter: Impeded Travelers in a Pine Forest, Upper Canada*, 1835-40
Watercolor over graphite on moderately thick, cream wove paper; watermark: J. WHATMAN
13⅞ x 10³⁄₁₆ in. (353 x 260 mm)
Gift of Mabel H. Cummings in memory of her sister Emma G. Cummings. 42.459

The immense white pine trees of North America were awe-inspiring to the English visitor. "The aspect of the forest of pine timber," Harvey wrote, "is solemn and grand in the extreme, owing to their stately loftiness, many measuring more than 150 feet, their tall, straight shafts attaining the height of full 100 feet without a wave or bend."[1] This evocative scene was reproduced in 1841 as a hand-colored etching and aquatint in *Harvey's Scenes of the Primitive Forest of America, at the four periods of the year, Spring, Summer, Autumn & Winter, engraved from his original paintings, Accompanied with Descriptive Letter-Press* (fig. 1). The aquatints were executed in New York by William James Bennett and hand-colored in London.[2] Harvey's accompanying text stated that, although the sketch was made in Upper Canada, "the scene is particularly characteristic of parts of the disputed territory, claimed by New Brunswick and the State of Maine [the northern half of Maine, ceded in 1842]; it is composed of a mixed growth of hard timber, that is to say, deciduous trees, and white, or soft, pine. The two trees on the margin of the marsh are commonly called buckwheat pines, from the branching of their limbs like the stems of buckwheat."

Dwarfed by the scale of the trees, a sleigh is delayed by a fallen branch in the road. "Winter is the time generally chosen for distant social visits," Harvey commented, "and when the journey passes through extensive forests, such impediments as the one represented in the view are not unfrequent; they are, however, thought trivial, for, with an axe, a passage is easily cleared. The jingle of sleigh bells attached to the harness of the horses throughout such journeys cheeringly breaks the otherwise awful stillness and death-like repose of these ancient forest solitudes."[3]

The natural surroundings are depicted in subdued shades of opaque gray, brown, green, and

Fig. 1. William James Bennett (1787-1844) after George Harvey, *Winter: Impeded Travelers in a Pine Forest, Upper Canada*, detail, 1841. Etching and aquatint, hand-colored. Museum of Fine Arts, Boston. Bequest of Mrs. Turner Sargent, 1889.

blue, while the clothing, the sleigh, and the two woodpeckers in the trees provide accents of bright red and green. Controlled, delicate scraping is used to suggest the steam rising from the horses and white highlights in the snow. Harvey employed the tiny brushstrokes and techniques of a miniaturist, both to give his forms structure and solidity, and to suggest atmospheric softness. Particularly subtle is his handling of the intricate web of branches and the dark spaces between the trees to imply the mysterious depths of the forest. In comparison the published print appears decorative: the rivulets in the snow are multiplied and regularized, while the bark on the trees has a monotonous pattern.

SWR

1. George Harvey, *A Descriptive Pamphlet of the Original Drawings of American Scenery*, (London: privately printed, 1850), p. 14. Harvey's pamphlet includes a brief autobiography. For additional biographical information on the artist, see Donald A. Shelley, "George Harvey, English Painter of Atmospheric Landscapes in America," *American Collector* 17 (April 1948), pp. 10-13.

2. Harvey exhibited two watercolors entitled *Winter: Impeded Travellers* in New York in 1843 and at the Boston Athenaeum in 1844. The Museum's watercolor is most likely the one listed as no. 44 in the New York catalogue, *An Index to the Original Water Color Drawings and Oil Paintings Executed by Mr. Harvey* (New York: n.p., 1843). The catalogue notes that no. 44 had been the model for the engraver. The size of the watercolor sheet and the printed image (13⁹⁄₁₆ x 10⅜ in.) are virtually identical.

3. Harvey, *A Descriptive Pamphlet*, p. 14.

George Harvey

6. *An Autumnal Fog. A Cataract on the estate of R. Donaldson Esqr. Dutchess County, New York*, 1835-40

Watercolor over graphite on moderately thick, cream wove paper, mounted on thick, pale yellow cardboard
8⅜ x 13⁷⁄₁₆ in. (210 x 345 mm)
Signed lower right in gray wash: G. HARVEY
M. and M. Karolik Collection. 51.2530

Harvey intended *An Autumnal Fog* to be part of his series of forty aquatint landscapes of North America, but it was never made into a print.[1] After moving to Westchester County in 1835, Harvey painted at several homes attractively situated on the Hudson, including that of Washington Irving, and the Astor estate at Hyde Park. *An Autumnal Fog* is one of two watercolors he made at Robert Donaldson's estate, Blythwood, located on the Hudson River about one hundred miles north of New York City at what is now Annandale. The other is *A Morning Rainbow* (1835-40, The New-York Historical Society).[2] Donaldson, a Southerner, purchased the property in 1835 and engaged Andrew Jackson Downing to landscape it.[3]

In *An Autumnal Fog*, as in all of his "atmospheric landscapes," Harvey sought to capture a particular season or specific time of day. "A fog in America rarely occurs," he wrote, "but when it does it is mostly in the fall of the year."[4] Here a modest waterfall is framed on the left by gently curving eroded earth, and on the right by a rocky outcrop. The color and motion of the falling water is suggested by reserved white paper accented with many small strokes of pale blue and gray. Thousands of tiny brushstrokes in subdued opaque colors seem to emulate the minuscule droplets of water that compose fog and its accompanying velvety hush. The muted tonalities of most of the composition serve as a foil for the few stronger touches of color in the autumn leaves and in the foreground clump of wildflowers.

SWR

1. *An Autumnal Fog* is listed on the back cover of *Scenes of the Primitive Forest* (New York: George Harvey, and London: Ackermann & Co., 1841) with the other proposed subjects. The hand-lettered title on the mount is identical in style to the printed titles of the four published prints (see cat. 5).

2. See Donald A. Shelley, "George Harvey and His Atmospheric Landscapes of North America," *New-York Historical Society Quarterly* 22 (April 1948), pp. 104–113.

3. The information about Donaldson and his estate accompanied the watercolor when it was purchased by the

Museum from Kennedy and Co. The Blythwood (or Blithewood) property now belongs to Bard College.

4. George Harvey, *A Descriptive Pamphlet of the Original Drawings of American Scenery*, (London: n.p., 1850), p. 17.

Eunice Pinney

Born Simsbury, Connecticut, 1770;
died probably Simsbury, Connecticut, 1849

Eunice Pinney was one of the first artists to be rediscovered during the resurgence of interest in folk painting in this century. She was one of only seven artists considered noteworthy enough to merit a profile in Jean Lipman's pioneering study, *American Primitive Painting* (1942). The next year, Lipman published a biographical account in which Pinney was described as "the earliest and certainly the most remarkable primitive water-colorist whose life and work may be recorded. . . . Her product . . . stands out from the body of nine-teenth-century water colors as a unique and origi-nal performance." More than fifty of her water-colors have now been identified; these include not only the memorial pictures and family registers that were traditional subjects of schoolgirl art, but also such literary themes as *Lolotte and Werther* from Goethe's *Sorrows of Werther* (National Gallery of Art, Washington, D.C.), which attest to Pinney's intellectual achievement, and subjects drawn from everyday life, which demonstrate her compositional inventiveness and facility for observation.

Pinney was born to Eunice Viets and Elisha Griswold; their marriage joined two of the wealthiest and most prominent families of Sims-bury. Eunice was one of eight children; her broth-er Alexander Viets Griswold became one of the leading bishops of the Episcopal Church. She mar-ried Oliver Holcombe of Granby, Connecticut, about 1789, and had two children. After the death of her first husband, Eunice married Butler Pinney of Winsor in 1797 and had three children – two sons and a daughter.

Unlike many American women artists of the early nineteenth century (for whom painting began as a schoolgirl exercise), Pinney seems to have taken up watercolor painting only in her thirties. All of her known work post-dates her second marriage; probably none was made before 1805 and none is known after 1826. Her pictures are distinctive for their relatively strong color and bold delineation of form. Some – as was typical of the art of her day – were inspired by British engravings, while many others seem to have been original compositions.

Eunice Pinney
7. *For Eunice Pinney*, 1813
Watercolor and pricking on moderately thick, dark cream wove paper
16½ x 20 in. (420 x 510 mm)
Inscribed on tomb, in brown ink: In memory of / Eunice Pinney, who died aged . / We want but lit-tle; nor that little, long; / How soon must we resign our verry dust, / Which frugal nature lent us for an hour, / What, tho we wade in wealth, or soar in fame? / Earth's highest station ends in, "Here he lies, / And "Dust to dust" concludes her noblest song. / Heav'n gives the needful but neglected call / What day, what hour, but knocks at human hearts / To wake the soul to singe [?] of future scenes"
M. and M. Karolik Collection. 60.472

For Eunice Pinney is one of two mourning pictures Pinney made for herself in the summer of 1813 (see fig. 1). It may be that some illness or injury made her feel particularly concerned about her own mortality, as the inscription on the verso of the watercolor implies.[1] However, no such diffi-culties are recorded in surviving biographical accounts. In fact, Pinney had made a number of undedicated memorials in the years preceding the painting of *For Eunice Pinney* and, reflecting her generation's matter-of-fact attitude toward death, may simply have prepared these with a realist's eye toward future use. It was not uncommon for memorials to be prepared in advance, with inscrip-tions awaiting completion, as here.[2]

Pinney dedicated the memorial to her oldest son, Oliver Holcombe, who presumably is the young man leaning on the tomb in the center of the watercolor. The young woman opposite him is probably Sophia Holcombe, Pinney's other child by her first marriage. Two of the younger chil-dren, Emeline Minerva Pinney and Norman Pin-ney, complete the group of mourners. The same four figures, similarly posed, recur in the second memorial to herself, painted a month later; rather than carrying a spray of roses – when held down-ward, as here, a symbol of life cut short – Sophia holds the hand of an even smaller child.[3] The costumes have also changed. Although the girls' gowns are similarly cut, in the later watercolor, they are of a patterned fabric, rather than white, and Oliver's waistcoat is now striped.

Fig. 1. *Memorial for Herself*, 1813. Watercolor on paper. New York State Historical Association, Cooperstown, New York.

Fig. 2. *Willow, Grave, and Woman Weeping*, about 1815. Water-color on paper. Abby Aldrich Rockefeller Folk Art Center, Williamsburg, Virginia.

Pinney frequently repeated details in her wa-tercolors. The weeping willow is a common fea-ture of mourning pictures, and Pinney used it of-ten, sometimes as a central element, as here, and sometimes arching over the bereaved figures from the side. The vignette of the figure rowing a boat on a river or lake (another traditional symbol of passage to the netherworld), with houses and a church on the shore beyond, was repeated in an-other mourning picture (fig. 2) painted a few years

Mary S. Chapin

Date and place of birth and death unknown

later. Several of Pinney's watercolors are known in this oval format, with a border painted yellow to simulate a gold frame – a device probably suggested by engravings of the period.

Although it has been observed that Pinney's sturdy figures and architectonic designs distinguish her watercolors from most schoolgirl art of the early nineteenth century,[4] some features of her technique ally her work with that tradition. The short parallel brushstrokes emulate the fine, feathery stitches of embroidered pictures, and the pinpricking in the older girl's gown and her sister's collar imitates the lusterless texture of fabrics such as crepe customarily worn by mourners.[5]

CT

1. The inscription reads, "For Oliver Hector Holcombe if he will get it framed: / Dear children pray now and then cast / A sorrowful thought upon me / You see where you'r coming at last / Prepare you for eternity / This piece is the product of one week. Finished / by your disponding mother June 13- 1813 / Who worships the great God; that instant joins / The first in heav'n, and sets foot on hell./ Faith builds a bridge from this world to the next, / O'r death's dark gulf; and all its horror hides;"

2. Beatrix T. Rumford, "Memorial Watercolors," *Antiques* 104 (October 1973), p. 688.

3. The fifth figure may have been meant to represent Pinney's child Viets. For the roses and other symbols frequently appearing in mourning pictures, see Phoebe Lloyd, "Posthumous Mourning Portraiture," in Martha V. Pike and Janice Gray Armstrong, *A Time to Mourn: Expressions of Grief in Nineteenth Century America* (Stony Brook, New York: Museums at Stony Brook, 1980), pp. 89-104.

4. Jean Lipman, "Eunice Pinney – An Early Connecticut Water-Colorist," *The Art Quarterly* 6 (summer 1943), p. 215.

5. All black or all white costume was decreed for the deepest degree of mourning, to be worn only by close relatives. See Barbara Dodd Hillerman, "Chrysallis [sic] of Gloom: Nineteenth Century Mourning Costume," in *A Time to Mourn*, p. 92.

Mary S. Chapin

8. *Solitude*, 1815-20

Watercolor over graphite on moderately thick, slightly textured, dark cream wove paper; fragmentary watermark: T GILPIN &
15¼ x 13½ in. (387 x 344 mm)
Inscribed verso in pen and brown ink: Solitude Mary S. Chapin
M. and M. Karolik Collection. 60.469

This splendid example of American folk art, probably executed by a schoolgirl in her late teens, dates from the first quarter of the nineteenth century.[1] Had Mary Chapin been a decade or two older, her picture most likely would have been meticulously embroidered with silk threads on silk fabric, an accomplishment that began to lose importance after the mid-1820s. Because her watercolor bears close ties to the embroidery tradition, both in its subject matter and in its technique, it must be considered in the light of that tradition.

Around 1800 American schoolgirls began to learn to make pictorial silk embroideries. For the next two decades they stitched pictures mourning the death of George Washington and of family members of all ages. They also depicted religious, pastoral, and fancy subjects – even scenes from novels – whose designs were frequently based on English or Continental prints.[2] The young woman in *Solitude*, stylishly dressed, book (perhaps a novel) in hand, but idly daydreaming, sums up the sentimental taste then in fashion. In her pose and position beneath a shady tree she resembles the figure in an embroidery titled *Maria*, which depicts the heroine of Laurence Sterne's popular novel of 1768, *A Sentimental Journey* (fig. 1).[3] In *Solitude*, Chapin has modernized Maria's voluminous eighteenth-century garments, dressing her figure in a fashionable, slim neoclassical dress, draped with a long stole. Yet she maintained the general outline and shapes, replacing the old-fashioned peplum of Maria's skirt with an up-to-date straw bonnet and repeating the forms of Maria's sash and the dog's ribbon leash in the modern stole. A landscape setting, including river and distant town, appears in the embroidered *Maria*, but becomes more important in *Solitude*, with an iron-railed bridge leading to a town that might be identifiable.[4]

Fig. 1. Anonymous needlework picture of Maria, the heroine of Laurence Sterne's *A Sentimental Journey*, 1800-25. Silk, wool, and sequins. Courtesy, The Henry Francis DuPont Winterthur Museum.

Fig. 2. Archibald Robertson (1765-1835), *New York from Long Island*, about 1795. Watercolor. Columbia University. Gift of J. Pierpont Morgan.

Designs for embroideries produced by schoolgirls were usually drawn on the silk by the teacher, sometimes with the assistance of a professional artist. Mary Chapin may have received the design for *Solitude* already sketched in graphite, or she may have copied it from a model provided by her teacher; one other similar watercolor on paper is known.[5] Chapin executed much of the picture in brushstrokes that resemble the varied stitches of embroidery, including featherstitch or fern stitch for the foliage of the small trees, and French knots (for the distant hills and for the dotted Swiss pat-

for the foliage of the small trees, and French knots (for the distant hills and for the dotted Swiss pattern on the dress, made with tiny dabs of white paint). The opposition of rust and green for the foliage is the same as that found in silk embroideries from the first two decades of the century[6] and also in watercolors of that period. Mary Chapin's manner of painting the foliage of the large tree is less "stitched" and more "brushed." The most likely sources for models are the watercolor landscapes (fig. 2) and drawing manuals of the Robertson brothers, Archibald (1765-1835) and Alexander (1772-1841), Scottish immigrants to New York who founded the Columbian Academy of Painting in the 1790s.[7] The Robertsons' formulaic generalizations of natural forms were well known by 1810-20 through their publications and the work of their students. *Solitude's* hybrid appearance is due to its maker's reliance on two separate traditions – silk embroidery and watercolor – both imported from England in the late eighteenth century.

SWR

1. The date is based, in part, on the watermark. Thomas Gilpin's first initial first appears in 1800; his mill ceased to make handmade paper after a fire in 1825, and it closed in 1837. See Thomas L. Gravell and George Miller, *A Catalogue of American Watermarks 1690-1835* (New York: Garland Publishing, 1979).

2. "Silk embroidery . . . appears to have been undertaken . . . at most of America's fashionable girls' schools in the year 1800. . . . A pictorial silk embroidery on silk became the epitome of needlework accomplishment. . . . [after the 1820s] painting on paper and velvet became increasingly popular. . . and pictorial embroidery was on the wane." Betty Ring, *American Needlework Treasures: Samplers and Silk Embroideries from the Collection of Betty Ring* (New York: E.P. Dutton in association with the Museum of American Folk Art, 1987) pp. 59-60. For a social history of American needlework, see Susan Burrows Swan, *Plain & Fancy: American Women and Their Needlework, 1700-1850* (New York: Rutledge Books, 1977).

3. The embroidery was published in Swan, *Plain & Fancy*, fig. 96; it was kindly brought to my attention by Ruth Szalasny. A watercolor *Maria* in the Colby College Museum of Art wears the eighteenth-century dress of the embroidery; illustrated in *A Group of Paintings from the American Heritage Collection of Edith Kemper Jette and Ellerton Marcel Jette* (Waterville, Maine: Colby College Press, 1956), p. 32. Both of these images appear to have been based on the same English print, as yet unidentified.

4. Comparable to *Solitude* in their topographical elements, though not in their style, are silk embroideries from Portland, Maine, illustrated in Ring, *American Needlework Treasures*, p. 79.

5. Private collection, New Jersey. According to its owner, the work came from the South Hadley/Holyoke area (object file, Department of Prints, Drawings, and Photographs; Museum of Fine Arts, Boston). The Museum acquired *Solitude* from a dealer in New Haven, possibly signifying a Connecticut River valley teacher as a common source.

6. See Ring, *American Needlework Treasures*, color pls. pp. 59-105.

7. The Robertsons' ideas were derived from the English artist, the Rev. William Gilpin, whose influential writings appear in the 1780s and 1790s; see Edward J. Nygren, *Views and Visions, American Landscape before 1830* (Washington, D.C.: The Corcoran Gallery of Art, 1986), pp. 18-20, and pl. 26.

9. *Giraffe*, about 1836

Stencil and watercolor over graphite on moderately thick, cream wove paper; watermark: J. WHATMAN TURKEY MILL / 1836
12⅛ x 12½ in. (326 x 335 mm)
M. and M. Karolik Collection. 52.1562

With its charming subject, pleasing design, and well-preserved colors, this outstanding example of American folk art speaks eloquently for the voiceless giraffe, long a creature of fascination to man. As early as 1443 an enthusiastic and observant traveler wrote: "When I came to Cairo in Egypt . . . we saw a giraffe . . . an exotic animal and marvelous to look upon; for it towered with its neck of misshapen length and its front legs one-and-one-third higher than the rear. . . . Its back and the color of its spotted skin seemed very like [that of] stags and does."[1] The visual source for the giraffe depicted here may have been an illustration in a book on natural history, or quite possibly an image of the first live giraffe to enter France in 1826. That celebrated animal, which survived for almost twenty years, was reproduced in popular prints and even inspired textile designs.[2] The giraffe's distinctive shape, patterned hide, and gentle gaze appealed to the creator of this watercolor, who set the animal between two arching trees surrounded by a lushly fruited grape vine and other leafy plants and groundcover.

Waxed-paper stencils were used to define the body of the giraffe, the grape leaves, grapes, and spiky plant. One by one the stencils were laid on the paper, and watercolor was applied sparingly or stippled from a stiff-bristled brush into the cut-out shape. The soft, dry brushstrokes provide a satisfying contrast to the crisp edge created by the stencil. The giraffe's spots were painted freehand and the setting finished in a variety of techniques. The artist suggested tree foliage by twisting a round stencil brush as it stippled dark green paint over a pale green wash, and painted the veins on leaves with a very fine brush.

It is very likely that this is the work of a woman. Its neat workmanship recalls embroidery techniques (as does Mary Chapin's *Solitude*, cat. 8), and the crisply stenciled areas emulate such cut and appliqued textiles as quilts. Stencil and water-

John Mackie Falconer

Born Edinburgh, Scotland, 1820;
died Brooklyn, New York, 1903

color designs were sometimes executed on cotton velvet, further emphasizing the link to the textile arts.

In the nineteenth century, stencil-painting was termed theorem painting, for it enabled the artist to "theorize" or break down an existing design into its component parts. Through the use of the resulting stencils, the image could be recreated in a methodical way. Examples have come down to us of several paintings made from the same stencil patterns.[3] This giraffe, however, appears to be unique; no other version has come to light.[4] With its combination of imaginative concept and skillful execution, the work is unlikely to have been painted by a schoolgirl. It is probably the work of a school mistress or a housewife.

SWR

1. Cyriacus of Ancona writing to Filippo Maria Visconti in 1443 about his visit to Egypt in 1436, as cited in Phyllis Williams Lehmann, *Cyriacus of Ancona's Egyptian Visit and Its Reflections in Gentile Bellini and Hieronymus Bosch* (Locust Valley, New York: J. J. Augustin, 1977), p. 10.

2. Berthold Laufer, *The Giraffe in History and Art* (Chicago: Field Museum of Natural History, 1928), pp. 88–89. Laufer also cites a giraffe that was introduced into England in 1827 and recorded in paintings, but did not survive for more than a few months. Our *Giraffe* may share a common source with the giraffe on a later Van Amburgh circus poster lithographed by Sarony, Major and Knapp in the mid 1850s; illus. *American Heritage* 7 (December 1955), p. 39.

3. For three still lifes executed from similar stencils see *M. & M. Karolik Collection of American Water Colors & Drawings 1800-1875* (Boston: Museum of Fine Arts, 1962), nos. 1302-1304.

4. I am grateful to Betty Ring, author of several books on American needlework, for her consultation, and to Ruth S. Szalasny, who is preparing a book on theorem painting, for generously sharing her expertise.

Hardware merchant and amateur painter John Mackie Falconer did much to encourage the recognition of watercolor as a legitimate medium in New York's artistic circles. He was a member of the short-lived New York Society for the Promotion of Painting in Water Colors (1850-55) and in 1866 helped found the American Watercolor Society (called, until 1877, the American Society of Painters in Water Colors). Two years later he collaborated on a defense of the medium, *Water Color Painting and Some Facts and Authorities in Relation to its Durability* (1868). He also practiced and promoted etching. Falconer's oil sketches of old Brooklyn houses and his watercolors of New York street types provide a fresh and lively visual record of the ordinary places and people of his generation. He was a friend and correspondent of such notable professional painters as Thomas Cole, Asher B. Durand, William Sidney Mount, and Jasper F. Cropsey, and he collected paintings by these and other American and European artists.

After receiving a high school education in Edinburgh, Falconer emigrated to the United States in 1836, and by 1847 had begun his long career at the J.B. Windle hardware company of New York (a business he took over in 1874). In the 1840s Falconer belonged to several New York sketch clubs; he exhibited a watercolor landscape for the first time at the National Academy of Design in 1848 and was elected an "honorary member amateur" in 1851. In 1853 he helped the New York Society for the Promotion of Painting in Water Colors organize its only exhibition.

The next summer Falconer went to Europe to sketch and to buy art for his collection. He moved to Brooklyn in 1857 and became a member of a number of art associations in that city, including the Brooklyn Sketch Club, to which Samuel Colman also belonged (see cats. 30, 31). In 1872, Falconer organized the Brooklyn Art Association's first historical exhibition of American paintings, lent to it generously, and wrote for the catalogue. He retired from business in 1880. In 1886 Falconer sold more than 1200 lots of his prints and art books, and moved to a modest home with a studio where he could paint, etch, and restore pictures. His collection of paintings and drawings, however,

was only dispersed at his estate sale in 1904. From that sale came an album of sixty sketches, including watercolors by Samuel Colman, John Henry Hill, and Thomas Moran, now in the Museum of Fine Arts, Boston.

John Mackie Falconer
10. *Bearded Man in Tall Hat and Long Coat*, 1851
Watercolor over graphite on moderately thick, smooth, cream wove paper
9 9/16 x 7 7/16 in. (243 x 189 mm)
Signed and dated lower right in graphite: 2/9 / JMFalconer / Nov 19 1851
M. and M. Karolik Collection. 59.97

11. *Young Man in White Apron*, probably 1851
Watercolor over graphite on medium thick, smooth, cream wove paper
9 15/16 x 7 1/2 in. (249 x 191 mm)
Inscribed lower right in brush and brown wash: JMF / 2/17 / Decr 20/5
M. and M. Karolik Collection. 59.102

The New York Society for the Promotion of Painting in Water Colors organized informal classes for "the study of local life character."[1] Falconer's two watercolors almost certainly resulted from these classes, whose models were men and boys from the neighborhood, hired to pose in the studio. Other subjects by Falconer include a cleaner leaning on his broom, a sidewalk vendor with his basket of wares, and a clerk in his apron.[2] An album consisting of twenty-five sketches made in 1840-41, entitled "Types of New Yorkers" (location unknown) was described in the catalogue for Falconer's estate sale.[3] Falconer may have been prompted to suggest the same topic for the watercolor school a decade later.

Bearded Man in Tall Hat and Long Coat and *Young Man in White Apron* were executed over slight but well-observed pencil sketches that indicate the contours of the figures and their props. The restricted palette of each (black, gray, brown, red) suggests that there was little time or inclination to experiment with the color scheme. Layers of transparent watercolors were applied in the traditional manner, from light to dark. The brushstrokes gradually built up the face and hands, the

Fitz Hugh Lane

Born Gloucester, Massachusetts, 1804;
died Gloucester, Massachusetts, 1865

shadowed folds, and the highlights of the clothing that suggest the body underneath. Compensating for some weakness in drawing anatomy, Falconer demonstrates fine technical skill in handling his watercolors, allowing no unwanted bleeding of color into color. One of the great charms of these sketches is their lack of finish. Falconer completed coloring the figures, but left unpainted the studio seating and props. These were undoubtedly timed exercises, and the sketchers were required to go on to the next pose when the allotted time was up. Direct and understated, Falconer's watercolors remain fresh and lively today.

SWR

1. See Linda S. Ferber, "Our Mr. John M. Falconer," in *Brooklyn Before the Bridge, Paintings from the Long Island Historical Society* (Brooklyn: The Brooklyn Museum, 1982), p. 18.

2. There are altogether nine watercolor studies of single figures in this genre in the Karolik Collection (*M. & M. Karolik Collection of American Water Colors & Drawings 1800-1875* [Boston: Museum of Fine Arts, 1962], cats. 279-287). In addition to dates, three of these bear numerical notations – 2/9, 2/17, and 2/12 – which may indicate something akin to the number of the pose and its duration in minutes.

3. Ferber, "Our Mr. John M. Falconer," pp. 16 and 18.

Like many American artists, Fitz Hugh Lane began his career working for a commercial printmaker. He became a landscape painter whose marine views, austere and poetic, are among the most admired of the nineteenth century. He was a prolific draftsman and occasional watercolorist, for the most part using those media as preparation for compositions in oil. Lane was largely self-taught, and his work has the charm of naiveté. At the same time it has come to be viewed as a quintessential expression of American romanticism.

Lane was the son of a sailmaker in the fishing town of Gloucester, Massachusetts. A childhood illness – probably polio – left him partially paralyzed, a condition that did not, however, significantly inhibit his artistic career. At the age of twenty-eight he began working for a local lithographic firm, but soon left for Boston, where he served an apprenticeship with W. S. Pendleton, the proprietor of the most important lithographic firm in the city. He worked as a lithographer for some fifteen years, producing trade cards and sheet music covers, but soon developed a specialty in topographical views. The example of Robert Salmon, then America's foremost marine painter and a former co-worker at Pendleton's, inspired Lane to work in oils as well, and by the early 1840s he was active as a painter, exhibiting marine views at the Athenaeum in Boston and the American Art-Union in New York.

Lane's topographical interests led him to paint many views of the major harbors of New England – Boston, Salem, and Gloucester (to which he would return permanently in 1848) – as well as views of New York and Baltimore, the result of a trip along the coast in 1850. These subjects, along with ship portraits, stormy seas pictures, and yacht races (most famously the first America's Cup contest, which he observed from New Bedford, Massachusetts, in 1851), became his standard fare until the Maine coast captured his imagination. Lane first visited Maine in the summer of 1848, and made a more extensive tour in 1850, exploring the Penobscot Bay area. He made three more visits to Maine between 1855 and 1860, and painted numerous views of such local landmarks as Owl's Head, Blue Hill, and Somes Sound. In these pictures, compositions become spare; the

palette, once based on bright, local color, becomes pale and subtle, and the anecdotal detail that animated Lane's early work gives way to an emphasis on light that is extraordinarily clear and serene.

Fitz Hugh Lane
12. *Castine Harbor and Town*, 1851
Watercolor over graphite on moderately thick, cream wove paper
10¼ x 31¼ in. (260 x 794 mm)
Inscribed upper left in brown ink: Castine harbor and town from American battery of 1779 at Hainey's Point, a short way northerly of Henry's Point of later time. / Fitz Henry [sic] Lane of Gloucester, Mass., made this sketch for Noah Brooks in August 1851, and on its acceptance an oil painting. / In his will of date Nov. 30, 1900 Mr. Brooks bequeathed the painting to the town of Castine "for the public library."
M. and M. Karolik Collection. 54.1727

As the inscription at upper left attests,[1] Lane made this watercolor to introduce a design for an oil painting to a prospective patron. The painting (fig. 1), left to the Witherle Memorial Library in Castine, was one of at least three views of the town Lane produced following a tour of the Penobscot Bay area in the summer of 1850.[2] Although Lane's preparatory sketches frequently functioned as fairly exact templates for his oils, here he used only the right half of the watercolor – the part showing the cluster of houses on the hill jutting into Penobscot Bay – and eliminated the foreground entirely. For the lone vessel at left, Lane substituted a variety of sailing ships, large and small; for the attenuated balance of the watercolor – bare tree and boat at far left, busily detailed townscape at far right – he evolved an openended composition in which the only real focal point is the setting sun, just right of center, so that the viewer's attention is divided between the regularly spaced ships in the harbor and the swirling clouds in the sky.[3]

Although Lane's earliest known work is a watercolor (*The Burning of The Packet Ship "Boston,"* 1830, Cape Ann Historical Association, Gloucester, Massachusetts), the medium rarely seemed to engage his interest. *Castine Harbor and Town* may be the only other full-fledged watercolor to survive, and in fact, he only very occasionally

augmented his pencil drawings with watercolor.[4] Lane preferred to use pencil to make sketches; these range from tiny landscape details to panoramas in pale outline, often extending over several sheets joined together, as here. As a draftsman, Lane was careful and economical. As a watercolorist, he was somewhat naive. In his rendering of the town, color washes simply fill in pencil outlines, and that part of the image is quite precise and sharp. The foreground, however, is far more loosely painted, and hatching strokes laid over a simple wash provide textural variety. The ship is slightly awkward, with the distant shore visible through its sails.

As are most of Lane's panoramic drawings, *Castine Harbor and Town* is quite spare, and the foreground particularly empty. Such a rudimentary design could have been made in preparation for the kind of dense, animated topographical pictures Lane had been painting for the previous six or seven years (see, for example, *Gloucester from Rocky Neck*, 1844, Cape Ann Historical Association, Gloucester, Massachusetts), with sailors, children, dogs, and other anecdotal details to be added to the bare foreground in the final version. Instead, he chose to base his oil on the more fin-

Fig. 1. *Castine*, 1850s. Oil on canvas. The Putnam Foundation, Timkin Art Gallery, San Diego, California.

ished part of the watercolor, the townscape at right. Yet the very factors that may have caused Lane (or his patron) to discard the left half of the watercolor give it appeal now: the absence of figures and other foreground detail, the single bare pine, the unoccupied ship whose translucent sails give it a ghostly presence, all create an impression of loneliness that foreshadows the austerity of Lane's late work.

CT

1. The inscription may well have been added by Lane's good friend and touring companion, Joseph L. Stevens, Jr., who annotated many of Lane's drawings. See John Wilmerding, *Fitz Hugh Lane* (New York: Praeger Publishers, 1971), p. 51.

2. The other two paintings of Castine, *Castine, Maine* (1850, Museum of Fine Arts, Boston) and *Castine from Fort George* (1856, Thyssen-Bornemisza Collection, Lugano, Switzerland), were derived from the pencil drawing *Castine from Fort George* (1850, William A. Farnsworth Library and Art Museum, Rockland, Maine).

3. Neither watercolor nor oil documents the historic landmark referred to in the inscription: the fort from which the Revolutionary army attempted to ward off a British invasion in 1779. Their defeat resulted in the four-year British occupation of Castine.

4. See, for example, *Gloucester from the Outer Harbor* (1852, Cape Ann Historical Association, Gloucester, Massachusetts).

Edwin Whitefield

Born East Lulworth, Dorset, England, 1816;
died Dedham, Massachusetts, 1892

Whitefield was primarily a topographical artist, producing some sixty lithographic views of North American cities between 1845 and 1878, as well as a set of twenty-eight small lithographs, "North American Scenery." While some of these were printed with color and some issued hand-colored, nearly all of the preparatory drawings were executed in graphite, sometimes with monochromatic wash added. Whitefield occasionally painted finished watercolors, and even less frequently oils, but rarely exhibited them. Of his extant watercolors, most were made in the 1850s and early 1860s; they include views of Canada and Minnesota, as well as the eastern United States.

The peripatetic nature of Whitefield's early career is due in part to his constant search for new subjects and new markets for his city views. Wherever he lived, Whitefield supplemented his income by teaching drawing and painting. Between 1838 and 1853 he lived along the Hudson River, in Troy, Albany, Hudson, and Yonkers. Whitefield began his career as a flower painter; he exhibited for the first time in 1842 at the American Institute of New York, and in 1845 he produced *American Wildflowers in Their Native Haunts*, a book illustrated with lithographs of flowers set before landscapes. He then turned to depicting the North American city.

After spending a year or two in Ontario and Quebec, in 1857 Whitefield moved to Minnesota Territory where he acquired land as a speculator. He made numerous brightly colored watercolors of the sites to promote their sales. When this venture proved unsuccessful, Whitefield went to Chicago (1861-63), and made a series of lithographs of that city and other Midwestern sites. After another Canadian stay during the Civil War, Whitefield settled permanently in the Boston area in 1866. As well as continuing to produce his large city views, he published a series of books, *The Homes of Our Forefathers* (1879-86), illustrated with lithographs of colonial buildings. He spent time in New York drawing the Cypriot antiquities at the Metropolitan Museum of Art (1882-83), for a project never realized in print.

Edwin Whitefield

13. *The Starrucca Viaduct from the Southeast Side of the Susquehanna River*, 1853

Watercolor over graphite, with pen and black ink, on moderately thick, dark cream wove paper
10½ x 26⅛ in. (256 x 676 mm)
Folios 14 (verso) and 15 (recto) in a sketchbook
Signed inside front cover in graphite:
Edwin Whitefield / Yonkers / Westchester Co. / N.Y.
M. and M. Karolik Collection. 53.2522

In the fall of 1853 Whitefield made a trip on the New York and Erie Railroads, during which he executed a particularly fine group of graphite drawings in this sketchbook, many of them amplified with watercolor.[1] The artist probably hoped to produce a set of prints depicting this recently completed stretch of railroad, whose triumphs of engineering included the Canawacta Bridge at Lanesboro, Pennsylvania, and the nearby Starrucca Viaduct. Whitefield had been making lithographic views of American towns and cities since 1845, and his skill and accuracy at capturing a landscape was fine-tuned by 1853. In his extensive manuscript journal, intended to accompany these drawings, he wrote:

> On we rush, and all at once another splendid view meets our delighted senses. We see the villages of Lanesboro and Susquehanna with the river winding around in a sharp curve, and beautiful hills on every side; while a massive and enduring structure, the Starucca [sic] Viaduct, is seen spanning with its numerous arches a deep valley which lies in our course, and which we speedily cross. Half a mile farther, and we come to the Canawacta Bridge, from which we can look down in the chimneys of Lanesboro; and after passing another mile we enter the new village of Susquehanna. . . .
>
> But the Starucca Viaduct requires some notice, as it is the most expensive and imposing structure. Describe on this page the Starucca Viaduct, and copy this off. [Whitefield neglected to follow his own instructions.]
>
> The Canawacta Bridge, built over the creek of the same name, and rising some 30 or 40 feet above the tops of the houses in Lanesboro, is a beautiful and substantial structure, built of wood. It is 450 feet long, and between 70 and 80 feet above the waters of the creek which run beneath it.[2]

Whitefield's panoramic view of the site of the Starrucca Viaduct is one of three two-page spreads in this sketchbook to treat this remarkable feat of engineering, accomplished in 1848. The subject was pictured by other artists at the time, including William McIlvaine and Jasper Francis Cropsey (see fig. 1).[3] While their images are picturesque, Whitefield's is topographical. He spells out with clarity out with clarity the disposition of hills and river valley and the distances between them, and pays special attention to the Roman-arched viaduct and the train that crosses it. Whitefield drew the entire scene delicately in fine-pointed graphite, jotting down notes as aids to memory: "trees," "field," "a valley here," "dam," and so forth. He then applied light watercolor washes to the small settlement's modest number of houses and a church, the fields and their fences, and the wooded hills, suggesting local colors little affected by atmosphere. Using a fine pen and black ink he clarified the crossed timbers of the fences and the rooflines of the buildings. At the upper left appear two close-up sketches of the Canawacta Bridge, which the artist also pictured more completely in this sketchbook. Whitefield's finished lithographs, though accurate, are often dry, and lack the evocative power of such on-the-spot drawings as this one, vitalized by its luminous washes.

SWR

Fig. 1. Jasper Francis Cropsey (1823-1900), *Starrucca Vale*, 1853. Graphite and wash. Museum of Fine Arts, Boston. M. and M. Karolik Collection.

The Starucca Viaduct (N. Y. & Erie R.) from the
south-east side of the Susquehanna River

Antonio Zeno Shindler

Born Bulgaria (?), 1823;
died Washington, D.C., 1899

1. Internal evidence suggests that Whitefield used this undated sketchbook from the mid 1840s until 1853. It includes sketches of the lower Hudson not far from Yonkers, where he lived during this period. There are also numerous drawings of waterfalls and scenery in the Finger Lakes district, especially near Ithaca, probably made during the artist's trip to Rochester and Buffalo in 1846. These drawings are less skillful than the 1853 series that includes *The Starrucca Viaduct*.

2. The journal, now in the Boston Public Library, is inscribed by Whitefield, "Trip on the N. Y. & Erie R. R. etc. in the Summer of 1854." The year was actually 1853; see Bettina A. Norton, *Edwin Whitefield: Nineteenth-Century North American Scenery* (Barre, Massachusetts: Barre Publishing, 1977), p. 146.

3. Two 1851 watercolors by McIlvaine are illustrated in Roger B. Stein, *Susquehanna, Images of the Settled Landscape* (Binghamton, New York: Roberson Center for the Arts and Sciences, 1981), figs. 4 and 5. For two Cropsey drawings of 1853 and a chromolithograph, see *M. & M. Karolik Collection of American Water Colors & Drawings 1800-1875* (Boston: Museum of Fine Arts, 1962) cats. 207-210.

For generations the Zeno family feuded with neighbors in a small village in the Transylvanian mountains, and early in his youth Antonio found himself "the last living male of his progeny." Outnumbered by his enemies, the young boy left his country and traveled across Europe to Paris, where he studied art for several years. Zeno adopted "Shindler" as his surname after being taken in by a wealthy man of that name.

By the time Shindler arrived in Philadelphia in the 1840s, he already possessed diverse skills. Between 1852 and 1863, he exhibited thirty-nine pictures at the Pennsylvania Academy of Fine Arts; these included landscapes, portraits, and flower studies in a variety of media, among them pastel, watercolor, and oil. A few watercolors have survived from this phase of the artist's career, including several picturesque views of Philadelphia and surrounding areas.

Shindler was extremely active during the post-Civil War years. In the late 1860s, he took over the James E. McClees photography studio in Washington, D.C., which for several years had been photographing envoys from Native American tribes to the United States Congress. In 1869 he published his and McClees's work in a catalogue for the Smithsonian Institution. The next year, Shindler was hired by William Blackmore, a British ethnographer, and the two traveled through the Midwest gathering Native American artifacts for Blackmore's museum in Salisbury, England. Shindler lost all of his possessions in the Great Chicago Fire of 1871, and moved back to Philadelphia soon after.

In 1876, Shindler began work at the Smithsonian Institution in Washington, D.C., where he remained until his death in 1899. His obituary states that he "had a peculiar and valuable appreciation of animal life, and for many years was engaged in coloring life castes [sic] of fishes, reptiles and other living things. In order to truly portray the delicate shades of his subjects, he would frequently keep in his rooms specimens of the living animals, which he would copy with remarkable precision." Shindler also painted ethnographic portraits, depicting "the various races and nationalities in native costumes."

Antonio Zeno Shindler
14. *Laurel Hill Cemetary, Philadelphia*, 1850s
Opaque watercolor over graphite on moderately thick, light beige wove paper
16¹⁄₁₆ x 20½ in. (419 x 520 mm)
Signed lower left in opaque white: ZS (in monogram)
Inscribed center left in gray wash: IN MEMORY OF / ALFRED THEODORE MILLER / son of / MATTHEW T. AND CAROLINE MILLER
M. and M. Karolik Collection. 50.3872

During his early residence in Philadelphia, Shindler completed a series of large watercolors depicting picturesque scenes in the area (fig. 1).[1] *Laurel Hill Cemetery* is among these views, and portrays one of the city's most popular tourist attractions.[2] Located four miles north of the city on the Schuylkill River, Laurel Hill was a common destination for steamboat passengers from the city seeking a spot for picnics and other outdoor activities.[3]

Fig. 1. *The Fairmount Water Works*, 1850s. Watercolor. Atwater Kent Museum, Philadelphia.

For his view of Laurel Hill, Shindler focused on a particularly popular area within the cemetery. The Gothic chapel in the rear of the picture was completed from a design by John Notman in 1838, and soon became the most admired structure on the grounds.[4] William Strickland's monument to the memory of Alfred Theodore Miller, a child who died in 1840, is prominently portrayed at left. This tomb, still extant, was particularly recom-

mended to viewers. An 1844 guidebook to Laurel Hill illustrated the tomb, and noted: "Our woodcut exhibits the general appearance of a monument to a lovely child, the figure of which, cut by the celebrated sculptor Pettrich, is a portrait taken after death. It is much visited, and generally admired."[5]

Shindler's picturesque view is part of a tradition of topographical watercolors that flourished in America in the first half of the nineteenth century. Many of these (see, for example, cats. 5 and 6) were produced by English-trained painters who worked for the most part in a transparent wash technique. In contrast, Shindler's Parisian education apparently encouraged a more liberal application of gouache, which he used for small impasto accents and also to add body throughout the sheet.[6] Gouache is used here in the background washes that form paths, greenery, architecture and sky, and is also used, partially diluted, to create misty atmospheric effects in the upper half of the picture.

The popularity of Laurel Hill Cemetery from the 1840s on reflects the important role of the funerary arts in Victorian culture. Washington Irving wrote that "the grave should be surrounded by everything that might inspire tenderness and veneration for the dead, or that might win the living to virtue,"[7] and accordingly Laurel Hill's founders created a cemetery that was also an arboretum and a sculpture garden. As Shindler's watercolor demonstrates, the buildings and monuments were designed to be grand and inspiring, and the landscaping was selected to lend pastoral beauty to the site, attracting tourists as well as mourners.

ABW

1. In addition to the Fairmount Water Works (like Laurel Hill, also along the Schuylkill; see fig 1), these include a view of Trenton in the collection of the Museum of Fine Arts, Boston, and a view on the Wissahicken River in a private collection. The Trenton view has traditionally been dated "before 1851," and the Fairmount Water Works view to 1842, suggesting an 1840s date for *Laurel Hill Cemetery*. However, Shindler did not exhibit at the Pennsylvania Academy of the Fine Arts before 1852, showing his first Philadelphia view in 1853,

and two subsequent views along the Schuylkill River in 1861 and 1863. While a lack of documentation makes dating difficult, the density of monuments depicted in *Laurel Hill Cemetery* as compared with earlier views makes a later date likely. The watercolor probably dates from the 1850s.

2. Tourists were in fact so numerous that by 1839 the president of the cemetery was forced to restrict the number of carriages allowed. For more information on the cemetery, see Richard Webster in *Philadelphia: Three Centuries of American Art* (Philadelphia: Philadelphia Museum of Art, 1976), pp. 302-303.

3. R.A. Smith, *Smith's Illustrated Guide to and Through Laurel Hill Cemetery, with . . . a tour up the Schuylkill* (Philadelphia: C. Sherman, Printer, 1852), p. 31.

4. An architectural study for the chapel is housed at the Philadelphia Athenaeum. The chapel was demolished in 1883.

5. *Guide to Laurel Hill Cemetery* (Philadelphia, 1844), p. 38.

6. Marjorie B. Cohn, *Wash and Gouache: A Study of the Development of the Materials of Watercolor* (Cambridge, Massachusetts: The Center for Conservation and Technical Studies, Fogg Art Museum and The Foundation of the American Institute for Conservation, 1977), pp. 49-51.

7. Washington Irving, quoted by Richard Webster, in *Philadelphia: Three Centuries of American Art*, p. 302.

Trained as a wood engraver and skilled as a draftsman, George Loring Brown soon began to design prints as well as cut blocks. He studied painting in part by copying old masters in European collections and became famous for his copies of Claude Lorrain's landscapes, acquiring the nickname "Claude Brown." By mid-century he was living in Rome and known on both sides of the Atlantic for his Italian views. Many of Brown's watercolors were executed in Europe as preparatory studies for oils. He did not exhibit or sell his watercolors until late in life; more than one hundred were included in an auction of his work held in 1879.

After an apprenticeship with the Boston wood engraver Alonzo Hartwell, Brown studied with Washington Allston and with the portrait painter G.P.A. Healy, who helped him find funds to go to Europe in 1832. Following brief visits to Antwerp and London, Brown went to Paris, where he studied with the landscape painter Eugène Isabey, and supported himself by drawing and cutting woodblocks for a French periodical. He also copied paintings on commission for the Boston Athenaeum. In 1834 Brown returned to the United States and continued to design and cut wood engravings as well as painting portraits and miniatures.

By 1840 Brown was again in Europe, where he stayed for twenty years working in Italy, Germany, France, and Switzerland, and gained an international reputation for his landscapes. On his return to America in 1859 Brown was singled out as a colorist. Although American critic Henry T. Tuckerman recognized the unevenness of his work, in 1861 the *London Observer* praised him for his "faithful portrayal of nature, for his color, and above all for his luminous skies." Known primarily for his paintings of New Hampshire scenery and retrospective views of Italy, Brown maintained studios in the Boston area for the rest of his life. In 1879, hoping to obtain funds to return to Italy, he held an auction of his pictures (handled by Doll & Richards in Boston). The catalogue stated "Especial attention is called to the water colors, Mr. Brown never before having offered one for sale. They were all done for his own portfolio and study, and cover the whole term of his artist life."

George Loring Brown
15. *View of The Mythens near Schwyz*, 1858
Watercolor over graphite on thick, moderately tex-
tured, dark cream wove paper
10⅜ x 17⅛ in. (264 x 435 mm)
Signed and dated lower right in pen and black ink: G.L.
Brown 1858
M. and M. Karolik Collection. 61.263

George Loring Brown's mentor, Washington Allston, wrote that the Swiss alps at dawn "seemed
literally to rise from their purple beds and put on
their golden crowns."[1] Brown's colorful, late-af-
ternoon view was based on his own observations
in Switzerland in the late summer of 1857.[2] The
1879 catalogue of an extensive auction of Brown's
work listed fourteen Swiss subjects: eleven watercolors and three oils. From their titles it is clear
that Brown traveled around the eastern side of the
lake of Lucerne, painting towns and mountains.[3]
He spent some time in the port of Brunnen and in

the nearby village of Schwyz, which gave its name
to the Swiss confederation. A nineteenth-century
English writer described the locale:

> Schwyz. . . is built at the foot of the Mythen, a dou-
> ble-crested mountain 5868 feet in height. . . . The
> town itself, but particularly the vicinity, offers many
> neat and even elegant specimens of domestic archi-
> tecture, and abounds in beautiful situations, of which
> the wealthier inhabitants have availed themselves, to
> construct villas and summer houses – all in harmony
> with the natural landscape.[4]

In its restrained and formulaic composition *The*

Mythens near Schwyz may be said to recall landscapes by Claude Lorrain, well-known to Brown
through his copies, but in its colorful palette and
atmospheric washes the watercolor more closely
resembles watercolors by J.M.W. Turner, some of
which were painted in the same area of Switzerland in the 1840s.[5] The composition retreats in a
stately way into the distance by means of horizontal bands of landscape elements. These begin in
the foreground with the water's edge and progress
across a field and the buildings of Schwyz nestled
in the trees to the base of the mountains shrouded

Alfred Jacob Miller

Born Baltimore, Maryland, 1810;
died Baltimore, Maryland, 1874

in shadow, ending with the roseate peaks and blue sky. Using opaque pigments in the sky and mountain shadows, and in the foreground vegetation, the artist quickly brushed in the elements of his composition. Using a sharp tool, such as the point of a knife, he scratched fine lines to suggest the grass growing along the bank and on the field. Scraping more broadly he created highlights on the mountain tops and white accents in the blue shadows at the base of the mountains. The surface texture of this watercolor is far more successful than that of his excessively encrusted canvasses. While lacking Turner's cosmic breadth, Brown captures some of that great painter's coloristic and atmospheric effects in his watercolor.

SWR

1. Cited in Henry T. Tuckerman, *Book of the Artists: American Artist Life* (New York: G.P. Putnam & Sons, 1870), p. 353.

2. Brown did not travel outside Italy in 1858, as his expense accounts verify; see *Account Book of George Loring Brown, 1851-1859*, in the William Morris Hunt Library, Museum of Fine Arts, Boston.

3. *Catalogue of Oil Paintings, Water Color Drawings, by George L. Brown, Pupil of Washington Allston and Isabey (Louis Gabriel Eugène). American, Roman, Venetian, Neapolitan, Florentine Views. Now on Exhibition by Doll & Richards, At No. 2 Park Street [Boston], To be sold at auction at the Hawthorne Rooms, On Wednesday, Thursday, Friday, and Saturday, May 7, 8, 9, and 10, 1879, at half past 2 o'clock, Leonard & Co., auctioneers.* Of 333 lots of American and European subjects, only fourteen were Swiss (nos. 4, 73, 134, 154, 207, 252, 280, 290, 296, 303, 309, 323, 332, and 333), half of them from the vicinity of Brunnen. All but one (no. 207, 1863) are dated 1857. In 1879 Brown was so well known for his reminiscences of Italy, that Swiss views are not even mentioned on the title page. Even in the later fifties the demand for Brown's standard Italian subjects must have overshadowed interest in new themes, for he sold no Swiss pictures between 1857 and 1859, as his account book attests (see note 2). *View of The Mythens near Schwyz* was a gift, as the inscription on its original mount indicated: "View of the Mittens-near Swyzt / Lake of Lucerne painted from nature Switzerland 1858 / presented to M. G. Whitlock by the artist Boston 1860."

4. William Beattie, *Switzerland* (London: George Virtue, 1835), p. 152.

5. See Joseph R. Goldyne, *J. M. W. Turner, Works on Paper from American Collections*, (Berkeley: University Art Museum, 1975), especially cat. 42, *The Lake of Zug – Early Morning* (1843, Metropolitan Museum of Art, New York), sold to John Ruskin by its owner because it was "too blue."

Alfred Jacob Miller was a successful painter of portraits and other figure subjects, and was one of the earliest Americans to depict the West. He made numerous sketches of the landscape and its inhabitants, from which he subsequently produced and sold oil paintings and hundreds of watercolors.

The son of a wealthy merchant, Miller's social connections served him in his career as a portrait painter. The extent of his early art education is not known, although Baltimore was an artistic center in the early nineteenth century: the Peale family had a museum there and Thomas Sully made regular visits from Philadelphia to paint portraits. In 1833 Miller went to Paris, where he attended life classes at the Ecole des Beaux-Arts, and copied paintings in museums. He seems to have been particularly attracted to the painterly aspects of the Venetians, the seventeenth-century Dutch, and Eugène Delacroix. The influence of Delacroix's energetic line and colorful palette is evident in Miller's subsequent work; like Delacroix, Miller was fascinated with animals in action, and he sketched at the animal combats then popular in Paris. Miller also visited Rome and sketched in the Alps. Returning to Baltimore, he sent his original work and his copies of European paintings to the Boston Athenaeum exhibitions of 1834 and 1835.

Miller moved to New Orleans, where late in 1836 William Drummond Stewart, a Scottish baronet, fortuitously visited his studio and invited the artist to accompany him on his fifth trip west on the Oregon Trail. In the following spring and summer Miller sketched his way across the plains to the Rockies with Stewart's party. Stewart engaged Miller to paint a series of oil paintings of the American West as decorations for Murthly Castle, his home in Perthshire. Miller began these large canvases in America and completed them at Murthly Castle between 1840 and 1842. Miller also brought Stewart a number of drawings recalling their western adventures, which Stewart kept in a "drawing room portfolio."

His Scottish commission ended, Miller returned to Baltimore in 1842. There he continued to paint portraits and also found a new market for his western subjects. Sanctioned by European taste, images of the Indian and the American West

Alfred Jacob Miller
16. *Snake Indian Pursuing a Crow Horse Thief,*
      about 1860

Transparent and opaque watercolor over and under
graphite on very thick, smooth, cream wove paper
7⁷/₁₆ x 10¹³/₁₆ in. (190 x 275 mm)
Signed lower right in graphite: Miller
M. and M. Karolik Collection. 58.1149

had become acceptable to American collectors.
Miller made hundreds of watercolors based on the
sketches he retained from his trip with Stewart. Two
large commissions still intact are two hundred images made for William T. Walters (now Walters Art
Gallery, Baltimore) and forty for Alexander Brown
(now Public Archives of Canada, Ottawa).

This spirited scene of horse thievery is one of the
many watercolors Miller based on the sketches he
made during the summer of 1837, when he traveled with William Drummond Stewart to the Far
West. Unlike other artists of the West such as
Thomas Moran (see cat. 29) and Walter Paris (see
cat. 32), who depicted its natural splendors, Miller

Fig. 1. *A Snake Pursuing a Crow Horse Stealer*, 1837–40. Graphite and watercolor on paper. Private collection.

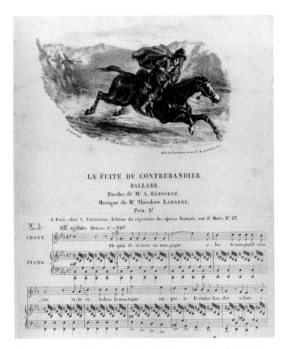

Fig. 2. Eugène Delacroix (1798–1863), *La Fuite du Contrebandier*, 1826. Lithograph. Museum of Fine Arts, Boston. Bequest of W.G. Russell Allen.

was commissioned to record the personal adventures of Captain Stewart, an eccentric Scottish baronet who had served in the British army under the Duke of Wellington. This was Stewart's fifth trip to the American West and he was eager to have Miller record it. They traveled with a party of fur traders along the Oregon Trail, from St. Louis to a valley near the Wind River Mountains (in present-day Wyoming), to attend the raucous annual reunion of traders with trappers and their Indian cohorts.

No field sketch by Miller is known for *Snake Indian Pursuing a Crow Horse Thief*.[1] However, by 1840, Miller had made a watercolor of the subject for Stewart (fig. 1).[2] The episode was probably envisioned rather than observed, and served as an expression of the fur trade's opinion of the Crows as untrustworthy and the Snakes as reliable allies.[3] In Stewart's version, the generalized setting, fluid forms, and sleek, elegant horses speak more of romantic imagination than gritty reality. Miller's dashing horses demonstrate his continued high regard for the work of Eugène Delacroix, which he had seen in Paris some seven years earlier. He could possibly have owned a print by Delacroix, readily available in the form of a sheet music cover (fig. 2).

Snake Indian Pursuing a Crow Horse Thief is more visually credible and pictorially unified than Stewart's version; the landscape setting is more developed, and the two horsemen are better integrated into their surroundings. Stewart's elegant mounts have been replaced with sturdy ponies, with shorter legs and rougher coats. The riders' trappings and buckskin attire – beaded, fringed breeches, red and yellow capes, and quiver – are given more prominence. Miller probably referred to the costumes and artifacts he had acquired on his trip and retained in his studio. This work is similar in style, and was probably executed at the same time as the group of 200 watercolors Miller made for William T. Walters of Baltimore between 1858 and 1860 (now Walters Art Gallery).[4]

The artist began with a graphite drawing, over which he painted thin washes, and then added thick accents of opaque paint. He also drew with graphite over certain painted areas. Under the washes, nervous, energetic graphite lines describe the forms of the rugged mountains, while lines drawn over the paint define the sharp-needled boughs of the fir trees.

Miller created a number of atmospheric effects in this watercolor, including the cloud of dust that rises convincingly from the hooves of the horse at the right. He suggested the dust by applying a thin layer of paint without discernible brushstrokes. This technique is known in oil painting as "scumbling," and Miller had been experimenting with it in 1836, when Stewart first visited his studio. Miller owed much of his future reputation to the fact that Stewart "liked the management of that picture."[5]

SWR

1. The field sketches, generally executed in pencil and wash, were retained by Miller and descended through the family; they are now mostly dispersed. A group is on loan to the Jocelyn Art Museum, Omaha, Nebraska, and a number were reproduced by Bernard DeVoto in *Across the Wide Missouri* (Boston: Houghton Mifflin Co., 1947). For additional information see Marvin C. Ross, *The West of Alfred Jacob Miller, from the Notes and Water Colors in The Walters Art Gallery*, rev. ed., (Norman, Oklahoma: University of Oklahoma Press, 1968), and *Alfred Jacob Miller: Artist on the Oregon Trail*, Ron Tyler, ed. (Fort Worth, Texas: Amon Carter Museum, 1982).

2. It was one of the group in Stewart's portfolio, which was sold after his death in 1871. Eighty-three of the drawings were sold at auction by Parke-Bernet, New York, May 6, 1966; this subject was lot 46, measuring 5⅞ x 7 in. (148 x 178 mm). It is no. 385 in the catalogue raisonné section of *Alfred Jacob Miller: Artist on the Oregon Trail*, Ron Tyler, ed.

3. Miller's notes, written to accompany the watercolors he made for William T. Walters (1858-1860), refer to actual events when they occurred. The text accompanying this subject consists of generalized comments relating to the poor relationship between Crows and Snakes (Ross, *The West of Alfred Jacob Miller*, opposite pl. 145).

4. All of Walters's watercolors are illustrated and Miller's notes quoted in Ross, *The West of Alfred Jacob Miller*. The only other significant group was made for William C. Wait (fifteen in 1858, and twenty-two in 1859), as recorded in Miller's account book (ibid., p. xxvii). The location of Wait's watercolors is unknown today; Ross posits that the fifteen now in the Beinecke Rare Book and Manuscript Library, Yale University, may be the 1858 group.

5. Ibid. Miller's account of the visit, written many years afterward, is quoted on pp. xvi-xvii.

James Hamilton

Born Entrien, near Belfast, Ireland, 1819;
died San Francisco, California, 1878

James Hamilton's romantic themes, dashing technique, and wide range of media earned him the sobriquet, the "American Turner." He was to become one of the most popular marine painters of his time, in watercolor as well as in oil. While his subjects tended to be based on historical or literary incidents, he also made studies from nature during his trips along the Eastern seaboard, and used wash and watercolor to prepare book illustrations; those he made for the publications of the arctic explorer Elisha Kent Kane were particularly well known.

Hamilton came to Philadelphia at the age of fifteen with his family. He attended school and studied drawing; afterwards he worked briefly in a countinghouse and also taught drawing. Among his students were Edward and Thomas Moran (see cat. 29). Encouraged by John Sartain, the painter and engraver, to become a professional artist, Hamilton exhibited oils for the first time in 1840 at the Artists' Fund Society. *A Scene on the Delaware* (location unknown), shown in 1843 at the Pennsylvania Academy of the Fine Arts, caught the public's eye and his career was launched. Hamilton exhibited regularly at the Pennsylvania Academy and was elected an academician in 1861; he also exhibited in New York, Baltimore, Washington, and Boston, occasionally including watercolors as well as oils. Hamilton made an extended trip to England in 1854–55, where he was able to study Turner's work in the original. His paintings found a ready market in Philadelphia and other eastern cities from the mid-1840s to the mid 1870s. In 1875 he sold more than one hundred paintings at auction to finance a trip around the world. He got only as far as San Francisco, where he died in 1878.

James Hamilton
17. *Sunset on the Jersey Flats*, 1861

Transparent and opaque watercolor on moderately thick, light gray wove paper, mounted on cardboard
8⅞ x 16⅝ in. (226 x 424 mm)
Signed and dated lower left in brown wash:
J. Hamilton / 1861
M. and M. Karolik Collection. 61.283

Hamilton painted the seacoasts of New Jersey, New York, Maryland, Delaware, and Massachu-

setts. Here the subject is the luscious color of the sky that illuminates the placid waters of the New Jersey marshes and the varied and changing clouds rolling above them.[1] The artist had a particular affection for clouds, and left notes and pencil sketches prepared for a lecture he delivered on the subject.[2]

The execution of this small picture is surprisingly complex. Hamilton covered the lower half of the sheet with a thick coat of white paint, over which he worked both additively and subtractively. A thick layer of yellow overlies the white in some areas, while the reds and blues are more thinly and transparently applied, often in multiple layers. In many places the artist wiped off one color to reveal another beneath, or scraped through one or more layers to get back to the white ground, which he then painted over again in a different hue.

Many of the stylistic elements of this picture – breadth, color, selectivity – can be said to have been learned from Turner, and passed on to Thomas Moran (see cat. 29). Hamilton may also have been inspired, directly or indirectly, by the success of Frederic Church's *Twilight in the Wilderness* (1860, The Cleveland Museum of Art). One of the most influential paintings of its time, this spectacular view, lit by a vivid sunset, spoke to the promise of America and fulfilled the "Transcendentalist longing to surrender the soul and become one with Nature."[3] It inspired emulation by many American painters, including Hamilton's exact contemporary, Martin Johnson Heade (1819-1904), whose work Hamilton could easily have known. In scale and subject, Hamilton's *Sunset on the Jersey Flats* is much closer to Heade's small marsh scenes than to Church's large mountainous landscape.[4]

SWR

1. Although more recently called "Marshes, New Jersey," the title used here is that used by a previous owner; see *The W.P. Wilstach Collection Catalogue* (Philadelphia: Commissioners of Fairmount Park, 1900), no. 336. See also Arlene Jacobowitz, *James Hamilton* (Brooklyn: The Brooklyn Museum, 1966), no. 30.

2. Jacobowitz, *James Hamilton*, p. 21 and fig. 8.

3. Trevor J. Fairbrother in Theodore E. Stebbins, Jr., Carol Troyen, and Trevor J. Fairbrother, *A New World: Masterpieces of American Painting 1760-1910* (Boston: Museum of Fine Arts, 1983), p. 242.

4. These similarities have also been noted in Theodore E. Stebbins, Jr., *The Life and Works of Martin Johnson Heade* (New Haven: Yale University Press, 1975), pp. 69-70.

James Hamilton
18. *Moonlight*, about 1864
Opaque watercolor on thick, smooth, cream wove paper
15½ in. (394 mm) diam.
Signed lower center in black wash: Hamilton
M. and M. Karolik Collection. 55.746

This watercolor most likely represents an imaginary scene: the mosses dripping from the dead trees suggest a locale farther south than Hamilton is believed to have traveled. He was, however, known to paint exotic subjects based on images by other artists, and was perhaps inspired here by a depiction of a swamp or bayou of the deep South. The circular format of the watercolor, like that of vignetted illustrations popular at the time, supports this idea. Whether Hamilton, in turn, intended this for a book illustration is not known, but the limited palette – primarily blue, black, and white – would be appropriate for an engraver to follow.

The tiny crouching figure on the spit of land at the left provides scale and implies narrative content. This suggestion of a story, taken in connection with the desolate trees and cool illumination, succeeds in creating an image that is haunting and evocative.

The technique of *Moonlight* is very similar to that of *Sunset on the Jersey Flats* (cat. 17).[1] The paints are sufficiently opaque to obliterate any sign of underdrawing. Hamilton applied washes and then wiped them off so as to define horizontal bands in the water, wispy clouds in the night sky, and reflected moonlight. Fine lines scraped along the horizon help to distinguish sky from water, and narrow brushstrokes describe the shaggy mosses and curling vines on the trees, and the grasses on the shore.

SWR

1. This watercolor has been entitled "Bayou in the Moonlight." As is the case with *Sunset on the Jersey Flats*, the title here is that used in *The W.P. Wilstach Collection Catalogue* (Philadelphia: Commissioners of Fairmount Park, 1900), no. 337. See also Arlene Jacobowitz, *James Hamilton* (Brooklyn: The Brooklyn Museum, 1966), no. 42.

Frances Flora Bond Palmer

Born Leicester, England, 1812;
died Brooklyn, New York, 1876

Fanny Palmer was the first woman to be employed as a creative artist and lithographer on the staff of Currier & Ives. Even though it was the firm's practice to publish lithographs emblazoned solely with its own name, Palmer was so esteemed that, like A. F. Tait and a very few others, she was allowed to sign some 170 prints she produced in the course of her seventeen-year tenure at Currier & Ives. Palmer was an innovative designer and a superb technician. She created countless compositions of her own as well as providing landscape backgrounds for other artists' prints. With Charles Currier, she developed an improved type of lithographic crayon, and introduced to the firm the technique of using a background tint in colored lithographs. Her own designs encompass a broad variety of subjects: picturesque views, country houses, farm and small-town life, battles, seasonal scenes, and railroad trains. These images present a sentimental view of American life that has retained its popularity to this day.

Palmer was the third daughter of a Leicester, England, solicitor. She was educated at Miss Linwood's School for young women in Leicester, an institution typical of those dedicated to the education of the daughters of the upper middle class. However, instruction in drawing and watercolor there must have been considerably above the average, for the director, Mary Linwood, was an accomplished artist herself (famed for her "stitchery pictures" of compositions by Gainsborough, Rembrandt, Raphael, and others) and patron of such painters as Constable and Hoppner. Linwood's embroidery style may well have influenced Palmer's feathery, stitchlike foliage; more significant was the model she provided of a woman as professional artist.

At age twenty, Fanny Bond married Edward Seymour Palmer, and by 1841 she was conducting drawing classes as well as providing the designs for prints for her husband's lithography firm in Leicester. That business failed, due to a local economic decline and Edward Palmer's lack of business acumen. By January of 1844, the Palmers had emigrated to New York, where they established another printing business, this time bearing Fanny's name as well as her husband's ("F. & S. Palmer") in tribute to her talents as an artist.

These talents were soon recognized by Nathaniel Currier, who in 1846 reissued a Fanny Palmer print, in 1849 published two of her original compositions, and in 1851, when F. & S. Palmer failed, bought out their stock and hired her for the firm. Edward Palmer (who subsequently operated a tavern in Brooklyn) died in 1859; Fanny worked for Nathaniel Currier, and later for Currier & Ives, until 1868. Thereafter, and until her death in 1876, she worked independently as a lithographer.

Frances Flora Bond Palmer
19. *The Mississippi in Time of War*, 1862
Opaque watercolor and colored crayons over graphite on moderately thick, moderately textured, gray wove paper
18 x 28¹⁄₁₆ in. (459 x 713 mm)
Signed lower left in black ink: F F P / 1862
M. and M. Karolik Collection. 53.2450

This image, of a guerilla attack on a paddleboat traveling on the Mississippi, is one of a pair of large watercolors Palmer produced in 1862 in preparation for lithographs issued by Currier & Ives three years later.[1] The other, *The Mississippi in Time of Peace* (fig. 1), documents a similar voyage in a more idyllic time. It shows the same red-shirted woodboatmen,[2] several big paddle-wheelers and other boats (but not the sinister iron-clads), and graceful trees framing the picture on one side. *Peace* takes place in the late afternoon, and *War* under the light of the full moon; the landscapes and buildings along the shore of each print, while not identical, are sufficiently similar to underscore the narrative connection between the two watercolors. *The Mississippi in Time of War* does not seem to represent any particular engagement[3] – in fact, Palmer does not specify whether the victims of the attack are citizens of the Union or the Confederacy, for although the sultry atmosphere and dripping foliage suggest a southern locale, the big paddlewheeler in *Peace* flies a Union flag. It is likely that Palmer was inspired by accounts of the Union forces' capture of Fort Donelson in Tennessee (a Confederate stronghold and key to its defense of the junction of the Ohio and Mississippi Rivers) early in 1862, and the retaliatory strikes by southern vessels, in-

Fig. 1. *The Mississippi in Time of Peace*, 1865. Watercolor and colored crayons. Museum of Fine Arts, Boston. M. and M. Karolik Collection.

cluding armored gunboats, along the Mississippi in subsequent months.[4] The incisive topicality of Palmer's designs was somewhat muted by the three-year delay between the execution of the watercolors and Currier & Ives's publication of the lithographs. In 1862, the images had value as propaganda. By the end of the conflict, they offered a more universal statement about the horrors of war.[5]

Palmer's watercolor technique is rather conventional, and reflects both her early exposure to the British landscape tradition and the requirements of commercial practice.[6] Thin translucent washes cover the whole of the sheet; some textural variety is provided by short, dense, fringelike strokes, alternating with wavy ribbons of color, especially in the foliage, and by opaque white in such areas as the masts of the foundering boat and the underbellies of the clouds. *The Mississippi in Time of Peace* is naturalistically colored. *The Mississippi in Time of War* is painted almost in grisaille, with accents in the acid, electric colors beloved of an earlier generation of topographical painters in watercolor, among them Nicolino Calyo and Michele Felice Corné. This dramatic palette, unusual for Palmer, translated well into hand-colored lithography, and demonstrates her adaptability: although most of the subjects she painted are picturesque, charming views, here she successfully employs the ingredients of the horrific sublime. Her colors are the violent tones of Vesuvius erupting; her trees are a shocked and

shattered reflection of the human cataclysm; and her sky, eerily animated by the full moon, is heavy with clouds.

    CT

1. Harry T. Peters, *Currier & Ives: Printmakers to the American People*, (New York: Doubleday, Doran & Company, Inc., 1929), vol. 2, nos. 3949 (*Peace*) and 3950 (*War*).

2. These figures are drawn directly from the river pictures of George Caleb Bingham, and the many prints after them circulated in Palmer's time. See especially Bingham's *Jolly Flatboatmen #1* (1846, The Manoogian Collection).

3. Peters, *Currier & Ives*, vol. 2, p. 62.

4. See Samuel Eliot Morrison, *The Oxford History of the American People* (New York: Oxford University Press, 1965), pp. 639, 644–45.

5. These Mississippi pictures were not Palmer's only essays in Civil War subjects. In 1862, Currier & Ives issued her *Terrific Engagement between the Monitor and the Merrimac*, and in 1865, her *Victorious Attack on Fort Fisher*.

6. For an account of Palmer's early training, see Charlotte Streifer Rubenstein, "The Early Career of Frances Flora Bond Palmer (1812–1876)," *The American Art Journal* 17 (autumn 1985), pp. 71–88.

William Martine Harding

Active 1865-1869

20. *New York Harbor from Brooklyn Heights Window*, 1869

Watercolor over graphite on moderately thick, cream wove paper.
9½ x 7½ in. (241 x 191 mm)
Signed lower left in gray wash: From my room window / May 1869 / W.M. Harding / Fecit; inscribed lower right in gray wash: 55 Columbia St. / Brooklyn Heights
M. and M. Karolik Collection. 61.286

Harding's biography remains as mysterious as this watercolor: except for a listing in the New York City Directory for 1865, which describes him as a commission merchant and agent for the Eureka Segar [Cigar] Machine, with offices at 184 Water Street in Manhattan, no other information about him has come to light.[1] Judging from this watercolor (the only identified example of his work), he probably had little formal training. Whether by instinct or through acquaintance with more high-style art, in *New York Harbor from Brooklyn Heights Window*, Harding was drawn to a favorite theme of romantic painters of the late eighteenth and early nineteenth centuries: the open window, whose view onto nature from the artist's own room symbolizes a pair of ambivalent emotions – the simultaneous longing for adventure and fear of the unknown, and the delight in domestic comforts and the frustration of their confinement.[2] By mid-century, the subject was treated by amateur painters as well. A drawing by an unknown artist active a generation before Harding shows an even more carefully rendered interior and a view into the distance marked by strict, even compulsive, symmetry (fig. 1).

While Harding's watercolor is not nearly as anxiety-producing as the earlier rendering, the odd angle from which the view is presented and the complicated window treatment contribute to the eerie atmosphere. There are multiple panes, shutters, a valence, and a scalloped drape hanging imposingly across the window as though to shroud the view. The view Harding depicts – across Buttermilk Channel to Governor's Island, with the shoreline of Jersey City in the far distance – combines a view of a busy harbor with the charm of a colorful sunset sky. The channel is

Fig. 1. Anonymous, *View from the House of Henry Briscoe Thomas, Maryland*, about 1841. Pen and black ink, black crayon, gray wash heightened with white on paper. Metropolitan Museum of Art, New York. Gift of Mrs. Lydia Bond Powel.

shown as a lively jumble of lines and angles, punctuated by the ships' spiky masts and the long, low buildings with their staccato windows in the middle distance. Beyond is the horizon, which neatly parallels the line of the window sill and so gives the vista an odd, disconcerting tilt. Harding's handling shows the painstaking deliberation of the amateur artist. Pale washes were carefully applied within graphite outlines, made, in most cases, with the aid of a straightedge. Only the curtain, with its ascending vines, and the sky, rendered with small strokes of transparent paint, were spontaneously rendered. And as though to acknowledge the romantic antecedents of his theme, Harding has restricted the use of color to the view of the harbor. His interior is rendered almost entirely in shades of white, gray, and taupe.

CT

1. *M. & M. Karolik Collection of American Water Colors and Drawings, 1800-1875* (Boston: Museum of Fine Arts, 1962), vol. 1, pp. 174-175.

2. The classic discussion of this theme is Lorenz Eitner, "The Open Window and Storm-Tossed Boat: An Essay in the Iconography of Romanticism," *Art Bulletin* 37 (December 1955), pp. 281-287. In the twentieth century, artists such as René Magritte, Marcel Duchamp, and Charles Sheeler have given the theme a surreal interpretation that resonates with the bizarre atmosphere of these nineteenth-century amateur drawings.

John William Hill

Born London, England, 1812;
died West Nyack, New York, 1879

A member of the middle generation of a family of artists, John William Hill was trained by his father, the etcher and engraver John Hill (1770-1850), who emigrated with his family to Philadelphia in 1819 and moved to New York in 1823. John William assisted his father with the production of the aquatints for the *Hudson River Portfolio* (1820-1825) after landscape watercolors by William Guy Wall. Working primarily in watercolor throughout his life, Hill spent the first three decades of his career painting the American landscape and city. At first his broad technique and picturesque style resembled those of Wall; later they became more precise and reportorial. Exhibiting as early as 1828 at the National Academy of Design – which made him an associate in 1833 – he helped found the short-lived New York Society for the Promotion of Painting in Water Colors in 1850 and exhibited frequently in New York in the 1860s and 1870s.

In 1833 he visited London to study old master paintings. From 1836 to 1841 he was a topographical artist for the New York State Geological Survey, then illustrated natural history publications, and in the late 1840s made watercolor views of cities in New England and upstate New York for lithographs published by the firm of Smith Brothers.

About 1855 Hill read John Ruskin's *Modern Painters* and followed Ruskin's advice to study nature and record it meticulously without rearrangement, using the brilliant colors and stippling and hatching techniques of the English Pre-Raphaelite painters. Applying Ruskin's theories, Hill continued to paint landscapes, and added close-up studies of plants and birds to his repertoire. In 1860 Hill helped to found the Association for the Advancement of Truth in Art, the Ruskinian movement based in New York. He rarely traveled to New York City, preferring to stay at his farm in West Nyack, New York, where he continued to work in the same style for the rest of his life.

John William Hill
21. *Study of Fruit*, 1877
Watercolor over graphite on very thick, smooth, cream wove paper
6⅛ x 10⅝ in. (156 x 270 mm)
Signed and dated lower right in red paint: J.W. Hill 1877
M. and M. Karolik Collection. 55.753

This informal arrangement of fruit rendered in glowing tones of the spectrum from red to violet is one of a number of similar images painted after Hill's conversion to the theories and practices of John Ruskin.[1] In its clear colors and fine technique it reflects Ruskin's ideas that, "you *ought* to love color, and to think nothing quite beautiful or perfect without it" and "all great art is delicate."[2] The composition is in fact more "artificial" and arranged than recommended by Ruskin, who wanted flowers or fruit depicted still on their living branches. "A cut off branch of fruit thrown upon the ground is not dignified," wrote a Ruskinian purist in 1866. "It is a good study but poor picture making. Even the great and authoritative example of William Hunt proves only that a picture may be made admirable in spite of a poor subject; for a poor subject cut flowers and plucked fruit must always remain."[3] The English watercolorist William Henry Hunt (1790-1864), much admired by Ruskin, painted brilliant, detailed studies of fruit, flowers, and bird's nests, becoming so popular for the last, that he was nicknamed "Bird's-nest Hunt." His work is likely to have inspired Hill to paint the same subjects. Although the press criticized Hill for painting and exhibiting "plucked fruit," his middle-class public probably found the subjects, scale, and color of his pictures appealing.[4]

Using small brushes and a miniaturistic technique Hill painted this portrait of a yellow apple with its red and orange blush, a large purple plum, small blue damson plums still on their leafy stems and a less clearly identifiable orange or peach. The fruits are set on an irregular surface, against a background that is painted with a slightly broader brush in a hatched pattern that suggests basket weave. The fruit forms are built up of many tiny brushstrokes of pure colors overlying washes, and the artist took advantage of the smooth white pa-

per to suggest the jewellike qualities of the fruits. No white paper is left untouched, although where the paint is thinly applied one can detect such underdrawing in graphite as the line dividing one color from another on the yellow apple or the veins in the pale yellow leaf at the lower left. A few strokes of thick opaque white pigment were applied to add highlights to the apple, a technique favored by Ruskin and used by William Henry Hunt.

SWR

1. For a succinct account of the style and practices of the Pre-Raphaelites, see William H. Gerdts, "Through a Glass Brightly: The American Pre-Raphaelites and Their Still Lifes and Nature Studies," in Linda S. Ferber and William H. Gerdts, *The New Path: Ruskin and the American Pre-Raphaelites* (Brooklyn: The Brooklyn Museum and Schocken Books Inc., 1985) pp. 40-41.

2. John Ruskin, *The Elements of Drawing*, (New York: Wiley, 1884), pp. 137 and ix. The book was first published in 1857.

3. Russell Sturgis in *The Nation* 3 (November 1866), p. 435, as cited in Ferber and Gerdts, *The New Path*, p. 188.

4. Hill noted that he sold a picture of pineapples to a Mrs. Parker, and a bird's nest picture was in private hands in 1879. See Ferber and Gerdts, *The New Path*, cats. 29 and 31.

John Henry Hill

Born West Nyack, New York, 1839;
died West Nyack, New York, 1922

Grandson of the English emigrant engraver John Hill and son of watercolorist John William Hill, John Henry was trained by his father (see cat. 21). John Henry's artistic education was carried out in accordance with Ruskin's theories; his precisely executed drawings and etchings, and his carefully rendered watercolors are textbook examples of Ruskin's instructions in *The Elements of Drawing* (1857). Hill first exhibited at the National Academy of Design in 1856, became an associate in 1858, and frequently exhibited watercolors and prints there and at various New York watercolor exhibitions until 1891. He also showed at the Brooklyn Art Association between 1865 and 1885. In 1860 he and his father were founding members of the Association for the Advancement of Truth in Art.

During 1864–65 Hill spent eight months in England and on his return joined a Ruskinian group in Ashfield, Massachusetts. He executed twenty-two still-life and landscape etchings in 1866, which were published (along with two earlier prints) as *Sketches from Nature* in 1867. Hill served as artist for two western surveys led by the geologist Clarence King in 1868 and 1870; he traveled to England and the Continent in 1878 and 1879 on an itinerary suggested by Ruskin, with whom he corresponded regularly. The American Pre-Raphaelites' precision and finicky execution began to look old fashioned with the emergence of Impressionism. Returning to West Nyack on his father's death in 1879, Hill continued to paint in watercolor and to etch, often reproducing and promoting his father's work. His lavish illustrated volume, *John William Hill, An Artist's Memorial* (1888), remains the basic biography of that artist.

John Henry Hill
22. Sunnyside, 1860
Watercolor over graphite on thick, moderately rough textured, dark cream wove paper; watermark: WHATMAN / TURKEY MILL
10 x 13½ in. (254 x 343 mm)
Signed and dated lower right in brown wash: J. Henry Hill / 1860
On verso in broad graphite: Lettie [?] / Sunnyside / Painted by J. Henry Hill 1860
M. and M. Karolik Collection. 60.414

The picturesque architecture and attractive setting of Sunnyside, home of celebrated author Washington Irving (1783–1859) made it a popular subject for artists beginning in the late 1830s.[1] Hill drew, etched, and painted the house numerous times between 1857 and 1884, and declared it "one of the prettiest cottages on the Hudson."[2] This watercolor was executed shortly after Irving's death, when Hill also made drawings for an illustrated edition of the author's works.

Like many others of his time and since, Hill enjoyed the quaint charm and individualistic features of this turreted "little Dutch-Spanish snuggery,"[3] set on a sloping green lawn, and shaded by trees, shrubbery, and vines. Glimpsed through the trees at the left is a miniature view of the Hudson River, several sailboats, and the highlands of the far shore. The motion of the feathery foliage and scudding clouds and the vivid green shadows on the grass suggest a breezy summer day. In the right foreground two young women, one with a parasol and the other reading or sketching, enliven the scene and affirm the continued enjoyment of the house by Irving's resident nieces and their many relatives.[4]

The neat underdrawing, fine brushstrokes, and bright colors characterize Hill's Ruskinian style. He followed Ruskin's rules and painted areas of wash broadly, and then added finely detailed leaves and blades of grass in varied shades of green, the dominant color of this picture. The brilliant greens can be compared to those in *Study of Elms* (cat. 25) by Henry Roderick Newman, also a follower of Ruskin. The point of view, vegetation, and figure arrangement resemble those in an etching Hill made in 1884 (fig. 1), which reproduces a

Fig. 1. *Sunnyside in Tarrytown*, 1884. Etching after a drawing by John William Hill. Museum of Fine Arts, Boston. Gift of J. Henry Hill.

drawing by his father and underscores the interdependence of their art.

SWR

1. Sunnyside was renovated with the help of George Harvey and is the subject of one of his "atmospheric landscapes" of 1835–40 (see cat. 5). The long British tradition of depicting gentlemen's estates was imported to America where its more modest architecture and land holdings were celebrated not only in such series as William Birch's *The Country Seats of the United States of North America* (1808), but also in innumerable individual house portraits. See Edward J. Nygren, *Views and Visions, American Landscape before 1830* (Washington, D.C.: The Corcoran Gallery of Art, 1986), pp. 22–23.

2. From Hill's *Sketches from Nature*, 1867, quoted in Linda S. Ferber and William H. Gerdts, *The New Path: Ruskin and the American Pre-Raphaelites* (Brooklyn: The Brooklyn Museum and Schocken Books Inc., 1985), cat. 15. John William Hill made a pencil sketch of Sunnyside in 1857, and John Henry Hill made an etching in the same year. John Henry made several drawings of the house in 1860 and 1878, and two additional etchings in 1867 and 1884.

3. Stanley T. Williams, *The Life of Washington Irving* (New York: Oxford University Press, 1935), vol. 2, p. 46.

4. Ibid., pp. 46–47.

Jasper Francis Cropsey

Born Rossville, Staten Island, New York, 1823;
died Hastings-on-Hudson, New York, 1900

Although Cropsey is known primarily as an oil painter, he was active as a watercolorist throughout his career. He first learned to use watercolor during his apprenticeship to the architect Joseph Trench, who provided lessons in the medium to enable Cropsey to supplement architectural drawings with landscape and figurative elements. Thereafter he would turn to watercolor not only for architectural renderings, but also for travel sketches, preliminary designs for oil paintings, and formal exhibition pieces. During the last two decades of Cropsey's life, watercolor was his preferred medium, and he continued to paint the kind of landscape scenes popular during the heyday of the Hudson River School in a relatively tight, topographically precise style long after the vogue for both had passed away.

As an architect in the 1840s, Cropsey executed numerous designs in wash and watercolor; at the same time, he was developing a reputation as a landscape painter. His earliest landscapes exhibit a familiarity with English watercolor conventions, and in accord with English practice, he used watercolor to record his observations during travels in Italy, England, and France in 1847-49. In 1853 he exhibited one of the sketches made on that trip in the New York Society for the Promotion of Painting in Water Colors' section of the New York Crystal Palace exhibition. Between 1856 and 1863, Cropsey was again in London, where he saw the Turners recently given to the National Gallery, attended shows at the Royal Society of Painters in Watercolor, and met Ruskin, who would be a lasting influence.

A member of the short-lived New York Society for the Promotion of Painting in Water Colors (1850-1855), Cropsey was elected to membership in the newly founded Society of American Painters in Water Color in 1867. He served on the three-artist hanging committee for the society's first exhibition, in December 1867; nonetheless, for the next ten years Cropsey's participation in the society's shows was sporadic, for during this period financial difficulties mandated a resumption of his architectural practice. But by 1880 he was once again active as a watercolor painter and for the remainder of his career he exhibited regularly with the society. If these late paintings failed to excite critical interest, it may have been because Cropsey retained from his earlier work the formal, highly detailed and finished manner (with much use of opaque pigment) that emulated the look of his oils, while more progressive painters were experimenting with a sketchier, more luminous style. Nonetheless, Cropsey regarded these watercolors highly and found in them a great source of satisfaction.

Jasper Francis Cropsey
23. *Summer Cottage, Front Elevation II*, 1866-67
Watercolor over graphite, with pen and black ink on thick, slightly textured, cream wove paper
18¾ x 24⅝ in. (476 x 636 mm)
Inscribed on chimney at right in brown ink: 1867
M. and M. Karolik Collection. 52.1600

24. *City House, Front Elevation*, 1873
Watercolor over graphite, with pen and red and black ink on moderately thick, slightly textured, cream wove paper; watermark: J. WHATMAN / 1866
22 x 17½ in. (558 x 448 mm)
Signed and dated lower right in black ink:
J. F. Cropsey. 1873.
M. and M. Karolik Collection. 52.1601

Between 1866 and 1873 Cropsey executed at least six designs for townhouses and three for summer cottages. This burst of activity marked a return to Cropsey's first profession, architecture, which by the late 1840s he had essentially set aside in favor of landscape painting. Cropsey's renewed interest in architecture may have been prompted by seemingly contradictory personal circumstances: the purchase, in 1866, of some forty acres of land near Warwick, New York, on which he intended to build a summer cottage, and straitened finances, resulting from heavy debts incurred in Europe and a diminished market for his paintings.

Nonetheless, in 1866, Cropsey began plans for Aladdin, his exotically titled (and furnished) home with a spectacular view of the Catskill Mountains. Unlike his rivals Frederic E. Church and Albert Bierstadt, who were building showplaces of their own at the same time, from the beginning Cropsey was his own architect. His inspiration seems to have been the picturesque bracketed style of cottage architecture codified by Alexander Jackson Downing.[1] Aladdin exhibited the love of ornament, varied outlines, and rich surface texture that were characteristic of the architecture of the age. The house's delightful eclecticism was much admired in Cropsey's time; it was described as a whimsical structure "in which gable and tower and balcony blend in harmonious confusion."[2] Despite the apparent simplicity of the design (the main house was a two-story, symmetrical unit), it was far from modest: the main house contained

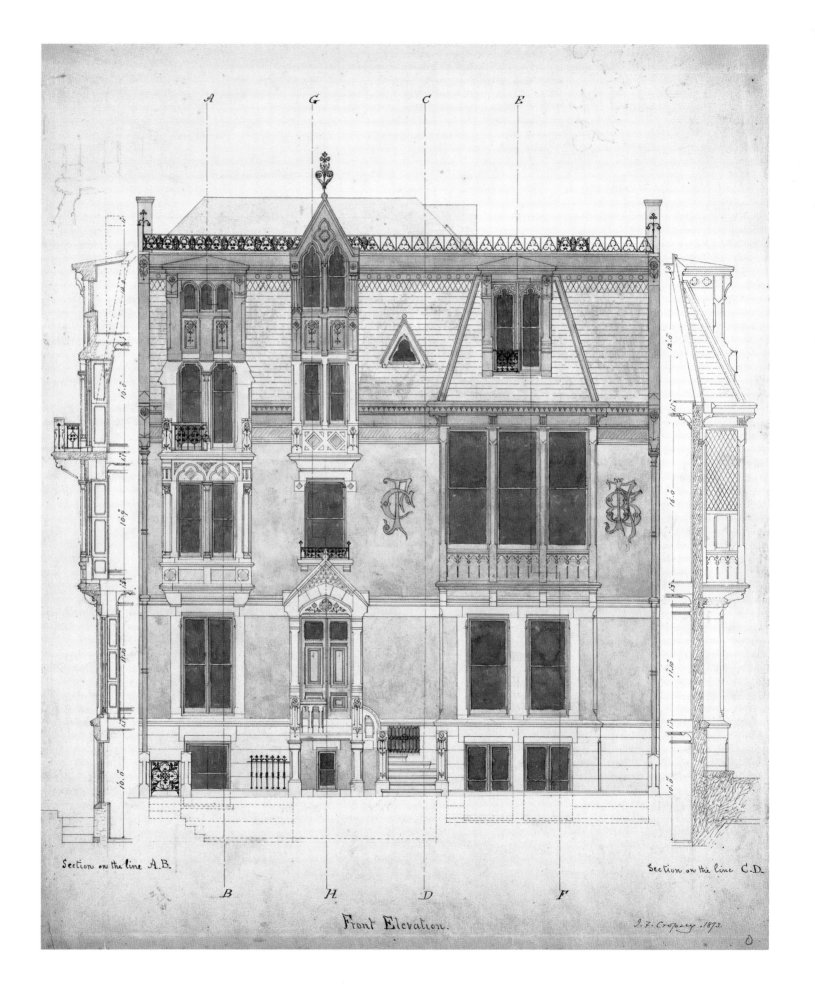

Section on the line A.B.

Section on the line C.D.

Front Elevation.

J.F. Cropsey .1873.

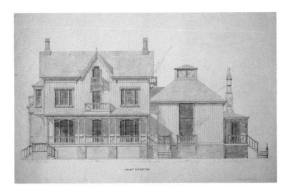

Fig. 1. *Summer Cottage, Front Elevation I*, 1866. Watercolor, pen and ink, and graphite on paper. Museum of Fine Arts, Boston. M. and M. Karolik Collection.

Fig. 2. *Front Elevation, Town House*, 1866. Watercolor and ink on paper. Newington-Cropsey Foundation, Hastings-on-Hudson, New York.

twenty-nine rooms, and was adjoined by a thirty-foot square studio wing with floor to ceiling windows and a cupola to admit light into the painting space.

Summer Cottage II represents Cropsey's most finished drawing for Aladdin, and other than some changes to the main house's veranda and window treatment on the second story, it seems to represent the house as it was actually built and lived in by the Cropsey family.[3] Two earlier drawings (Museum of Fine Arts, Boston [fig. 1], and Newington-Cropsey Foundation, Hastings-on-Hudson, New York), both dated 1866, show Cropsey's evolving design; the present drawing is virtually identical to the more elaborate of these,[4] but is more richly colored and more fully detailed. Furthermore it lacks the measurements and penciled notations that *Summer Cottage I* contains, making it clear that it was intended not as a working plan but as a presentation drawing or a souvenir of the final design.

City House, drawn in 1873, is one of a group of town house designs of increasing sophistication that Cropsey produced over a seven-year period. These, too, reflect the most modish styles of American architecture, combining elements of the Queen Anne and Gothic Revival styles. Several of the drawings probably represent designs (never realized) for property on West 49th Street that Cropsey acquired in 1866, and contain features that suggest the houses may have been intended for his own use. There are large studios, with generous projecting window bays; one of the earlier designs (fig. 2) features a palette and brush finial on the second-story oriel.[5] The Museum's watercolor is embellished with Cropsey's monogram and, in cipher, the date 1873, as ornaments on the facade.

Both *Summer Cottage II* and *City House*, in addition to being handsome documents of ambitious architectural projects, are elegant watercolors in their own right. They display Cropsey's refined color sense and, although the washes are transparent and applied evenly, subtle variations in texture reveal Cropsey's interest both in mass and in surface decoration. The projecting balconies and porches in the summer cottage cast rich gray shadows on the ocher walls, giving the flat façade

an active, three-dimensional quality and conjuring up the long shadows of a sunny afternoon. The city house, decoratively colored in rose, light yellow, purple-gray, and pale orange, was painted with smooth washes for the most part. However, the dark greens of the building's many windows were applied rather wetly, and so have a shimmery surface that evokes the reflective properties of glass.

CT

1. For a discussion of the architects who influenced Cropsey, and for the inspirations for Aladdin in particular, see Barbara Finney, "Jasper F. Cropsey: Architect," in Ella M. Foshay and Barbara Finney, *Jasper F. Cropsey, Artist and Architect* (New York: New-York Historical Society, 1987), especially pp. 139-141.

2. William Henry Forman, "Jasper Francis Cropsey, N.A.," *The Manhattan* 3 (April 1884), p. 379, quoted in William Nathaniel Banks, "Ever Rest, Jasper Francis Cropsey's House in Hastings-on-Hudson, New York," *Antiques* 130 (November 1986), p. 1001.

3. A multistoried tower on the eastern side of the house, balancing the studio wing, is visible in a photograph of Aladdin made in the early 1900s (reproduced in William S. Talbot, *Jasper F. Cropsey 1823-1900* [Washington, D.C.: National Collection of Fine Arts, 1970], p. 42). This tower would have appeared at the left in *Summer Cottage II*, whose edge has been cropped; however, it was not pictured in either of the other two surviving drawings for Aladdin, suggesting that there were other drawings for Aladdin, now lost. The Cropseys were forced to sell their Warwick home in 1884. It burned to the ground in 1909.

4. Among the very minor differences in detail are the fully colored windows on the foundation level, which in the earlier drawing are only sketched in, and the substitution of brick pilasters for rough timbered posts on the foundation level of the porch at far right.

5. Finney, "Jasper F. Cropsey: Architect," p. 139.

Henry Roderick Newman

Born Easton, New York 1843;
died Florence, Italy, 1917

Like the Hills (see cats. 21 and 22), Henry Roderick Newman was one of a small number of painters known as American Pre-Raphaelites who fervently embraced John Ruskin's theories of art. These men and women helped to validate watercolor as a professional medium, both by the seriousness of their intent and by their exhibition of finished works in the medium. Newman, who rarely painted in oil, used watercolor for many large and significant works throughout his long career.

Newman's father was a physician and surgeon who moved his practice to New York City when his son was young. Newman spent two years in medical school, but after his father's death in 1861, he persuaded his mother to allow him a year to become an artist. At the end of the year, his work was exhibited at the National Academy of Design. In 1864 he was elected to the Society for the Advancement of Truth in Art, and through one of its members, Thomas Farrer, procured a job teaching at the School of Design for Women at the Cooper Institute in New York City (1865-66). In Stockbridge, Massachusetts, between 1866 and 1868, he produced his earliest extant watercolors.

In 1870 Newman was advised to go abroad for his health. Settling first in Paris, he was able to study in Gérôme's classes for less than a month before the Franco-Prussian war broke out. After a brief stay in Chartres, he went to Italy, arriving in Florence in September 1870. He married an Englishwoman in 1883 and made that city his home, painting its architectural monuments and the flowers of the Tuscan countryside. Newman also painted in Venice, in Egypt in the 1880s and 1890s, and in Japan between 1896 and 1898.

John Ruskin was deeply impressed by one of Newman's watercolors of Santa Maria Novella, Florence, which he was shown in 1877. The men corresponded and eventually met in England in 1879. Ruskin commissioned Newman to record the architectural monuments of Florence for his St. George's Museum in Sheffield, England, and purchased four studies of anemones as well. This support and encouragement from his mentor no doubt helped Newman to maintain his Pre-Raphaelite style, whose importance had begun to wane in America. The subject matter of his pictures kept them popular items with travelers, and images of Italian churches and landscapes were brought back to New York and Brooklyn, as well as to Boston by Sarah Choate Sears, Mrs. Samuel Hooper, and Denman W. Ross, among others.

Henry Roderick Newman
25. *Study of Elms*, 1866
Watercolor over graphite on thick, cream wove paper
16¾ x 19¼ in. (426 x 489 mm)
Signed and dated lower left in red wash:
H R Newman / 66
M. and M. Karolik Collection. 1973.380

26. *Mt. Everett from Monument Mountain in April*, 1867
Watercolor over graphite on thick, smooth, dark cream wove paper
10⁷⁄₁₆ x 13⅞ in. (266 x 351 mm)
Signed and dated lower center in red wash:
H.R. NEWMAN / 67
Gift of Mrs. Harriet Ropes Cabot. 50.2630

Study of Elms is Newman's earliest known watercolor. It is almost certainly the watercolor entitled *Study of Elms, South Manchester, Connecticut*, that was shown at the fall 1866 Artists' Fund Society exhibition.[1] That watercolor was criticized in the press for its "extremely unpleasant" color.[2] Indeed, the excessively earnest description of every leaf on every tree in brilliant hues of yellow-green, green, and blue-green, bedazzles the eye. And yet, the high color values and clarity of vision convey the actual look of such trees viewed in the blazing light of summer sun, and the watercolor fullfils the dictates of the American Pre-Raphaelite movement.

Mt. Everett from Monument Mountain, painted the following April, depicts a site about fifteen miles southwest of Stockbridge, Massachusetts. It has a more subdued palette, due largely to Newman's faithfulness to the look of the season, but perhaps in part as a response to the earlier criticism of his color extremes. The composition may have been influenced by a winter view of the Catskills by fellow Ruskinian Charles Herbert Moore (1840-1930), which was described in 1865 as "a very little picture of a great deal of country."[3]

Newman found beauty not only in the shapes of the hills, but in the muted grays and pinks of the branches of early spring, budded but not yet in leaf. He painted each tree, each branch, each twig, with the scientific thoroughness prescribed by Ruskin for a single rock or plant. Looking down, he painted the mill and other buildings set at the river's edge in a precise, miniaturistic fashion, showing exactly what he observed. Throughout the picture tiny areas of untouched paper between the strokes of paint contribute to the image's translucency. The colors are local, virtually unchanged by the cool New England light and clear atmosphere. Only on the mountain did Newman delicately lift color to soften the stippled strokes and make the forms appear slightly hazy and more distant.

Mt. Everett belonged to Mrs. Samuel Hooper of Boston in 1867, when it was exhibited in New York at the first annual exhibition of the American Society of Painters in Water Colors (after 1877, The American Watercolor Society).[4]

SWR

1. See James L. Yarnall and William H. Gerdts, *The National Museum of American Art's Index to American Art Exhibition Catalogues from the Beginning through the 1876 Centennial Year* (Boston: G.K. Hall & Co., 1986), vol. 4, p. 2577, no. 65915.

2. "Paletta," the pseudonymous art critic for the *American Art Journal* 6 (Nov. 29, 1866), p. 87, as quoted in Kathleen Adair Foster, "Makers of the American Watercolor Movement, 1860-1890" (Ph. D. diss. Yale University, 1982), pp. 114-115. Although Foster was not able to locate a copy of the 1866 Artists' Fund Society catalogue, she was the first to equate the Museum's watercolor and the object criticized.

3. Linda S. Ferber and William H. Gerdts, *The New Path: Ruskin and the American Pre-Raphaelites* (Brooklyn: The Brooklyn Museum and Schocken Books Inc., 1985), no. 47.

4. Ibid., p. 196. Mrs. Hooper also lent two Stockbridge subjects to the 1867 exhibition. Newman himself submitted a view of Monument Mountain.

Henry Roderick Newman
27. *Wild Flowers*, 1887
Watercolor over graphite on thick, smooth, cream wove paper
15⅜ x 10½ in. (390 x 265 mm)
Signed and dated lower left in brown wash:
H.R. Newman / 1887
Gift of Denman Waldo Ross. 17.1418

Wild Flowers is a superb example of the meticulous studies of flowers Newman made in Tuscany. He was especially known for his renderings of wild anemones: pencil drawings and watercolors of single blossoms, and plants growing in their natural setting. While he most often depicted the *Anemone coronaro* as seen in *Anemones* (1876, Amon Carter Museum, Fort Worth), the red flower in this picture is also a variety of anemone.[1]

Around 1856 American Pre-Raphaelite painters had begun to follow Ruskin's instructions to paint weeds, grass, and wild flowers as they grew in nature, as opposed to artifical interior arrangements.[2] Newman's *Wild Flowers* presents an unedited close-up of vibrant red anemones set against weeds and yellow-green grasses. He created the complex mesh of plants and grasses not only by drawing with paint, but also by lifting pigments, easily carried out on the smooth paper. He met the challenge of depicting a fluffy dandelion gone to seed by using minuscule strokes of paint and the white of the paper to evoke its downy texture and pale translucence.

Although Newman painted out of doors, he was careful to make adjustments for indoor viewing. A visitor to his studio wrote:

> Most pictures find their home on the walls of dwelling-rooms, and are seen in a side light from ordinary windows on a level with the pictures themselves; and on this ground Mr. Newman rightly maintains that, except for pictures expressly painted for high-lighted galleries, all landscape and flower pieces, should be worked at in the open air with only such screen or shelter as is positively needed for the artist. To adapt them to be fitly seen in rooms, all pictures begun under these conditions should be finished and carefully gone over indoors in a well-lighted, ordinary windowed, room, not in a high north light. . . . Such being Mr. Newman's convictions, he works in his house at a large window screened from

actual sun-rays simply by fine cambric blinds, and sedulously avoids north light as cold and depressing.[3]

SWR

1. Walter Punch, librarian of the Massachusetts Horticultural Society, identified these flowers as anemones. The Amon Carter Museum's watercolor is illustrated and discussed by Erica Hirshler in Theodore E. Stebbins, Jr., *The Lure of Italy: American Artists and the Italian Experience, 1760-1914* (Boston: Museum of Fine Arts, 1992), cat. 85.

2. See, for example, John Henry Hill's *Dandelions* (1858, private collection) and especially *Fringed Gentians* (about 1867, private collection). Others, like Newman's *Milkweed*, shown at the National Academy of Design in 1865, are known today only by their titles. See William H. Gerdts, "Through a Glass Brightly," in Linda S. Ferber and William H. Gerdts, *The New Path: Ruskin and the American Pre-Raphaelites* (Brooklyn: The Brooklyn Museum and Schocken Books Inc., 1985), and fig. 13 and pl. 4.

3. H. Buxton Forman, "An American Studio in Florence," *The Manhattan* 3 (June 1884), pp. 536-537.

Henry Roderick Newman
28. *Wall Enclosing the Mausoleum of Ieyasu at Nikko, Japan*, 1897
Watercolor over graphite on thick, smooth, cream wove paper, affixed to paper mounted on a wooden panel
16½ x 9 in. (420 x 230 mm)
Signed and dated lower left in red wash:
HR NEWMAN / Nikko / June 1897
Purchased from General Funds. 99.143

By the time Newman traveled to Japan in the late 1890s, he had spent more than twenty years painting architectural monuments in Italy and Egypt in the precise Pre-Raphaelite manner. He visited Nikko several times and recorded sections of the outer wall of the mausoleum of Ieyasu with its colorfully painted carvings (fig. 1). John La Farge had been in Nikko in 1886, and described the site as follows:

> Great lanterns (toro) of stone, capped with green and yellow moss . . . are disposed in rows along the great stone wall, which is streaked by the weather and spotted with white and purple lichens. Along its upper edge runs the red-lacquered wall, heavily roofed, of the cloister which surrounds the farther court above. Its face is paneled between the metal-fastened beams and posts with two rows of deep carvings of innumerable birds and trees and waves and clouds and flowers. All these are painted and gilded, as are the frieze above and the intervals between the gilded rafters. On all this space, and on the great white gate, the "Gate Magnificent," the full sun embroidered the red and white and colored surfaces with millions of stitches of light and shadow.[1]

This is one of four watercolors of identical format in the Museum that Newman made showing sections of the wall surrounding the shrine.[2] In each he depicted two courses of the massive stone wall and two carved panels of birds, recording with absolute fidelity the wonderfully carved and colorfully painted decoration. Here, the top panel contains a peacock surrounded by flowers and foliage. The peacock's shoulder is stippled in contrasting warm and cool colors, marvelously suggesting its iridescence. Below, a carving depicts a crane in swirling, stylized water. It is framed above and below by wooden beams whose smooth lacquered surface is suggested by minute brushstrokes of vermilion and other red pigments. A

Fig. 1. Wall surrounding the Mausoleum of Ieyasu. Photograph. Department of Asiatic Art, Museum of Fine Arts, Boston.

stone lantern, cropped at the right, adds weight and depth to the composition. Newman recorded the grainy surfaces of the stone wall and lantern, using varied stipples and dashes to evoke the mottled gray, brown, and pink of the stone, and the yellow-green moss adorning the lantern.

Painstaking as the technique is, this work is handled in a softer, more painterly way than the linear *Mount Everett* (cat. 26). Newman brushed in color over color, and lifted pigments to reveal the white of the paper. A more diffuse light than that described by La Farge permitted Newman to record color "with millions of stitches," but without the distortions of bright sunlight.

SWR

1. La Farge, *An Artist's Letters from Japan* (London: T. Fisher Unwin, 1897), p. 69.

2. The other three are dated "Oct. 21, 1896," "Sept. 1897," and "1898."

Thomas Moran

Born Bolton, Lancashire, England, 1837;
died Santa Barbara, California, 1926

Early in his career as a landscape painter and illustrator, Thomas Moran found a market for his small romantic watercolors. He adopted the medium, using it both to color the pencil sketches he made on his travels, and as a vehicle for finished compositions based on these field sketches. Hundreds of both types of watercolors are known today; the best known relate to Moran's explorations of the Rocky Mountain states and their unique geological formations.

Thomas Moran's father, a weaver, resettled his family in Philadelphia in 1844. There Moran attended school and in 1853 was apprenticed to the wood-engraving firm of Scattergood and Telfer. He also shared a studio with his older brother, Edward, a painter, who taught him to use oil paints. Both young men were encouraged in their artistic careers by James Hamilton, a Philadelphia marine painter (see cats. 17, 18). Moran exhibited for the first time at the Pennsylvania Academy of the Fine Arts in 1856, showing one oil and five watercolors. He sketched avidly from nature and in 1860 experienced his first taste of wilderness at Lake Superior. Moran spent 1861-62 in England studying J.M.W. Turner's oils and watercolors in London, and drawing sites in the British Isles. He returned to Philadelphia to marry Mary Nimmo (who became a prominent etcher) and they spent a year in France and Italy (1866-67) where he came to know Corot. After 1871 the Morans lived in or near Manhattan; in 1884 they built a picturesque summer home and studio in East Hampton, Long Island, which became a center for their artistic family and friends.

In 1871 Moran's career took a significant turn with his first trip west. He was commissioned to serve as staff artist for F.V. Hayden's expedition to explore the Yellowstone region. This experience laid the foundations for Moran's favorite subject matter, the mountains and waters of the Rockies. During the next two decades he traveled eight times to the frontier, recording the geography of the Colorado River, Grand Canyon, Yosemite, Lake Tahoe, the Tetons, and sites in New Mexico and Arizona. Moran's prominently exhibited paintings and thousands of illustrations enabled Americans to visualize the West; they also helped persuade Congress to designate the Yellowstone

area as the country's first national park. Sketches from these trips provided Moran with visual resources for illustrations, watercolors, and oils throughout his life. In his later years the artist traveled to Europe, favoring Venice, and returned to favorite places in the American West, often wintering in Santa Barbara, California.

Thomas Moran
29. *Cliffs, Green River, Wyoming*, 1872
Watercolor over graphite on thick, smooth, beige wove paper
6³⁄₁₆ x 11¹¹⁄₁₆ in. (158 x 297 mm)
Signed lower right in brush and brown wash: (monogram) TMoran. / 1872.
M. and M. Karolik Collection. 60.428

In June 1871, on his way to join F.V. Hayden's Yellowstone exploration party, Moran descended from the Union Pacific train at Green River, Wyoming. Before he continued his trip north by stagecoach, he made a rapid watercolor study of the cliffs along the river, inscribing it: "First Sketch Made in the West at Green River, Wyoming 1871" (fig. 1). That sketch, retained by Moran throughout his life, provided the composition for this finished watercolor, executed in the studio the following year.[1] Though the scene is devoid of human habitation, on the horizon at the far left appears the smoke of a steam locomotive, a reminder of the new method of travel to the area. Sites along the Green River remained favorite subjects for Moran; some thirty watercolors of the area are recorded, ranging in date from 1871 to 1923.[2]

On this small sheet of paper – just over six by eleven inches – Moran implied a breathtaking monumentality. Over broad washes of tan and blue, he built up the landscape components using fine brushes and opaque pigments – predominantly blue, pink, and white – to suggest the local hues of rocks, land, and water, as well as the clear air and magnificent cloud formations. He selected certain elements of the landscape to describe in detail and dealt with others in more generalized terms. Precise brushstrokes capture the geological history of the sentinal butte and the river bank at right – their pink and yellow limestone strata, and the irregular patterns of their subsequent erosion. In

Fig. 1. *First Sketch Made in the West at Green River, Wyoming,* 1871. Watercolor on dark cream paper. Thomas Gilcrease Institute of American History and Art, Tulsa, Oklahoma.

order to blur and coalesce the mounds and gullies of the low-lying foreground, Moran dragged a partially dry brush full of purple pigment over them, forcing the viewer to look to the brilliantly colored buttes beyond. This manipulation of focus may have derived in part from Moran's experience working closely with the photographer William Henry Jackson at Yellowstone.

Cliffs, Green River, Wyoming is one of Moran's best watercolors of the subject, when the excitement of discovery was still fresh. With his breadth of conception, selectivity, and painstaking construction he succeeds in conveying the emotional impact of the landscape. Later in life he stated: "Zola's definition of art exactly fills my demands when he said that 'art is nature seen through a temperament.' The old idea that art is best defined as 'painting nature as it looks, and not as it is,' will not satisfy me. An artist's business is to produce for the spectator of his picture the impression produced by nature on himself."[3]

SWR

1. The 1871 sketch, measuring 9¼ x 13¼ in., is appreciably larger than the Museum's watercolor. The watercolor came to the Museum entitled *Cliffs, Green River, Utah*, a title that has been maintained erroneously. The original mat was dedicated, "To John Duff, Esq. with regards of T. Moran." No information has been found on John Duff.

2. Carol Clark, *Thomas Moran, Watercolors of the American West* (Fort Worth, Texas: Amon Carter Museum, 1980), pp. 155-158. See also Thomas S. Fern, *The Drawings and Watercolors of Thomas Moran* (Notre Dame, Indiana: The Art Gallery, University of Notre Dame, 1976), p. 11: "[Moran's] daughter, Ruth, reported that it was a family joke that when they needed money, one of them would say, 'Well, it's time Father painted another Green River.' "

3. From Moran's article, "Knowledge a Prime Requisite in Art," *Brush and Pencil* 12 (April, 1903), p. 15, quoted in Thurman Wilkins, *Thomas Moran, Artist of the Mountains* (Norman, Oklahoma: University of Oklahoma Press, 1966), p. 223.

Samuel Colman

Born Portland, Maine, 1832;
died New York City, 1920

An enthusiastic traveler, Samuel Colman used watercolor to record his trips to the American West, Europe, and North Africa. His dedication to the medium and his belief that it was a serious vehicle for American artists led him to join others in founding the American Society of Painters in Water Colors (later the American Watercolor Society) in 1866. Its first president, Colman maintained a life-long interest in the society and regularly exhibited at its annual exhibitions.

The artist's father, Samuel Colman, Sr., had moved to New York by the late 1830s, and became a successful publisher. Henry Tuckerman called him "one of the first tasteful dealers in fine engravings . . . [whose] store on Broadway was a unique depository of pictures, and a favorite resort of artists and litterateurs." Perhaps this family business had some influence on Colman, who took up landscape painting and first exhibited at the National Academy of Design when he was eighteen or nineteen years old. His subjects included views of the White Mountains and the Hudson River. He became an associate of the academy in 1855 and a full member after his return from two years of study in France, Spain, and Morocco in 1861-62.

Colman traveled west in 1870, stopping at Laramie and Green River, Wyoming, and possibly going as far as Yosemite. From 1871 to 1875 he traveled in northern Europe and North Africa. By the late seventies he was considered the leading American watercolorist, and his prices were up to ten times as much as those of any other exhibiting artist. Colman had many artistic interests: he helped organize the Society of American Artists, and was a member of the New York Etching Club. He collected oriental art and artifacts, and was an active member of the Society of Decorative Arts. He worked for an interior design firm that included Louis Comfort Tiffany, and he decorated his own house in Newport, Rhode Island, which had been designed by McKim, Mead and White.

Colman went west again in 1886, 1888, and between 1898 and 1906, visiting Colorado, Texas, California, Mexico, and the Canadian Rockies. After 1900 he exhibited less, and in 1904 he paid his last visit to Europe to paint mountains. His illus-

trated book, *Nature's Harmonic Unity, a Treatise on its Relation to Proportional Form*, was published in 1912.

Samuel Colman
30. *The Green River, Wyoming*, 1871
Transparent and opaque watercolor over graphite, with pen and brown ink, on thick, moderately rough, cream wove paper
16⅛ x 21¹³⁄₁₆ in. (410 x 554 mm)
Signed and dated lower left in brown ink:
Saml Colman. 1871
M. and M. Karolik Collection. 53.2442

Like Thomas Moran (cat. 29), Colman depicted one of the spectacular areas of the West recently made accessible from the East by rail. Colman was not as strongly identified with western subjects as Moran; however, he helped familiarize the New York art public with the genre by regularly exhibiting important finished watercolors. This large and imposing view of the eroded limestone cliffs of the Green River was most likely exhibited at the American Society of Painters in Water Colors in the year of its creation. It embodies Colman's belief that a watercolor could have the presence and status of an oil.[1]

The Green River was almost certainly executed in the studio from sketches made on the spot. A complete graphite underdrawing is visible, outlining the tops of the cliffs and even the shapes of the clouds. The artist covered the upper part of the sheet with a pale yellow wash (visible in the sky) that both unifies the image and suggests a time of day – probably late in the afternoon – when the cliffs show off their warm red and yellow hues and the clouds appear pinkish-orange. Cleverly placed cool accents – smoke rising from a campfire and vertical reflections on the water's surface – heighten the dominant warmth of the image. The cliffs were painted in washes, which were more extensively blotted and blended at the far left than at the near right and center. There, to create greater texture and detail, Colman dragged a partly dried brush over the rough paper surface and painted deep shadows and small clumps of vegetation with darker, glossier paints. (He even pushed aside little areas of paint with the end of his brush to suggest

the foliage of the bush at the lower right.) Using pen and brown ink, he outlined the sentinel butte and the rock columns in the center foreground. The contrast between the sharply defined foreground elements and the smoky softness of the distant cliffs heightens the effect of atmospheric recession.

Colman's watercolor emphasizes the natural state of this spectacular setting. Almost unnoticed, several groups of Native Americans go about their daily activities – scouting, canoeing, camping. They are one with the land. Moran, on the other hand, invests his uninhabited landscape with the smoke of an approaching locomotive – a symbol of change.

SWR

1. It is very likely the work entitled *Cliffs on the Green River, Rocky Mountains*, which Colman exhibited at the 1871 exhibition of the American Society of Painters in Water Colors. See Kathleen Adair Foster, "Makers of the American Watercolor Movement: 1860-1890" (Ph.D. diss., Yale University, 1982), p. 347 and note 14. A watercolor entitled *Green River, Rocky Mountains* was shown at the 1872 exhibition as well.

Samuel Colman
31. *Sycamore Canyon*, 1888
Opaque watercolor over graphite on moderately thick, slightly textured, gray-pink wove paper
11⅝ x 15 in. (296 x 381 mm)
Inscribed lower right: Sycamore Canyon Feb 20th 1888 (in brown wash); by Saml Colman / 77 (in black ink)
M. and M. Karolik Collection. 61.355

This watercolor of leafless sycamore trees was probably painted in or near Santa Barbara, California, as were two similar studies, also on colored papers in the Karolik Collection.[1] After Colman returned from his second European sojourn in 1875, his style became looser and more suggestive.[2] In its direct execution, lack of finish, and expressive use of light and color, *Sycamore Canyon* demonstrates Colman's continued response to recent trends in French painting.

In *The Green River, Wyoming* of 1871 (cat. 30) Colman colored the paper with a pale yellow wash. Here, he uses pinkish paper to create overall at-

mosphere and color, and even to evoke a time of day. The long shadows cast on the ground at the left suggest late afternoon. The broad strokes of the graphite underdrawing can be easily seen; however the legibility of the image depends largely on the assured strokes of the brush, fully loaded with paint. Over a generalized background broadly washed in, the artist defined the twisted limbs of the sycamores with dark browns and creamy whites. Although textured and fibrous, the paper is well sized and has a relatively hard surface. The washes dried slowly, permitting Colman to create

small clumps of grass by adding touches of intense color that bled suggestively into the wet washes in the left foreground. The bold contrast between the large areas of exposed pink paper and thickly applied, opaque pigments of pale tonalities lends a modern air to this rapid study from nature.

SWR

1. *Ojai Valley: Sycamore Trees*, on yellow-green paper and *Mission Canon, S. Barbara*, on gray-pink paper, (both undated, Museum of Fine Arts, Boston). While the date of this watercolor has been read as 1868, there

is no evidence to indicate that Colman visited Santa Barbara at this time. *Old Tree, Santa Barbara* (The Fleming Museum, University of Vermont, Burlington), is clearly dated February 27, 1888. (Wayne Craven, "Samuel Colman (1832-1920): Rediscovered Painter of Far-Away Places," *The American Art Journal* 8 [May 1976], p. 36, fig. 27).

2. Kathleen Adair Foster, "Makers of the American Watercolor Movement: 1860-1890" (Ph.D. diss., Yale University, 1982), p. 348. She notes that George Inness and W.T. Richards, European travelers in the 1870s, also began to use colored papers late in that decade. See cat. 36.

Walter Paris

Born London, England, 1842;
died Washington, D.C., 1906

Relatively little is known about English-born Walter Paris, outside of his watercolors of the American West. He was educated at the Royal Academy in London in the early 1860s where he may have learned a highly detailed watercolor technique suitable for architectural subjects. Paris is said to have taught drawing at the Royal Military Academy, Woolwich, and to have worked as an architect for the British government in India. Around 1872 he came to the United States and traveled west. He was the first artist to maintain a studio in Colorado Springs, Colorado. The town was founded in 1871 by the railroad promoter William J. Palmer, and newly accessible by rail from the East, it shortly became a health resort and tourist town. During the 1870s so many young Englishmen were in evidence, that the town was nicknamed "Little Lunnon." Paris resided there frequently during the 1870s and, less regularly, into the 1890s. His watercolors of Colorado subjects were exhibited at the Corcoran Gallery in Washington as early as 1875. Paris also maintained a studio in Union Square, New York City, where the Tile Club was founded in 1877. The club included men of letters and musicians (Paris was an amateur violinist), as well as artists. Among the most distinguished of the latter were Winslow Homer, Edward Austin Abbey, J. Alden Weir, and R. Swain Gifford. Each had a club nickname; Paris was quite logically "The Gaul." In the 1890s Paris settled in Washington, D.C., where he exhibited with the Washington Water Color Club and other watercolor societies. He became an American citizen in 1894, twelve years before his death.

Walter Paris
32. *Pike's Peak and the "Gateway" to the Garden of the Gods*, 1874
Opaque and transparent watercolor over graphite on thick, slightly textured, cream wove paper
12¹³⁄₁₆ x 20⅛ in. (326 x 510 mm)
Signed and dated lower right in brown wash:
W. Paris / 1874
M. and M. Karolik Collection. 52.272

Paris had only a short walk or buggy ride from his studio in Colorado Springs to view the astounding landscape depicted here. In the distance, snow-covered Pike's Peak rises above the foothills of the Rockies and the red rock "walls" surrounding the Garden of the Gods (see fig. 1). Beyond these walls were the extraordinary natural formations that have attracted tourists since Paris's time. One author described them as "red rocks of every conceivable and inconceivable size and shape . . . queer, grotesque little monstrosities . . . colossal

monstrosities . . . all motionless and silent, with a strange look of having been stopped and held back in the very climax of some supernatural catastrophe." Another writer called the site "a pale pink joke."[1]

The bright hues and elaborately detailed surface of this painting suggest the lavish encrustations of a Victorian artifact. Despite his almost microscopic attention to the scene and his eccentric, "total recall" vision, Paris's handling of the watercolor medium, learned in England, is skillful.[2] Varying the application of paint, he used flat washes of color for the meadow and sky, and applied opaque colors with fine brushes to describe the varied shapes of the rock formations, the vegetation of the foothills, and the plants growing in the foreground. A man with a walking stick surveys a world in miniature lying in the valley below. It includes a farmhouse, laundry hanging on a washline, a corraled horse, and grazing cattle. In the distance a horsedrawn carriage

Fig. 1. William Henry Jackson (1843-1942), *The Gateway & Pike's Peak*, 1880s. Photograph. Courtesy Amon Carter Museum, Fort Worth, Texas.

approaches the "gateway." The distant mountains and cloudless sky provide visual relief from the dizzying foreground, with its countless dabs of contrasting colors.

Paris's Colorado watercolors must have appealed to the Victorian taste for the colorful, the exotic, and the particular. In 1873 he had a chromolithograph produced in England that replicated another, presumably similar, watercolor of the Garden of the Gods.

SWR

1. *Colorado, A Guide to the Highest State*, Harry Hansen, ed. (New York: Hastings House, 1970; originally WPA Guide, 1941), p. 222. The first writer is Helen Hunt Jackson, and the second is Julian Street. Another watercolor by Paris in the Karolik Collection (undated, Museum of Fine Arts, Boston) depicts some of the formations within the "Garden."

2. An architectural subject by Joseph Nash, Paris's teacher at the Royal Academy, also shows a lively surface pattern; see Martin Hardie, *Water-colour Painting in Britain, III The Victorian Period* (London: B.T. Batsford Ltd., 1968), pl. 118.

William Stanley Haseltine

Born Philadelphia, Pennsylvania, 1835;
died Rome, Italy, 1900

Despite Haseltine's proficiency in watercolor, he seems to have regarded the medium as one for private expression. He was not a member of the American Watercolor Society, and probably showed with them only once, in 1877, as a benefit for the American Church in Rome. Nor did he make an attempt to promote his watercolors later in his career: at his death more than 500 remained in his studio. Nevertheless, he used watercolor and wash from the outset of his career to augment the pencil sketches that recorded his observations during his many travels. By the 1880s and nineties, he used the medium frequently for more elaborate, formal images that reflect his many working holidays.

Born into a prosperous Philadelphia family, Haseltine began his artistic training there under the landscape painter Paul Weber, a German immigrant whose romantic sensibility had a lifelong effect on Haseltine. Haseltine studied at the University of Pennsylvania and at Harvard, but after graduation from the latter in 1854, he returned to Philadelphia, persuaded his parents to allow him to pursue an artistic career, and accompanied his mentor to Germany. There he settled in Düsseldorf and, under the tutelage of the landscape painter Andreas Achenbach, mastered the clear color and precise draftsmanship that was characteristic of the Düsseldorf school. There too he met a group of American artists, among them Worthington Whittredge, Emanuel Leutze, and Albert Bierstadt, who became sketching companions and lifelong friends. He returned to New York briefly in the late 1850s, but by the mid-1860s he was back in Europe, settling temporarily in Paris. In France he associated with much-admired academic painters, such as Adolphe William Bouguereau, Benjamin Constant, and Jean-Léon Gérôme, but was equally intrigued by the new vogue for *plein-air* painting. He began spending a great deal of time sketching in the countryside, and his style in both oil and watercolor loosened accordingly. An interest in light and atmosphere supplanted the precise rendering of natural forms, particularly the rocks of the New England coastline, that had earlier been his mainstay.

By 1874, Haseltine and his family had established a permanent residence in the elegant Palazzo Altieri in Rome. He also maintained a presence in the New York art world by exhibiting regularly at the National Academy of Design (to which he had been elected in 1861) and at the Century Association. He was equally active in artists' organizations in Munich and Rome, and was a founder of the American School of Architecture, later the American Academy, Rome. Shortly after Haseltine's death in Rome in 1900, a memorial exhibition of his oils and watercolors was mounted in his rooms at the Palazzo Altieri.

William Stanley Haseltine
33. *View of Cannes with Parasol Pines*, 1869
    or later
Opaque watercolor over graphite on moderately thick, blue-gray wove paper
15¼ x 28⅛ in. (386 x 560 mm), irregular
Inscribed lower right in purple ink:
W. S. Haseltine / Cannes
Bequest of Mrs. John Gardner Coolidge. 63.176

When Haseltine visited Cannes in 1869, the once-sleepy fishing village was rapidly becoming a fashionable resort. Its gentle climate, picturesque old town (the subject of several of Haseltine's sketches), and beautiful view of the Esterel mountains attracted the wealthy during the colder months. Haseltine toured the Riviera in the fall of 1869, and for this watercolor took as his subject a site just outside of town, identified in a popular guidebook as the "magnificent Bocca Wood, a glorious grove of gigantic umbrella pines extending for some distance along the shore towards the W[est], a paradise of artists, and the admiration of Europe."[1]

A Haseltine sketchbook of Cannes and Venice in the M. and M. Karolik Collection at the Museum of Fine Arts contains two drawings, one in pencil, the other in pencil and wash, that anticipate the composition and main motif of *View of Cannes with Parasol Pines*.[2] The wash drawing (fig. 1), introduces the towering umbrella pines – a

Fig. 1. Sheet from Cannes sketchbook, 1869. Wash on paper. Museum of Fine Arts, Boston. M. and M. Karolik Collection.

Fig. 2. Sheet from Cannes sketchbook, 1869. Pencil on paper. Museum of Fine Arts, Boston. M. and M. Karolik Collection.

single, tall, somewhat twisted tree at right, and at left a pair of trees growing so close together that their foliage appears as a single mass. The figure with a pole over his shoulder posed prominently at water's edge in the wash drawing is moved to the middle distance in the watercolor, and becomes a woman hoeing a patch of land framed by the two groups of trees. The hilly terrain of the sketch becomes a flat plain. The pencil drawing (fig. 2) which, like the wash drawing, is simply inscribed "Cannes," records the main features of the finished watercolor's composition; that is, a road winding through the center foreground through the two groups of trees into the far distance, with mountains on either side.

Several of the Cannes drawings in this sketchbook are inscribed, "October 17, 1869," and it is possible that the watercolor was also made at that time. However, its highly finished, formal manner and assured style suggest a slightly later date. The palette – pale greens, browns, and yellows, highlighted with a salmon-colored gouache – and Haseltine's use of a blue textured paper are all features of his mature watercolor style; the soft tonalities and highly controlled, abbreviated brushstrokes give this watercolor a pastellike delicacy that would mark Haseltine's work in watercolor for the remainder of his career. Therefore it is possible that (although Haseltine used watercolor frequently on his travels and loved to paint *en plein air*) *View of Cannes with Parasol Pines* was

not completed on the spot but was worked up – or even executed entirely – in the studio some time after Haseltine's visit to the Riviera.[3]

CT

1. Augustus J. C. Hare, *South-eastern France* (London: G. Allen, 1890), p. 519. Hare notes that "The greatest injury which has been done to Cannes of late years has been the destruction of the greater part" of the Bocca Wood.

2. For other, similar images of these majestic trees, see *Cannes* (about 1868; oil on canvas; Indiana University Art Museum, Bloomington), *Cannes in the Sixties* (1860s; pen and ink and wash on paper; Mead Art Museum, Amherst College, Amherst, Mass.), and *Cannes* (about 1875; watercolor and gouache on blue paper; Memphis [Tennessee] Brooks Museum of Art.

3. I am grateful to Marc Simpson for sharing with me his knowledge of Haseltine's watercolor practice. See also Andrea Henderson, "Haseltine in Rome," in Marc Simpson, Andrea Henderson, and Sally Mills, *Expressions of Place: The Art of William Stanley Haseltine* (San Francisco: The Fine Arts Museums of San Francisco, 1992), pp. 39-41.

Hailed in 1873 as one of the "best-known watercolor painters in America," Richards began to work actively in the medium by the late 1860s, at about the same time he took up marine painting. By the 1870s, Richards had become well known for his watercolors of seacoast scenes; these were critically acclaimed, imitated by several lesser painters, and avidly collected. George Whitney, a Philadelphia manufacturer, was an enthusiastic supporter of Richards's work, and eventually owned more than 275 watercolors. Another collector, the Reverend Elias Magoon of New York, whom Richards met while sketching in Atlantic City in 1870, amassed a group of some eighty-five watercolors over the next decade. Magoon gave a number of these – the celebrated "History of England Series" – to Vassar College. He donated another fifty-four to the Metropolitan Museum of Art in 1880 in an effort to establish the American equivalent of London's celebrated Turner bequest. But by the mid-1880s, critical support for Richards's refined technique began to wane, and he was further discouraged by the deaths of his two most ardent supporters, Magoon and Whitney. Nevertheless, he continued to paint and exhibit watercolors to the end of his career.

Richards taught himself to draw as a young man, and by age seventeen was profitably employed as a designer of lighting fixtures for a Philadelphia manufacturing firm. At the same time, he was studying with the German-born landscape painter Paul Weber, whose precise style was good grounding for the Ruskinian manner Richards would later adopt.

In 1855 Richards made his first trip to Europe, traveling in France, Switzerland, Italy, and Germany. Soon after his return in the spring of 1856, he gave up his job as an industrial designer and devoted himself entirely to art. He was named an academician by the Pennsylvania Academy in 1863. That same year he joined the newly formed Association for the Advancement of Truth in Art, a group of painters, writers, and architects dedicated to reforming American art according to the teachings of John Ruskin. Oddly, Richards did not join the American Society of Painters in Water Colors until 1874, by which time the organization had been in operation for eight years.

In 1867 Richards went again to Europe; a dramatic storm on the return voyage is reported to have inspired him to take up marine painting. For the rest of his career, Richards dedicated himself to depicting the beauty of the sea in all weathers and seasons. While maintaining a studio in Germantown, Pennsylvania, he made summer pilgrimages to many sites along the eastern seaboard, particularly Atlantic City and Newport. The latter became his permanent residence from 1890 to his death in 1905.

If he was rebuffed by the avant-garde later in his career (the Society of American Artists excluded him from its first exhibition in 1878), Richards was generally well received by the establishment. He won medals at the 1876 Centennial Exhibition and at the 1889 Exposition Universelle in Paris, and showed regularly at the National Academy of Design and at the Pennsylvania Academy, which in 1905 awarded him their Gold Medal of Honor.

William Trost Richards
34. *Seascape with Pines and Overhanging Clouds*, 1870

Opaque watercolor over graphite on moderately thick, slightly textured, light beige wove paper
6^{11}/$_{16}$ x 13 in. (167 x 329 mm)
Signed lower right in black ink: Wm T Richards 1870
M. and M. Karolik Collection. 60.1059

35. *Beach with Sun Drawing Water*, 1872

Opaque watercolor over graphite on moderately thick, slightly textured, light beige wove paper
6¾ x 13^{15}/$_{16}$ in. (172 x 353 mm)
Signed lower left in brown ink: Wm. T. Richards. 1872
M. and M. Karolik Collection. 60.1058

Seascape with Pines and Overhanging Clouds and *Beach with Sun Drawing Water* were bought by Maxim Karolik from Edith Ballinger Price, his Newport neighbor and the artist's granddaughter. Karolik was an ardent collector of Richards's watercolors (although he seems never to have bought an oil) and eventually owned at least ten. Clearly, these simple, nearly monochromatic compositions had great appeal for Karolik, whose painting collection emphasized the work of Lane, Heade, Kensett, and other Luminist masters. Like many of their works, the small scale of these watercolors belies their spatial grandeur.

Neither location depicted in these watercolors can be identified with certainty. In the summer of 1870, when he painted *Seascape with Pines*, Richards worked on Cuttyhunk Island, Massachusetts (just west of Martha's Vineyard) and at Atlantic City, the more probable location for the picture. The watercolor may be the picture entitled *Evening, Atlantic City, New Jersey* Richards exhibited at the fifth annual exhibition of the American Society of Painters in Water Colors in the winter of 1871, but this is by no means certain. His itinerary in the summer of 1872 included the Adirondacks, Biddeford Pool in Maine, the Isles of Shoals, Gloucester, and Narragansett; *Beach with Sun Drawing Water* could have been produced at any of these sites. Despite the precision and high degree of finish of these watercolors, topographical specificity was clearly not Richards's intent. Rather, it was the mesmerizing effect of mist and cloud and rhythmic advance of the waves that fascinated him (as his son noted, "he stood for hours in the early days of Atlantic City or Cape May, with folded arms, studying the motion of the sea, until people thought him insane"[1]) and that he tried to evoke in these watercolors.

The radical simplicity of Richards's compositions and the sureness of his touch prevent these meticulous watercolors from seeming labored. Choosing a slightly textured beige paper, in *Beach with Sun Drawing Water* Richards further enhanced the tonal unity of his picture by laying down a broad, even blue-gray wash over almost the entire sheet. Color contrasts and textural accents were added within a very narrow range. In the sky, Richards gently lifted up some of the gray wash, then applied a yellow tone to create the dazzling effect of the sun breaking through the clouds. In *Seascape with Pines and Overhanging Clouds*, a similar monochromatic softness prevails, interrupted only by the band of salmon-pink clouds along the horizon, and by the three pines, seemingly pushed to the edge of the sheet by the prevailing winds.

CT

1. Harrison S. Morris, *William T. Richards. Masterpieces of the Sea* (Philadelphia and London: J.P. Lippincott Company, 1912), p. 10.

William Trost Richards
36. Near Paradise, Newport, 1877
Opaque watercolor over graphite on very thick, rough textured, pink-buff wove paper ("carpet paper"), stretched and tacked on a wooden panel
23 x 37 in. (584 x 940 mm)
Signed and dated on lower left in black wash: Wm T. Richards. 1877, and on reverse of panel: Near Paradise, Newport / Wm T. Richards
Gift of Mrs. Arthur Astor Carey. Res. 27.154

Aware that his previously successful watercolor style was becoming outdated, Richards in about 1877 experimented with new materials and a new scale. After years of producing watercolors of modest dimensions, he painted a group of water-colors of so ambitious a size – nearly two by three feet – that they could successfully vie for attention with oil paintings.[1] He set aside his conventional watercolor papers and worked instead on rough and fibrous carpet paper,[2] whose texture he suc-

cessfully exploited and whose color, ranging from bluish-gray to a warm pinky brown, allowed Richards to work as though he were using a tinted paper. In this picture, the warm earthy hue of the paper both provides a middle tone and represents the bare ground at the base of the outcropping at left. Extensive use of dry-brush strokes in the foreground combined with the coarseness of the paper describes the lichen on the rocks with extraordinary effectiveness. Richards was delighted

Fig. 1. John La Farge (1835-1910), *Bishop Berkeley's Rock, Newport*, 1868. Oil on canvas. Metropolitan Museum of Art. Gift of Dr. Frank Jewett Mather, Jr.

with the result: "The principal events of the week have been another visit from Mrs. Astor, and a visit from Miss Wolfe of New York, and they each bought a drawing! hurray!! With such a start the carpet paper ought to be a success. I do find that the drawings are very popular, and they certainly are more important looking than the small drawings of previous summers."[3] And indeed these watercolors, which seemed to represent a marked change from his previous work in the medium, were much talked about in the press and sought after by collectors.

Near Paradise, Newport was one of four works Richards submitted to the Eleventh Annual Exhibition of the American Watercolor Society, held in February of 1878. It was a popular favorite;[4] however, the press expressed some ambivalence. John Moran, writing for the *Art Journal*, was typical in both his admiration for Richards's effects and his concern that the new scale exposed a deficiency in content: "Mr. W. T. Richards contributes a transcript of 'Paradise Rocks,' near Newport (5) which

has more breadth than his ordinary work, with a truth of local colour and a well rendered distance, but we find a want of meaning and sympathy in it."[5]

Moran's comment may reflect the fact that, despite its larger scale and the relative looseness of handling, this watercolor is not really a departure from Richards's former style, but remains true to his Ruskinian roots. *Near Paradise, Newport* is crammed with geological and botanical detail, and contains numerous focal points. Although he painted the far distance fairly freely, Richards's loyalty to opaque pigments and the care he lavished on every facet of foreground rock locates the painting squarely within the Pre-Raphaelite watercolor tradition. The lone gull soaring through the barren outcroppings (whose importance Richards advertised by making it the lightest value against the darkest value in the watercolor) adds a slightly sentimental note that is equally Victorian.

The setting for this watercolor was most likely the Paradise Valley region in Middletown, just north of Newport, overlooking Paradise Rocks with a view south toward Second Beach.[6] On some of this land was a farm rented by John La Farge in the late 1860s, and La Farge produced a number of large oil sketches of the area during this period (fig. 1).[7] In contrast with Richards, who carefully described the empty, rugged countryside to expose its primeval nature, La Farge conveyed the mystery of the region in a spare, atmospheric composition. When La Farge's Newport landscapes were first exhibited, they were criticized for their lack of finish. By the mid-1870s, however, their suggestive, fluid style had become part of the mainstream of American painting, while Richards's more literal rendering of the same site had begun to seem somewhat old fashioned.

CT

1. These include *A Rocky Coast* (1877, Metropolitan Museum of Art, New York); *Paradise, Newport* (1877, National Gallery of Art, Washington, D.C.), *Cove and Conanicut Island* (about 1877, Cooper-Hewitt National Museum of Design, Smithsonian Institution, New York), *Cormorant Cliff, Jamestown, Rhode Island* (1877, Cleveland Museum of Art), *Coast View at Newport* (1877, private collection, Wellesley, Massachusetts); and *Old Fort, Conanicut Island* (1877, Wadsworth Atheneum, Hartford, Connecticut).

2. Carpet paper or carpet felt is a wide, soft, thick paper, made from used paper, rags, wool, and similar waste materials, and placed under carpets. It is highly textured; its wool or linen fibers are often visible. See E. J. Labarre, *Dictionary and Encyclopedia of Paper and Paper-Making* (Amsterdam: Swets & Zeitlinger, 1952), p. 41. Such a support leads almost inevitably to looser handling and to the increased use of opaque pigments in order to bring up highlights.

3. Richards to George Whitney, October 1877, quoted in Linda Ferber, *William Trost Richards, American Landscape and Marine Painter* (Brooklyn: The Brooklyn Museum, 1973), p. 84, cat. 68.

4. The watercolor reportedly sold immediately (see Kathleen Adair Foster, "Makers of the American Watercolor Movement: 1860-1890," [Ph.D. diss., Yale University, 1982], p. 152). It was subsequently owned by Arthur Astor Carey, a dedicated Ruskinian and for some years president of the Boston Society of Arts and Crafts. Carey's aunt was the Mrs. Astor mentioned in Richards's letter; she may have kindled his interest in the painter. Cynthia Fleming kindly provided the information on Carey.

5. John Moran, "The American Water-Colour Society's Exhibition," *Art Journal* 4 (1878), p. 91.

6. Richards made several drawings of this picturesque ravine, including an undated pencil sketch, also owned by the Museum of Fine Arts, and a watercolor, *From Paradise to Purgatory, Newport* (1878, Metropolitan Museum of Art, New York).

7. Robert G. Workman, *The Eden of America, Rhode Island Landscapes, 1820-1920* (Providence: Museum of Art, Rhode Island School of Design, 1986), p. 44.

George Inness

Born Newburgh, New York, 1824;
died Bridge of Allan, Scotland, 1894

George Inness worked in watercolor for some thirty years, from the early 1850s to about 1883. Compared to his prodigious output in oils (the 1965 catalogue raisonné by Leroy Ireland documents nearly two thousand works) the fewer than four dozen watercolors form a tiny fraction of his oeuvre. Nonetheless, these watercolors show a remarkable development from handsome, if rather conventional, landscape compositions to an extraordinarily free and lush use of the medium.

Inness's family was relatively prosperous and cultivated, and he enjoyed some exposure to art even in childhood. He had several opportunities to study art as a teenager, training first with an itinerant painter and in an engraving firm, and then with the French painter Regis Gignoux. He made a precocious debut in New York, showing at the National Academy of Design and at the American Art-Union when barely twenty. The promise shown in these early works encouraged a New York auctioneer, Ogden Haggarty, to send Inness to Europe in 1851. By this time, Inness's interest in classical composition and idealized treatment of landscape forms had already begun to distinguish him from the topographically oriented painters of his day. His interest in watercolor further deviated from most contemporary landscape painters, who for the most part preferred sketching in pencil.

In 1853, Inness visited France, where he was strongly affected by the warm tonalities, looser brushwork, and informal compositional style of the Barbizon painters. He returned to the United States the next year, and for over a decade painted landscapes that reflected the formal properties of the Barbizon school and, as Inness embraced Swedenborgian beliefs, were increasingly meditative and spiritual.

In April of 1870, sponsored by his dealers, Williams and Everett of Boston, Inness returned to Europe. For the next four years he lived in Rome and toured the surrounding countryside, as well as Perugia, Venice, and the Tyrol. These sites inspired many of his most successful pictures in oil and his most original watercolors. His first Italian watercolors were rather conventionally picturesque, but soon his handling became freer, his compositions more dramatic, and his color richer and more expressive.

By the late seventies, Inness was back in the United States, living in New Jersey, and maintaining a studio in New York. The art dealer and collector Thomas B. Clarke became his agent in 1878; from this point Inness's financial situation and reputation were secured. He remained an independent spirit, however: he was a founding member, in 1878, of the dissident Society of American Artists; that same year he published some of his controversial artistic theories in *Harper's New Monthly Magazine.* During this period, he produced only about seven watercolors, and like his oils, these were innovative in technique – often mixing watercolor, body color, and chalk – and, in the case of the majestic Niagara series, epic in scale. He abandoned watercolor by the mid-1880s, perhaps because the spiritual content of his pictures was best expressed in the weightier oil medium.

Inness only occasionally made watercolors in preparation for oils. Nor did he seem to intend them for public display: he did not show with the American Watercolor Society (although he was a friend of its president, Samuel Colman; see cat. 30), and sold only a handful of watercolors during his lifetime. Most of Inness's work in the medium became known only at the sale of his daughter's estate in 1927.

George Inness
37. *Castle in the Mountains*, about 1873
Transparent and opaque watercolor over graphite on moderately thick, light tan wove paper
8⅞ x 12⅛ in. (224 x 308 mm), irregular
Signed lower left in graphite: Geo. Inness
Inscribed verso in graphite: G Inness
M. and M. Karolik Collection. 60.1026

Inness's second trip to Italy, made between 1870 and 1874, accounted for more than two hundred paintings and about half of his documented watercolors. The watercolors in particular reflect his summer travels: to the environs of Rome (where he was based for those four years), to Venice, to Perugia, and to the Tyrolean Alps, which he probably visited in the summer of 1873, and which inspired his most spontaneous and fluid watercolors.

Based in Pieve di Cadore, Titian's birthplace, Inness made at least seven watercolors of the village and surrounding mountains that summer.[1] *Castle in the Mountains* and a somewhat smaller watercolor, known as *Barberini, Italy* (private collection), feature the same sharply profiled mountains and the castle at far left, but *Barberini, Italy* was observed from a greater distance, converting an immediate and magical view into a panorama. These, and a third watercolor of the mountains, *The Dolomites* (fig. 1) exhibit the same jagged edged trees and the unusual pink and green palette that Inness began to use just before he left for Italy.[2]

Castle in the Mountains was probably based on a pencil sketch made on the spot.[3] However, Inness imposed upon his observations a compositional pattern that he would use for years, one especially well suited to the depiction of mountain scenery. An empty wedge of color in the immediate foreground is succeeded by a series of overlapping diagonals that define progression into space; these culminate in the steep, castle-surmounted hill at left and the loftier mountains in the far distance at right. This formula provides a deliberate structure to a picture otherwise given over to free abstract washes and generalized forms.

Despite its origins in an actual site and the spatial logic imposed by Inness's compositional

Edward Alfred Sargent

Born 1842;
died Staten Island, New York, 1914

Fig. 1. *The Dolomites*, about 1873. Watercolor, gouache, and graphite on paper. Wadsworth Atheneum, Hartford, Connecticut. Gift of Philip L. Goodwin.

2. For a comprehensive discussion of Inness's watercolors, see Robert S. Mattison, *George Inness, Watercolors and Drawings* (New York: Davis & Long Company, 1978), cat. 21.

3. Kathleen Adair Foster, "Makers of the American Watercolor Movement: 1860-1890" (Ph.D. diss., Yale University, 1982), p. 173.

pattern, *Castle in the Mountains* is a romantic fantasy, quite distinct from the descriptive travel sketches made by American fellow travelers in Italy. Painters such as Gifford, Bierstadt, Casilear, and many others visited the Alps from the 1860s on, and produced sketches and formal compositions that celebrated the natural drama of the scenery or – especially in comparison with Inness's imaginative treatment – remained topographically earthbound. Almost none of them used watercolor, while conversely, Inness seemed to have worked only in watercolor that summer, for no oils of the mountains have been identified. His preference for watercolor, and his concern for the pictorial poetry of his subject, ally him instead with earlier British painters such as John Robert Cozens and especially Turner, whose work he admired and whose Alpine watercolors he may have known.

CT

1. "We spent two summers at Perugia, one at Albano, and one at Pieve di Cadore, the birthplace of Titian, whom my father thought the greatest colorist that ever lived." George Inness, Jr., *Life, Art, and Letters of George Inness* (New York, 1917; reprint edition, New York: Kennedy Galleries, Inc., Da Capo Press, 1969), p. 75.

Between 1870 and 1894, Edward Alfred Sargent is listed in *Trow's New York City Directory* under three professional headings: draftsman, architect, and artist. These titles, used almost interchangeably, indicate the character of Sargent's life and work. While most of the artist's known watercolors are renditions of the designs of other architects, Sargent also designed several buildings himself, including a high school in Flushing, Queens, and the Ninth Regiment Armory in New York, a rambling castle on West 14th Street. Sargent also exhibited four studies of architectural interiors and exteriors at the National Academy of Design between 1861 and 1864.

Little is known of Sargent's personal life. His obituary requests that "English papers please copy," suggesting that he might have been born in England. Sargent is first documented in New York at the age of nineteen, when he exhibited a watercolor at the National Academy of Design. The watercolor, titled "Village Chapel, Gambrill and Post," probably represented a British church. By 1871, Sargent is recorded as living in Staten Island, where, after a brief sojourn in New Jersey, he spent the rest of his life.

In his architectural drawings, Sargent ambitiously combined precise perspectival draftsmanship, abundant surrounding detail, and skillful handling of watercolor. Sargent's skills must have been highly prized in his day, for he executed many drawings for Calvert Vaux and George B. Post, two prominent New York architects. Several watercolors by Sargent for Vaux and Post are in the collection of the New-York Historical Society.

Edward Alfred Sargent

38. *Suggestions for the Public Supply of Steam,*
    about 1870-78

Transparent and opaque watercolor over graphite on
moderately thick, cream wove paper
12⅞ x 17⁹⁄₁₆ in. (328 x 445 mm)
Inscribed lower left in brown wash: E.A. Sargent. Del.;
lower left in white gouache: - REFERENCE- / GREY, SEW-
ER - / RED, STEAM - /BLUE, FRESH WATER- / GREEN,
SALT WATER.; lower center in white gouache: SUGGES-
TIONS FOR THE PUBLIC SUPPLY OF STEAM/ FOR HEATING,
COOKING, EXTINGUISHING FIRES, MELTING SNOW & C. /
WITH IMPROVED SUBWAYS FOR PIPES, SEWERS, TELE-
GRAPH WIRES &c.; lower right in white gouache: LEWIS
LEEDS / 110 BROADWAY N.Y.; right margin in graphite:
Typesetting / Grinding / do / Folding / Folding /
Printing / Printing / Show
M. and M. Karolik Collection. 61.314

Designed to entice municipal and corporate cus-
tomers to use the services of the engineer Lewis
Leeds, Sargent's watercolor is a masterful adver-
tisement for the steam heating services offered by
the firm.[1] Soon after the Civil War, many buildings in New York began to use steam heat. It was
regarded as an enormous improvement over the
coal stoves used in most apartments and houses at
mid-century. "The waste was terrific, the smoke
dense and full of soot, and the sidewalks dirty with
uncollected ashes often exposed to the wind."[2]
The building shown in cross-section at right is
efficiently heated by a series of subterranean
steam boilers, linked by pipes to the ten-story
structure above.

Sargent's watercolor demonstrates the means
for solving many other mid-century civil engineering problems as well. At left, in a small
vignette, Sargent depicts a snow storm that has
downed telegraph wires, and created a hazard for
pedestrians in the form of falling snow and ice. Also shown is a building burning out of control, for
which little help is evident. Sargent's "improved
subways for pipes, sewers, telegraph wires &c.,"
shown at lower right in the cross-sectioned building provide a solution for all of these problems.
Firefighters are shown dousing flames with a
high-pressure hose, while a workman at rooftop
also uses water to clear the area of dangerous
masses of snow.

Fig. 1. *Long Island Historical Society, Pierrepont and Clinton
Streets, Brooklyn*, about 1877-81. Watercolor. The New-York
Historical Society.

Although this watercolor probably depicts
Madison Square in Manhattan, a large intersec-
tion at the corner of Broadway and Twenty-Third
Street, none of the buildings depicted ever
existed.[3] In an inventive spirit, Sargent has not
only replumbed and rewired this busy area, but
has also redesigned all of its structures. A much
more typical example of Sargent's work is the
*Long Island Historical Society, Pierrepont and Clin-
ton Streets, Brooklyn* (fig. 1), where the artist has
provided a detailed study of a proposed building
designed by George B. Post between 1877 and
1881. Even this strictly functional watercolor was
enlivened, however, by a variety of textural effects
produced by pigment laid on with a dry brush,
and heavy applications of gouache. In *Suggestions
for the Public Supply of Steam*, Sargent's vigorous
imagination transformed a commercial application
of the watercolor medium into an intriguing work
of art.

ABW

1. Leeds, a civil engineer and architect who practiced in
New York from 1860 until 1898, started his career in
partnership with Calvert Vaux, later Sargent's employer.
Since Vaux's name does not appear along with Leeds's
in the lower margin, this watercolor most likely dates
between 1870 and 1878, when Leeds was a solo practitioner at 110 Broadway. Sargent was only a few doors
away during these years; he is listed as working
at 152, 98 and 102 Broadway between 1871 and 1880.

2. Harry Granick, *Underneath New York* (New York:
Rinehart & Company, 1947), p. 56.

3. Photographs in the architectural collections of the
New-York Historical Society show that throughout the
late nineteenth century, this site was occupied by very
different structures.

SUGGESTIONS for the PUBLIC SUPPLY of STEAM
FOR HEATING, FOR POWER, COOKING, EXTINGUISHING FIRES, MELTING SNOW &c.
WITH IMPROVED SUBWAYS for PIPES, SEWERS TELEGRAPH WIRES &c.

REFERENCE
GREY. SEWER
RED. STEAM
BLUE. FRESH WATER
GREEN. SALT WATER

LEWIS W. LEEDS
110 BROADWAY N.Y.

James Wells Champney

Born Boston, Massachusetts, 1843;
died New York City, 1903

Known primarily for his black and white line illustrations, Champney also worked in a variety of painterly media. He tended to produce and exhibit in one medium at a time, moving from oils early in his career to pastels later on. Throughout his life, however, he consistently used watercolor to paint a wide range of subjects, including preliminary studies, landscapes, travel sketches, and family portraits. In contrast to many of his oils and pastels, whose Victorian subjects appear dated today, Champney's direct and spontaneous watercolors remain fresh and appealing.

Art education for Champney was a fruitful combination of academic training and practical experience. While he attended secondary school, Champney took art lessons at the Lowell Institute in Boston, including the study of anatomy with the physician, Oliver Wendell Holmes. In 1859 he was apprenticed to the Boston wood-engraving firm of Bricker & Russell and continued to develop his drawing skills. After serving with the 45th Massachusetts Regiment of Volunteers during the Civil War he taught drawing at Dr. Dio Lewis's academy for girls in Lexington, Massachusetts. From 1866 to 1870 and again in 1871 Champney studied painting in Europe. He was a pupil of the genre painter Edouard Frère in Ecouen, near Paris, and of Joseph Henri François van Lerius at the Royal Academy in Antwerp, where he won a top prize for his drawings. During this period he often used watercolor to augment a black and white sketch. Returning to the United States in 1872, Champney was commissioned in 1873 by *Scribner's Monthly* to accompany Edward King on his tour of the reconstructed South. Champney's illustrations to King's prominent series of articles, "The Great South," were his first important contributions in that genre.

By the early 1880s Champney had ceased to illustrate periodicals on a regular basis, but continued to illustrate children's books written by his artist wife, Elizabeth Williams, a Vassar College graduate, whom he married in 1873. Between 1876 and 1903 he illustrated twenty-six of her books, among them *Three Vassar Girls Abroad* and nine sequels. The Champneys maintained studios in New York City, at their summer house in Deer-field, Massachusetts, and in Europe when they visited from time to time.

From 1875 to 1903 Champney exhibited regularly with the American Watercolor Society. Beginning with the 1875 Paris Salon and the 1876 Philadelphia Centennial he also showed oil paintings of contemporary genre subjects, anecdotal in content and highly finished. From 1877 to 1881 Champney was professor of drawing and painting at Smith College and later taught at the Hartford Society of Decorative Arts. He was elected to associate membership in the National Academy of Design in 1882. By the mid-1880s he was working extensively in pastels and became known for his New York society and theater portraits. Ever responsive to the changing demands of the art market, in 1898 he undertook mural decorations for New York's Hotel Manhattan. Champney was also an amateur photographer who not only used his images as aids to painting landscapes and portraits but also gave lectures on photography as an independent art form.

Fig. 1. Champney with two students in the meadow by his house in Deerfield, Massachusetts.
Photograph courtesy Deerfield Academy.

James Wells Champney
39. *Self-Portrait*, 1880-85

Transparent and opaque watercolor on moderately thick, slightly textured cream wove paper
13¾ x 9½ in. (349 x 242 mm)
M. and M. Karolik Collection. 58.1081

This excellent likeness probably dates from the early 1880s: Champney, with his healthy complexion and reddish-blond beard, but graying hair, appears to be close to his fifth decade (see fig. 1). It is an unusual and highly successful example of a large-scale, realistic portrait executed in watercolor. This broad and fluid medium does not lend itself to the accurate definition of facial features, and nineteenth-century watercolor portraits were more commonly small and often handled with the fine brushstrokes of the miniature technique (see cat. 3).

The background and clothing are sketchy and unresolved, focusing attention on the face. Like a sculptor using clay, Champney worked both additively and subtractively; brushing on and wiping off pigments to model his features. Particularly effective was the way he rubbed the pigment from the forehead and around the eyes, to reveal the underlying bony structure and suggest the play of light across the surface of the skin. He used opaque white paint to highlight the tip of the nose, the pupils of the eye, and hairs in the beard.

In the 1880s a number of American artists, among them Champney and Childe Hassam (cat. 64) revived the medium of pastel. By the early 1890s Champney was producing many pastel portraits, taking advantage of the medium's capacity for modelling flesh and capturing the subtleties of texture and light. The opaque pigments and liberal use of white in this watercolor, in combination with the extensive manipulation, anticipate the matte, blended appearance of Champney's pastel portraits.

SWR

James Wells Champney
40. *An Artist in His Studio*, probably 1880s

Transparent and opaque watercolor over graphite on
moderately thick, slightly textured, cream wove paper
11 1/16 x 15 3/8 in. (281 x 391 mm)
M. and M. Karolik Collection. 58.1083

41. *An Artist Sketching*, probably 1880-90
Opaque watercolor on moderately thick, slightly textured, blue wove paper
5 x 9 in. (126 x 228 mm)
M. and M. Karolik Collection. 58.1082

These two watercolors depicting fellow artists – one indoors, the other out – show two different aspects of Champney's style. *An Artist in His Studio*, though unfinished, was carefully prepared with a complete graphite underdrawing, and then filled in with color, while no such understructure remains visible in the loosely, though thickly painted *An Artist Sketching*.

The heavy beams and windowless interior of *An Artist in His Studio* suggest a barn or outbuilding. While all the trappings are well defined by relatively heavy application of dark, opaque pigments, the artist himself and the large canvas before him contrast abruptly as mere sketches on the white paper. This very likely depicts a fellow artist, for the huge easel, large canvases, and enormous frame are not typical of Champney's small-scale works. Neither do the architecture and accessories resemble any of Champney's several studios in New York, Deerfield, and Paris, which are recorded in photographs.[1] Nor was he an animal painter, as the stuffed gazelle and dove that serve as studio props and the subjects of the smaller canvases seem to suggest. On the whole, the ambiance is more European than American, and it probably records a studio Champney visited on one of his many trips abroad.

The evocative outdoor scene, *An Artist Sketch-ing*, was very likely painted at Deerfield, where Champney's summer studio was located. A similar fence appears in a photograph of the artist himself at work at an outdoor easel, also using an umbrella to modulate the bright daylight (see cat. 39, fig. 1). Here a painter of substantial build dominates his minuscule camp stool; his pad of paper or portfolio leans casually against a tree. It has been suggested that the artist depicted is William Gedney Bunce (1842-1916), a Hartford, Connecticut friend of Champney.[2]

Working with opaque pigments, Champney nearly covered the blue paper, even painting in the whites of the sky. His sketchy, impressionist paint

John La Farge

Born New York City, 1835;
died Providence, Rhode Island, 1910

application and lively yellow-greens suggest dappled light filtering through the trees and animating the image.

The three watercolors included here are Champney's personal expressions, rather than commissioned illustrations or exhibition pictures. They demonstrate the strengths of his informal subjects: a keenly observed self-portrait, a complete record of a business-like studio, and a light-filled landscape. They were purchased for the Museum by Maxim Karolik from a granddaughter of the artist.

SWR

1. See American Studies Group, *James Wells Champney* (Deerfield, Massachusetts: Deerfield Academy, 1965), illus. on pp. 14, 15, 17, 25, 47, and 51.

2. In a letter of 1988 from Lincoln Bunce Spiess, Bunce's distant cousin, to the Department of Prints, Drawings, and Photographs, Museum of Fine Arts, Boston.

John La Farge received watercolor lessons as a child, but it was not until he undertook his first stained glass commission in 1876 that he began to use the medium with regularity. For the rest of his career, he employed watercolor to develop designs for all his decorative projects, including glass, murals, and embroideries, as well as for independent works. Beginning in the late 1870s he gained mastery in the medium by painting exquisite floral subjects, and used it to record his travels to Japan (1886) and the South Pacific (1890-91). La Farge began to exhibit his watercolors in 1879, and for several decades thereafter he sold them – along with oils – at auction and through dealers to supplement his irregular income from decorative projects.

Born to wealthy French emigré parents, La Farge had a cultured upbringing that included drawing instruction from his maternal grandfather, Louis Binsse (1774-1844), a miniature painter, and lessons from an English watercolorist. After graduating from college and studying law, La Farge visited Europe in 1856 where he drew from the old masters and trained in the Parisian studio of Thomas Couture. He moved to Newport, Rhode Island, in 1859 in order to study painting with William Morris Hunt. That area would remain home for the La Farge family, although the artist often lived in New York or Boston when undertaking extensive decorative commissions.

La Farge began his professional career as a landscape painter in oils, working in the subdued colors and loosely brushed manner of the Barbizon School as practiced by Hunt. During the seventies his compositions became more decorative and he began to employ brighter and more contrasting colors, based on his studies of Japanese prints, color theory, and direct contact with English Pre-Raphaelite art.

La Farge's mature career began in 1876 with the prestigious commission for murals and windows for Trinity Church, Boston. It continued past the turn of the century with the design and execution of hundreds of similar commissions for churches, public buildings, and private homes. In his later years, La Farge published extensively on the theory, criticism, and appreciation of art, and on his travels. One of his closest artistic friends was Winslow Homer. Although La Farge's watercolors were eagerly collected during his lifetime, after World War I his elegant work was perceived as old fashioned and its popularity waned. In recent years, scholars have taken a renewed interest in this rich period of American decoration, focusing attention once again on the special qualities of La Farge's work.

John La Farge
42. *Wild Roses in an Antique Chinese Bowl*, 1880
Transparent and opaque watercolor on thick, slightly textured, cream wove paper
10⅞ x 9¹/₁₆ in. (276 x 229 mm)
Initialed and dated lower right in black wash:
JLF / 1880
Bequest of Miss Elizabeth Howard Bartol. Res. 27.96

Flowers were a favorite subject for La Farge and one he handled with ease, whether painted in watercolor or oil, or executed in stained glass. The artist gradually developed a personal style by working out his theories and practices of color and composition in the many floral still-lifes he painted in oil between 1859 and the early 1870s. Around 1878 La Farge transferred his study of flowers to the medium of watercolor.[1] These works on paper were filled with light and color, more brilliant than any preceding oil. Common flowers – hollyhocks, apple blossoms, iris, waterlilies, wild roses – were painted in a relaxed and naturalistic manner in compositions that were graceful and firmly designed. La Farge's floral watercolors are among his most beautiful and confident works in the medium.

Wild Roses in an Antique Chinese Bowl presents a handful of pink blossoms informally placed in a Chinese ceramic container with a celadon (pale gray-green) glaze.[2] The short-stemmed arrangement is casual, as is the off-center placement of the bowl. La Farge was particularly adroit in capturing the translucency of the fragile petals by using reserves of white paper, washes of pale pink, and touches of bright red. The surrounding leaves, painted in greens and blues, provide a contrast to the warm-hued blossoms. The margins of the sheet reveal the multiple layers of wash that comprise the background. La Farge could well have

been referring to such complex washes when he identified his own working methods with the "veilings and sequences" that he discovered in an ancient Japanese flower painting.[3]

The same interplay of opacity and transparency, of light and shadow, of quiet and bright colors, also characterizes La Farge's stained glass. In particular, the milky layers of wash on the bowl and in the background call to mind opalescent glass, whose manufacture in the United States La Farge succeeded in patenting in 1880. The color trials in the margins of the sheet recall the words applied to his earlier floral oils: "He delighted in juggling with the magic colors: with lake and crimson overlaying blues and vermilions, and with the darks of all colors warmed and enriched by glazings of blue and green and purple: – it was simply flower painting, but a development and education of a color sense which has accented every work of his after artistic life."[4]

La Farge made his first significant appearance in the watercolor medium at the 1879 American Watercolor Society exhibition. His floral still-life, *Roses in a Pi-tong* (about 1879, Fogg Art Museum, Harvard University Art Museums, Cambridge, Masachusetts), depicting cultivated roses in a figurally decorated Chinese vase, was considered the outstanding work in the exhibition. One critic commended it for its highly fashionable "Oriental bric-a-brac" and for its "roses made of a breath or a blush."[5] La Farge's pictures from that exhibition sold, as did a number of floral watercolors included in an auction of his work held in Boston in December of that year. These subjects appealed to a growing number of private collectors who found them appropriate for home decoration. After 1880 La Farge did not paint for exhibition, but sold his watercolors through private dealers or at auction. Although *Wild Roses in an Antique Chinese Bowl* was offered for sale at intervals starting in 1887, it was not sold until 1909, when Elizabeth Bartol, a student of Hunt, purchased it from the Boston dealers, Doll & Richards.[6]

SWR

1. For a detailed discussion of this genre, see Kathleen A. Foster, "The Still-Life Paintings of John La Farge," *American Art Journal* 11 (July 1979), pp. 4–37.

2. The three-footed flowerpot with a simple ornament of three raised rectangular bars dates from the sixteenth or seventeenth century. I appreciate the help of Wu Tung, Matsutaro Shoriki Curator in the Department of Asiatic Art at the Museum of Fine Arts, Boston, who identified the type and color of the container. When exhibited at Doll & Richards in 1890 the title was *Wild Roses in a White Antique Chinese Bowl*; in 1909 it was *Wild Roses in an Ancient Chinese Bowl*. The same pot, or one very similar to it, appears in *Roses* (about 1880, private collection); see James L. Yarnall, *John La Farge: Watercolors and Drawings* (Yonkers, New York: The Hudson River Museum of Westchester, 1990), pl. 19.

3. Speaking of a painting he purchased in Osaka in 1886, La Farge wrote, "But I was yet to find something old that would be directly meant for me, – a painting by the legendary painter of Japan . . . Kose-no-Kanaoka. The painting is still in fair condition, though injuries of time reveal, as usual, the methods used by the painter. And it was a delight in me . . . to recognize in the veilings and sequences of this painting of the lotus methods I had used myself . . . when I had tried to render the tones and the transparency of our fairy water-lily." John La Farge, *An Artist's Letters from Japan* (London: T. Fisher Unwin, 1897), p. 242.

4. Candace Wheeler, "The Painters of Yesterday," typescript copy of manuscript written about 1900, Department of Prints, Drawings, and Photographs, Museum of Fine Arts, Boston, pp. 7–8; also cited in Foster, "Still-Life Paintings," p. 10.

5. Earl Shinn, *Nation* 28 (March 1879), quoted in Kathleen A. Foster, "John La Farge and the American Watercolor Movement: Art for the 'Decorative Age'," in *John La Farge* (Pittsburgh: Carnegie Museum of Art, 1987), pp. 136–138, and notes 36, 37.

6. I am most indebted to James L. Yarnall for providing manuscript entries from Henry A. La Farge and James L. Yarnall, *Catalogue Raisonné of the Works of John La Farge*, forthcoming, which includes exhibition and provenance records for this and the other La Farge watercolors included here.

John La Farge
43. *Moonlit Seascape*, about 1883
Transparent and opaque watercolor on moderately thick, smooth, cream wove paper
6 11/16 x 4 13/16 in. (170 x 123 mm)
Bequest of Miss Mary C. Wheelwright. 59.688

This small, but richly executed watercolor explores the light of the moon, seen through various thicknesses of cloud cover and reflected on the surface of the ocean. The subtle tilt of the horizon, implying the water's movement, contributes to the transitory impression of the image. Although La Farge worked to create a sense of specific time and place, probably the coast of Newport, Rhode Island, at the same time he succeeded in evoking a sense of wonder at the powers of the moon and the ever-changing illumination of the moving clouds.[1] Landscape studies such as this one and others (see cats. 44 and 46) contributed to La Farge's ability to render unusually naturalistic landscape backgrounds in his stained glass windows (see cat. 47).

La Farge painted in multiple layers of transparent and opaque washes; he applied stroke after stroke to suggest the dark green water and wash over wash in various shades of blue to create the sky. A sharply contrasting lemon yellow defines the moon and its reflections on the rippled surface of the water, and tinges the palest patch of clouds. To suggest both the shape and movement of the clouds, La Farge wiped away pigment, and also took advantage of the serendipitous pooling and drying of the white washes.

Contemporary taste for the sketch enabled the artist to exhibit and sell small studies such as this one, and although the precise exhibition and sale history of *Moonlit Seascape* is not known, it was acquired by Mrs. Arthur Cunningham Wheelwright (Susan Cabot) before her death in 1917. She passed it on to her daughter, Mary Cabot Wheelwright, who left it to the Museum after her death in 1958.

SWR

1. There is a watercolor study of the coast at Newport, Rhode Island, dated 1883 (W1883.21 in Henry A. La Farge and James L. Yarnall, *Catalogue Raisonné of the Works of John La Farge*, forthcoming). *Moonlit Seascape* was probably painted at the same place and time. La Farge also made oil sketches and pencil drawings of cloud movement at Newport: *Clouds over Sea; From Paradise Rocks* (oil on canvas, 1863, private collection), and *Study of Cloud Movement* (graphite on paper, 1865, Museum of Fine Arts, Boston).

John La Farge
44. *View Over Kyoto From Ya Ami*, 1886

Transparent and opaque watercolor over graphite on thick, slightly textured, cream wove paper
10½ x 14⁹⁄₁₆ in. (268 x 369 mm)
Inscribed in pen and black ink: Sept 17.86 (lower left); LF / Kioto / 86 (lower right); other notes in graphite
Gift of William Sturgis Bigelow. 21.1441

Although La Farge began collecting Japanese prints and oriental objects in the 1860s, and wrote about Japanese art in the 1870s, it was not until 1886 that he made his only visit to Japan in the company of Henry Adams. Both men wanted to escape: Adams from the memories of his wife's suicide and La Farge from the problems associated with the dissolution of his decorating firm. During their three months in Japan La Farge painted and bought photographs and an occasional object while Adams purchased what he referred to as "tons of porcelain, pottery and bronze."[1] They enjoyed their two weeks in Kyoto (September 8-22), staying at a hotel located above the city to the east, in the vicinity of Kiyomizu temple complex. From the hotel grounds they looked over the city lying in a valley surrounded by a ring of mountains.

This watercolor, when first exhibited at Doll & Richards in 1893, was described as: "View over Kiyoto From Ya Ami. Morning. Sunrise, 6 to 7 o'clock. Part of the city in the foreground in night fog." La Farge wrote about the circumstances of the painting of this and several similar water-colors:

Early on most mornings I have sat out on our wide veranda and drawn or painted from the great panorama before me – the distant mountains making a great wall lighted up clearly, with patches of burn-

ing yellow and white and green, against the western sky. The city lies in fog, sometimes cool and gray; sometimes golden and smoky. The tops of pagodas and heavy roofs of temples lift out of this sea, and through it shine innumerable little white spots of the plastered sides of houses . . . near us, trees and houses and temples drop out occasionally from the great violet shadows cast by the mountain behind us.[2]

Painted on the spot, this watercolor displays the freshness and immediacy not always present in the Japanese subjects La Farge executed later with the aid of photographs. The artist captured a moment in time, as the Impressionists sought to do; the pastel colors of his palette echo those of that movement, which he appreciated. He handled the washes with breadth and rapidity, using pale luminous colors to suggest the sky, the mountains, and the mist that hangs over the low-lying city. He employed richer tones of blue and green for the verdant foreground, where smaller brushwork effectively implies the shapes of trees and rooftops. The artist's intention to convey delicacy and refinement is supported by the words, "pinkish as silk," among his marginal notes.

The watercolor was purchased from Doll & Richards in 1893 by William Sturgis Bigelow (1850-1926), a Boston collector – primarily of Japanese art – and a major benefactor of the Museum of Fine Arts. Bigelow lived in Japan from 1882 to 1889 and spent time with La Farge and Adams during their stay. *View Over Kyoto From Ya Ami* is one of twelve La Farge watercolors that Bigelow presented to the Museum in the 1920s.

SWR

1. Quoted in James L. Yarnall, "John La Farge and Henry Adams in Japan," *American Art Journal* 21 (no. 1, 1989), p. 62.

2. John La Farge, *An Artist's Letters from Japan* (London: T. Fisher Unwin, 1897), p. 231. The illustration on this page, *Kioto in Fog – Morning* is a wood engraving derived from the watercolor, dated September 10, in the Currier Gallery of Art, Manchester, New Hampshire. Henry A. La Farge and James L. Yarnall, *Catalogue Raisonné of the Works of John La Farge*, forthcoming, will include at least two other such views.

John La Farge

45. *Chiefs and Chiefesses Passing on Their Way to a Great Conference. Evening. Samoa.*, 1891

Transparent and opaque watercolor over graphite on thick, moderately textured, dark cream wove paper
11¾ x 14⅞ in. (300 x 379 mm)
Inscribed lower right in pen and black ink: Vaiala / Upolu. Samoa. / JLF February. 91
Bequest of E. Adelaide Sargent Mason in memory of Arthur Hewes Sargent. 1981.505

In 1890 La Farge set forth again with Henry Adams; their main objectives were the Polynesian islands of Samoa and Tahiti. Departing from San Francisco in August, they sailed around the world, stopping first in Hawaii, and afterwards in Fiji, Ceylon, and elsewhere, before returning via Europe to New York in November 1891.[1] They arrived in Samoa in early October 1890 where they stayed for nearly four months, based in the village of Vaiala near Apia on the island of Upolu, not far from where Robert Louis Stevenson and his wife lived. They were the guests of the great chief, housed in a spacious thatched native structure "just by the shore, here fringed with trees and palms, and only some six feet above the inland sea of the reef. . . . Blue sea outside; green inside."[2] In that peaceful place, with its gentle climate and "sweet light," La Farge and Adams were treated as honored guests and were invited to witness native ceremonies and dances.

Aware of the opportunities Samoa offered him to improve his ability to draw the human figure, La Farge made many watercolors of Samoan men and women at work and play, in ritual and casual encounters. He had heard that in Tahiti, the next stop, the inhabitants assumed European dress, "And that is why I am lingering here, as I see for the first time, and probably for the last, a rustic and Boeotian antiquity, and if I live to paint subjects of the 'nude,' and 'drapery,' I shall know how they look in reality."[3] This watercolor may have been one of La Farge's last Samoan efforts, and was probably completed on board ship between his departure from Samoa on January 28 and his arrival in Tahiti on February 3.

Chiefs and Chiefesses Passing on Their Way to a Great Conference represents a procession of men and women, backlit against a view of trees and ocean, who stride purposefully toward their goal. Their rhythmic disposition on the page recalls that of an ancient Greek frieze. In his writings La Farge idealized the physiques of the Samoans and made frequent references to parallels with Greek sculpture.

As I write in our Samoan house . . . I see passing against the background of sea, figures which at a little distance and in shifting light are nearer to the little terra cottas that you like than anything one could find elsewhere. Young men naked to the waist, with large draperies folded like the Greek orator's mantle, garlanded, with flowers in their hair, pass and repass.[4]

He also noted:

There is nothing nearer to the drapery of the Greek statue than the Samoan wrap of cloth or of tappa, which is merely a long rectangle wrapped about the body, either as high as the chest, like the cloak of the Greek orator, or merely around the waist and thighs, always carefully arranged in special sets of folds which designate both the sex and the social position of the wearer; with this the wreaths and flower and leaf girdles and the anointed body, which belong to our vague conception of the Greek and Roman past.[5]

In this watercolor the man at the center wears the bulky native bark cloth (*tapa*), and the two figures at the left have applied coral lime to their hair, which appears stiff and yellow. One of the most successfully drawn figures is the woman at the right, her legs visible beneath a transparent white fabric. La Farge recorded his first impressions of Samoan women: "Then entered another . . . with the same splendid walk and swing, the same beauty of the setting of the head on the neck. These people had cultivated art in movement and personal gesture, because they had no other plastic expression."[6] La Farge generalized the faces of these men and women. He wrote, "Fine too, as some of the heads were, they were only relatively important, as with the Greek statues that we have, and that we know quite well and intimately, even though their heads be missing. The whole body has had an external meaning, has been used as ours is no longer, to express a feeling or to maintain a reserve which we only look for in a face."[7]

Exhibited by Doll & Richards in 1898, the watercolor was purchased the following year by a Bostonian, Arthur Hewes Sargent. It remained in the hands of his daughter Adelaide, later Mrs. Charles E. Mason, who left it to the Museum in 1981. *Chiefs and Chiefesses Passing* has not been previously exhibited or published.

SWR

1. For an excellent reconstruction of the trip and the art it inspired see James L. Yarnall, "John La Farge and Henry Adams in the South Seas," *American Art Journal* 20 (no. 1, 1988), pp. 51-109.

2. John La Farge, *Reminiscences of the South Seas* (Garden City, New York: Doubleday, Page & Co., 1916), p. 97.

3. Ibid., pp. 272-273.

4. Ibid., p. 273.

5. Ibid., p. 112.

6. Ibid., pp. 71-72.

7. Ibid., p. 177.

John La Farge
46. *View in Ceylon, near Dambulla, Looking Down Over Rice-Fields*, 1891
Transparent and opaque watercolor on moderately thick, smooth, dark cream wove paper (possibly imitation Japanese vellum)
16 15/16 x 13 3/8 in. (430 x 342 mm)
Inscribed lower right: LF.91. (in black wash); near Dambulla Ceylon (in graphite); and other notes in graphite
Gift of William Sturgis Bigelow. 26.784

This breathtaking landscape is the largest and most important watercolor La Farge painted on the lush tropical island of Ceylon, where he spent two weeks with Henry Adams on their return voyage. They visited sites of ancient culture, including caves filled with Buddhist sculptures at Dambulla. In a letter Adams recorded the execution of this watercolor on September 14, 1891.[1]

A plain dotted with flooded rice paddies is framed by a pair of cliffs and screened by exotic trees. In the distance moisture-laden clouds settle over the hills. La Farge imbued the landscape forms with a sinuous grace that contributes to the decorative aspect of the image. The dominant colors are jewel-like blues and greens interspersed with white, but red plays an important role, for example, in the pale washes of the sky and clouds, and in the more densely painted cliffs and rocks. La Farge brushed one color over another, often in multiple layers. The illuminated face of the cliff at the left openly shows its variegated hues. The cliff at the right, in deep shadow, reveals its sequences of washes only in the margin, where shades of gold, green, blue, and purple may be seen separately. La Farge's ability to delight the eye is further displayed in the piquant contrast between the bright white cloud that rises behind this cliff and the deep green silhouetted shrubs growing on the summit.

The forms of the tall rounded cliffs, the trees, and the hovering clouds are reminiscent of Chinese and Japanese paintings. Further emphasizing the orientalizing character of the watercolor is the paper, which imitates Japanese vellum. The soft fibers and silken surface were particularly receptive to the colored washes, and to the artist's slightest touch. When he wiped paint from the sky at the upper left, the fibers rolled up into little balls, creating a slightly pebbly texture.

In Samoa, La Farge painted the human figure (see cat. 45), but in Tahiti he shifted his attention to landscape. What Adams wrote about the Tahitian watercolors applies equally well to this view of Ceylon. "He has a wonderful faculty for getting light into his color. . . . He splashes in deep purples on deep greens till the paper is soaked with a shapeless daub, yet the next day, with a few touches, it comes out a brilliant mass of color and light. Of course, it is not an exact rendering of actual things he paints, though often it is near enough to surprise me by its faithfulness; but whether exact or not, it always suggests the emotion of the moment."[2]

SWR

1. James L. Yarnall, "John La Farge and Henry Adams in the South Seas," *American Art Journal* 20 (no. 1, 1988), p. 97 and note 203.

2. Ibid., p. 78.

Winslow Homer

Born Boston, Massachusetts, 1836;
died Prout's Neck, Scarborough, Maine, 1910

John La Farge

47. *Christ and the Pilgrims*, about 1896

Transparent and opaque watercolor over graphite on thick, cream wove paper

14½ x 10½ in. (368 x 266 mm)

Inscribed upper center in graphite: Buffalo? (and other notes)

Special Picture Fund. 12.348

In 1896 the children of William and Martha Allen Means commissioned La Farge to design a memorial window to their parents, for Mount Vernon Church, Boston.[1] Restating a theme he had previously used for two windows,[2] he chose as his subject the twenty-third psalm, in which the Shepherd leads his followers to eternal life: "Yea, though I walk through the valley of the shadow of death, thou art with me; thy rod and thy staff they comfort me."

In designing his stained glass windows La Farge drew upon his work in other media. Here, the monumental figures demonstrate a greater competence than was present in the Samoan subjects of 1891 (see cat. 45) and reflect his more recent experiences with such mural decorations as *Athens* (1893-98, Walker Art Building, Bowdoin College, Brunswick, Maine). La Farge also drew upon his watercolor landscapes; though simplified in form and color, the trees and towering cliff in the background of this window recall *View in Ceylon* (cat. 46).

This watercolor is a fully developed design that could be shown to the patron for approval, and could also serve as a reference during the manufacture of the window. Because La Farge supervised every stage of the production, he was able to use these small watercolors as guides for the color and type of glass. He used "coded meanings in the watercolor washes that corresponded to specific choices of glass."[3] In this watercolor, for example, the rose and mauve tones of the woman's garments suggest a range of opalescent glass, while the changeable blue-green and pink of Christ's cloak suggests iridescent glass. Henry Adams's comments on La Farge's attempts to capture effects of light in Tahiti point out the close relationship between the artist's watercolors and glass: "Every evening, La Farge and I . . . wait for the

after-glow, which lasts about half an hour, and gives a succession of lights that defy imitation or description. La Farge is trying to suggest them in water-color . . . but glass is the only possible medium for such tones, and even glass could not render all."[4]

SWR

1. The church, on Beacon Hill, was converted to condominiums in 1975, and the window is now installed at the James Parker Masonic Home, Charlton, Massachusetts. Another window in a similar format, dedicated to James Ayer (1898), is now in the Worcester Art Museum; see *John La Farge* (Pittsburgh: The Carnegie Museum of Art, 1987), pl. 159.

2. Channing Memorial Church, Newport (1880-82) and Trinity Church, Buffalo (1886), as noted in Henry A. La Farge and James L. Yarnall, *Catalogue Raisonné of the Works of John La Farge,* forthcoming. The design for the Means window remained in the artist's estate, and his marginal note *Buffalo?* indicates his uncertainty as to which window this was.

3. Henry A. La Farge in *John La Farge* (Pittsburgh: The Carnegie Museum of Art, 1987) p. 159, note 79.

4. Adams to Elizabeth Cameron, February-March, 1891, quoted in James L. Yarnall, "John La Farge and Henry Adams in the South Seas," *American Art Journal* 20 (no. 1, 1988), p. 78.

Winslow Homer revolutionized the art of watercolor painting in America. Early in his career as an illustrator, he learned to distill an image into a few telling forms rendered in bold patches of light and dark; his intimate knowledge of tropical seas and northern streams led him to use pure transparent colors, which he employed with unequaled mastery to evoke the everchanging waters of these locales. Above all, he recognized watercolor's exceptional capacity to be simultaneously descriptive and expressive. The watercolors from his mature years retain their impressive power today.

Homer learned to use watercolor from his mother, Henrietta Benson Homer, an accomplished amateur. In his late teens he was apprenticed to J.H. Bufford & Sons, a Boston lithographic firm. He became a freelance illustrator in 1857 and two years later moved to New York. He continued working as an illustrator until 1874, becoming particularly well known for the work that appeared in *Harper's Weekly* both during and after the Civil War. Homer also pursued a career in painting, first exhibiting in 1863 at the National Academy of Design, where he was elected an associate in 1864 and the following year an academician. In 1867 Homer spent ten months in France, where he painted oils in Paris and in the countryside, sending back sketches to *Harper's.* His oil painting, *Prisoners from the Front* (1866, Metropolitan Museum of Art, New York) was displayed at the 1867 Exposition Universelle in Paris and was one of only a handful of American works singled out for special mention. Throughout the 1870s Homer maintained a studio in New York, where he socialized with a number of fellow artists including his life-long friend John La Farge (see cats. 42-47), and exhibited regularly at the National Academy.

His first intensive campaign in watercolor took place during the summer of 1873 at Gloucester, Massachusetts, and until 1880 he painted watercolors only when he left New York City in the summertime. These watercolors – many of which bore close stylistic ties to his popular paintings and illustrations of children – were well received at the American Watercolor Society exhibitions. Homer also organized auctions of his watercolors in Boston, Chicago, and New York between 1878 and 1880. Late in 1880 the Boston dealers Doll & Richards gave Homer his first one-man show of watercolors, all painted at Gloucester that summer.

Homer spent most of 1881-82 in England, mainly at Cullercoats, a fishing village and artists' colony near Tynemouth on the Northumberland coast, where he worked almost exclusively in watercolor. His subjects were the fishermen and their families, and their daily routines in fair weather and foul. These watercolors were larger and had greater monumentality than his previous work in the medium. He sent back nearly forty of them to Boston, where the dealer J. Eastman Chase, formerly of Doll & Richards, gave him a one-man exhibition in February 1882. The next year, however, Homer returned to Doll & Richards, who gave him one-man shows in 1883, 1884, and 1886.

In 1884 Homer moved to Maine, where he maintained his studio and residence at Prout's Neck for the rest of his life. His oils dealt more and more with the sea, and he was considered America's finest marine painter. His watercolors, however, reflected sites he favored for fly fishing. Summers and autumns might find him in the Adirondacks or Quebec; he often spent winters in the Bahamas, Bermuda, or Florida, painting the landscape and waters of these areas, their fishermen, hunting guides, and sponge divers. Following the success of his Adirondack subjects, which sold out almost immediately in New York in 1890, his watercolors were much in demand and he sent them a few at a time to his dealers in New York (first Reichard's and later Knoedler's) and to Doll & Richards in Boston. Homer was also represented by dealers in Chicago, where he won a gold medal at the International Exposition of 1893, one of many honors he would receive in his lifetime.

Winslow Homer
48. *Boy and Girl on a Hillside*, 1878
Watercolor over graphite on thick, rough-textured, cream wove paper
8¹⁵⁄₁₆ x 11⁵⁄₁₆ in. (225 x 288 mm)
Signed and dated lower right in black wash:
HOMER 1878
Bequest of the estate of Katherine Dexter McCormick.
68.568

Homer spent much of the summer of 1878 at Houghton Farm in Mountainville, New York (not far from West Point). The farm belonged to Lawson Valentine, a family friend, who owned a successful varnish manufacturing firm for which Homer's brother Charles was the chief chemist. Both of these men helped support Homer by buying his work in the 1870s, and a number of Houghton Farm subjects were originally owned by Valentine.[1]

Homer made many watercolors and drawings that summer depicting rural children chatting over a fence, picking fruit, leaning against a tree, or lying in the grass, lazily enjoying their pastoral surroundings. These works develop themes introduced earlier in the decade in his popular book and magazine illustrations, and in such paintings as *Snap the Whip* (1872, Butler Art Institute, Youngstown, Ohio) and *Breezing Up* (1876, National Gallery of Art, Washington, D.C.). They follow the watercolor studies of children at play painted at Gloucester, Massachusetts, in 1873, and in subsequent summers, many of which served as the basis of wood-engraved illustrations. These display clearly demarcated tonal areas, and rely heavily on the use of opaque white for highlights. Watercolors such as *Boy and Girl on a Hillside* demonstrate Homer's movement away from his illustrative style and his increasing concern with painting the figure in the more complex lighting of an atmospheric landscape. They reveal Homer's commitment to painting not only *from* nature, but *in* nature. "This is the moment when Homer spoke so adamantly about *plein air* method."[2]

Using quiet, mixed, relatively opaque colors, Homer varied the handling of the paints. He used broad washes for the hillside, enlivening the foreground with dabs of green paint and fine lines in

graphite or opaque white to suggest vegetation. He built up the foliage of the large tree with overlying strokes of different intensities. The two figures, well defined by graphite underdrawing, were subtly painted; Homer lifted color to lighten and model the girl's pink dress. The heavily textured paper allowed minute indentations of untouched white paper to show through some washes. These pinpoints of white contribute to the look of mown stubble in the field and of the pale sky behind the leaves of the distant trees, while the white paper provides a reflective base for this evocation of hazy, shadowless light.

In another watercolor, *On the Hill* (1878, collection of Mr. and Mrs. Alistair Bradley Martin), Homer depicted a boy and girl on the same grassy hill, reclining with their backs to the viewer. In both cases, the relationship between the figures, implied but not stated, lends an anecdotal aspect to the picture.[3] Here, the boy is absorbed into the hillside, while the girl, standing erect and watchful, gazes into the distance. Her small figure presages the heroic fisherwomen of Homer's mature works.

SWR

1. At least twenty-four watercolors, as well as seven oils and eight drawings, belonged to Lawson Valentine. See John Wilmerding and Linda Ayres, *Homer in the 1870s, Selections from the Valentine-Pulsifer Collection* (Princeton, New Jersey: The Art Museum, Princeton University, 1990), appendix, p. 43, and the essays in that catalogue.

2. Kathleen Adair Foster, "Makers of the American Watercolor Movement: 1860-1890" (Ph.D. diss., Yale University, 1982), p. 83.

3. In the mid-seventies Homer was learning to distinguish between the awkwardness of an adolescent girl and the grace of a young woman. In these individual figure studies – less closely tied to illustration – he often used thinner washes and handled them delicately.

Winslow Homer

49. *Driving Cows to Pasture*, 1879

Watercolor over graphite on thick, slightly textured,
cream wove paper
8⁹⁄₁₆ x 13⅝ in. (217 x 345 mm)
Signed and dated lower left in black wash: HOMER '79
Bequest of the estate of Katherine Dexter
McCormick. 68.569

Homer spent part of 1879 in rural West
Townsend, Massachusetts, not far from the New
Hampshire border. He stayed with his brother,
Charles, and sister-in-law, Martha (Mattie)
French. Best known of his work from this summer
are the numerous drawings of children, including
sunbonneted girls swinging or going berrying,
typically drawn with graphite and heightened
with white on gray paper. A few watercolors of
farm men and boys are also dated 1879, but work
in this medium is scarcer than it was in 1878.

Driving Cows to Pasture differs from the posed
subjects of the previous summer at Houghton
Farm.[1] Homer's use of fluid, uninterrupted washes on a smooth surfaced paper marks an advance
over the drier and more controlled technique of
works from 1878 such as *Boy and Girl on a Hillside* (cat. 48). Here, the distant view and the casually dabbed red-brown cows in the middleground
are broadly painted, while the treatment of the
foreground is quite explicit: Homer scraped and
lifted pigment to create pale rocks and delicate
ferns. The clouded sky and quiet hues give a serious tone to this little watercolor. In spite of its
size, *Driving Cows to Pasture*, with its treatment of
man at work in his environment, contains the
seeds of the large and powerful Adirondack
images of a decade later, such as *Woodsman and
Fallen Tree* (fig. 1).

This is one of eight watercolors, including *Boy
and Girl on a Hillside*, purchased in Chicago by
Mrs. Wirt Dexter from an auction Homer held
there in 1879.[2] Her daughter, Katherine Dexter
McCormick (Mrs. Stanley), who maintained resi-
dences in both Chicago and Boston, left the eight
watercolors to the Museum.

SWR

Fig. 1. *Woodsman and Fallen Tree*, 1891. Watercolor. Museum
of Fine Arts, Boston. Bequest of William Sturgis Bigelow.

1. Other 1879 watercolors include *Harrowing* (private
collection) and *Boy and Fallen Tree* (Museum of Fine
Arts, Boston).

2. The uncatalogued exhibition and auction was held
from December 7 through 10 at a gallery, as yet
unidentified, on Wabash Avenue. This information was
kindly provided by Abigail Booth Gerdts from the manuscript, catalogue raisonné of the works of Winslow
Homer by Lloyd Goodrich, courtesy of the City University of New York, Lloyd Goodrich and Edith Havens
Goodrich, Whitney Museum of American Art Record
of the Works of Winslow Homer.

Winslow Homer

50. *Children Playing under a Gloucester Wharf*,
1880

Watercolor over graphite on thick, rough-textured,
cream wove paper
8⁴⁄₁₆ x 13½ in. (205 x 342 mm)
Signed and dated lower right in black wash: HOMER
1880; on verso in graphite (in Homer's hand): 41. (outlined); No 19 [?] - A / 13¾ x 8½ / mat to come close
to / edge not cove at all
Hayden Collection. Charles Henry Hayden Fund.
21.2554

Homer spent the summer of 1880 in Gloucester,
Massachusetts, living in isolation at an island
lighthouse in the center of the harbor.[1] He painted many watercolors, including some extraordinarily brilliant sunsets with schooners in the
harbor, but by and large he kept to the familiar
subject of children at play. During this period
Homer's palette lightened and brightened, his
brushwork loosened, and his ability to convey
lighting and atmospheric conditions grew
stronger.

Children Playing under a Gloucester Wharf
depicts four mischievous youngsters who have
waded into the water to play beside a boat. The
bold composition precludes any suggestion of
sentimentality. The rectilinear pilings and deck, as
well as a distant band of land and boats, frame the
scene. Light falling from the left casts slanted
shadows on the pilings and water, further subdi-
viding the composition into well-defined geometric forms. Homer chose paper with a rough
surface that left tiny specks of white paper bare
of pigment, thus animating the image with
sparkling, impressionistic light.

The sketchy, somewhat unfinished appearance
of *Children Playing under a Gloucester Wharf* may
have prevented its immediate sale, and it remained
in Homer's possession.[2] Around 1896 he gave it
to another accomplished watercolorist, Ross
Turner (see cat. 71), when that artist paid a visit
to the Prout's Neck studio. Some twenty-five years
later the Museum purchased the watercolor from
Turner's son.

SWR

1. For more on Homer's stay in Gloucester see D. Scott Atkinson in *Winslow Homer in Gloucester* (Chicago: Terra Museum of American Art, 1990).

2. When the 1880 Gloucester watercolors were exhibited at the Century Association in New York in November of that year, they received critical attention, but sales were modest. Sales were better at Doll & Richards in Boston in December, and at the American Watercolor Society exhibition in New York early in 1881. See Helen Cooper, *Winslow Homer Watercolors* (New Haven: Yale University Press, 1986), p. 75.

Winslow Homer

51. *Girls on a Cliff*, 1881
Opaque and transparent watercolor over graphite on very thick, rough-textured, cream wove paper
12⅝ x 19⅛ in. (322 x 485 mm)
Signed and dated lower left in gray wash: Winslow Homer / 1881
On verso in pen and brown ink (probably Homer's hand): 19 (crossed out)
Bequest of David P. Kimball in memory of his wife, Clara Bertram Kimball. 23.522

52. *Fisherman's Family (The Lookout)*, 1881
Watercolor over graphite on thick, moderately textured, cream wove paper
13½ x 19¾ in. (342 x 492 mm)
Signed and dated lower left in brown wash: Winslow Homer 1881
On verso in pen and brown ink (probably Homer's hand): 13
Bequest of John T. Spaulding. 48.726

In a move that would shape his future as a marine painter and watercolorist, Homer sailed for England in March 1881. He settled for the summer at Cullercoats, a small fishing community and artists' colony on the Northumberland coast not far from Tynemouth. Apparently he had planned to stay only until the fall, but he changed his mind and remained for another year, returning to New York in November 1882. These two watercolors were painted during his first summer in Cullercoats.[1]

In *Girls on a Cliff* two young women, dressed in the local costume of full skirt and shawl, pick yellow flowers growing on a cliff high above the sea. The clear light, bright blue sky, and billowing white clouds suggest a fine, breezy summer day. The simple diagonal division of the composition and the peacefulness of the scene continue Homer's style of the late seventies, as seen in *Boy and Girl on a Hillside* (cat. 48). So does his use of opaque pigments, particularly noticeable here in the quantities of white that suggest the clouds of varying densities. However, the larger size of the picture indicates that Homer felt capable of making a more ambitious statement. At the same time, his technique remained rather conventional. He was still dependent on a fairly complete preparatory drawing, and let traces of it remain visible, defining contours of the cliff, blades of grass, and details of clothing. He enlivened the paths and vegetation with the traditional English techniques of blotting, lifting, and scraping.

Fisherman's Family presents a more striking composition, with its abruptly cropped cliff, large open space, and closely knit figures. Moreover, its content differs: Homer is beginning to move away from his anecdotal, Victorian approach to subject matter. His figures are quietly heroic, as they await the return of male family members; however, the sky is clear, and there is no air of anxiety or danger. Their difficult lives are not sentimentalized; rather, they evoke universal feelings of admiration and understanding. These figures parallel the peasants depicted in contemporary and very popular European paintings by such artists as J.-F. Millet, Jules Breton, and Josef Israels.

In working up this watercolor, Homer made a number of adjustments to the figure group. He painted the little girl's face over a scraped out area, and added a small child in dark clothing to close the gap between the two seated figures. In contrast to these deliberate revisions, Homer handled the setting with great spontaneity. He allowed loosely applied washes to suggest the billowing column of smoke that arises from the steam-driven boat on the horizon, and defined its hull with a single evocative stroke of red. To create the face of the cliff, he overlaid wet washes of orange and gray, and freely dabbed and blotted the pigments to suggest the seams and textures of the stone.

Homer appears to have been satisfied with his work from the first summer at Cullercoats, for he was ready to show a watercolor at the August 1881 exhibition of the Newcastle Art Association.[2] He also took advantage of the increasing appreciation of his work at home and sent nearly forty watercolors to the Boston dealer J. Eastman Chase for a one-man exhibition held in February 1882.[3] *Girls on a Cliff* may well have been in the group shown by Chase; it was subsequently purchased by Mr. and Mrs. David P. Kimball of Boston, who also collected landscapes by Monet.

SWR

1. For more on Homer at Cullercoats see Helen Cooper, *Winslow Homer Watercolors* (New Haven: Yale University Press, 1986) pp. 92-123; and William H. Gerdts, "Winslow Homer in Cullercoats," *Yale University Art Gallery Bulletin* 36 (spring 1977), pp. 18-35.

2. Entitled simply *Cullercoats;* Cooper, *Winslow Homer Watercolors*, pp. 87-88.

3. Chase, who only represented Homer during his English stay, remained a close friend and correspondant for life. The numbers "19" and "13" written on the backs of these watercolors, apparently in Homer's hand, could relate to a list sent to Chase.

Winslow Homer
53. *Girl with Red Stockings (The Wreck)*, 1882
Watercolor over graphite on very thick, slightly textured, cream wove paper
13⅜ x 19½ in. (342 x 495 mm)
Signed and dated lower right in brown wash:
HOMER / 1882
On verso in graphite (in Homer's hand): Girl with Red Stockings; 48. (outlined)
Bequest of John T. Spaulding. 48.727

A contemporary account of an incident at Cullercoats could well have been written about Homer's watercolor: "As the storm begins to gather, the very air seems charged with possibilities of tragic disaster. The women, gathering bait among the rocks, look up with startled faces as the sky darkens, and the sharp blasts from the northeast, forerunners of the tempest, whistle past."[1] Also called *The Wreck*, this watercolor depicts a young fisherwoman who steadies her baskets as she pauses to gaze at a boat foundering on the rocks. In contrast to the sunny scenes in the previous watercolors (cats. 51, 52), *Girl with Red Stockings* evokes Homer's own experiences of fall and winter storms on the English coast. He sketched a shipwreck and dramatic rescue at sea in October 1881 and painted it in his largest watercolor to date, *The Wreck of the Iron Crown* (1881, collection of Carlton Mitchell).[2] Other watercolors derive from this episode, including *Watching the Tempest* (1881, Fogg Art Museum, Harvard University Art Museums, Cambridge, Massachusetts), which depicts lifeboats and crews setting out for the rescue, and *Perils of the Sea* (1881, Sterling and Francine Clark Art Institute, Williamstown, Massachusetts), in which women anxiously wait for news. Less specifically associated with the incident, but probably affected by it, is a group of watercolors, which includes *Girl with Red Stockings*, that represents one or more fisherwomen who stand on a rocky shore and look out to sea under stormy skies. The motif of a boat in distress, which occurs in a number of these watercolors, is introduced with particular subtlety here: the boat is pushed to the far left of the picture, its gray silhouette barely distinguishable from the color of the sea and sky.

Fig. 1. *Spoondrift*, undated. Graphite on paper. Cooper-Hewitt National Museum of Design, Smithsonian Institution, New York. Photograph: John Parnell.

Homer based many of these watercolors — as if they were oil paintings — on carefully prepared charcoal studies. *After the Storm* (undated, The Art Museum, Princeton University, Princeton, New Jersey) is such a drawing, depicting the figure and central portion of *Girl with Red Stockings*. The watercolor itself, on the other hand, reveals relatively little graphite underdrawing. Working with fairly transparent, somber colors, Homer deliberately built up the image. He applied multiple washes to the sky to suggest the churning motion of the storm clouds, and made them darker in value to contrast to the pale blue heaving sea. Subsequently, by scraping away the dark gray sky to reveal the white of the paper, he created the foaming spray that crashes over the wrecked ship and higher ocean waves. In the foreground he worked both negatively and positively, lifting pigment to lighten some parts of the rocks and painting dark accents on others. Homer's extensive manipulation of the paint — applying, blotting, and reapplying pigments — results in a smooth, rounded appearance in many of the forms. He paid close attention to the figure, defining her clothing and baskets with care, and deftly painting a stray lock of hair and the tip of her shawl to indicate the velocity of the wind.

The rust colored globules scattered along the rocky shore and floating on the water are Homer's shorthand representations of spindrift or spoondrift, the foamy spray that is driven by a violent wind along the surface of the sea. A graphite drawing labeled in his hand "Spoondrift" (fig. 1) reveals his bubble-like interpretation of the natural phenomenon in a setting of heaving waves, billowing surf, and rectangular rocks.

SWR

1. R. J. Charlton, "Cullercoats," *Magazine of Art* 9 (1886), p. 458, quoted in Helen Cooper, *Winslow Homer Watercolors* (New Haven: Yale University Press, 1986), p. 100, note 17.

2. Clearly, Homer considered it an important picture. After exhibiting it in a Newcastle art dealer's window, he sent it to J. Eastman Chase's gallery in Boston in February 1882, asking $250, a high price for his watercolors at the time. The watercolor was purchased by Edward W. Hooper of Boston, an avid Homer collector, who left it to his daughter, Mabel (Mrs. Bancel La Farge), in whose family it remained until the early 1940s.

Winslow Homer
54. *An Afterglow*, 1883

Watercolor over graphite on thick, moderately textured, cream wove paper, with partial watermark: J. WHATMAN
15 x 21½ in. (380 x 547 mm)
Signed and dated at left (on transom of boat) in black wash: HOMER 1883
On verso in pen and brown ink (probably in Homer's hand): No 21 (outlined)
Bequest of William P. Blake in memory of his mother, Mary M. J. Dehon Blake. 22.606

An Afterglow is one of about twenty watercolors of Cullercoats that Homer completed after his return from England. Like most of them, it is large in scale and deliberately executed, but it is unusually serene and devoid of anxiety. Homer depicts a quiet moment at the end of the day, when fisherfolk have a moment to chat while tending their boats and drying sails in the afterglow of the setting sun.[1] In its conversational aspects, *An Afterglow* looks back to such anecdotal paintings as *Breezing Up* (1876, National Gallery of Art, Washington, D.C.). However, in this watercolor, Homer treated the image with greater monumentality, giving the boats a heroic character. The two primary broad-beamed fishing boats are powerfully sculptured and arranged with a bold symmetry that leaves a void in the center of the composition. The boats are riding high; their full, rounded shapes create rhythms that echo throughout the image – in the sails, the billowing skirt of the woman at the right, and the fisherman in yellow oilskins at the left. The serenity and sobriety of *An Afterglow* mitigate the subject's potential for Victorian sentimentality.

The sheet shows evidence of major compositional changes. Most easily recognizable among these are the forms of the hulls and sails of the two main boats. Their bows were originally higher, and Homer scraped the darker pigments off the paper and repainted each sail in a different configuration. Especially in these areas, but also elsewhere on the sheet, there is evidence of wiping, lifting, blotting, scraping, and repainting. This process created granular textures characteristic of this period of Homer's watercolors, which are far

more studied and less directly observed than his later ones. Reflections in water – whether salt or fresh, still or moving – provided a continuing artistic challenge for Homer. Here they are varied in color and range from cool darks to warm bright hues.

Thomas Wigglesworth, an important Boston collector, purchased *An Afterglow* from Homer's Boston dealer, Doll & Richards, in December 1883. The watercolor passed through the hands of Henry S. Grew and was once again with Doll & Richards in February 1900, when William Payne Blake acquired it; he left it to the Museum in 1922.[2]

SWR

1. The boats are not under way, for their rudders and tillers are not in place. *Returning Fishing Boats* (1883, Fogg Art Museum, Harvard University Art Museums, Cambridge, Massachusetts) shows one of these boats under sail.

2. *An Afterglow* once lived up to its name better. Highly esteemed and frequently on view, both before and after its acquisition by the Museum, it bears evidence of overexposure to light. The sky and its reflection in the water no longer have their original color, which suggested the rosy purple hue visible just after sunset.

Winslow Homer
55. *Adirondack Lake*, 1889

Watercolor over graphite on moderately thick, slightly textured, cream wove paper
14 x 20 in. (355 x 508 mm)
Signed and dated lower right in black wash:
HOMER 1889
On verso in graphite: M E Homer[1]
William Wilkins Warren Fund. 23.215

Peace, solitude, and satisfaction pervade *Adirondack Lake*. These were the qualities that attracted Homer repeatedly to the wilderness region where he sketched, painted watercolors, and took part in his favorite sport, fly fishing. Beginning in 1889 Homer stayed frequently at the North Woods Club, a private association for wealthy but serious sportsmen. Not far from Minerva, New York, its lodge was located on Mink Pond, well populated with trout.[2] Homer painted nearly ninety watercolors of the Adirondacks between 1889 and 1892, depicting its forests, mountains, and waterways, and the local inhabitants – guides, woodsmen, hunters, and fishermen; these are among his finest works (see cats. 56-60).

As in nearly all of Homer's fishing subjects, in *Adirondack Lake* the vantage point is low, suggesting that the watercolor may have been painted from a boat. At what appears to be a cool early morning hour a lone man glides in a canoe over the shadowed surface of a lake; the taut arc of his fishing line and waiting net indicate a successful catch. At first the watercolor gives the impression of having been painted almost entirely in monochromatic, blue-black wash; however, touches of warm, bright hues invade the dark layers of pigment, adding richness and depth of color especially in the lushly painted screen of trees. The white paper plays an important role in the brightening sky and its reflection on the surface of the lake. Homer achieved these reflections by broadly scraping away pigment to reveal the paper. He scratched more precisely to define the slender wake of the canoe and the delicate silk filament of line. Although they are small in scale, the fisherman and boat are finely detailed, and provide a fo-

cal point of human activity that serves to emphasize the broader forms of the evocative landscape.

SWR

1. The inscription almost certainly refers to Homer's
sister-in-law, Martha (Mattie) E. French, Mrs. Charles
Savage Homer, Jr., who must have been a former owner.
Many of the watercolors Homer gave to his family
gradually appeared on the market. This one was purchased by the Museum of Fine Arts from Boston dealer
Frank Bayley in 1923.

2. Homer first visited the Adirondacks in 1870 and
1874, but by 1889 he had joined the North Woods Club
and became a frequent visitor. He usually came in the
late spring and summer months, but returned for a second stay in the autumns of 1889, 1891, and 1892. See
David Tatham, "Winslow Homer at the North Woods
Club," in *Winslow Homer, A Symposium*, Studies in the
History of Art 26 (Washington, D.C.: National Gallery
of Art, 1990), pp. 115-130. The club was located on the
site of the former Baker family farm, where Homer
boarded during his visits of the 1870s.

Winslow Homer
56. *Leaping Trout*, 1889
Watercolor over graphite on moderately thick, slightly
textured, dark cream wove paper
14 x 20 in. (355 x 507 mm)
Signed lower left (pigment scraped off): HOMER;
upper right (pigment lifted): W. H.
William Wilkins Warren Fund. 99.24

One of Homer's most exquisite and magical
watercolors, *Leaping Trout* presents an intriguing
visual dialogue between the lucidly rendered fish
and their mysterious surroundings. It is close in
mood to the imaginative *Mink Pond* (1891, Fogg
Art Museum, Harvard University Art Museums,
Cambridge, Massachusetts). *Leaping Trout* is not
dated and for many years was assigned to the year
1892. Recently, however, it has been identified as
the watercolor described in the press when it was
shown at Reichard's, Homer's New York dealer, in
February 1890.[1] Several other watercolors, more
straightforward in treatment and showing only a
single trout, are clearly dated 1889 (Museum of
Fine Arts, Boston, The Cleveland Museum of Art
and Portland [Maine] Museum of Art,).

Homer painted the trout in their natural colors,
predominantly silvery gray with iridescent spots,
against an indeterminate background composed of
layer after layer of wash, applied and wiped off
again and again. From beneath cool dark tonalities
emerge warm hues, suggesting the sun's heat at-
tacking the damp mists that rise from the water's
surface. By contrast, the color notes on the dark
water are transparent and cool – blue, purple, and
pink. These lustrous gemlike colors glow amid a
rhythmic arrangement of interwoven bands of
dense, almost black, pigments and an occasional
patch of scraped white paper. The reflections and
the lily pads demonstrate not only Homer's inventive use of color, but also how little brilliance is
necessary to create a coloristically effective
image.[2]

Leaping Trout parallels contemporary work by
Homer's close friend John La Farge, who used
similar overlays of cool and warm colored washes
in *View of Dambulla, Ceylon* (cat. 46). Moreover,
the fragments of brilliant jewel-toned colors isolated by black boundaries find a parallel in La
Farge's stained glass. In its attention to formal design and surface pattern, and even its subject matter, *Leaping Trout* – like La Farge's windows that
depict carp – brings to mind Japanese prints.[3]

The first Homer watercolor to enter the collection of the Museum of Fine Arts, *Leaping Trout*
was bought at the end of a decade in which the
Museum made major acquisitions of Japanese art.
Originally the property of Homer's greatest patron (and sometime dealer), Thomas B. Clarke of
New York, the watercolor was purchased directly
from his auction sale in 1899, and must have
pleased connoisseurs and sportsmen alike.

SWR

1. In *The Critic*, February 22, 1890, it was described as
"a brace of speckled trout leaping out of the dark waters
of a pool in which wave pink lily pads." Information
kindly provided by Helen Cooper in a letter of December 13, 1984, to the Department of Prints, Drawings,
and Photographs, Museum of Fine Arts, Boston.

2. To achieve the iridescent spots on the fish, Homer
painted a dot of pink wash, blotted it, painted a dot of
blue wash, blotted that, and finally added a speck of vermilion. He created the extraordinary purple reflection at
the lower right by laying a transparent blue wash over a
red one.

3. For example, Hokusai's woodcut *Carp* (1813); see
Helen Cooper, *Winslow Homer Watercolors* (New Haven:
Yale University Press, 1986) fig. 159.

Winslow Homer

57. *The Blue Boat*, 1892

Watercolor over graphite on very thick, slightly textured, off-white wove paper
15⅛ x 21½ in. (386 x 546 mm)
Signed, dated, and inscribed lower left in pen and brown ink: Winslow Homer N. A. 1892 / This will do the business
On verso in pen and brown ink (Homer's hand): K 15 x 21; in graphite (possibly Homer's Hand): On the Trail
Bigelow Collection. Bequest of William Sturgis Bigelow. 26.764

In *The Blue Boat* Homer reinterprets the subject and composition of *Trapping in the Adirondacks*, a wood-engraved illustration he had designed in 1874 (fig. 1). In contrast to that close-up image, in which the trappers pull a mink from the pond, the canoers in this watercolor occupy a spacious landscape and are just starting out on a hunting adventure (suggested by the rifle butt glimpsed between them).

Though less explicit than the watercolors that depict deer-hunting, *The Blue Boat* shows the same pair of guides – one old, the other young – who appear in many of those scenes.[1] Homer's Adirondack models were almost certainly guides employed by the North Woods Club: bearded Rufus Wallace and youthful Michael Flynn.[2] In order to complete his watercolors at Prout's Neck, Homer hired his Maine neighbors, John Gatchell and his son Wiley, to pose for him.[3] In the generalized features of the men in *The Blue Boat*, Homer portrays types, not individuals. Even a more specific face, such as that of *The Adirondack Guide* (cat. 60), cannot be associated with a single personality. Rather, the older guides stand for teachers of wilderness lore, and the younger men their students.

Homer was extremely confident in the execution of *The Blue Boat*. He prepared the composition with a light sketch in graphite, and made no major changes after he began to paint. (The little scraping and reworking he did was mainly to create reflections in the water around the canoe.) He applied rust colored wash over the green middleground, allowing its granularity to suggest dense and complex vegetation without any descriptive brushstrokes. He produced reflections on the

Fig. 1. *Trapping in the Adirondacks*, 1874. Wood engraving. Museum of Fine Arts, Boston. Gift of W.G. Russell Allen.

water, which include an extraordinary stroke of Prussian blue painted across the foreground from left to right. At first the paint was dense and wet, while at the end the drying brush skimmed across the paper; Homer blotted some pigment from the beginning of this stroke. The reflection he created is darker where the boat blocks the light and tails off into the brightness of the water's surface. This single brushstroke demonstrates Homer's mastery of watercolor, and his ability to paint both descriptively and expressively, yet without pretense or virtuosity. His satisfaction is recorded in the words he penned on the sheet, "This will do the business."[4]

The Blue Boat is one of Homer's greatest watercolors, owing to its audacious execution and its exceptional condition, which permits us to see today the clear and luminous colors as they were when Homer painted them. But its success lies deeper, not only in its virile subject matter and strength of composition, but in its mood and invitation to escape to the unspoiled wilderness. The serenity of *The Blue Boat* and its meditational qualities may have appealed to its Bostonian owner, William Sturgis Bigelow, who was a major collector of Japanese and Chinese art, and a practicing Buddhist.

SWR

1. See Helen Cooper, *Winslow Homer Watercolors* (New Haven: Yale University Press, 1986), pp. 174ff.

2. See David Tatham, "Trapper, Hunter, and Woodsman: Winslow Homer's Adirondack Figures," *American Art Journal* 22 (no. 4, 1990), pp. 40-67, which includes photographs of Wallace and Flynn.

3. See Philip Beam, *Winslow Homer at Prout's Neck* (Boston: Little, Brown and Company, 1966), pp. 102-103, which includes a photograph of John Gatchell.

4. The inscription on the verso of the sheet, "On the Trail," is a logical title, but one that is used for another watercolor depicting a hunter and dogs in the forest (1892, National Gallery of Art, Washington, D.C.).

Winslow Homer

58. *Old Settlers*, 1892

Watercolor over graphite on very thick, moderately textured, dark cream wove paper
21½ x 15⅛ in. (547 x 386 mm)
Inscribed on verso in pen and brown ink (Homer's hand): P — 15 x 21
Bequest of Nathaniel T. Kidder. 38.1412

The growing lumber industry in the Adirondack wilderness was causing its natural resources to diminish. This was a subject discussed widely at the time *Old Settlers* was painted.[1] In it, Homer conveys the awe and respect he felt for the gigantic old pines of the forests (see also cat. 5). Two years later he would express his feelings more poignantly in *Old Friends* (1894, Worcester [Massachusetts] Art Museum), depicting an aged woodsman and a scarred giant of a tree. Here, with a bit of humor, Homer designates the old settlers as a pair of black bears. Although they blend into the landscape (as did the cows in *Driving Cows to Pasture*, cat. 49), their presence not only animates the image, but provides the sense of scale needed to appreciate the height of the trees.[2]

This watercolor demonstrates particularly well Homer's ingenuity in using the subtractive method. He began by painting the background mountains and trees in loose, wet washes, similar to those he used in *The Blue Boat* (cat. 57). He then reduced the density of some pigments, scraping the clouds and foliage to suggest forms dissolving in light. In the lower left he scraped a light-reflecting lake at the base of the mountain, and lifted pigment to create a pale naked branch whose abstract forms seem out of a Japanese print.

Old Settlers holds great appeal in its straightforward depiction of the wilderness. Bostonian Nathaniel T. Kidder purchased it the year after its creation and retained it for the remaining forty-five years of his life.

SWR

1. See Helen Cooper, *Winslow Homer Watercolors* (New Haven: Yale University Press, 1986), pp. 187 ff.

2. Homer painted the larger bear on a roughened patch of paper that he had scraped vigorously, which gave the animal the appearance of a shaggy coat.

Winslow Homer

59. *The Fallen Deer*, 1892

Watercolor over graphite on moderately thick, rough-textured, dark cream wove paper
13¾ x 19¾ in. (352 x 503 mm)
Signed and dated lower right in black wash:
1892 / HOMER
On verso in graphite (Homer's hand): No 4 A miserable Pot hunter; just shot; in pen and brown ink (Homer's hand): D — 14 x 20; in blue crayon (probably Homer's hand) 6 and 26 (each in a circle)
Hayden Collection. Charles Henry Hayden Fund. 23.443

It is likely that Homer painted *The Fallen Deer* as one of a pair with *Deer Drinking* (fig. 1).[1] Both animals are at the water's edge, one alive, the other dead.[2] These are the only representations of does that Homer painted, and their treatment in close-up portraits sets them apart from the numerous Adirondack watercolors devoted to stag hunting.[3]

Homer depicted the doe in pale transparent washes, opposing her clear, delicate form to an indeterminate, impressionistic background, heavily painted in opaque pigments. Tender, graceful curves suggest the softness and vulnerability of her body.[4] Homer painted her head with detailed care, endowing her with a sense of individuality that makes her death more poignant.

In all his hunting watercolors Homer portrayed not the visiting city sportsman, but the local inhabitants. Some used the meat for food, others were "pot hunters" who sold the antlers and hide for money to buy food for the pot.[5] It was considered unsportsmanlike to kill does (whose loss depleted the deer population). Homer's words, "a miserable pot hunter," written on the reverse of this watercolor, should be interpreted not as a condemnation of pot hunting *per se*, but as an expression of his own feelings at the death of a female deer. By contrast, in *A Good Shot* (1892, National Gallery of Art, Washington, D.C.), Homer portrays the heroic death of a stag.

The subject of *The Fallen Deer* may have had an effect on its history. It once belonged to William T. Evans of New York, a prominent collector, but changing attitudes toward hunting may have decreased its desirability. It appears to have

Fig. 1. *Deer Drinking*, 1892. Watercolor. Yale University Art Gallery. The Robert W. Carle Fund.

been on the market for nearly a decade before the Museum of Fine Arts purchased it in 1923.[6]

SWR

1. See Eleanor Lewis Jones, "Deer Drinking, Reflections on a Watercolor by Winslow Homer," in *Smithsonian Studies in American Art* 2 (fall 1988), pp. 55–65.

2. Deer were commonly killed in a lake because transportation by water was easier than hauling the carcass out of the woods.

3. These include *An October Day* (1889, Sterling and Francine Clark Art Institute, Williamstown, Massachusetts), *Sketch for "Hound and Hunter"* (1892, National Gallery of Art, Washington, D.C.), and *The End of the Hunt* (1892, Bowdoin College Museum of Art, Brunswick, Maine). For a discussion of these and other watercolors placed in an instructive narrative sequence, see Helen Cooper, *Winslow Homer Watercolors* (New Haven: Yale University Press, 1986), pp. 174–178.

4. Homer refined the form of the doe, reshaping the contours of her belly and tail by painting over them with background colors.

5. See David Tatham, "Trapper, Hunter, and Woodsman: Winslow Homer's Adirondack Figures," *American Art Journal* 22 (no. 4, 1990), p. 61.

6. According to the Museum's records, after its ownership by Evans, *The Fallen Deer* was sold at auction by the American Art Association, March 1913, lot. 33; it was then with Moulton and Ricketts, New York, and with Frank W. Bayley, Boston, from whom the Museum purchased it in 1923.

Winslow Homer
60. *The Adirondack Guide*, 1894
Watercolor over graphite on very thick, rough-textured, cream wove paper
15⅛ x 21½ in. (384 x 545 mm)
Signed and dated lower left in black wash: HOMER / 1894

On verso in graphite (Homer's hand): No 5 Picture for a dark corner
Bequest of Mrs. Alma H. Wadleigh. 47.268

With its bold composition, painterly execution, and inventive use of color, *The Adirondack Guide* exemplifies Homer's mature watercolor style.

Against broad patches of wooded background and reflective water is set the figure of a man rowing a boat, both viewed from the back. A large tree appears to shelter the boatman, its drooping branches echoing his long gray beard. Here, Homer seems to combine the imagery of two more reportorial watercolors: *The Guide* (1889, Portland

Fig. 1. *Camp Fire, Adirondacks*, 1894. Watercolor. The Art Institute of Chicago. Mr. and Mrs. Martin A. Ryerson Collection.

[Maine] Museum of Art), showing a canoer, and *Camp Fire, Adirondacks* (fig. 1), where an uprooted tree much more literally shelters the guide.

Homer was extremely concerned with formal qualities in *The Adirondack Guide*. The pair of raised oars daringly bisects the composition. The blue tree trunk with its cascade of dead branches, almost abstractly decorative, parallels in visual interest the man and his boat whose forms are refined with controlled brushstrokes and delicate scraping. Vivid touches of pure red, yellow, and blue, accent the man's facial features. Many layers of brushwork activate the amorphous depths of the dark woods and the shadowed water where reflections of tree, boat, and rower enliven the surface. The central elements of the image are painted in clear transparent colors in response to the light that enters this open space.

Homer stayed at the North Woods Club from June 3 to July 8, 1894.[1] While he surely began *The Adirondack Guide* there, using a local man as his model, it is equally certain that he brought it to completion in Maine. He probably reconstructed the pose and lighting conditions at Prout's Neck, using a neighbor and a Maine skiff as his models.[2]

Homer's note on the back of this sheet, "Picture for a dark corner," indicates his canny grasp of the market for his watercolors in the late 1890s. It was probably written to his Boston dealers, Doll & Richards, when he sent *The Adirondack Guide* to

them in mid-March, 1897. In just over six weeks the picture was sold to George C. Wadleigh of Haverhill, Massachusetts, and for fifty years presumably brightened a dark corner of the house until his widow left it to the Museum in 1947.

SWR

1. David Tatham, "Winslow Homer at the North Woods Club," in *Winslow Homer, A Symposium*, Studies in the History of Art 26 (Washington, D. C.: National Gallery of Art, 1990), p. 128.

2. A great deal of research has surrounded the identities of the models for Adirondack subjects. At one time it was proposed that the model for *The Adirondack Guide* was Harvey Holt, a well-known woodsman, whom Homer may have known in Keene Valley in the 1870s. Holt, born in 1808, died in January 1893, and it is highly improbable that he actually posed for this watercolor. However, photographs of Holt show him to be stockier than either Rufus Wallace or John Gatchell, the other models Homer was likely to have used, and Holt's features are remarkably similar to those depicted in the watercolor. For photographs of Holt see Ashton Sanborn, "Winslow Homer's 'Adirondack Guide'," *Bulletin of the Museum of Fine Arts, Boston* 46 (February, 1948), pp. 48-51. For Homer's other models see notes to cat. 57.

Winslow Homer
61. *The Sponge Diver*, 1898-99
Watercolor over graphite on moderately thick, moderately rough, cream wove paper; partial Whatman watermark: MAN 1898
15 x 21⅜ in. (380 x 543 mm)
Inscribed in brush and black wash: H. and Bahamas 1889 (lower left); Homer / 1889 (lower right)
On verso in graphite (in Homer's hand): No 18
Gift of Mrs. Robert B. Osgood. 39.621

Among Homer's most brilliant Bahamian subjects is *The Sponge Diver*. In an expanse of clear blue water whose gentle motion is suggested by broad, wet brushstrokes, a half-submerged diver seen from the back grasps a sponge in one hand and with the other clings to the stern of a boat. The dark oar jutting out over the pale stern draws the eye to the central part of the image. Homer played the forms of man and boat against each other, boldly contrasting the rich brown, glistening back to the broad, white stern. With seemingly artless brushstrokes he modeled the hull, and with an evocative squiggle suggested the reflected light shimmering on its surface.

Although Homer twice wrote the date of 1889 on *The Sponge Diver*, he must have done so years later, and had to have been mistaken.[1] A recent examination of the sheet reveals a Whatman watermark with a date of 1898, coinciding with Homer's visit to Nassau that winter.[2]

Homer reworked the sheet in the studio, strengthening the formal design in several ways. He scraped away the upper part of the land mass at the right to suggest greater recession into depth. To bring the bold forms of diver and boat into even greater prominence he marked the image for cropping, nearly an inch in on both sides and the lower edge.[3] With its close-up view, vivid coloration, and broad confident handling *The Sponge Diver* relates closely to such loosely brushed contemporary watercolors as *The Turtle Pound* (1898, The Brooklyn Museum) and *West India Divers* (1899, Helen F. Spencer Museum of Art, University of Kansas, Lawrence).

SWR

126 / AWASH IN COLOR (cat. 61)

1. The watercolor was a gift from Homer to a Dr. William Allen Bartlett, otherwise unidentified, in 1906.

2. The first three digits are unquestionable, the last somewhat indistinct.

3. Protected by an overmat, these margins show evidence of a deep pink hue in the water, now almost entirely faded elsewhere in the image.

Winslow Homer
62. *Palm Trees, Florida*, 1904
Watercolor over graphite on moderately thick, slightly textured, cream wove paper
19¾ x 13⅞ in. (502 x 352 mm)
Inscribed lower right in graphite: Sketch W. H.
Bequest of John T. Spaulding. 48.731

Homer first visited Florida in January 1886. As he grew older its mild climate, exotic landscape, and fishing opportunities drew him back for several winters. The landscape of *Palm Trees, Florida* resembles several other watercolors dated 1904 that Homer made during a visit to Homosassa, Florida, in the early months of that year. The vegetation is very like that in *Homosassa Jungle* (1904, Fogg Art Museum, Harvard University Art Museums, Cambridge, Massachusetts), which includes men fishing from a flat-bottomed boat. Located on a river near the Gulf of Mexico, Homosassa was a fisherman's paradise where Homer cast for bass and painted watercolors. As in some earlier Adirondack subjects, the viewpoint of *Palm Trees, Florida* could be that of a fisherman in a boat on the water. Indeed, the only human inhabitant of the picture is just such a one, glimpsed against the distant sandy shoreline.

Palm Trees, Florida demonstrates Homer's consistent ability to evoke a keen sense of place and its accompanying mood. Here it is the placid waters, humid atmosphere, and exotic flora of the Gulf Coast. Three diagonal bands of sky and clouds suggest the upward motion of the air.[1] As in *Old Settlers* (cat. 58), Homer depicted a stand of trees. Here, they are a diverse lot of tropical growth. Tall palms reach into the sky; Homer wiped the paint so that the soft fronds blur into the adjacent clouds and seem to sway in the wind. He painted the jungle at the water's edge thickly and opaquely, wiping and lifting pigment to suggest the dense growth and its spiky, idiosyncratic shapes. On earlier trips to Florida, Homer had portrayed its exotic animals in considerable detail and included alligators and egrets in such watercolors as *In a Florida Jungle* (1886, Worcester [Massachusetts] Art Museum). Here, two bright red birds draw attention to the dark tangled growth, but merely hint at the wildlife that inhabits its depths.

SWR

1. The sky was once pinker in hue as attested to by a narrow marginal band protected by the overlapping mat. Homer may have used a mixed color called Payne's gray, which combined with black and blue the light-sensitive pigment alizarin crimson. His two extant color boxes contain two moist pans each of Payne's gray. See the analysis of the paints by Craigen Weston Bowen in Marjorie B. Cohn, *Wash and Gouache, A Study of the Development of the Materials of Watercolor* (Cambridge, Massachusetts: The Center for Conservation and Technical Studies, Fogg Art Museum and The Foundation of The American Institute for Conservation, 1977), pp. 68-69 and by Judith C. Walsh in *American Traditions in Watercolor, The Worcester Art Museum Collection*, Susan E. Strickler, ed. (New York: Abbeville Press, 1987), pp. 64-65. Walsh's essay, "Observations on the Watercolor Techniques of Homer and Sargent," provides much information on this topic.

128 / AWASH IN COLOR (cat. 62)

James Abbott McNeill Whistler

Born Lowell, Massachusetts 1834;
died London, England, 1903

Although Whistler produced his first watercolors in the early 1850s, while still in secondary school in Pomfret, Connecticut, he worked only sporadically in this medium during the following thirty years. During the 1860s and 1870s, when he was making his reputation in London, Whistler used thin watercolor washes in decorative studies for interior design projects, such as the sketches for Aubrey House in Kensington, bought by his patron William Alexander in 1873. In the late 1870s, Whistler was hired to produce a set of wash drawings to illustrate a catalogue of Sir Henry Thompson's collection of Nankin porcelain, a project that reinforced his interest in oriental design.

Whistler began his work in watercolor in earnest during his 1879-80 trip to Venice. Nearly insolvent after his disastrous libel suit against the critic John Ruskin (for which he was awarded the token compensation of a farthing), and the overly lavish decoration of his new home (the White House in Chelsea), Whistler fled to Venice with a commission for etchings from the Fine Arts Society of London as his sole source of income. While there, Whistler not only made prints, but also produced a series of delicate pastels that illustrate the untouristed sights of Venice. At the same time, he took up watercolor, and shortly after his return to London he began to work seriously in the medium, apparently inspired by discussions with the watercolorist Charles Edward Holloway.

Whistler's first major exhibition to include watercolors, "'Notes' – 'Harmonies' – 'Nocturnes'," was held at Dowdeswell Gallery in 1884. It included oils and pastels as well as watercolors, and marked the full integration of the medium into his oeuvre. The innovative nature of his achievement was recognized by several critics, among them Frederick Wedmore, who noted in *The Academy*, "When Mr. Whistler speaks it is because there is something fresh to be said; a new pretty thing has been seen, or a thing has been seen newly, and clamours to be recorded." By 1886, when Whistler held his second exhibition of "notes," more than two-thirds of the works exhibited were watercolors. The artist continued to produce small watercolors through the 1890s.

Whistler's watercolors closely relate in style, subject matter, and mood to his mature oils and pastels. City views, land and seascapes, and figure studies are all rendered in a manner more suggestive than descriptive. The watercolors are generally small, and extremely sophisticated in their use of transparent and opaque washes. Whistler often combined watercolor with other media, such as graphite, chalk, and even pastel.

Whistler produced about 450 watercolors during his lifetime; they document visits to Venice, Amsterdam, Dieppe, Trouville, and Paris, among other locales, and have proved difficult to date because of Whistler's habit of returning to places, and artistic styles, at various points throughout his career. The best of the watercolors are fresh and engagingly inventive, and were enthusiastically pursued by Whistler's patrons, especially Charles Lang Freer.

James Abbott McNeill Whistler
63. *"Little Scheveningen:" Grey Note*, 1880s or
    1890s
5 x 8½ in. (127 x 215 mm)
Opaque watercolor on thin, brown wove paper, affixed overall to cardboard
Inscribed verso, in graphite: Grey note - Mouth of Scheveningen [and graphite sketch of female figure]
Gift of Walter Gay. 23.251

"Little Scheveningen:" Grey Note is one of the "notes," "harmonies," and "nocturnes" Whistler painted from the late 1870s through the 1890s. These works, including watercolors, oils, and pastels, are noted for their small size, atmospheric moods, sophisticated color arrangements, and subtle variations intechnique. *"Little Scheveningen:" Grey Note* is typical of the watercolors Whistler produced during this period. It has the appearance of a quick, effortless study; an abbreviated impression of sea, sky and boats is conveyed with bold brushwork on a small scrap of brown paper.[1]

Whistler covered his sheet with large areas of gray, in which tonal and textural shifts are extremely subtle. He applied wash to moistened areas in the clouds at upper left, achieving seamless, fluid transitions between close shades of gray. At right, he laid individual brushstrokes on top of already-dried washes, leaving crisp edges. The few brushstrokes of mauve in the sails of the boats at center lend a subtle note of contrast. The brown paper adds to the sober mood of the scene.

Whistler made at least a half-dozen trips to Holland in the 1880s and 1890s and returned to Scheveningen many times, perhaps because of its soaring skies and misty weather. A fishing and resort town on the coast of Holland near The Hague, Scheveningen was one of the most popular upper-middle class tourist resorts in the late nineteenth century, and was especially favored by the painters of the Hague School. Whistler's restless travels and consistency of style make it difficult to date individual works executed in Scheveningen, or even identify their locations with certainty. The artist's first biographer wrote in 1908 that he had "touched perfection in many a little angry sea at

Dieppe, or note in Holland, or impression in Paris, but . . . not many of them are dated."[2]

"Little Scheveningen:" Grey Note was purchased from the artist by Whistler's fellow expatriate, the painter Walter Gay. Gay lent it to a memorial exhibition of Whistler's works at Boston's Copley Society in 1904 (where it was identified as representing the mouth of the Thames) and to the larger retrospective at the New Gallery, in London, in 1905. It may also have been among the pictures Whistler showed at the Dowdeswell Gallery two decades earlier;[3] it is similar to those color studies, which received mixed reviews. In defense of these nearly abstract works, Whistler wrote that "a picture is finished when all trace of the means used to bring it about has disappeared" and told a fellow painter that "a perfect thing is a perfect thing, whether large or small."[4]

ABW

1. Whistler often used brown paper as a support for his watercolors.

2. Elizabeth and Joseph Pennell, *The Life of James McNeill Whistler* (London: W. Heinemann, and Philadelphia: J.B. Lippincott Company, 1908), vol. 2, pp. 80-81. The Pennells also note that Whistler could not remember any dates or places when interviewed.

3. The exhibition was subtitled, "Arrangement in Flesh Colour and Grey." A reviewer noted that the color-coordinated gallery included an attendant dressed in gray and pink who handed out copies of the brown-paper catalogue. See Ruth E. Fine, "Notes and Notices:

Whistler's Watercolors" in *Essays in Honor of Paul Mellon* (Washington, D.C.: National Gallery of Art, 1986), pp. 115-116. For an additional discussion of the exhibition, see review by Frederick Wedmore, "Mr. Whistler's Arrangement in Flesh Colour and Gray," in *The Academy: A Weekly Review of Literature, Science, and Art* 25 (May 24, 1884), p. 374.

4. Margaret MacDonald, "Notes, Harmonies & Nocturnes," (New York: M. Knoedler & Co., 1984), pp. 10-11.

Frederick Childe Hassam

Born Dorchester, Massachusetts, 1859;
died East Hampton, Long Island, 1935

One of the best-known American Impressionists, Childe Hassam was also an enthusiastic painter of watercolors throughout his career. He reportedly made watercolors as a child. While working as a wood engraver and an illustrator in Boston in the 1870s and 1880s, Hassam was encouraged to pursue his interest in the medium by the example of watercolorist Ross Turner (cat. 71). In 1882, the Boston gallery of Williams and Everett gave Hassam his first solo show; it featured fifty-four watercolors of picturesque and historically evocative sites around Boston. Hassam's second show at Williams and Everett, in 1884, once again consisted entirely of watercolors; these were landscapes and figure sketches he made while touring Europe the preceding year. In 1886, Hassam returned to Europe. Based in Paris, he studied at the Académie Julian where many American artists trained, and witnessed the increased impact of Impressionism on mainstream painting styles. As a result of his years in France, his palette lightened, his strokes became brisker, his handling more assured; in watercolor he became the master of the transparent wash technique.

Hassam returned to the United States, settling in New York, in 1889. At about that time, he began to make summer pilgrimages to Appledore, Isles of Shoals, New Hampshire, where poet Celia Thaxter presided over a salon that attracted many of the brightest artists and writers of the era. Hassam greatly admired her celebrated gardens, and he painted them repeatedly in a vibrant tapestry of color, with slanted strokes evoking the island's breezes, and liberal use of white paper suggesting the summer sun. Many of these watercolors were used to illustrate Thaxter's book, *An Island Garden* (1894).

By the 1890s, Hassam was working extensively in pastels, an interest that affected his watercolor technique: he experimented with gouache, with mixed-media effects, and with dry strokes of opaque pigment that imitated the look of pastel. Hassam's innovative use of watercolor led him to organize the New York Water Color Club in 1890 (one of many artists' associations in which the sociable Hassam would be active) as a progressive alternative to the American Watercolor Society.

Hassam served as president of the club from 1890 to 1895.

In 1897, Hassam and several other artists formed the dissident group Ten American Painters. Although among The Ten only Frank Benson would share Hassam's dedication to watercolor, he continued to insist on the medium as an important vehicle for significant works of art. Hassam consistently showed his oils and watercolors side by side, especially at the Montross Gallery in New York, and encouraged museums and private collectors to buy watercolors.

Hassam continued to paint almost until his death in 1935. His style, which before the turn of the century had been relatively adventurous, did not change appreciably after World War I, and his reputation was eclipsed by the advent of modernism. The renewed enthusiasm for American Impressionism has once again brought Hassam's work into public view, and the 1990 exhibition of his Isles of Shoals work has rekindled awareness of Hassam's strengths as a watercolor painter.

Childe Hassam
64. *Chatou near Bougival*, 1889
Transparent and opaque watercolor on thick, moderately rough-textured, cream wove paper
9¹⁵⁄₁₆ x 13⅞ in. (253 x 352 mm)
Signed and dated lower left: Childe Hassam. 1889 (in gray watercolor) / Chatou near Bougival (in pen and black ink)
Gift of Miss Kathleen Rothe. 58.598

Although Hassam would later deny the impact of Impressionism on his work ("when I lived in Paris I knew nothing of Monet, . . . etc."),[1] his exposure to the French style during his three years in Europe (1886–89) had a marked effect on his palette and technique. At the same time, the French painters' example solidified his dedication to two themes – the modern city and the picturesque countryside – that would sustain him, in watercolor and oil, for the remainder of his career.

Hassam's subject here is a pleasant village on the Seine some eight miles west of Paris (fig. 1), frequented by pleasure-loving city dwellers and immortalized by Renoir in his *Luncheon of the Boating Party* (1881, Phillips Collection, Washington, D.C.).[2] Whereas Hassam generally shared Renoir's interest in themes of bourgeois conviviality, here it was the peaceful, somnolent beauty of Chatou that attracted him, and in this modest watercolor he depicts the domesticated countryside of Chatou as an ideal of repose. Not only is there no trace of the commercial traffic that plied the deeper channel of the Seine,[3] but there are also none of the holiday makers, the cheerful boaters and picnickers who so charmingly inhabit Renoir's pictures. Hassam's river is glass-smooth. No boats can be seen, as though the picture were painted out of season, or in the early evening hours. Yet the brilliance of the light contradicts this notion, and so it would seem that Hassam chose to absent the figures in order to emphasize the setting's idyllic nature.

The placid mood of the watercolor is furthered by Hassam's use of cool tonalities and even application of wash. There is little emphasis on stroke here – the antithesis of Hassam's later, staccato style – and the smoothness adds to the effect of calm. The only modulation of the water is the broad band of cerulean blue, skimmed over the

pale blue wash and then softened with a subsequent damp stroke, causing the color to soften and dissolve, an effect as ephemeral as the wake it represents. Equally soothing is the organization of the composition into a series of horizontal bands, interrupted only by the trees at left, and by the bird and its reflection on the pale blue water at center.

Hassam's characterization of Chatou foreshadows the environment he would find so attractive in the 1890s at the Isles of Shoals: rural, yet readily accessible by train or boat; natural, yet domesticated; isolated, yet always with the promise of stimulating company. Chatou's origins as a sleepy riverside village gave it the kind of quaintness and link with the past that always appealed to Hassam. He discovered Chatou late in his European sojourn (otherwise his only notable excursions out of Paris seem to have been to Villiers le Bel, some ten miles north of the city, where he had friends); nonetheless, it is surprising that he did not paint this part of the Seine repeatedly, as he would Appledore.[4]

CT

1. Hassam, interview with DeWitt McClellan Lockman, January 25, 1927, quoted in H. Barbara Weinberg, *The Lure of Paris: Nineteenth-Century American Painters and Their French Teachers* (New York: Abbeville Press, 1991), p. 246.

2. Chatou was a twenty-minute train ride from the Gare Saint-Lazare. It was near La Grenouillère, where Monet and Renoir painted, and Bougival. It was already something of a haven for artists and writers by the mid-1850s, when its resident population was a mere 1,200; in the next decades it population swelled to 3000 and it became the preferred locale for the increasingly popular sport of rowing. It was known as well for its restaurants. See Robert L. Herbert, *Impressionism: Art, Leisure, and Parisian Society* (New Haven and London: Yale University Press, 1988), pp. 211-212, 246-248.

3. West of Paris the Seine is divided by a long band of narrow islands, beginning at Bezons, just south of Argenteuil, and continuing for several miles past Chatou and Bougival to Port-Marly. River traffic used the deeper channel on the Rueil side, while pleasure boaters used the channel between Chatou and Chiart islands (Herbert, *Impressionism*, p. 248). Hassam probably painted this watercolor from the riverbank at Rueil, looking

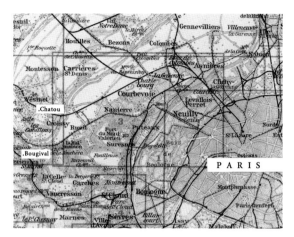

Fig. 1. *The suburbs west of Paris.* Engraving from Karl Baedeker, *Paris et ses environs* (Leipzig and Paris, 1903).

across the Seine past the narrow sandbar island toward the hamlet of Croissy, with Chatou just beyond. Susan Vrotsos graciously provided this information.

4. According to Weinberg (*The Lure of Paris*, p. 246), before Hassam's return to America in the fall of 1889, he rented Renoir's old studio — which may have inspired him to tour that master's haunts along the Seine, although in general he seems not to have emulated the Impressionists' activities while in Paris. His failure to travel during this period has been attributed to financial constraints (Donelson F. Hoopes, *Childe Hassam* [New York: Watson-Guptill, 1979], pp. 13-14). Kathleen Burnside (who, with Stuart Feld, is preparing a catalogue raisonné of Hassam's works) notes that Hassam was concentrating on urban subjects at this time, producing some garden pictures (more often in oil than watercolor) and only a few suburban landscapes. He seems to have painted only one other watercolor of this area, *The Seine at Chatou* (about 1889, private collection, Mamaroneck, New York). I thank Kathleen Burnside for this information. The mere handful of titles in exhibition catalogues of the period (such as *The Seine at Bougival*, in a Noyes and Cobb exhibition of the late '80s, *In the Country*, in Doll & Richards's 1889 Hassam exhibition, or *The Village of Suresnes, Distant Paris, across the "Bois de Boulogne"* in their 1891 Hassam show) further attests to the infrequency of such painting excursions.

Childe Hassam

65. *Nocturne, Railway Crossing, Chicago*, 1893
Opaque watercolor on thick, rough-textured cream wove paper
16 x 11¾ in. (406 x 298 mm)
Signed lower left in black watercolor: Childe Hassam
Inscribed verso in black ink: Nocturne / Railway Crossing Chicago / Childe Hassam
Hayden Collection. Charles Henry Hayden Fund. 62.986

Acquired in 1962 as *"Wet Night, Boston,"* and then assigned a date of 1902, this watercolor's original title was revealed during conservation treatment, and redated to 1893, when Hassam was in Chicago for the World's Columbian Exposition. A recent reexamination of the watercolor revealed another mystery, for to the right of the signature on the recto, painted out by Hassam but still partially visible in transmitted light, is the inscription *Iles* [sic] *of Shoals*.

This is probably the watercolor Hassam exhibited at the Fourth Annual Exhibition of the New York Water Color Club in 1893 as *Nocturne. At the Crossing*, and again under the same title at Doll & Richards Gallery, Boston, in November of 1894.[1] *Nocturne* typifies the mixed-media look aspired to by many members of the New York Water Color Club. The whole sheet is covered with dark blue washes, layer upon layer, to imitate the slick, rain-soaked streets and murky sky.[2] Streaks of dry brush representing tire tracks have the look of pastel, and dabs of pigment in yellow, white, salmon, and orange, possibly applied directly from the tube, are so thick and glossy as to be reminiscent of oil (see detail). The halos formed by the subsequent application of water suggest headlights seen through fog and mist. Handsome and evocative, *Nocturne* draws upon watercolor's ability to capture the moment; at the same time, it resembles an oil painting in its complexity.

While Hassam developed the impressionist side of his art in the many watercolors he produced during summers at the Isles of Shoals (see cat. 71, fig. 1), this picture exhibits his interest in tonal, poetic effects. In titling the watercolor, he may well have been paying homage to Whistler, whose work he clearly admired, and whose virtuoso

Fig. 1. James McNeill Whistler, *Nocturne: Grey and Gold – Canal, Holland (Amsterdam Nocturnes)*, 1883-84. Watercolor on paper. Freer Gallery of Art, Smithsonian Institution, Washington, D.C.

manipulation of the medium to create mysterious effects is an important precedent for Hassam's accomplishment here (fig. 1).[3] The subject – city streets on a rainy or snowy night, often featuring a ghostly, top-hatted cab driver emerging from the mist – is one Hassam addressed frequently beginning in the 1890s. In the 1894 Doll & Richards exhibition, for example, he showed a "nocturne" and three other rainy day or evening scenes, in addition to the present picture.[4]

CT

1. By the 1890s, the American Watercolor Society had become quite conservative, resisting the full and equal participation of women in the organization and, in technical matters, favoring the traditional English manner of working only in pure transparent washes. The New York Water Color Club was founded in 1890 to provide a forum for more varied techniques in watercolor than the Watercolor Society welcomed in their shows. See Donelson F. Hoopes, "The Emergence of an American

Charles Herbert Woodbury

Born Lynn, Massachusetts, 1864;
died Boston, Massachusetts, 1940

Medium," *American Traditions in Watercolor: The Worcester Art Museum Collection* (Worcester: Worcester Art Museum, 1987), p. 32, and Ralph Fabri, *History of the American Watercolor Society: The First Hundred Years* (New York: American Watercolor Society, 1969), p. 29.

2. Hassam also employed a great deal of rubbing and lifting of color to suggest the softening effects of the damp atmosphere. He used the edges of the wash to provide contours (and in the case of the tall buildings, he may have blotted those edges so the buildings seem to dissolve into the mist) in order to suggest shape without being literal. And he distinguished sky from street not by means of tone – for the two areas are the same deep blue – but by texture: the washes in the street were left relatively smooth, but the sky exhibits a grainy texture, caused by rubbing away one layer of wash, leaving visible the pigment of another in the hollows of the paper.

3. As Hassam noted after a visit to the collection of Charles Lang Freer, "I admired his Whistlers so much. The smaller street things are very interesting, the things I have painted, the little shop windows." At Whistler's death, he wrote to J. Alden Weir, "I am sorry that I never knew him – He is surely one of the big men." Quoted in David Park Curry, *Childe Hassam. An Island Garden Revisited* (Denver: Denver Art Museum, 1990), p. 164.

4. *Exhibition and Private Sale of Water Color Drawings by Childe Hassam at the Gallery of Doll & Richards*, November 2-14, 1894, cats. 1, *Nocturne [At the Crossing]*; 3, *Rain, Mist and Electric Light [Madison Square]*; 31, *Nocturne [A Balcony, Venice]*; 34, *Rainy Evening [A Fifth Avenue Flower Shop]*; 35, *Rainy Day [Fifth Avenue at the Park]*.

Although Charles Herbert Woodbury displayed talent as an artist from an early age, his family encouraged him to pursue a more lucrative profession. In 1882, Woodbury enrolled in the Massachusetts Institute of Technology to study engineering. Despite the rigors of MIT's program, he continued to attend life classes at the Boston Art Club, to exhibit and sell his paintings, and even to teach art. Only a few months after receiving his bachelor's degree in 1886, Woodbury opened his first studio and art school in Boston.

In 1890, Woodbury married one of his students, Marcia Oakes; the two painters made an artistic excursion of their year-long honeymoon in Europe. Woodbury studied at the Académie Julian in Paris for several months. During the couple's stay in Holland, Marcia Oakes Woodbury began her career as a painter of Dutch genre scenes. The Woodburys traveled frequently between Boston and Europe during the next few years, and Charles began to specialize in dramatic marine views. He was particularly attracted to the New England coast, painting the explosive motion of ocean waves in both oil and watercolor. Woodbury took up watercolor painting in 1885, using it for both preparatory studies and finished works; it became one of his favorite media.

In 1895, the Woodburys built a studio and summer home in Ogunquit, Maine, and opened it two years later as a summer art school. During the winter, Woodbury taught at Wellesley College and at the Pine Hill School for Girls in Boston. Both artists sold their popular oil paintings and watercolors in Boston galleries.

In 1913, Marcia Woodbury died, and as World War I approached, Charles closed the Ogunquit school. To assist in the war effort, Woodbury created posters for the U.S. Government. He also began to make etchings. After the war, he published his first manual, *Painting and the Personal Equation* (1919), an effort followed by two other books published in 1922 and 1925. Woodbury also returned to active teaching in this period, reopening the Ogunquit Summer School in 1923. He founded the Woodbury Training Institute in Applied Observation in 1928, in collaboration with Elizabeth Ward Perkins, a friend and fellow art instructor.

Although still relatively little known outside of New England, Woodbury was influential both as a painter and as a teacher, and his work received critical acclaim during his lifetime. Retrospectives of his work were held at the Museum of Fine Arts, Boston, in 1945, and at the MIT Museum in 1988.

Charles Herbert Woodbury
66. *Canal Scene, Holland: The Green Mill*, 1894
Transparent and opaque watercolor over graphite on thick, slightly textured, dark cream wove paper
20 x 25⅝ in. (508 x 651 mm)
Signed and dated lower right in gray wash: Chas H Woodbury '94
Gift of Mary W. Bartol, John W. Bartol, and Abigail W. Clark. Res. 27.99

Between 1891 and 1894, Charles and Marcia Oakes Woodbury spent many months in Holland. Entranced by the gray skies and verdant farmland of the Dutch countryside, Charles Woodbury began a series of paintings depicting a windmill next to a wide canal, culminating in a large oil, *The Green Mill* (fig. 1). The watercolor version of *The Green Mill* falls in the middle of this series, predating the oil by two years, but most likely following a group of pencil and oil sketches and a photograph of the scene.[1] Painted in an ambitious size and in an unusual palette, this watercolor was clearly intended as a finished presentation piece. In some respects, it reflects Impressionist practice, for Woodbury recorded his careful observation of the scene with vigorous strokes in graphite and watercolor that suggested rapid execution. The radical cropping of the windmill at the top so that water is the featured element of the picture suggests an awareness of the Impressionist penchant for unusual viewpoints.[2] At the same time, the watercolor reveals an aesthetic-movement sensibility, one concerned with decoration and pattern. While Woodbury's subject – a peasant pulling on a barge line – is picturesque, *Canal Scene, Holland* is above all a color study, a carefully orchestrated mix of harmonious greens. With its strongly articulated vertical and horizontal elements, the composition is abstract and graphic.

Woodbury's oil painting of the subject elicited mixed responses from critics. One critic com-

W. Dodge Macknight

Born Providence, Rhode Island, 1860;
died East Sandwich, Massachusetts, 1950

Fig. 1. *The Green Mill*, 1896. Oil on canvas.
The MIT Museum.

plained in 1896 that *The Green Mill* was not as original or spontaneous as the artist's marine studies. Many American painters were drawn to Holland in these years, and were inspired by such Hague School artists as Anton Mauve and Jacob Maris to paint rural landscapes and scenes of peasant life. The originality of Woodbury's image is found in its unusually bold composition and, as another critic noted, in its Whistler-like harmonies of color: "Mr. C.H. Woodbury is beginning to take an important place in the various exhibitions, through his landscapes. This time it is a harmony in greens, "Green Mill," green reflection, green grasses, green water, in Holland."[3]

ABW

1. These studies are discussed by Erica Hirshler in her essay "The Art of Charles H. Woodbury," in *Earth, Sea and Sky* (Cambridge: MIT Museum, 1988), pp. 97-98. Two oil sketches of figures pulling ropes are in the collection of the MIT Museum, and are dated about 1893. One sketch depicts the woman shown in the watercolor. The second sketch depicts a second male figure, as in the oil painting. A photograph of the scene, differing slightly from both the oil and watercolor, and with no figures, is preserved in a scrapbook of clippings now in a private collection.

2. The oil painting reflects similar efforts. See Hirshler, "The Art of Charles H. Woodbury," p. 97.

3. It is unclear whether these reviews are based on the oil or the watercolor. Woodbury exhibited works titled

"The Green Mill" in several gallery exhibitions between 1896 and 1905, but catalogues do not specify the medium of the work shown. The reviews quoted here are located in an unpaginated scrapbook compiled by the artist's mother and still in the collection of the Woodbury family. The first review is marked "NY Times Apr 3 96." The second review is unmarked.

Except for a small number of pastels produced in the 1880s and early 1890s, Dodge Macknight worked exclusively in watercolor. During his lifetime, he became famous for his winter landscapes, which often featured a violet and red palette that some critics found shocking (his work was dubbed "Macknightmares") while others proclaimed his pictures masterpieces. Macknight's reputation flourished amid this controversy: from the 1890s on, his annual shows made headlines for the rapidity with which his pictures sold; his pleasing subjects and his engaging personality attracted such important local collectors as Desmond FitzGerald (his first biographer), Denman Ross, and Sarah Choate Sears. In 1915, Isabella Stewart Gardner created a "Macknight Room" at Fenway Court to display her watercolors by the artist. He was the only contemporary painter she so honored.

Macknight began his artistic career as an apprentice to a theatrical designer, and beginning in 1878, he was employed for several years by the Taber Art Company of New Bedford, Massachusetts, which made reproductions of paintings and photographs. A friend financed a trip abroad in 1883. Macknight went first to Paris, where he studied with Fernand Cormon, a follower of Léon Bonnat. He exhibited in the salons of 1885, 1886, and 1887. For the next decade he traveled widely in Europe and North Africa in the company of various French and American painters; he worked in Brittany, southern France, Spain, and Algeria. At Arles, he renewed his friendship with Van Gogh, whom he had met in Paris in 1886.

In 1888, while still in Europe, he sent thirty-five watercolors to Doll & Richards in Boston, beginning an exclusive relationship with the gallery that would continue for the rest of his career. He returned to the United States in 1897 and settled in East Sandwich, Cape Cod; summers were spent in search of picturesque subject matter in Mexico, Morocco, Jamaica, the Grand Canyon, and other exotic locations. The resulting watercolors became the focus of his annual shows. Bostonians considered him one of the nation's greatest watercolorists: his work was teamed with that of Homer and Sargent in an exhibition at the Boston Art Club in 1921; a similar exhibition was sent to Paris in 1923. He retired from painting in 1930.

Dodge Macknight
67. *Haystack: Belle Ile, Brittany,* about 1890

Transparent and opaque watercolor over graphite on very thick, moderately textured, white wove paper 15½ x 15¹⁵/₁₆ in. (394 x 404 mm.), irregular
Signed upper left in red watercolor: Dodge Macknight
Bequest of David P. Kimball in memory of his wife Clara Bertram Kimball. 23.540

Haystack traditionally has been associated with Macknight's painting campaigns on Belle Ile, off the Brittany coast, where he spent the summers of 1889 and 1890.[1] He had been preceeded there by Monet, whose Belle Ile subjects had been shown in Paris in June 1887. Those pictures – of the water churning around the island's peculiar "needle rocks," and of waves crashing against the cliffs – were called "savage" by the critics and were admired by Macknight's friend Van Gogh;[2] the excitement they caused in Paris may well have inspired the American artist to explore the site himself. However, once there, he was apparently not attracted to the dramatic subjects that appealed to Monet. Rather, if the titles of watercolors Macknight sent to his 1891 exhibition at Doll & Richards (in which *Haystack* was probably shown) are any clue, it was picturesque, domestic themes that engaged him. Such pictures as *Yellow-Roofed Cottage*, *Sunny Morning in the Wheat Field*, and *Returning from Market* no doubt had great appeal for Bostonians, whose interest in peasant subjects stemmed from their long-standing admiration for Millet.

Nonetheless, these watercolors were perceived as radical when they were first shown in Boston. The *Boston Evening Transcript's* reviewer noted of the previous year's Belle Ile scenes, "After being duly shocked by his excessive and violent tones, which startle and amuse more than they gratify at first, we cannot fail . . . to be struck by the success with which he reproduces the phenomena of sunlight, the vitality of his landscapes, the pure and unadulterated quality of his color, and the utter originality of his point of view. If he keeps on in this way he will make a great name for himself; such is our prediction."[3]

Macknight chose an unconventional format for this watercolor – the paper is nearly square – and designed an unusually empty composition, consisting of some scrabbly trees and a lumpy haystack (whose scale is difficult to ascertain) in the immediate foreground, a tiny farmhouse along the horizon in the center of the picture, a bare field between, and a nearly cloudless sky above all. He employed an intense palette of pure color (one commentator called his color scheme "brutal"),[4] with drybrush used to imitate the look of pastel. Macknight's technique is as audacious as his palette: the field, for example, consists of a green wash layered, not over closely related tones to create a rich, resonant effect, but over bright yellow to suggest grain just beginning to emerge from the barren ground. He used scraping out to describe the ladders leaning against the stack and some of the tree branches. Elsewhere, branches are composed of deep blue and Macknight's favorite purple-red, creating a decorative effect that is evocative of trees just coming into bloom.

Although there is no evidence that Monet and Macknight knew one another, by 1891 they were already associated in the minds of the Boston public. According to the Boston *Post*, "It is worthy of note that the most saleable pictures in the market this season are of the impressionist type. The pictures of Claude Monet sell almost as fast as they can be obtained. Doll & Richards will soon show a collection of the unique watercolors of W. Dodge Macknight, who has lately exhibited in London, in Sargent's studio."[5] The Belle Ile pictures did indeed sell well, and marked the beginning of Macknight's association with important Boston collectors: Isabella Stewart Gardner, who would eventually own eleven Macknights, bought her first watercolor, *The Bay, Belle Ile*, from the 1891 Doll & Richards exhibition.[6]

CT

1. Desmond FitzGerald, *Dodge Macknight Water Color Painter* (Brookline, Mass.: privately printed by Riverdale Press, 1916), p. 24.

2. Robert L. Herbert, *Impressionism. Art, Leisure, and Parisian Society* (New Haven and London: Yale University Press, 1988), p. 302.

3. *Boston Evening Transcript*, March 24, 1890, quoted in FitzGerald, p. 25.

4. Jos. R. Brown, "To the Editor," *Boston Evening Transcript*, 1891, quoted in FitzGerald, *Dodge Macknight*, p. 26.

5. *Boston Post*, February 24, 1891, quoted in FitzGerald, p. 28. According to FitzGerald, in December 1890 Sargent offered Macknight the use of his London studio for an exhibition of the Belle Ile watercolors, which were shown at Doll & Richards the following spring.

6. Karen E. Haas, "Dodge Macknight - *painting the town red and violet..." Fenway Court 1982* (Boston: Isabella Stewart Gardner Museum, 1983), pp. 36-47, and Philip Hendy, *European and American Paintings in the Isabella Stewart Gardner Museum* (Boston: Isabella Stewart Gardner Museum, 1974), pp. 142-147.

Dodge Macknight
68. *Flags, Beacon Street, Boston*, 1918
Watercolor over graphite on thick, moderately rough-textured, white wove paper
17⅛ x 23¾ in. (435 x 603 mm)
Signed and dated lower left: Dodge Macknight (in red watercolor) / 1918 (in purple watercolor)
Bequest of Mrs. Edward Jackson Holmes, Edward Jackson Holmes Collection. 64.2114

Between 1917 and 1919, Macknight painted at least seventeen pictures of Boston streets bedecked with American flags. The decorations honored America's participation in the war, and were put up in conjunction with parades for the Red Cross, for Liberty Day, and, after the Armistice, to welcome home returning regiments. *Flags, Beacon Street* has been associated with the Yankee Division Parade on April 25, 1919; however, the watercolor is clearly dated 1918.[1] There were numerous parades in the summer of 1918 as well, and it is possible that the watercolor commemorates one of those events.

Macknight showed some of his flag paintings in his 1918 and 1919 Doll & Richards exhibitions. The *Boston Evening Transcript* described them as "a novel and stirring feature" of these annual shows, and praised Macknight's artistry in so vividly rendering Boston's streets "embowered in American flags and the flags of the Entente Allies – long, busy, crowded vistas, fairly glowing and glimmering with color. . . . No one who is at all familiar with Mr. Macknight's works will need to be assured that the color in these pictures is splendid in the strictest sense of the word. Childe Hassam has tried the same stunt in several pictures recently, with varying success."[2]

Hassam's well-known flag pictures, produced at exactly the same time, were the New York analogue to Macknight's festive and patriotic compositions. Hassam can claim precedence for the subject, since his first flag pictures were painted and displayed in 1916;[3] Macknight surely would have seen them. He may also have known French versions of the subject, such as Manet's *Rue Mosnier decorated with Flags* (1878, collection of Mr. and Mrs. Paul Mellon, Upperville, Virginia) and Monet's *The Rue Montorgueil, Festival of June 30, 1878*

(1878, Musée d'Orsay, Paris). Like Hassam and the French painters, Macknight reduces the marchers and spectators to lively flecks of color and light; his characteristic red and purple palette here becomes, in the words of the *Boston Herald*'s critic, "stains of wine color and orange [played against] the intensity of the Red, White and Blue . . . [resulting in] a vinous gayety of tone."[4] Macknight views the parade from a privileged vantage point: the balcony of a friend's townhouse on Beacon Street.[5] A mammoth flag, cropped at upper right, is tethered to the balcony railing, and billows like a sail on high seas. Its mast, slicing diagonally across the picture, forms a large X with the railing, and shapes a dramatic, telescoping view to the parade below. The dynamic juxtaposition of the looming flag, painted in bold, slashing strokes, and the marchers moving past on Beacon Street, rendered with bright staccato dabs, creates competing rhythms that convey the jubilation of the moment.

On the verso is an unsigned watercolor, *Floral Border*.

CT

1. The exhibition of Macknight's watercolors held at the Museum of Fine Arts, Boston, in 1950 assigned this work the title "Yankee Division Parade," and dated it 1919 (see *Dodge Macknight, 1860-1950, Loan Exhibition of Watercolors* [Museum of Fine Arts, Boston, 1950], cat. 83). The date, in purple, was painted after the signature, in red, most likely when Macknight completed the watercolor. However, it is possible that Macknight didn't inscribe the date on the picture until some time later, and misremembered the exact year as he did so. However, in the absence of further documentation, the picture is catalogued here with the date inscribed on it.

2. "Dodge Macknight Waves the Flag in Stirring Quartet of Watercolor Views of Boston Streets," *Boston Evening Transcript*, March 23, 1918.

3. See Ilene Susan Fort, *The Flag Paintings of Childe Hassam* (Los Angeles: Los Angeles County Museum of Art, 1988).

4. "Once More, Dodge Macknight," *Boston Herald*, March 24, 1918.

5. *Dodge Macknight, 1860-1950* suggests the watercolor was painted from the balcony of John T. Spaulding's house at 99 Beacon Street, a plausible location for the view depicted. Spaulding, a prominent Boston collector and supporter of Macknight's, seems never to have owned this watercolor. An inscription on the backing in Macknight's hand dedicates the painting to "my dear friends/Ned and Mary Holmes/with love." The Holmeses, prominent Bostonians, were also Macknight enthusiasts.

George Hawley Hallowell

Born Boston, Massachusetts, 1871;
died Boston, Massachusetts, 1926

Although he is just being rediscovered today, Hallowell received exuberant praise from colleagues during his lifetime. John Singer Sargent reportedly called Hallowell "the finest decorative talent in America today," and architect Ralph Adams Cram considered him "one of the greatest geniuses of his time." Hallowell's family was highly artistic. His father, Lewis Morris Hallowell, was an architect and his mother, Harriet Cordelia Hawley, was a pianist and artist. The family also included an aunt, sister, and cousin who were artists, as well as Stephen and Maxfield Parrish, who were distant yet influential relatives. In keeping with family tradition, Hallowell attended classes at Harvard in his mid-teens, studying watercolor and drawing with Harold B. Warren, and art and art history under professors Charles H. Moore and Charles Eliot Norton. This exposure is reflected in a Pre-Raphaelite penchant for detailed handling and minute observation of nature in his work (Moore and Norton were among the chief proponents of Ruskin's "truth to nature" philosophy in America.)

At the age of sixteen, Hallowell began an apprenticeship in the architectural firms of Rotch & Tilden and H. Langford Warren, but he changed course in 1890 and entered the School of the Museum of Fine Arts. There he studied painting for three years under Frank W. Benson and Edmund Tarbell, probably the best-known of the Boston School artists. While stylistically Hallowell's work retains the characteristic smooth surfaces of these Boston School painters, he also was influenced by the sinuous decorative manner of the international art nouveau movement, and by the stylized compositions of his cousin Maxfield Parrish. Hallowell's later preference for jewel-like colors owes a debt to Parrish and to the work of his Pre-Raphaelite mentors, especially Moore.

During the 1890s, Hallowell executed numerous book covers, poster designs, and drawings for such Boston clients as the *Atlantic Monthly*, the Tremont Theater, and the *Boston Herald*. In 1899, he embarked on a two-year trip to Europe, during which he made watercolors after Italian Renaissance paintings, architecture, and stained glass. After his return to Boston, and for the next six years, Hallowell spent much of his time designing decorative furnishings for churches, such as altar-

pieces and stained glass. He continued to paint in oil and watercolor, exhibiting his paintings in 1903 at the St. Botolph Club in Boston, and with the Copley Society, the Boston Water Color Club, the Boston Society of Arts and Crafts, and the New York Water Color Club for the remainder of his career.

Fig. 1. Katsushika Hokusai (1760-1849). *Amida Waterfall*, 1827-1830. Woodblock print. Museum of Fine Arts, Boston. William and John T. Spaulding Collection.

George Hawley Hallowell
69. *Brook in Vermont*, about 1901-06
Watercolor over graphite on very thick, moderately textured, off-white wove paper
9⅞ x 13½ in. (250 x 342 mm.), irregular
Gift of Denman W. Ross. 06.122

Critic William Howe Downes wrote of Hallowell's landscapes shown at his 1903 exhibition at Boston's St. Botolph Club that they were "glorified by the passion for color; they were the ardent, fiery, impulsive flights of a Byronic mind, overflowing with creative and dramatic potency. To me, the strong, abrupt contrasts of light and dark . . . rich and mysterious shadows full of color . . . strange and fascinating combinations of local color forming mosaics of the utmost brilliancy were the wonders that one recalled and that remained a source of profound pleasure."[1]

Downes could well have been speaking of Hallowell's *Brook in Vermont*. The heightened, saturated colors of this watercolor and the intense concentration on natural details are typical of the artist's landscapes in this medium. Here, Hallowell omits all trace of sky, and minimizes surrounding landscape elements in order to concentrate fully on his subject – water. Water is observed here in many states: patterned swirls of transparent liquid as it flows across the rocks at the center of the image, shadowed claw-like fingers of water crawling down the rocks at lower left, and, at lower center, foaming, bubbling water as it churns.

The close-up examination and highly specific rendering of natural phenomena derive from Hallowell's training with the American Pre-Raphaelites. His devices for portraying water in motion are reminiscent of nineteenth-century Japanese prints popular in Boston at the time, such as Katsushika Hokusai's *Amida Waterfall* (fig. 1), where patterned swirls of water turn into sinewy fingers. These textural variations in water are adroitly portrayed by Hallowell using a combination of linear drawing and colored washes. Although certain areas of the foam and the cloudlike rock at center are depicted by means of white paper reserves, the image is for the most part built up with thin layers of watercolor that have been applied and then lifted off with a sponge or other

144 / AWASH IN COLOR (cat. 69)

Charles Emile Heil

Born Boston, Massachusetts, 1870;
died Portland, Maine, 1950

absorptive material. This technique results in mottled, velvety washes reminiscent of the soft-focus style of Hallowell's Boston School mentors. These delicate washes, in some cases outlined by the incised point of a pencil, follow the graphic underdrawings. Hallowell's incorporation of a variety of artistic influences, and his penchant for decorative effects, puts him at the heart of Boston style of his time.

ABW

1. William Howe Downes, "George H. Hallowell's Pictures," *The American Magazine of Art* 15 (September, 1924), p. 452. For another comprehensive discussion of Hallowell's life, see "Hallowell and His Work," *Boston Herald*, February 1, 1903, p. 38.

Charles Heil first studied art in Boston's Free Evening Drawing Classes, and later continued his education at the Cowles Art School with Joseph De Camp and Ernest Major. Leading practitioners of the "Boston School" style of painting, De Camp and Major specialized in portraits and genre scenes rendered in an elegant, highly finished manner. Both artists had studied in Paris and, in keeping with their example, Heil followed his study at Cowles with two years under Gustave Courtois and Joseph Blanc at the Colarossi and Delecluse academies. He made his debut in Paris exhibitions with portraits, landscapes, and animal studies.

Heil continued to paint portraits and landscapes after returning to Boston, perhaps hoping to emulate the successful careers of De Camp and Major, but soon he turned his attention to an early childhood passion: drawing birds. In 1910, an exhibition of the artist's ornithological studies in watercolor proved quite popular, encouraging Heil to continue his work in this genre, and it is for his etchings, drawings, and watercolors of birds that he is best remembered today.

Whereas reviews of Heil's work generally emphasized his close observation of zoological detail, his work is not scientific in the tradition of such artists as John James Audubon. Rather, it is marked by elegant combinations of descriptive and decorative effects. It incorporates many of the decorative stylistic features of art-nouveau design, and exhibits the influence of the *fin-de-siècle* passion for Japanese prints.

Heil continued throughout his career to receive favorable notices from critics, and won a gold medal at the 1915 Panama-Pacific Exposition. He sold his work in numerous solo exhibitions at Doll & Richards and the Brooks Reid Galleries in Boston, and in New York. The National Gallery in Washington, the New York Public Library, and the Bibliothèque Nationale all acquired Heil's work during his lifetime. At his death in 1950, the Boston Public Library acquired a complete set of the artist's ornithological etchings; along with the Museum of Fine Arts, Boston, it is the major repository of the artist's work.

Charles Emile Heil
70. *The Lotus*, about 1912
Watercolor over graphite on thick, rough-textured wove paper mounted on thick cardboard
16⅞ x 22½ in. (428 x 571 mm)
Signed lower right in graphite and watercolor:
C E Heil
Purchased from an anonymous fund. 43.1310

The large size, unconventional composition, and startling magnification of its subject distinguishes *The Lotus* from the majority of Charles Heil's watercolors. Works like *Phoebe* (fig. 1) are more typical: small in scale, in a vertical format with the bird floating decoratively on the center of the sheet, and the white of the paper forming the background. Here the sheet is filled completely with form and color. The viewer is shown not a single specimen, but a close-up view of a pond from which exotic water plants emerge dramatically.

Fig. 1. *Phoebe, Profile to Left, on Grass*
Watercolor. Museum of Fine Arts, Boston.
Bequest of John T. Spaulding.

Ross Sterling Turner

Born Westport, New York, 1847;
died Nassau, the Bahamas, 1915

The striking effects of scale and composition in this work are heightened by Heil's choice of a vibrant pink and green palette. The intensity of these hues is muted somewhat by a fairly extensive lifting of color, leaving enough wash to fill the hollows of the wove paper, while revealing a complex layering of washes that yield a mossy texture and a shimmering iridescence. Heil intensifies this effect by applying his pigment thickly in the upper third of the picture to suggest the broken reflections of the flowers in the dark water.

Japanese influences, long prevalent in Boston, are evident here in the patterned mosaic of large, unbroken circular lotus pads in the lower half of the composition. The smooth and uniform handling of these shapes forms a simple, ornamental backdrop for the more descriptive rendering of the stems and flower buds, whose crisp edges are preserved with wax resist. This combination of decorative simplification and close observation is a hallmark of the artist's work and of the Boston School artists with whom he trained.

Designed clearly as a "presentation watercolor," this work is most likely the one exhibited as *The Lotus* in 1912 at the Third Exhibition of the Society of Odd Brushes, Boston. It remained in Heil's possession and was shown at least four times between 1936 and 1939, including a large solo show at the Portland (Maine) Art Museum in 1936.[1] An admiring reviewer of that show singled out this watercolor for special mention, finding it "a glimpse of the exotic" in a show marked by "purity and brilliance of color and a marvelous sense of pattern and spatial relations. Other outstanding qualities are [Heil's] close observance of Nature and his ready perception of beauty in fields unexplored by the majority of artists."[2] *The Lotus* was purchased from the artist seven years later.

ABW

1. The other three shows were: the Boston Society of Water Color Painters, "Fiftieth Anniversary Exhibition" at the Museum of Fine Arts Boston, April 18 to May 14, 1939, cat. 130; the "Thirty-Fifth Annual Water Color Exhibition" at the Pennsylvania Academy of the Fine Arts, November 7 - December 12, 1937, cat. 604; and the "Exhibition of Paintings" at Jordan Marsh Gallery, April 26 to May 8, 1937.

2. "Charles E. Heil Has One Man Exhibit at Museum" *Portland, Maine Sunday Telegram* (October 4, 1936). This review, and others, are preserved on microfilm in the Archives of American Art.

Although proficient in oils and pastels, Turner always enjoyed greatest success as a watercolorist. Frank T. Robinson, writing in 1888, claimed that "Turner is best seen and felt in his water-colors. With this medium he excels in graphic ability and tact, and finds more freedom and a readier vehicle for his imagination." In a February 6, 1909 review of an exhibition of Turner's oil paintings and watercolors, The *Boston Evening Transcript* noted:

> Mr. Turner is distinctively a water-color painter, and it only requires a comparison such as this exhibition affords between his oils and watercolors to demonstrate that he is much more at home with the lighter medium. Although his oil paintings are not by any means without merit, they are painted with a water-color touch and in a watercolor style. . . . His watercolors, on the other hand, are distinguished by the qualities which properly belong to the medium, a certain crispness, a sparkle, a bright, clear, staccato style, and a personal charm.

Turner's artistic beginnings were somewhat belated: although after high school he was employed for a year as a mechanical draftsman for the U.S. Patent Office in Washington, D.C., it was not until 1876, at the age of twenty-nine, that he began his formal education in the fine arts. That year he traveled to Paris and then to Munich, where he studied with Frank Currier and was also influenced by Frank Duveneck and William Merrit Chase. His earliest works are thickly painted, following their example; however, after a trip to Italy in 1879, his palette and touch lightened, as he recognized his natural gift for watercolor.

Returning to the United States in 1883, Turner settled in Boston. He began to exhibit regularly at the Boston Art Club (which he would eventually serve as vice president), the Boston Water Color Club, and the New York Water Color Club. By the late 1880s he had a show almost annually at Doll & Richards, which, as Homer's watercolor gallery, had become known as a showcase for the medium. In 1883, he began offering instruction in watercolor in his Boston studio. Among his pupils was poet Celia Thaxter. At about the same time, he met Childe Hassam. The two painters spent many summers as Thaxter's guests on the Isles of Shoals, New Hampshire. Whereas Turner had earlier inspired Hassam to develop his interest in

watercolor, by the mid-80s Hassam's vibrant style affected Turner's.

Turner was an avid traveler: his watercolors record views in Italy, Mexico, and Bermuda, as well as the environs of his summer home in Wilton, New Hampshire. His watercolors were shown at the World's Columbian Exposition in Chicago in 1893. A natural teacher, Turner published several instruction manuals, among them *The Use of Watercolor for Beginners* (Boston: Louis Prang and Company, 1886). He also held posts at the Massachusetts Institute of Technology and from 1909, at the Massachusetts Normal Art School. Turner died in 1915, and a memorial exhibition was organized that year at the Guild of Boston Artists.

Ross Turner
71. *A Garden Is a Sea of Flowers*, 1912

Transparent and opaque watercolor on slightly textured, dark cream commercially prepared illustration board
20¾ x 30⅝ in. (527 x 780 mm)
Inscribed lower right in pale blue watercolor: a garden is a sea of flowers / Ross Turner / 1912
Gift of the Estate of Nellie P. Carter. 35.1690

This dazzling watercolor was painted on the Isles of Shoals, most likely at the Appledore property of poet Celia Thaxter, whose famous garden had been celebrated by many painters, including Childe Hassam, Ellen Robbins, and J. Appleton Brown. Turner had been a frequent visitor to Appledore, first staying at the guest house Thaxter ran and then, to her delight, building a studio next to her cottage. Thaxter, who had studied painting with Turner in the early 1880s, was enthusiastic about his work, and encouraged him to use her studio as a gallery for his watercolors: "You must not forget to bring frames and mats and have one of your pictures always for sale in my room, on the easel, and others beside. That is the place where they will sell best, because so many eyes will see them."[1]

Turner was particularly adept at flower subjects (one critic noted, "this intimacy with flowers gives him the power to interpret their language to

Fig. 1. Childe Hassam (1859-1935), *The Island Garden*, 1892. Watercolor on paper. National Museum of American Art, Smithsonian Institution. Gift of John Gellatly.

us"[2]), and painted individual species as well as garden views. His preference for informal gardens, rather than the more manicured kind, was established early and was no doubt influenced by Thaxter. He was showing views of such gardens as early as 1888, when a watercolor entitled *In the Summer Time* was singled out from among the twenty works in Turner's Doll & Richards show for its successful depiction of "a natural growth of semi-wild flowers in their simple, unaffected beauty, growing in a rural garden."[3] *A Garden is a Sea of Flowers* is a reprise of this vision. Like his friend Childe Hassam, Turner continued to visit and paint Appledore for some years after Thaxter's death; this late view of her garden is one of Turner's best-loved works.

Turner's debt to Hassam has been noted frequently. *A Garden is a Sea of Flowers* exhibits the

coloristic brilliance and the short, energetic brush strokes of many of Hassam's watercolors of Thaxter's garden, as well as his characteristic high horizon line and worm's eye perspective (see fig. 1). But whereas Hassam's pictures are painted with quick strokes of transparent color, Turner here makes extensive use of gouache, and while Hassam lets the white of his paper express the dazzling light of a summer's day, Turner covers his cream-colored support almost completely, and for sparkle relies on generous dabs of an opaque pigment, most likely Chinese white. Hassam's preferred palette for his pictures of Thaxter's garden was red, yellow, and blue; his favorite flower was hers, the poppy. Here, though species are difficult to identify, one can perhaps discern the mallow and the lanky hollyhock, swaying slightly in the island's breeze, and the hot pink *rosa rugosa* that grew profusely on Appledore. Finally, Turner takes to the extreme some of the compositional devices Hassam employed in his Appledore views. Hassam often showed Thaxter's garden as a wall of color, the space anchored only by "picturesque tidbits of architecture,"[4] or a strip of sea or sky at the very top of the picture in order to suggest romantic contrast between immediate pleasure and a longing for the remote and unknown. In Turner's watercolor, the wall of blossoms covers the entire sheet save for the corner of sky at upper right. The space is barely penetrable; the viewer instead is plunged into a jungle of blossoms so dense and brilliant that he is nearly overcome by their perfume.

A Garden is a Sea of Flowers made its debut in a Doll & Richards exhibition of about 1913. Painters and collectors of the period were enthusiastic about such riotous garden views, but the subject was not without its detractors. Already in 1893 a critic sniffed, "[After years of painting scenic panoramas, landscape painters] sprang to the other end of the see-saw and began picturing French gardens, fence corners, bits of swampy meadows, with cottony trees and malarious atmospheres. Distance was wiped out by a high sky line or smothered in fog or mist."[5] Although he was astute in recognizing the essential conservatism of such images,[6] this critic was moving against the current of popular taste. The vogue for such

a garden is a sea of flow

John Singer Sargent

Born Florence, Italy, 1856;
died London, England, 1925

informal, wild gardens as Celia Thaxter's, often conceived in painterly terms themselves, took shape in the 1890s and continues to this day.[7]

CT

1. Celia Thaxter to Ross Turner, March 14, 1888, in Rosamund Thaxter, *Sandpiper: The Life and Letters of Celia Thaxter* (Francestown, New Hampshire: Marshall Jones Co., 1963), quoted in David Park Curry, *Childe Hassam: An Island Garden Revisited* (Denver: Denver Art Museum, 1990), p. 34.

2. Frank T. Robinson, "Ross Turner," *Living New England Artists* (Boston: Samuel E. Cassino, 1888), p. 177.

3. Ibid., p. 176.

4. Curry, *Childe Hassam*, p. 68.

5. *New York Evening Post*, April 27, 1893, as quoted in John I. H. Baur, *The Inlander: Life and Work of Charles Burchfield, 1893-1967* (Newark, Delaware: University of Delaware Press, 1982), pp. 259-260.

6. Trevor J. Fairbrother, *The Bostonians, Painters of an Elegant Age, 1870-1930* (Museum of Fine Arts, Boston, 1986), p. 46.

7. See Curry, *Childe Hassam*, p. 108 and Fairbrother, *The Bostonians*, p. 47.

Although Sargent deprecatingly described his watercolors as "snapshots" and "making the best of an emergency," they are among his greatest achievements. Generally made while on holiday and away from the pressures of formal commissions, Sargent's watercolors are freer, more experimental, and more personal than most of his work in oil. Although their subjects are not unusual – they are, for the most part, landscapes, genre scenes, and figure studies – the watercolors often take an unconventional point of view, and are typically marked by dazzling renditions of light and shadow. Not for the purist, they display an extraordinary mixture of opaque and transparent pigments, and numerous tricks of the trade – scraping, wiping, and lifting out color; the use of resist, drybrush, and wet-in-wet techniques; and the application of color straight from the tube – all so deftly handled as to seem effortless.

Sargent's first exposure to art came from his mother, who was a capable watercolorist; as a consequence, he was encouraged to sketch as a child. He studied art as a youth, perhaps with the German watercolorist Carl Welsch. As a teenager, he produced a remarkable series of sketchbooks (Fogg Art Museum, Harvard University Art Museums, Cambridge, Massachusetts and the Metropolitan Museum of Art, New York), filled with accomplished watercolor records of his family's constant travels. In the 1880s and 1890s he made watercolors on various trips to Spain, North Africa, and Venice, as well as on holiday in the Cotswolds; these were often in preparation for other projects. After the turn of the century he began to regard his watercolors as independent compositions, worthy of exhibition. His first major show to include watercolors seems to have been in 1903, at the Carfax Gallery in London; he joined the Royal Society of Painters in Water-Colours the next year. However, at first he chose not to sell his watercolors, and gave away only a few to friends.

After the death of his mother in 1906, Sargent regularly dedicated two or three months in the late summer and fall of each year to travel and watercolor painting. With his sister Emily and a handful of close friends, he visited at various times the Swiss Alps, Spain, Majorca, Corfu, and many sites in Italy. His friends, sometimes posed naturally and sometimes in elaborately costumed tableaux, were the subjects of a large number of watercolors and quite a few oils produced until the outbreak of World War I. He subsequently dedicated himself to mural painting, save for a handsome group of watercolors painted in Florida in 1917. Sargent's watercolors formed the basis of several large and critically acclaimed exhibitions that he arranged at M. Knoedler and Co. in New York; he also stipulated that the works be sold as a group, and arranged favorable prices (less than $250 per watercolor) as an inducement. As a result, his various series of pictures – the 1905-06 Bedouin subjects, the charming genre scenes done at the Simplon Pass, the Carrara quarry watercolors – remained united. The Brooklyn Museum virtually bought out the first Knoedler show (acquiring eighty-three of eighty-six pictures); the Museum of Fine Arts bought all forty-five watercolors displayed in 1912; the Metropolitan Museum acquired ten in 1915 and the Worcester Art Museum eleven in 1917. These institutions remain the major repositories of Sargent's watercolors.

Watercolors played a large role in the retrospective shows held toward the end of Sargent's life, and in the memorial exhibitions mounted in Boston, New York, and London immediately after his death in 1925. Sargent's reputation was severely damaged by the advent of modernism, and in particular by a scathing review published shortly after his death by Roger Fry; only recently has he resumed his rightful place alongside Winslow Homer as one of America's greatest masters of watercolor.

John Singer Sargent
72. *Genoa: The University*, about 1908

Watercolor over graphite, with wax resist on thick, rough-textured, cream wove paper; watermark:
J. WHATMAN
20⅞ x 15¹⁵⁄₁₆ in. (530 x 405 mm)
Signed lower left in iron gall ink: John S. Sargent
Hayden Collection. Charles Henry Hayden Fund.
12.204

"Genoa is not a museum, and few travelers are tempted by her art or by her memories. Like Venice, she lived and grew by and for commerce. But whereas in Venice we saw magnificent collections of pictures by her own artists, that remain a precious memorial to the ages, and lend a charm to her commercial greatness, in Genoa we find only the fading record of the greatness without charm."[1] Sargent seems to have concurred with this view, expressed in a 1911 guidebook, *The Ideal Italian Tour*, for although he painted countless watercolors of Venice, only a few are known that clearly represent Genoa.

The University at Genoa, which began as a Jesuit college in 1623 and became a university in 1812, is at the cultural center of the city. Housed in a seventeenth-century building, it boasts statuary by Giovanni da Bologna, and is distinguished by a natural history museum, a botanical garden and, adjacent to the garden, a celebrated courtyard. Sargent gives us a view along the balcony of that court, looking toward the staircase that leads to the garden.[2] A few steps away is the Palazzo Balbi-Senarega, whose picture gallery contains works by Van Dyck, Titian, Rubens, Strozzi, Guido Reni, and Tintoretto, among others. But neither the artistic masterpieces nor the architectural splendors of this historic quarter of the city seemed as paintable to Sargent as this empty corridor in the university.[3] His interest was in the light, in the tinted shadows cast on the stone walls, and in the contrast with the riotous color of the gardens beyond.

Sargent conveyed the empty coolness of the colonnaded passageways with the palette he turned to so often for architectural subjects: a medium brown, accented with a soft gray-blue. This combination of warm and cool tones is espe-cially effective in the corridor's worn tiled floor where, by actually articulating only a few of the lozenges, he nonetheless created a rich impression of the receding space. Sargent used a straightedge for perspectival scaffolding, though he drew the vaults freehand. He felt free to disregard under-drawing as he was laying down his washes, some-times – as in the capital of the foremost column at right – changing his mind even after color had been applied, deftly scraping out the original capi-tal in order to achieve a clean silhouette. In con-trast to the quiet, restful tones of the university's stately architecture, the botanical garden, seen be-yond the screen of columns at right, is a profusion of green and yellow daubs. Sargent's strokes are alternately transparent and opaque, with scraping out and dry-brush strokes over top, to create the effect of scintillating light, of light breaking up color.

CT

1. Henry James Forman, *The Ideal Italian Tour* (Boston and New York: Houghton Mifflin Company, 1911), p. 391.

2. *Baedeker's Handbook for Travelers: Northern Italy* (Leipzig: Karl Baedecker, 1882), p. 97.

3. Sargent often found eloquence in uninhabited spaces and empty corridors. See, among many examples, *The Garden Wall* (cat. 77) and *Venetian Doorway* (Metropol-itan Museum of Art, New York).

John Singer Sargent
73. *Corfu: Lights and Shadows*, 1909

Transparent and opaque watercolor over graphite on thick, rough-textured, cream wove paper
15¾ x 20⅞ in. (403 x 530 mm)
Hayden Collection. Charles Henry Hayden Fund.
12.207

Even for the cosmopolitan Sargent, 1909 was an unusually international year. Based in London, and exhibiting portraits and genre paintings at the Royal Academy and the New English Art Club there, Sargent made his American debut as a wa-tercolorist in New York in February,[1] worked on the Boston Public Library murals, and was award-ed the Order of Merit by France and the Order of Leopold by Belgium. In the late summer he made his customary pilgrimage to the Val d'Aosta with his sister Emily. From there, they went to Venice, where they joined their close friends Jane and Wilfred von Glehn (later de Glehn) and Eliza Wedgwood. At the beginning of October they all moved to the Greek island of Corfu, where they rented the Villa Sotiriotisa.

Corfu, under British authority for much of the nineteenth century, had been restored to Greece in 1863. By the time of Sargent's visit it was an ex-tremely fashionable resort, patronized by well-born Britons, Austrians, and Germans, including Kaiser Wilhelm, who maintained a summer resi-dence there. In spirit, Corfu was closer to Italy and the west than to Greece and the east, having a long history as a trading outpost for the Vene-tians.[2] For Sargent, it was a natural extension of his usual itinerary. He painted a variety of subjects there, including the island's famed olive groves, orange trees, and cypresses, and their villa and its gardens. He also produced at least two watercolors in the park of the royal villa Monrepos, which commands a spectacular view of the town and fortress of Corfu, and of the sea beyond.

In both views of this modest stucco building, Sargent's primary interest was the pattern of col-ored shadows on the whitewashed surface of the building. In the smaller version (fig. 1), Sargent isolated the front façade, cropping it just below the roofline and showing only fragments of the landscape and side wall to left and right. This

Fig. 1. *The Green Door*, 1909. Watercolor on paper. Private collection. Photograph courtesy of Coe Kerr Gallery, New York.

closeup view, and the resulting magnification of the animated, translucent strokes of wash, make the picture quite abstract. In *Corfu: Lights and Shadows*, Sargent used a straightforward composition and technique to suggest the simple joys of a holiday on a Mediterranean island: the dazzling light and baking heat relieved by refreshing breezes and by a glimpse of an invitingly cool interior and the sea in the distance. He chose a conventional view, and the blue brushstrokes sweeping across the walls of the simple building give a sense of motion to what could have been a rather static composition. The watercolor is directly painted, and other than some wiping out on the façade, there are few technical flourishes. The warm tones used for the buildings and landscape contrast with the cool tones of the interior spaces. The leaves at upper left were described with short, crisp brushstrokes while the dissolving shadows they cast were painted quite wet to underscore their intangibility, in a bright blue (probably ultramarine) that has been mixed with white to suggest the chalky texture of the cottage walls. Although Sargent described his subject here as sunlight and shadow (the juxtaposition of direct, transmitted, and reflected light being one of his favorite effects), the watercolor is far richer than a simple descriptive exercise. In *Corfu: Lights and Shadows*, Sargent evokes the mood of a holiday idyll: the sun-dappled building in its siren setting conjures up an interlude of romance and repose.

CT

1. Sargent exhibited eighty-six watercolors and his friend Edward Darley Boit showed sixty-three watercolors at Knoedler's. See Trevor J. Fairbrother, *John Singer Sargent and America*, Outstanding Dissertations in the Fine Arts, (New York: Garland Publishing, Inc., 1986), pp. 328-329, and Annette Blaugrund, "'Sunshine Captured': The Development and Dispersement of Sargent's Watercolors," *John Singer Sargent*, ed. Patricia Hills (New York: Whitney Museum of American Art, 1986), pp. 224-230.

2. British royal connections with the island of Corfu continue. Prince Philip was born there in 1921 and maintains Monrepos as a summer residence. See Philip Sanford Marden, *Greece and the Aegean Islands* (Boston and New York: Houghton, Mifflin and Company, 1907), pp. 368-380, and *The Blue Guides: Greece*, ed. Stuart Rossiter (London: Ernest Benn Limited, 1967), pp. 453-458.

John Singer Sargent
74. *Under the Rialto Bridge*, about 1909
Transparent and opaque watercolor over graphite on moderately thick, moderately rough-textured, cream wove paper
10⅞ x 19 in. (276 x 484 mm)
Hayden Collection. Charles Henry Hayden Fund. 12.203

The Rialto Bridge, built in 1588, is one of the most famous landmarks in Venice. Sargent, who painted Venice more than any other place in Italy, initially (in the 1880s) avoided the tourist haunts, gravitating instead to the city's back streets and underclass populations. When he returned after the turn of the century, he focused for the most part on Venice's landmarks, seeking new approaches to hackneyed subjects.[1] Watercolor was an ideal vehicle, and Sargent's Venetian views evoke the sparkling light reflected off the canals onto the sculpted facades of the city's famous churches and palazzi, and seem to capture spontaneously the odd perspectives offered by its maze of alleys and waterways. The view Sargent chose of this site – the underside of the bridge – would have been familiar to the city's many gondola-riding tourists, yet it was not a vantage point promoted by Venice's commercial photographers or by the legions of artists who painted more conventionally picturesque scenes. *Under the Rialto Bridge* is a distinctly original view, one that captures the immediacy of Sargent's vision but at the same time perfectly illustrates Ruskin's poetic description of the bridge:

> At the extremity of the bright vista, the shadowy Rialto threw its colossal curve slowly forth from behind the palace of the Camerlenghi; that strange curve, so delicate, so adamantine, strong as a mountain cavern, graceful as a bow just bent.[2]

Although Sargent frequently painted similar subjects in oil and watercolor, rarely do images in the two media correspond as closely as do the watercolor and two oils (fig. 1 and private collection) he painted of the Rialto Bridge between about 1909 and 1911. *Under the Rialto Bridge* was the first of these, and is the simplest. In it, the ponderous curve of the bridge looms dark and massive overhead, filling almost half the sheet. It dwarfs

Fig. 1. *The Rialto*, about 1911. Philadelphia Museum of Art. The George W. Elkins Collection

the gondola passing off to the left, while throwing much of the Grand Canal into shadow. Its bulk is dematerialized, however, by the reflections dancing across its underside, the diagonal brushstrokes describing the angle of the light bouncing off the canal. In the oils, Sargent added to these elements several other gondolas carrying elegantly attired English or American tourists and, in the immediate foreground, a humbler vessel bearing working-class Venetians and their cargo of cabbages to the nearby produce market.[3]

Sargent tended to work on a watercolor block, and so most of his paintings are a uniform size – about 15¾ x 20¾ inches.[4] *Under the Rialto Bridge* is unusual both for its elongated shape and for its palette, which is based upon tan, teal, cobalt, and several other blues as well as his usual brown and purple tones. Compared to most of his watercolors, which exhibit an extraordinary range and variety of techniques, this work is quite straightforward in execution. It is based on fluid washes, with a few strokes laid on with a dry brush to delineate the lapping water, and opaque white to articulate the jaunty gondolier and the reflections on the bridge. It is a sketch, and as such, *Under the Rialto Bridge* offers insight into Sargent's method of picture-making. The artist's great nephew and biographer Richard Ormond describes a family photograph that records a scene nearly identical to that of the Rialto Bridge pictures, featuring Sargent's sister Emily and their friend Eliza Wedgwood in the gondola at center right.[5] The oils were informed both by the photograph, in which the foreground activity and the vantage point from the Fondamenta del Vin (the embankment on the southwest side of the bridge) were established, and by the watercolor, in which the patterns of light and shadow were worked out.

Despite its function as a preparatory sketch, Sargent presumably considered this watercolor entirely satisfactory as a work of art, for he exhibited it at the Royal Water-Colour Society in 1910[6] and again at Knoedler's Gallery in New York before selling it to the Museum in 1912.

CT

1. I am grateful to Erica Hirshler for sharing these ideas with me.

2. John Ruskin, *The Stones of Venice* (1851-53), edited by Jan Morris (Mount Kisko, New York: Moyer Bell Limited, 1989), p. 54.

3. For a thorough discussion of this district, see Margaretta Lovell, *Venice: An American View, 1860-1920* (San Francisco: The Fine Arts Museums of San Francisco, 1984), pp. 120-121.

4. Sargent also occasionally used a slightly smaller block (for example, for *Simplon Pass: The Lesson*, cat. 75), measuring 15 x 18 inches.

5. Richard Ormond, *John Singer Sargent: Paintings, Drawings, Watercolours* (London: Phaidon Press Limited, 1970), p. 257. The oil now in the Philadelphia Museum was exhibited frequently during Sargent's lifetime. The other, in which Emily and Eliza are shown more prominently, remained in the family until recently.

6. Ibid.

John Singer Sargent

75. *Simplon Pass: The Lesson*, 1911
Transparent and opaque watercolor over graphite, with wax resist, on thick, rough-textured, cream wove paper
15 x 18⅛ in. (381 x 459 mm)
Signed upper right in iron gall ink: John S. Sargent
Hayden Collection. Charles Henry Hayden Fund. 12.218

76. *Simplon Pass: The Tease*, 1911
Transparent and opaque watercolor over graphite, with wax resist, on thick, rough-textured, cream wove paper
15¾ x 20⅝ in. (401 x 524 mm)
Signed lower right in iron gall ink: John S. Sargent
Hayden Collection. Charles Henry Hayden Fund. 12.216

"Other travellers wrote their diaries; he painted his, and his sisters, his nieces and nephews, Miss Wedgewood [sic], the Misses Barnard, Mr. and Mrs. de Glehn, Mr. Harrison are all on its pages . . . Palestine, the Dolomites, Corfu, Italy, Spain, Portugal, Turkey, Norway, Greece, Egypt, France, and the Balearic Islands are on record."[1] Sargent's pictorial diary for the summer of 1911 consists of numerous watercolors of his family and friends at the Simplon Pass.[2] The paintings are, to be sure, brilliant essays on the rendering of colored shadows and dappled light and demonstrate Sargent's facility with an astonishing variety of watercolor techniques, all employed so as to seem effortless. Yet they are also a glimpse into intricate personal relationships as fascinating and appealing as are Sargent's surfaces.[3]

The Lesson features Sargent's sister Emily, herself an accomplished painter, demonstrating watercolor techniques to her two nieces, Rose-Marie, aged about eighteen, and Violet Ormond, about fourteen. Photographs from the period attest to Emily's genial bulk, and to her fondness for the dark, voluminous cloak secured with a silver brooch she wears here.[4] Her watercolor pan in her lap, she clenches one brush between her teeth (so as to preserve the delicate point), while painting the scene before her on a watercolor block resting on a tripod. Her technique and materials were not unlike her brother's: he, too, was not much interested in elaborate paints or papers, but

preferred the convenience of "box colors" and a watercolor block when painting out of doors.[5]

Rose-Marie plays a more active role in *The Tease*. Her slightly bored air (one suspects she holds the green parasol as much to preserve her delicate complexion as to shade her aunt's composition from the glare of the sun) provides an amusing foil to Emily's intensity. Her companion, Polly Barnard, was an old family friend; as a girl, she had posed with her sister for *Carnation, Lily, Lily, Rose* (1885-86, Tate Gallery, London). As a woman in her thirties (she is about thirty-seven here), she often joined the Sargent entourage for its Alpine vacation. She and Rose-Marie were frequently shown together in these watercolors and, despite the difference in their ages, were posed and outfitted interchangeably in pictures whose exotic, Near-Eastern costumes and languid air gave the pictures an intriguing note of sensuality. The mood in *The Tease* is much more playful, but it too is anecdotal, and deliberately ambiguous. Lounging in the Alpine grass, the younger woman pesters her companion, perhaps with an insect or piece of meadow grass in her hand. Polly Barnard, her expression shielded by her spectacles and the green-tinted shadows cast by her parasol, shrinks away; her body, though summarily painted, clearly describes her irritation. Yet the figures remain close: Sargent's flashing strokes merge their white dresses into a single mass of decorative white drapery; their forms are further blended by the diagonal blue-green shadow falling over both of them. Sargent referred to Rose-Marie and Polly (as well as their sisters Reine Ormond and Dorothy [Dolly] Barnard) as the "inter-twingles,"[6] an allusion to their willing interchangeability as models but also, perhaps, to the easy familiarity and affection among the young women.

CT

1. Mary Newbold Patterson Hale, "The Sargent I Knew," *World Today* 50 (November 1927); reprinted in Carter Ratcliff, *John Singer Sargent* (New York: Abbeville Press, 1982), p. 237.

2. Among these are *Reading*, *Simplon Pass: The Green Parasol*, and *Simplon Pass: At the Top* (all 1911, Museum of Fine Arts, Boston); *In the Tyrol* (1911, Fogg Art Museum, Harvard University Art Museums, Cam-

bridge, Massachusetts); and *In the Simplon* (1911, private collection). There are also numerous oils from the period in which these figures appear, and many that address the theme of the artist painting out of doors. *The Lesson* would be reprised in 1912 in Spain (*In the Generalife*, Metropolitan Museum of Art, New York); there Emily appears painting a watercolor observed by Jane von Glehn and an older Spanish friend known only as "Dolores."

3. For an important discussion of this aspect of Sargent's art, see Trevor J. Fairbrother, "Sargent's Genre Paintings and the Issues of Suppression and Privacy," *American Art around 1900: Lectures in Memory of Daniel Fraad, Studies in the History of Art* 37 (Washington, D.C.: National Gallery of Art, 1990), pp. 29-49.

4. Reproduced in James Lomax and Richard Ormond, *John Singer Sargent and the Edwardian Age* (Leeds: Leeds Art Gallery, 1979), figs. 21 and 24.

5. Sargent noted that "I find 'box color' very useful, and I use a great many brushes, keeping my fist full when I work." Sargent in Richard Ormond, *John Singer Sargent: Paintings, Drawings, Watercolours* (London: Phaidon Press Limited, 1970), p. 70. The remnants of glue on the edges of the sheet on which *The Lesson* was painted is clear evidence that it was painted on a watercolor block. For an excellent discussion of Sargent's materials and technique, see Judith C. Walsh, "Observations on the Watercolor Techniques of Homer and Sargent," Susan E. Strickler, ed., *American Traditions in Watercolor: The Worcester Art Museum Collection* (Worcester: Worcester Art Museum, 1987), pp. 45-65, especially pp. 60-61.

6. Quoted in David McKibben, *Sargent's Boston* (Boston: Museum of Fine Arts, 1956), p. 114. Fairbrother ("Sargent's Genre Paintings," p. 41) notes that "intertwingles" is a portmanteau blend of intertwine and intermingle, and suggests that it refers as well to the convoluted poses Sargent asked his models to assume.

John Singer Sargent
77. *Simplon Pass: The Foreground*, 1911
Transparent and opaque watercolor over graphite, with wax resist, on thick, rough-textured cream wove paper; fragmentary WHATMAN watermark
14 x 20 in. (357 x 509 mm)
Signed lower right in iron gall ink: John S. Sargent
Hayden Collection. Charles Henry Hayden Fund.
12.219

Between 1904 and 1913, Sargent spent almost every summer at the Simplon Pass or at Purtud in the Val d'Aosta on the Italian-Swiss border. He responded energetically to the purity of light and air at the high elevations, and produced numerous informal paintings, in oil and in watercolor, of family members and close friends posed langorously in Alpine meadows (see cat. 76), and of the Alpine landscape itself – of glacial streams, mountain boulders, and the delicate Alpine flora, often from a dizzily ascending perspective surmounted by a wisp of brilliant blue sky.

Six Simplon Pass landscapes were among the forty-five watercolors the Museum of Fine Arts acquired from Sargent's 1912 exhibition at Knoedler's in New York; his Boston friend and patron Sarah Choate Sears bought the oil *Glacier Stream: the Simplon* (about 1910, Museum of Fine Arts, Springfield, Massachusetts) at about the same time.[1] Of these, *Simplon Pass: the Foreground* is rare for recording a stormy, overcast day. Furthermore, it is the most unusual compositionally, and the most austere, for it includes no landmark or feature – no alpine hut, no figure sketching, no strip of sky at the top – to enable the viewer to judge scale or measure distance, or to give the scene a picturesque charm.[2] Instead, the focus is a muddy, rutted path that bisects the image (the frontality of *The Foreground* is unusual for Sargent, who typically preferred diagonal compositions) and leads the eye to a relatively near summit. Beyond are mountains so tall that they obscure the sky. *The Foreground* is particularized, with animated dry-brush strokes and judicious use of paper reserve as well as Sargent's customary deftly manipulated washes defining the boulders and muddy patches. Wax resist – applied between layers of wash in passages at left – repli-

Fig. 1. *Yoho Falls*, 1916. Oil on canvas.
Isabella Stewart Gardner Museum, Boston.

cates the texture of lichen on the rocks, and dol-
lops of white overlaid with red glazes are Alpine
roses. The mountains, on the other hand, are far
more softly painted to indicate the diffuse atmosphere and their greater distance. On the hillside at
upper left, a swath where color has been wiped
away evokes the reflection of the sun breaking
through storm clouds. In its intimate focus on
natural effects, and in its rootless composition,
Simplon Pass: The Foreground anticipates the oils
and watercolors Sargent painted in the Canadian
Rockies five years later (fig. 1).[3]

Sargent's critics, both in his own day and at
present, have frequently remarked that he was
preoccupied by formal concerns in these landscapes and indifferent to specifics of topography.[4]
Viewed up close, *Simplon Pass: the Foreground* appears a dazzling display of light and texture, with
little form or substance. Yet the emotional impact
of the animated surface and startling perspective
cannot be denied. Sargent supplies just enough
detail so that the view becomes recognizable in
feeling, if not in its geographical particulars and,
when the watercolor is seen at a distance, the
space resolves, the foreground appears traversable,
and the moisture-laden atmosphere is palpably
cool and fresh.

CT

1. Other Simplon landscapes from this period include a
dramatic oil owned by the Corcoran Gallery of Art
(*Simplon Pass*, 1910), *Simplon*, a watercolor at the Museum of Art, Rhode Island School of Design, and the
very wet and abstract watercolor, *Mountain Fire*
(1903-08, The Brooklyn Museum).

2. Sargent tended to avoid romantic vistas, confessing in
a letter to his friend Henry Tonks, "As you known enormous views and huge skies do not tempt me." (Ormond
family collection, quoted in Richard Ormond, *John
Singer Sargent: Paintings, Drawings, Watercolors* [Lon-
don: Phaidon Press Limited, 1970], p. 69.) Yet he was
capable of suggesting high drama in nature with just a
few strokes of the brush, as in the remarkable
Mountain Fire, mentioned above.

3. I thank Trevor Fairbrother for this suggestion.

4. Ormond notes, "It cannot be said that Sargent was indifferent to the subjects which he selected to paint, but
they are primarily vehicles for statements about colour
and light, and even paint itself." Ormond, *John Singer
Sargent*, p. 69. Carter Ratcliff defines these mountain
landscapes as "expanses of enveloping texture, woven
from phenomenally acute perceptions of tone and color"
(*John Singer Sargent* [New York: Abbeville Press,
1982], p. 221). And of a slightly earlier alpine picture,
The Hermit, a rather less sympathetic critic wrote in
1909, "[It is] a piece of extraordinary brilliant execution. The first impression is that of actual blinding sunlight and shadow. . . . If to represent the sensations of
the eye with the utmost possible vividness and com-
pleteness be the master aim of art, then this is among
the final masterpieces; but what is the effect on our
minds?" (Lawrence Binyon, "The New English Art
Club," *The Saturday Review*, 107 [May 29, 1909], p.
684, quoted in Patricia Hills, "Painted Diaries: Sargent's
Late Subject Pictures," *John Singer Sargent* [New York:
Whitney Museum of American Art, 1986], pp. 193-
194.)

John Singer Sargent
78. *The Garden Wall*, 1910

Transparent and opaque watercolor over graphite, with
wax resist, on thick, rough-textured, cream wove paper;
with fragmentary (Whatman?) watermark
15¾ x 20¾ in. (403 x 530 mm)
Signed upper left in red watercolor: John S. Sargent;
upper right in iron gall ink: John S. Sargent
Hayden Collection. Charles Henry Hayden Fund.
12.222

Sargent's subjects here are, at left, Jane Emmet
von Glehn (later de Glehn), wife of the painter
Wilfred von Glehn, and herself an accomplished
painter of portraits and landscapes, and at right
Lady Richmond, wife of the academic artist Sir
William Blake Richmond. These couples, along
with Sargent, his sister Emily, and Eliza
Wedgwood, another family friend, were frequent
traveling companions in the summer and autumn
months from about 1907 onward. In the early
autumn of 1910, this group rented Torre Galli, a
handsome villa near Florence owned by Sargent's
friend, the Marchese Farinola. The artists painted
and posed for one another frequently in those
years, and although Sargent occasionally was
exasperated by the progress of his work ("So
many studies have been started here with the
Richmonds figuring in corners that I feel tired"),[1]
the interval at Torre Galli was in fact rather fruitful. Sargent produced at least three oils and four
watercolors before decamping for Lucca in October;[2] these document the villa itself, the lush
Tuscan countryside and, in such paintings as
Breakfast in the Loggia (fig. 1) his friends posed in
various combinations against the cool stucco walls
of the villa, with its sun-dappled gardens visible
beyond.

The convivial mood of *Breakfast in the Loggia*
is not repeated in *The Garden Wall*, an elegant and
technically brilliant watercolor whose unconventional composition suggests personal relationships
of great complexity. Two companions, who chat so
animatedly in the oil, here do not converse or even
look at one another. Sargent posed them on either
side of the doorway in tactful acknowledgment of
their different ages,[3] but the separation also suggests an emotional gulf between them, however

Fig. 1. *Breakfast in the Loggia*, 1910. Oil on canvas. Freer Gallery of Art, Smithsonian Institution, Washington, D. C.

momentary. The younger woman, dressed in a gown of dazzling white, sports a cashmere shawl so particularized as to become a focal point, while her face and hair, because of a superimposed pale gray wash, recede somewhat into the background; she does not look at her friend or the viewer but appears to be daydreaming. Lady Richmond is far more conservatively dressed than Jane von Glehn; her hairstyle is more severe, as is her countenance. She perches on the edge of the stone bench, her arms crossed and propped on an unread book held facing outward in her lap; remnants of strokes wiped out at her right arm and hip reveal that her figure was once fuller, and therefore slightly closer to Jane von Glehn. For the most part, the foreground has been rendered in a cool, almost monochromatic palette – Sargent's familiar blues and browns – and in tones of even intensity: the shawl is about the only dramatic accent. The softly washed warm tones of the interior court make it seem the more inviting space. Its inclusion in the center of this composition, and the marked differences in handling between foreground and courtyard, not only make the space of the picture more legible, but, by pulling the eye beyond the picture's surface, raise the issue of interior thoughts and emotions. There is no evidence as to whether Sargent actually observed subtle tensions between these figures as they sat in the sun at Torre Galli, or whether he staged the tableau; however, he had created psychological mysteries before, as, for ex-

ample, in his well-known portrait of the daughters of Edward Darley Boit (1882, Museum of Fine Arts, Boston). As he had in that painting (and, ultimately, as had Velázquez, whom Sargent greatly admired), here he used the separate spaces of his composition and the physical attitudes of his figures to intimate a relationship and an emotional situation to which the viewer is not privy.

CT

1. John Singer Sargent to Vernon Lee, quoted in Richard Ormond, *John Singer Sargent: Paintings, Drawings, Watercolors* (London: Phaidon Press Limited, 1970), p. 76.

2. In addition to *Breakfast in the Loggia*, noted below, *At Torre Galli: Ladies in a Garden* (1910, oil on canvas, Royal Academy, London), *Florence: Torre Galli, Wine Bags*, *Florence: Torre Galli*, and *Vines and Cypresses* (all 1910, watercolor, Museum of Fine Arts, Boston) were painted at or near the Marchese's villa that autumn.

3. See Trevor J. Fairbrother, *The Bostonians: Painters of an Elegant Age, 1870-1930* (Boston: Museum of Fine Arts, 1986), p. 69.

John Singer Sargent
79. *La Biancheria*, 1910
Transparent and opaque watercolor over graphite, with wax resist on thick, rough-textured, cream wove paper; fragmentary watermark: WHATMAN 1905 [?] ENGLAND
15⅞ x 20¾ in. (403 x 530 mm)
Signed lower left in iron gall ink: John S. Sargent
Hayden Collection. Charles Henry Hayden Fund.
12.229

The watercolors Sargent made on his holidays in Italy and the Alps were not made on order, nor were they intended for exhibition or sale (he occasionally gave one to a friend). Thus there was no reason for the most fashionable portrait painter in England and America not to pursue such an unlikely, unglamorous subject as laundry drying on the line.

To be sure, many other artists had depicted laundresses – it was a timeless subject, figuring traditionally in representations of labors of the months. In Sargent's age, Millet (and in his wake, a host of American and Dutch artists) had painted peasant washerwomen scrubbing clothes at river's edge, and Daumier and Degas had painted numerous images of fatigued Parisian laundresses. But the laundry itself – breeze-stiffened sheets flapping on the line on a sunny day – was virtually unprecedented as a subject. For Sargent, of course, the attraction was not the linens, but the opportunity they afforded to paint sun and shadow, direct and transmitted light.

La Biancheria probably was painted in the autumn of 1910, when Sargent was on holiday in Italy. Most of the subjects that caught his eye that season were more conventional – the lush gardens surrounding Tuscan villas, handsome outdoor statuary and fountains. But for someone whose favorite theme had always been the rendering of white against white, the sight of laundry hanging on a line must have been irresistible. Sargent's love of making a subject out of white appeared early in his career, and in oils as well as watercolors: in *Artist in his Studio* (1910, Museum of Fine Arts, Boston), for example, it was the unlikely subject of rumpled linens (their folds affording Sargent the opportunity to paint highlights and deep shadows) that caught his eye. In this contemporary water-

color, the attraction is the same; the white of the paper and the translucency of Sargent's washes contributing to an even more dazzling effect.

Sargent brings all his technical expertise to bear, and although the casualness of the subject gives the watercolor an unpremeditated look, it was actually carefully orchestrated. Sargent used a rough-textured paper, whose twill pattern evokes the texture of the woven fabric on the line. His graphite underdrawing was casual, and in some areas defines the slack washline (which is also formed by the thinnest stripe of reserved paper) and the contours of the limp laundry. The expressively rendered background was painted rather opaquely. Wispy strokes of dry brush in the trees are punctuated with dots of pigment (possibly cadmium yellow) from the tube. The linens themselves are variously rendered, reserved paper being used for the most distant sheets, a pale yellow wash on the ones in the center, and watery blue on those in the foreground, so that one follows the tangled lines of laundry into the distance, rather than perceiving a flat, decorative pattern. And most remarkable of all, in the sheets closest to the viewer, Sargent was able to suggest not only light coming from behind, but also the sense of laundry still wet, and hanging limply. In the background, drier washes suggest drier sheets, and their squared-off contours indicate they've already stiffened in the crisp autumnal air. Sargent characterized his watercolors as "snapshots," and all his technical prowess was designed to make them seem intuitive, spontaneous, painted with an invisible hand.[1] The veracity of *La Biancheria* attests not only to Sargent's facility with the brush, but also to his subtle powers of observation; its status as one of Sargent's most frequently exhibited watercolors is a tribute to his mastery of compositional complexity and elegant surface.[2]

CT

1. Judith C. Walsh, "Observations on the Watercolor Techniques of Homer and Sargent," Susan E. Strickler, ed., *American Traditions in Watercolor. The Worcester Art Museum Collection* (Worcester: Worcester Art Museum, 1987), p. 56.

2. This watercolor made its debut at the New English Art Club in 1911. Like a number of the Museum of Fine Arts's Sargents, it was included in the 1923 exhibition of American watercolors in Paris ("Exposition d'Art Américain: John S. Sargent, R.A., Dodge Macknight, Winslow Homer, Paul Manship"), and in the memorial exhibitions in Boston (1925) and New York (1926). It has also been chosen to represent Sargent in a variety of more recent survey shows, notably "Eight American Masters of Watercolor" (Los Angeles County Museum of Art, 1968).

John Singer Sargent
80. *Villa di Marlia: Lucca,* 1910
Watercolor over graphite, with wax resist, on thick, rough-textured, cream wove paper; fragmentary WHATMAN watermark
15¹³/₁₆ x 20¹⁵/₁₆ in. (404 x 533 mm.)
Signed lower left in iron gall ink: John S. Sargent
Hayden Collection. Charles Henry Hayden Fund. 12.232

After spending the early autumn in Florence, in October of 1910 Sargent moved to nearby Varramista, outside of Lucca. There he was the guest of his friend the Marchese Farinola, who had also been his host in Florence. Ever eager to work, even when on holiday, Sargent explored the villas and gardens in the area, finding that "the mixture of dense vegetation, broken lights and garden sculpture provided endless motifs for his expansive and luxuriant style."[1] He was especially attracted to the Villa Garzoni at Collodi and the Villa di Marlia at Lucca, the latter's famous gardens providing subject matter for at least three watercolors, all in the Museum of Fine Arts (see fig. 1).[2]

When Sargent visited the Villa di Marlia, it was owned by the family of the Prince of Capua, and had a long and dramatic history. The Orsetti family built the estate in 1651, and retained it for more than 150 years. But in 1806 the family was forced to sell it to Elisa Baciocchi, Napoleon's sister, after Buonaparte had invaded Tuscany and presented the town of Lucca to her. She renamed the property "Villa Reale Marlia" and began an ambitious program of renovations designed to convert the baroque property into an English manor, with extensive gardens, vast lawns, and a deer park. Napoleon's defeat in 1814 curtailed her plans, fortunately before she was able to change the original design's most beautiful feature: a group of outdoor garden "rooms," defined by a series of interconnected alleys with surrounding walls of high boxwood hedges. These rooms contained reflecting pools, a nymphaeum, and even a "green theater."[3] It was the baroque part of the gardens at Marlia, and not Elisa's modernizations, that intrigued Sargent, and in these watercolors he skillfully conveyed the experiences of coming

Fig. 1. *Villa di Marlia: A Fountain*, 1910. Museum of Fine Arts, Boston. Hayden Collection. Charles Henry Hayden Fund.

3. For further information about Lucca, the Villa di Marlia, and the watercolor that is the companion to this one, see Erica Hirshler, "Villa di Marlia: A Fountain," in Theodore E. Stebbins, Jr., *The Lure of Italy, American Artists and the Italian Experience 1760-1914* (Boston: Museum of Fine Arts, 1991), cat. 73, pp. 321-323.

4. In its mate, *Villa di Marlia: A Fountain*, Sargent recorded a view some distance to the right: a complex and compressed arrangement that includes the pool (with the surrounding balustrade visible on three sides), a stone screen with sculpted niche, and the same statuary visible here. That watercolor may have been painted on a more overcast day, for the fountains, with their rushing water, rather than the sparkling light and deep shadow that so enlivens this picture, seem to have been Sargent's main interest.

upon these garden rooms: the sense of surprise, mystery, and delight.

In *Villa di Marlia: Lucca*, Sargent leads the eye down the boxwood-lined path at the north end of a long reflecting pool.[4] The two stone figures on the balustrade at right, representing the Arno and Secchia rivers that run through Tuscany, are seen from the side and behind. Their lumpy silhouettes are enlivened by the light playing over them, dazzlingly rendered in washes of ocher and blue and scintillating areas of paper reserve. Marking the progression on the other side are large terracotta pots of lemon trees, their lushness rendered with a few short strokes of green and yellow wash. But as the eye travels toward the back wall of the garden room (where lively calligraphic strokes of blue over wax resist evoke flickering light coming through the dense foliage), it is stopped by the shadows across the path. These liquid shadows, flowing from the rough masonry bases, form mysterious abstract shapes that are even more animate than the river gods who cast them.

CT

1. Richard Ormond, *John Singer Sargent: Paintings, Drawings, Watercolours* (London: Phaidon Press Limited, 1970), p. 76.

2. The others are *Villa di Marlia: The Balustrade* (12.228) and *Villa di Marlia, A Fountain* (12.232).

John Singer Sargent
81. *The Cashmere Shawl*, 1911
Watercolor over graphite, with wax resist, on thick, rough-textured, cream wove paper
20 x 14 in. (507 x 355 mm)
Inscribed verso, at center right, in graphite: To be cut / as marked / on other side.
Hayden Collection. Charles Henry Hayden Fund. 12.227

The Cashmere Shawl is one of Sargent's most dashing images, an elegant confection painted in the spirit of his friend Paul-César Helleu. Sargent's model is his niece, Rose-Marie Ormond, at about eighteen. She stands before an unidentified building with bits of foliage at her feet; the swirls of resist on the facade echo the fluid sweep of her pose, the insouciant turn of her head, and the dramatic billowing and bunching of her dress wrapped in the cashmere shawl. As the inscription on the verso indicates, Sargent intended that the picture be cut at the left margin, rendering the background more abstract while emphasizing the stylishness of the figure.

The shawl, one of a trunkful of exotic costumes Sargent used for his genre pictures in this period, was among his favorite props. It is probably an antique shawl, made in Kashmir about 1800-20. Interestingly, the cashmere shawl, which had been immensely popular in the mid-nineteenth century, was no longer fashionable in the Edwardian era, except among those who favored antique clothing and other modes of aesthetic dress. However, such high-style designers as Jacques Doucet and Paul Poiret appropriated oriental motifs for the borders of their garments, and Sargent's interest in exotic, Near-Eastern garb may well have been reinforced by contemporary costume design. *The Cashmere Shawl*, with its mask-like treatment of Rose-Marie's face, also echoes the style of fashion photographs of the period, in which models were often posed against dreamy, indefinite backgrounds. With its swirls of drapery and bravura surfaces, this image is as well a reprise in small scale of Sargent's own high-fashion portraits, such as *Mrs. George Swinton* (1896-97, Art Institute of Chicago), and was likewise conceived in terms of decorative effect.

The shawl was also an aspect of Sargent's neo-classicism (most obviously expressed in the murals he painted for the ceiling of the rotunda of the Museum of Fine Arts) and his interest in the work of J.A.D. Ingres. Beginning about 1907, it was featured in a group of portraits and figurative subjects that possess "a distinctly neoclassical mood."[2] Among these are several for which his nieces posed, notably *Woman in a Cashmere Shawl* (about 1910, private collection), and the mysterious *Cashmere* (about 1908, private collection), which features seven women wearing the same shawl, all modeled by his younger niece Reine Ormond. In this watercolor, mystery is replaced by élan, and by a kind of measured sensuality. The fabric clings alluringly to Rose-Marie's body, and her highly

Fig. 1. *Standing Woman*, Tanagra (?), 290-270 B.C. Museum of Fine Arts, Boston. Gift by Contribution.

artificial pose accentuates her figure. The triangle of drapery kicked out at left is in counterpoint to her elbow at right, and to her elaborate headgear. Rose-Marie exhibits a strong sculptural presence, her garments concealing yet revealing her form in a manner reminiscent of a Tanagra figurine (fig. 1).[3] With her curves thus accented, Rose-Marie exhibits the seductiveness of Sargent's exotic Javanese dancers of the late 1880s; swathed in white, she remains chaste.

CT

1. Nicola Shilliam of the Department of Textiles and Costumes graciously provided me with information on Kashmir shawls.

2. Richard Ormond, *John Singer Sargent: Paintings, Drawings, Watercolours* (London: Phaidon Press Limited, 1970), p. 66. Trevor Fairbrother has offered the suggestion that the shawl is also a token of Sargent's abiding interest in the style and spirit of the high Victorian period, the era of his youth.

3. Tanagra figurines, small painted terracotta sculptures from Boeotia dating from the Hellenistic period, were extremely popular with collectors in the last quarter of the nineteenth century. I am grateful to John J. Herrmann, Jr., for information about the figurines.

John Singer Sargent
82. *Lizzatori I*, 1911
Watercolor over graphite with wax resist on thick, rough-textured, cream wove paper; fragmentary WHATMAN watermark
20⅞ x 15¹³⁄₁₆ in. (530 x 400 mm)
Signed lower left in graphite: John S. Sargent
Hayden Collection. Charles Henry Hayden Fund.
12.239

83. *Carrara: Workmen*, 1911
Transparent and opaque watercolor over graphite with wax resist, on thick, rough-textured, cream wove paper
14 x 20 in. (355 x 507 mm)
Signed lower right in iron gall ink: John S. Sargent
Hayden Collection. Charles Henry Hayden Fund.
12.235

The quarries at Carrara, in the Apulian Alps about five miles from the Ligurian coast, yield some of the most sought-after marble in the world. Its whiteness (made all the more dazzling by the tiny crystalline specks that the local stoneworkers associated with the tears of Christ) and its unusually fine, uniform grain, make it especially desirable for sculpture. Michelangelo traveled to Carrara to choose his own blocks; Bernini and Canova sought out Carrara marble, as did Hiram Powers and many other nineteenth-century American neoclassical sculptors. By the mid-nineteenth century, the presence of artists from all over Europe lent a colorful aspect to this otherwise dull and dusty working-class village: "The town is a continuous *studio*, peopled with artists in various costumes, who affect mostly the shaggy aspect of the German Burschen, with a wild growth of hair, whiskers, mustachios, and beards, and every variety of head covering."[1] Sargent is known to have visited Carrara only once, in the autumn of 1911, at the urging of his friend the Marchese Farinola; by at least one account, it was an arduous experience.[2] Sargent nonetheless produced at least two oils and some sixteen watercolors depicting Carrara, eleven of which were bought by the Museum of Fine Arts the year following his visit.[3]

Sargent's initial impressions of Carrara are recorded in sketchbooks preserved at the Fogg Art Museum. Those drawings are for the most

Figs. 1, 2. *Sheets from Carrara Sketchbook*, 1911. Graphite on paper. The Harvard University Art Museums. Gift of Mrs. Francis Ormond.

part studies of the workers and their equipment, rendered in brusque pencil strokes. Several of the sketches (see figs. 1 and 2) rehearse the poses of the climbing figures in *Lizzatori I*. In the watercolors, however, figures and stone seem to have been of equal interest, as Sargent's attempt to understand the mechanics of cutting and hauling the huge blocks of marble was supplanted by an interest in recording the play of light over the sheer faces of the cut stone and the duller textures of dust and rubble.

The *lizzatori*, whom Sargent depicted in both these watercolors, were the workers who, by means of thick restraining ropes and soaped wooden skids (or *lizza*), would slide the mammoth blocks down the hillside. This method was both primitive and extremely hazardous, for a broken

rope would allow a block to tear down the mountain, crushing anyone in its path, and avalanches were not uncommon. A few months before Sargent's visit, ten workers eating their lunches among the rocks (much as the figures do in *Carrara: Workmen*) were killed when the face of a cliff collapsed above them.[4] Although the tragedy was still fresh when Sargent visited the quarries, he did not romanticize his subjects in these paintings, nor did he comment upon the arduousness of their labor. Rather, in most of the Carrara watercolors, rocks and men are rendered with a uniform palette, and the figures are subsumed into the landscape.

In *Lizzatori I*, the men are in deep shadow, pushed to the top left corner of the sheet. They are defined primarily by the coils of rope they carry; it is the dizzying climb up the white stone steps that is the focus of the composition. Sargent uses an astonishing variety of techniques in this watercolor to suggest by analogy the textures of the materials he is portraying: the glint of the white stone steps is suggested by slivers of reserved paper; thin, granular pigment applied over heavily textured paper, as well as the liberal use of resist, imitates the grainy surface of the rough-hewn rock faces at right; scraping out evokes the shaggy texture of the ropes; and subtle wiping of color in the sky hints at the thin, wispy clouds often visible at high altitudes. At the same time, Sargent works here with a rather limited palette, his signature ultramarine blue and Vandyke brown, rendering rocks and men in the same tones.

The same almost monochromatic color scheme, and the same array of techniques is seen in *Carrara: Workmen*, including the witty use of scraping out for such details as the soles of the workers' shoes. Strokes of red and creamy yellow – for a kerchief, for a straw-wrapped wine bottle – draw attention to the workers, who are much more prominent than the figures in most of the Carrara watercolors. Yet they are laid in with washes so wet and soft that they would nearly dissolve into the stone behind them, except that Sargent, with a masterful gesture analogous to a sculptor's, scrapes out contours and carves out telling details to give them form again.

CT

1. *Murray's Handbook for Travellers in Northern Italy*, part II (London: John Murray, 1858), p. 453.

2. As is often noted in connection with these images, at Carrara Sargent reportedly "slept for weeks in a hut so completely devoid of all ordinary comforts that his companions, far younger men, fled after a few days, unable to stand the Spartan rigors tolerated by their senior with such serene indifference." Unidentified author, *The Living Age* 325 (May 30, 1925), p. 446.

3. The Museum acquired its twelfth Carrara subject, *Carrara: A Quarry*, in 1921. Other watercolors are owned by The Tate Gallery, The Art Institute of Chicago, and two private collectors. The oils are *Bringing Down Marble from the Quarries to Carrara* (1911, The Metropolitan Museum of Art, New York) and *Marble Quarries at Carrara* (1913, collection of Lord Harewood, Leeds, Yorkshire).

4. For this and other tales connected with Carrara, see David Roberts, "When the Quarry is Marble," *Smithsonian* 22 (January 1992), pp. 98–110.

John Singer Sargent
84. *Alice Runnells James (Mrs. William James)*, 1921

Transparent and opaque watercolor over graphite on thick, rough-textured, cream wove paper
21 1/16 x 13 1/2 in. (534 x 342 mm)
Inscribed lower right in iron gall ink: to Alice James / John S. Sargent / Chocorua 1921
Gift of William James. 1977.834

Sargent seldom used watercolor for formal portraiture, reserving the medium for more casual likenesses of family and friends. Among those he did depict in watercolor was Alice Runnells James, one of many members of the James family with whom he had long and warm connections.[1] Alice Runnells James was the wife of Sargent's young colleague, the Boston painter William James, Jr., and a much admired friend of Sargent's sister Emily.[2] The watercolor was painted at the James family compound in Chocorua, New Hampshire, where Sargent was a guest in the summer of 1921.

Alice James too came from a distinguished family. Her mother came from venerable New Hampshire stock. Her father, John Sumner Runnells, was the president and general counsel for the Pullman Car Company and was based in Chicago. She probably met her husband (named for his father, the philosopher and Harvard professor) in about 1904 at Chocorua, where both families had summer homes; by 1910 they were engaged. The younger William James had abandoned an early commitment to the study of medicine for a career as a portrait painter, and shortly after their marriage in 1912, he joined the faculty and became a trustee of the School of the Museum of Fine Arts.

Alice James fit in well with the James family. She was close to her husband's uncle, the novelist Henry James, and was the acknowledged social arbiter and hostess for her generation of the family. Although she was an energetic and charming woman, Alice James was frequently ill,[3] and it is as an invalid that Sargent chose to portray her. The pale colors he used in the portrait – thinned-down ocher over white for her dress, a faded peach color for her bedjacket (whose aqua lining is echoed in the tints of the large pillows behind

Fig. 1. *Mrs. Gardner in White*, 1922. Watercolor on paper. Isabella Stewart Gardner Museum, Boston.

her), and a dull maroon for the backdrop – underscore the sitter's fragility. Yet – in contrast to the magical watercolor portrait of the aging Isabella Stewart Gardner painted the next year (fig. 1) – Alice James does not seem merely physically frail, wasting away in body while her spirit remained bright. Her face is pale, her mouth taut; her eyes lack sparkle and do not engage the viewer, who is cast in the role of visitor to the sickroom. The sense that Alice James was withdrawn physically and emotionally is enhanced by the unusual placement of the figure on the sheet: the head is high up on the page and pushed to the back of the sheet while the body (the lower half of which is barely articulated) slides off to the left.[‡]

Alice James's enervated posture, and the detachment and distance of her facial expression, obviously indicate her physical sufferings. They also may reflect her weariness with the Jamesian legacy, much as she reveled in it. R.W. B. Lewis reports her occasional impatience with the family's

Maurice Brazil Prendergast

Born St. John's, Newfoundland, 1858;
died New York City, 1924

intellectual intensity, and with its unceasing analysis of self and others; her directness no doubt conflicted with the Jamesian distance. Whereas Alice James could snap, "I'm getting goddam tired of the James-know-it-all," her father-in-law would pronounce that her "invalidism . . . wrought refinement in her inwardly."[5] Sargent's portrait is a brilliant evocation of these complex emotions and of the price paid by women in the James family.

CT

1. David McKibben lists another watercolor of Alice Runnells James, *The Quarry, Chocorua, New Hampshire*, in a private collection. See *Sargent's Boston* (Boston: Museum of Fine Arts, 1956), p. 103.

2. Stanley Olson, *John Singer Sargent: His Portrait* (New York: St. Martin's Press, 1986), p. 263.

3. R.W. B. Lewis offers the following description: "Alice Runnells James was a tall, good-looking woman; in her outward seeming, vigorous, smiling, and spirited; one who enjoyed social gatherings to the last guest's departure and who made of [the James family homes] inviting social and literary centers for decades. But she suffered from ailments, most of them real (there was a thyroid deficiency), though some imaginary, all her adult life, and had to remove herself regularly for rest and convalescence." *The Jameses, A Family Narrative* (New York: Farrar, Straus, and Giroux, 1991), p. 606.

4. The unusual elongation of the composition was tempered somewhat when Sargent drew a framing line two inches from the bottom of the sheet.

5. Lewis, *The Jameses*, pp. 608 and 606. Recapitulating the family's views of Alice James, Lewis reveals a disturbing lack of privacy. "The refinement grew stronger with time:" says Lewis, "it was hardly a secret among the James kinfolk that Alice had little taste for the sexual aspect of marriage, whereas her husband had an exceptionally energetic sexual nature" (p. 608). The James marriage suffered many storms; William separated from Alice for a time in the 1940s, and shortly after her death from a stroke in 1957, he married Mary Brush Pierce, the daughter of painter George deForest Brush.

Maurice Prendergast was one of the most sophisticated painters of his generation. Although his formal training was limited to study at the Académie Julian and at Colarossi's studio in Paris, he was well acquainted with the art literature of his day, particularly that detailing modern movements. He traveled frequently to Europe, and associated with such progressive artists as Arthur B. Davies, William Glackens, and Walt Kuhn who, as organizers of the Armory Show, helped shape modern art in America. Among Prendergast's earliest biographers were Walter Pach and Van Wyck Brooks; among his supporters were some of the most discerning patrons of his day. He was one of three watercolor painters (the others being Cézanne and Demuth) Albert Barnes collected in depth; Lizzie Bliss bought his work along with Picasso's and Matisse's; Duncan Phillips and John Quinn were also Prendergast enthusiasts. His light-hearted subject matter – strollers in the park, bathers by the seaside – belie a profound interest in the issues of modernism. That (like Demuth, Burchfield, Marin, and others) his primary medium was watercolor rather than oil is another link with the American avant-garde of the twentieth century.

Prendergast was the first of five children born to a grocer and a doctor's daughter. The children had only a limited education, and soon after the family moved to Boston in 1868, Maurice was employed in menial jobs in a drygoods store. Prendergast's younger brother Charles would be his lifelong companion and collaborator; by the 1880s the brothers' aptitude for art had attracted the attention of local patrons, who encouraged them to travel abroad. Maurice went to England (1886-87) and France (1891-94, during which time he studied at the Académie Julian). In 1898-99, sponsored by the prominent Boston collector Sarah Choate Sears, he toured Italy, painting many watercolors that are still considered his most glorious works.

In 1895, Prendergast made his artistic debut in Boston, submitting two watercolors to the Boston Art Club's spring annual. In his April 7 review of that show, the *Sunday Herald*'s critic singled out Prendergast's paintings from among the 150 works displayed, noting their "finely disciplined sense of pure and brilliant color, subordinated to a

vivacious and accurate style of depiction." A decade of critical support and widening exposure followed. Prendergast's solo exhibition of Venetian watercolors at Boston's J. Eastman Chase Gallery in 1899 prompted the noted art dealer William Macbeth to give him a show in New York. Museums in Chicago, Detroit, and Cincinnati began exhibiting his work as well. During this period Prendergast lived in Boston, and made frequent painting pilgrimages to such nearby resorts as Revere and Nantasket beaches, Annisquam, and Gloucester.

By about 1906, the Boston art community, previously so supportive, had begun to find Prendergast's work mannered and unrealistic. Although his subject matter – figures in an idyllic landscape – remained relatively constant, he was working more and more in oil, and in a classicizing style influenced by Cézanne and Puvis de Chavannes. After a trip to Paris and St. Malo in 1907, Prendergast became more involved in artistic events in New York, participating in the inaugural exhibition of The Eight (1908), the Exhibition of Independent Artists (1910), and the Armory Show (1913). He and Charles moved to New York City in 1914, after a last trip to France. During the next decade, Prendergast exhibited frequently in New York, and resumed his practice of taking working vacations on Massachusetts' North Shore. Prendergast died in 1924. Although his reputation rose and fell throughout his career, the memorial exhibition mounted by the Cleveland Museum of Art two years after his death, and the subsequent series of articles by such champions of American art as Duncan Phillips, Lloyd Goodrich, Margaret Breuning, and Van Wyck Brooks served to secure his standing as one of America's greatest practitioners of watercolor.

Maurice Prendergast
85. *Handkerchief Point*, 1896-97
Watercolor over graphite on thick, moderately rough-textured, cream wove paper
19⅞ x 13¾ in. (505 x 350 mm)
Signed lower right in graphite: Prendergast- / Pre
Gift of Francis W. Fabyan in memory of Edith Westcott
Fabyan. 31.906

With Demuth and Marin, Prendergast was the most generously represented of twentieth-century artists at the Whitney Museum's landmark exhibition, "A History of American Watercolor Painting."[1] The show included eight watercolors by Prendergast, divided between Italian subjects and views of the New England shore, *Handkerchief Point* (no. 151) being among the latter. His style was characterized as exhibiting "a fine mixture of shimmering tones, thick texture and loosely woven pattern, with which he accomplished effects paralleling those of Cézanne." Highlighting Prendergast's modernity, the exhibition catalogue downplayed his similarity to the American Impressionist painters (with whose work his subject matter nonetheless has clear affiliation), emphasizing instead his connection with "the younger men who were actually in closer contact with the French Movement – Marin, for instance, and Weber."[2]

Handkerchief Point is quite similar to a group of watercolors done at the same time on the rocky beaches of Nantasket, south of Boston, among them *Low Tide, Nantasket* (about 1896-97, Williams College Museum of Art, Williamstown, Massachusetts) and the slightly smaller *Rocky Shore, Nantasket* (fig. 1),[3] which is nearly a mirror image of this watercolor. *Handkerchief Point* traditionally has been associated with Marblehead, although there is no point in the area bearing that name. In fact, no "Handkerchief Point" could be found on either the North or the South shores – presumably the name was a local, and colloquial one, no longer used and not recorded in area histories, and was applied to a place where friends would stand to salute departing travelers.[4]

Like the other rocky coast watercolors painted in this period, *Handkerchief Point* shows an exaggeratedly vertical composition with a high hori-

Fig. 1. *Rocky Shore, Nantasket*, about 1896-97. Watercolor, pencil, and ink on paper. Collection of Mr. and Mrs. Granville M. Brumbaugh.

zon line. It is dotted with Prendergast's beloved perky little girls and white-frocked women carrying colorful parasols. Prendergast's extensive use of reserves, and his scattering of reds and a grainy textured emerald green across the picture causes it to read abstractly, like a brilliantly patterned mosaic. Yet he took pains to make the composition define a legible space, and so he arranged the figures in *Handkerchief Point* in a long chain, slowly snaking back toward the horizon through the mossy banks in subtly diminishing scale. The figures are for the most part Prendergast's generalized types, with raisin eyes and button noses (when their features are rendered at all). But as Carol Clark has noted, in the center of the picture is a working-class family (see detail) – a woman in a white dress and maroon parasol and a man behind her carrying a small child over the slippery rocks – who form a narrative vignette that

demonstrates both the new accessibility of the seashore for the city's wage earners and a new, more democratic tenor to family life.[5] And there are few faces that Prendergast has rendered with more specificity and tenderness than that of the husband.

CT

1. Including 234 watercolors by seventy-four artists, this exhibition was the first historical survey of the medium to be mounted by a major museum. It ran from January 27 to February 25, 1942.

2. Alan Burroughs, introduction to *A History of American Watercolor Painting* (New York: Whitney Museum of American Art, 1942), pp. 13-14.

3. Carol Clark, Nancy Mowll Mathews, and Gwendolyn Owens, *Maurice Brazil Prendergast. Charles Prendergast. A Catalogue Raisonné* (Williamstown, Massachusetts: Williams College of Art, 1990), nos. 640 and 642.

4. The watercolor has been known by this title since at least 1934. To add to the confusion, another watercolor of 1896 now known as *Handkerchief Point* (collection of Mr. and Mrs. Meyer Potamkin) was exhibited in the 1930s as *Nantasket Beach No. 2* (see Clark et al., *Prendergast*, no. 671). Jean Woodward, Virginia Gamage, Cynthia Fleming, Captain Al Swanson, Joseph Garland, and John Kosa, among others, graciously assisted in the search for Handkerchief Point.

5. Carol Clark, "Modern Women in Maurice Prendergast's Boston of the 1890s," in Clark et al., *Prendergast*, p. 32.

Maurice Brazil Prendergast
86. *Sunlight on the Piazzetta*, 1898-99

Watercolor over graphite on thick, moderately rough-textured, cream wove paper
12⅜ x 20⅝ in. (315 x 524 mm)
Signed lower left in graphite: Prendergast / Venice
Inscribed verso, lower right, in graphite: Venice 1899
Gift of Mr. and Mrs. William T. Aldrich. 61.693

87. *Umbrellas in the Rain*, 1899

Watercolor over graphite on thick, rough-textured cream wove paper
13¹⁵⁄₁₆ x 20⅞ in. (354 x 530 mm)

Signed and dated lower left: Prendergast (in black ink) / Maurice B. Prendergast Venice / 1899 (in purple ink) Hayden Collection. Charles Henry Hayden Fund. 59.57

In 1898, Maurice Prendergast made his first trip to Italy, financed by Boston photographer and patron of the arts Sarah Choate Sears. He remained in Italy for about eighteen months, visiting and painting in Padua, Florence, Siena, Orvieto, Rome, Naples, and Capri. None of these sites inspired him as did Venice which, as an early admirer noted, "was to play the greatest part in

the formation of the man."[1] While still in Italy, Prendergast sent sixteen watercolors made there to the J. Eastman Chase Gallery in Boston for what may have been his first solo exhibition (April 1899); some of these paintings had already been seen at the Twelfth Annual Exhibition of the Boston Water Color Club. Both displays were warmly received. As the critic for the *Boston Evening Transcript* wrote:

> Maurice B. Prendergast, who has been in Venice, exhibits eleven sparkling and gay pictures of that aqueous capital in its most festive moods. Mr. Prendergast was born to paint fetes, and he carries a

whole Fourth of July in his color-box. What an irresistible spirit of happy holiday activity pervades his scintillating and Watteau-like scenes! Flags fluttering, waves rippling, sun shining over all, brilliantly dressed throngs of men, women, and children, all moving, here and there, in a veritable kaleidoscope of life![2]

Sunlight on the Piazzetta and *Umbrellas in the Rain* were most likely among that group of pictures Prendergast sent to Boston. They were both painted in the area adjacent to the Piazza San Marco, then as now the most touristed square in all Venice. *Sunlight on the Piazzetta* depicts the adjoining Piazzetta directly in front of the elegant Ducal Palace, whose lacy arcades stretch across the entire picture surface. For *Umbrellas in the Rain* Prendergast positioned himself in front of the notorious prison, the Carceri, whose heavy first story is visible at upper right. Its ponderous form and somber tones contrast with the airy south facade of the palace at left. Spanning the narrow Rio di Palazzo that separates the prison from the palace is the Ponte della Paglia, the famous marble bridge; beneath it glides the graceful, attenuated form of a gondola, its gondolier hidden behind the lamppost.

Despite the specificity of Prendergast's renderings, in neither watercolor is Venice's majestic architecture his focus. Rather, in these pictures he introduces a thematic device that he would use repeatedly in the next decade: a fragment of an historic building – such as the Ducal Palace or West Church (see cat. 88) – serves as the backdrop for contemporary activity, and the colorfully dressed citizens from all social classes move pleasurably through the grand spaces, once the province of the elect.

The sense of pageantry that marks these watercolors had been a feature of views of Venice since the Renaissance; in describing one such picture, Henry James used language that could have applied equally well to Prendergast: "his subject was always a cluster of accidents; not an obvious order, but a sort of peopled and agitated chapter of life."[3] Prendergast's vision has often been associated with Carpaccio, whom he admired.[4] However, Carpaccio's paintings have the mood of a solemn processional, with individual figures clear-

Fig. 1. *Umbrellas in the Rain*, verso.

Fig. 2. *Umbrellas in the Rain, Venice*, about 1898-99. Watercolor over pencil on buff paper. The Metropolitan Museum of Art, New York. Bequest of Joan Whitney Payson, 1976.

ly portrayed. Prendergast's lightness of touch, the colorful animation of his figures, and their relatively small scale and undifferentiated features against the grand spaces of the plaza, is perhaps closer to the many views of the Piazza San Marco painted by Guardi.

Despite their freshly observed quality, these watercolors were clearly intended as major statements, and were carefully composed. On the verso of *Umbrellas in the Rain* is the pencil scaffolding for Prendergast's first attempt at the composition (fig. 1), presumably abandoned because the greater prominence given the Ducal Palace in that scheme would have proportionately diminished the space available for the wet pavement, Prendergast's real

subject. Another version of *Umbrellas in the Rain*, a smaller, unfinished watercolor now in the Metropolitan Museum of Art (fig. 2) is more symmetrical and as such less immediate. Both demonstrate the deliberateness of Prendergast's method, for in both sketches, Prendergast seems to have worked from the top to the bottom of his sheet, first laying in (over the palest of graphite diagrams) the lacy quatrefoils of the clerestory of the Ducal Palace, then the pedestrians on the bridge. The lower half of the picture, with its dazzling, improvised passages of pooled and layered washes, and its spidery yet sure strokes denoting the watery echoes of the balustrade and lamppost, was the last to be painted.

In *Sunlight on the Piazzetta*, Prendergast has animated his scene by subtly tilting the composition, a device he used often to prevent his architectural grid from seeming too static. His color scheme is surprisingly subdued here. Russets and deep blue-greens predominate, and the bright reds, ochers, and purple-blues of the parasols are confined to the central band of the picture, where there is sunlight. The tones in the shadowy foreground are far quieter. Even the little girls' white dresses, initially left as brilliant reserves, were dulled down with gray wash. The arcade, seemingly a screen of exactly repeated architectural shapes, in fact exhibits extraordinary variety. The reddish brown washes beneath the arches were allowed to puddle and pool; in some of the intervals a granular texture is evident. On the clerestory level, the façade is appropriately bright while the cool interior spaces are rendered in subtle, muted colors. No opening is given exactly the same tone or texture as its neighbor. Prendergast's technique is remarkably inventive here, and suggests the magical complexity of those interior spaces.

Although these watercolors seem to document the range and variety of modern life (*Sunlight on the Piazzetta*, in particular, has been called a "microcosm of *fin-de-siècle* Venice"[5]) their populations are surprisingly feminine – relatively few men appear in either picture. The stiff breeze that animated both these scenes provided an additional challenge to Prendergast's recurring interest in women's poses and costumes; the prevailing sense of urban bustle is gently counterposed by the

many charming, intimate vignettes he creates. Our attention is caught by little girls feeding pigeons, a child with a hoop (reminiscent of Bonnard, whose contemporary city views were infused with a like tenderness), and, in *Umbrellas in the Rain*, by several children who seem to regard us from across the plaza. Perhaps the most affecting of these figures is the young woman in green with auburn hair just to the left of the center of the picture in *Sunlight on the Piazzetta* (see detail). She is a definite type, of a poorer class than most of Prendergast's figures, and a type that was the object of some scorn:

> The Venetian women, as seen on the streets of their city, are untidy, dirty, although picturesque, often slight in youth, but dumpy and shapeless in middle life. Almost all of them wear black shawls, thrown over their heads, if the weather be cool, if warm, merely draped with careless grace over their shoulders. The beautiful red-gold hair one does sometimes find, however, but so untidily arranged.[6]

Prendergast views her far more sympathetically, dressing her in soft green (rather than the more typical harridan's black) to complement her reddish hair, and although her facial features are barely indicated, he shows her in a pensive pose that contrasts poignantly with the bright chatter all around her.

CT

1. William Mathewson Milliken, "Maurice Prendergast, American Artist," *The Arts*, 9 (April 1926), p. 182.

2. "The Fine Arts Twelfth Annual Exhibition of the Watercolor Club," *Boston Evening Transcript*, March 4, 1899, p. 10.

3. James is discussing Tintoretto's *Marriage at Cana* (Santa Maria della Salute, Venice). James, *Italian Hours* (1909) (New York: Horizon Press, 1968), pp. 49-50.

4. See Van Wyck Brooks, "Anecdotes of Maurice Prendergast," in *The Prendergasts* (Andover, Massachusetts: Addison Gallery of American Art, 1938), p. 38, and, more recently, Gwendolyn Owens, *Watercolors by Maurice Prendergast in New England Collections* (Williamstown, Massachusetts: Sterling and Francine Clark Art Institute, 1978),p. 48.

5. Margaretta M. Lovell, *Venice. The American View 1860-1920* (San Francisco: The Fine Arts Museums of San Francisco, 1984), p. 81.

6. Elise Lathrop, *Sunny Days in Italy* (New York: James Pott & Co., 1907), p. 296, quoted in Lovell, *Venice*, p. 82.

Maurice Prendergast
88. Sketchbook ("The Boston Water-Color Sketchbook"), 1897-98
Left page: Watercolor over graphite and black crayon on moderately thick, cream wove paper, affixed overall to blue gray paper (originally one of the flyleaves of the album).
Right page: Watercolor over graphite on moderately thick, cream wove paper affixed to a page of the album.
7 x 7½ in. (178 x 190 mm)
Gift of Mrs. Charles Prendergast in honor of Perry T. Rathbone. 59.957

Some eighty-seven of Prendergast's sketchbooks are known. Most of them are inexpensive memorandum books and contain notes, addresses, and miscellaneous comments. They are in several sizes, although few are larger than about 7½ x 5 inches; the present book is exceptional in being nearly square. The majority of the notebooks contain pencil drawings only, which were undoubtedly made by Prendergast as he moved through the city and visited his favorite summer resorts; some also contain a few watercolors. The "Boston Water-color sketchbook" is one of the most prized of Prendergast's books, for its ninety-six pages contain fifty-one watercolors (twenty-two of these are tipped in, and may have been painted earlier than the others) eleven pencil sketches, and one drawing in black crayon.[1] Its importance was recognized by Prendergast's brother Charles, who was probably the one who inscribed the legend "Sketches By / Maurice Prendergast / 1899" in red inside the front cover, and decorated the binding.[2]

Most of the watercolors were painted at Revere Beach, a resort popular among Boston's day-tripping working class. As in Prendergast's work as a whole, there are very few men in these watercolors; companionship among women (and their children) seems to be a recurring theme.[3] There are occasional sketches of single figures (which appear to have interested the artist because of costume or pose) and drawings of heads, though there are no portraits. Facial features are rendered summarily, if at all. Rather, the vast majority of the sketches are compositional studies featuring children bathing, and groups of women conversing, sitting

on the beach, or gazing out to sea. They are generally shown in profile or with their backs turned; they rarely show awareness of being observed by the artist. Although none of these vignettes has yet been identified as a precise study for a finished work, Prendergast was clearly interested that summer in developing programs for pictures, for many of the scenes are framed with a broad line of gray watercolor.

In several of the drawings, Prendergast experimented with different formats, most notable of these being a long, narrow shape, attributed to the influence of Japanese pillar prints. Affinities with Pierre Bonnard and Edvard Munch have also been discerned.[4] Technically, the sketches are bold and

assured; for the most part they were painted very wet, with rich, deep colors applied, often in several layers, over a scribbly pencil (or ink) outline. Occasionally, Prendergast used graphite on top of the washes as well. The sketches are dazzling and light-filled, in keeping with their subjects. They are also quite innovative: "for the first time [Prendergast] adroitly avails himself of the paper as a color,"[5] reserving it for the white of hats, parasols, and especially dresses.

CT

1. The sketchbook also has been referred to as the "Revere Beach Sketchbook." See Carol Clark, Nancy Mowll Mathews, and Gwendolyn Owens, *Maurice Brazil Prendergast. Charles Prendergast. A Catalogue Raisonné*, (Williamstown, Massachusetts: Williams College Museum of Art, 1990), no. 1478.

2. According to legend, Charles saved a number of the sketchbooks from a disastrous studio fire in the winter after Maurice's death. It is also likely that Charles was responsible for tipping in a number of the watercolors, in the hope of preserving their crumbling edges, and that he assembled the whole album from two or three surviving books. The presence of binding holes along the edge of several of the tipped-in watercolors (which also vary in size and shape) supports this hypothesis. *Maurice Prendergast Water-Color Sketchbook*, critical note by Peter A. Wick (Boston: Museum of Fine Arts, 1960), pp. 10-11.

3. Carol Clark, "Modern Women in Maurice Prendergast's Boston of the 1890s," in Clark et al., *Prendergast*, p. 30.

4. For examples of works exhibiting these influences, see pp. 42, 18, and 46–47, respectively, in Wick, *Prendergast Sketchbook*. See also Wick's comments, p. 7.

5. Charles Parkhurst, "Color and Coloring in Maurice Prendergast's Sketchbooks," in Clark et al., *Prendergast*, p. 78.

Maurice Prendergast
89. *West Church, Boston*, 1900–01

Watercolor over graphite on thick, slightly textured, cream wove paper
10¹⁵⁄₁₆ x 15⅜ in. (276 x 392 mm)
Signed lower right in brown ink: Prendergast
Hayden Collection. Charles Henry Hayden Fund.
58.1199

Old West Church, at Cambridge and Lynde streets in Boston, was the subject of three pairs of watercolors Prendergast painted at the turn of the century. The building was a monument to old Boston and a testament to change in the city's history: designed in 1806 by architect Asher Benjamin, for a congregation that had been in existence since 1737 (and whose original structure on this site had been used as a barracks during the siege of Boston), its pulpit had been occupied by such esteemed preachers as Jonathan Mayhew and Charles Lowell. By the 1890s the neighborhood had changed: as first Russian and Polish, then Italian immigrants settled in the West End, and as the earlier, Protestant residents moved elsewhere, Old West's congregation dwindled. The church finally was sold to the Boston Public Library, which in 1894 reopened the building as its West End Branch.[1] It is as a library that Prendergast painted it: a busy place whose handsome courtyard and fountain provided a vest-pocket recreation space for Boston's middle and working classes.

Prendergast may first have been asked to paint Old West Church by its former minister, Cyrus Bartol. According to legend, the artist's first attempt at the subject – presumably the composition represented by this watercolor and the nearly identical *Court Yard, West End Library, Boston* (fig. 1), presenting a broad view of the courtyard and the lower stories of the library – was rejected because too little of the building was shown.[2] Prendergast went on to paint two upright views showing the entire building behind a screen of leafy trees (fig. 2 [this was the version acquired by Rev. Bartol] and *The Bartol Church* [collection of Weil Brothers]). Prendergast's third treatment of the subject features the fountain (no longer extant) looking out from the steps of the library toward Cambridge Street (fig. 3 and *Courtyard, West End Library, Boston* [private collection]).

Fig. 1. *Court Yard, West End Library, Boston*, about 1900–01. Watercolor, pencil, and ink on paper. Metropolitan Museum of Art, New York. Gift of the Estate of Mrs. Edward Robinson.

Fig. 2. *West Church, Boston*, about 1900–01. Watercolor and pencil on paper. Collection of Mr. and Mrs. Arthur G. Altschul.

Fig. 3. *The Fountain, Boston*, about 1900-01. Watercolor and pencil on paper. Collection of Rita and Daniel Fraad.

In most of the watercolors, the season appears to be late summer, but in the Boston version, the feeling is definitely autumnal. The leaves on the trees are a mellow orange (in counterpoint to the bold blue doors of the library) and the flower beds, which in other watercolors are filled with red and yellow blooms, are bare. The courtyard, whose depth is exaggerated in the vertical compositions, is compressed in the Boston and Metropolitan Museum versions; the projecting central block of the church is also flattened, and the figures are arranged, friezelike, in a series of horizontal bands.

Although it is difficult to determine the exact sequence in which the six watercolors were produced, it seems likely that the Metropolitan Museum's watercolor preceded the Boston version. Prendergast made a number of changes in the Metropolitan's picture. He folded under about an inch of the paper at the botton, thereby eliminating the cobblestone street. He also left incomplete two figures in the immediate foreground (their ghosts are still visible; the sheet has since been reopened to its full size), in order to arrive at a composition he would then replicate in the Boston watercolor.[3] Furthermore, *West Church, Boston* shows no evidence of revision and is in general more tightly and confidently painted.

Prendergast's masterful handling of crowds and groups of figures suggests the constant random motion of people in public spaces, and gives his scene a spontaneous, just-observed quality. In fact,

West Church, Boston is carefully structured. Prendergast deliberately placed figures emerging from the library's central door and at the entrance to the courtyard, and distributed figures along the fence in rhythmic groupings (the same narrative clusters occur in the Metropolitan Museum's picture). Some of the same characters – for example, the man in blue at the far left – reappear in other watercolors of the series. Though clearly presenting a slice of modern urban life, the courtyard of the West End Library, circumscribed by the brick façades and the decorative iron fence, was a controlled space and served Prendergast like a stage set: his colorfully costumed players move across our field of vision generating countless little dramatic incidents.

CT

1. Walter Muir Whitehill, *Boston: A Topographical History*, 2nd ed. (Cambridge, Massachusetts: The Belknap Press of Harvard University Press, 1968), pp. 177-178. In 1962, the Methodist Church bought the building and restored it to religious use.

2. According to William Milliken, "the one he did first, on order for the minister of the church, showed the street with the church an incidental part of the composition. This did not suit the client and a second was done in which the church played a more prominent role." "Maurice Prendergast, American Artist," *The Arts* 9 (April 1926), p. 182.

3. Stephen Rubin, "Courtyard, West End Library, Boston" in *American Watercolors from the Metropolitan Museum of Art* (New York: The American Federation of Arts in association with Harry N. Abrams, Inc., Publishers, 1991), p. 159.

Maurice Prendergast
90. *The End Men*, about 1914

Watercolor over graphite on thick, moderately textured dark cream wove paper
12⅜ x 16⅜ in. (313 x 415 mm) irregular
Signed lower left in red watercolor: Prendergast
Hayden Collection. Charles Henry Hayden Fund.
58.980

The world of theater and cabaret, a subject popular with many French and American painters of Prendergast's generation, was not readily accessible to him because of his deafness. Although biographers speak generally of his interest in theater (he and Charles were believed to own stock in a cinema company),[1] such subjects appear very rarely in his art. While in Paris in 1907, he made two watercolors of cabaret scenes (both now Williams College Museum of Art, Williamstown, Massachusetts; see especially *La Vie Moderne* [fig. 1]). He seems not to have taken up the subject again (or to have depicted any other interior scene) for some seven years. *The End Men*, probably painted around 1914, most likely represents a theatrical performance in New York City, where the Prendergast brothers moved late in 1914, after spending the spring and summer in France.

Several studies for *The End Men* are found in a pocket sketchbook from this period.[2] These pencil sketches, undoubtedly made during a performance, record the end men in various poses, the orchestra in the pit (fig. 2), the proscenium and upper boxes, and the dancers (singly and in groups) with their off-the-shoulder dresses and flouncy skirts. The hasty, energetic line of the sketches is carried over into the finished watercolor, where reserves of white paper form the dancers' dresses, their contours drawn with brush and watercolor over a very sketchy graphite underdrawing.

End men, who give the picture its title, were the two comedians on the flanks of the blackface chorus of a minstrel troupe.[3] The members of the chorus here are not in blackface – in fact, they have no facial features at all – but the presence of the end men, as well as the small orchestra in the pit at the foot of the stage, makes it clear that this is a variety show, a new and increasingly popular

Fig. 1. *La Vie Moderne*, about 1907. Watercolor and pencil on paper. Williams College Museum of Art, Williamstown, Massachusetts. Gift of Mrs. Charles Prendergast.

Fig. 2. Sketchbook study for *The End Men*, 1914. Pencil on paper. Museum of Fine Arts, Boston. Gift of Mrs. Charles Prendergast in Honor of Perry T. Rathbone.

form of theatrical entertainment. That it was nonetheless a relatively respectable performance (rather than one including burlesque) is indicated by the presence of the two women in the audience at lower right. Those figures, clearly reminiscent of similarly placed spectators in Degas's café-

Fig. 3. *Seascape* (verso of *The End Men*). Watercolor and pencil on paper.

concert pictures, locate the viewer in the audience, and generate a sense of measurable space in an otherwise flat composition. At the same time, the compositional density of *The End Men*, the loose, watery washes bleeding into one another, and the seeming casualness of the execution generally, look ahead to Charles Demuth's cafe and vaudeville pictures (see cat. no. 97), begun at almost the same time. But whereas the slinky dancers in Demuth's watercolors make those images seem risqué, Prendergast's demurely arranged chorines, in their somewhat old-fashioned costumes, suggest a more sedate entertainment.

On the verso is a seascape (fig. 3), unfinished and unsigned.

CT

1. Nancy Mowll Mathews, *Maurice Prendergast* (Williamstown, Massachusetts: Williams College Museum of Art, 1990), p. 34.

2. Museum of Fine Arts, Boston, 1972.1149. The first two-thirds of this sketchbook contain sketches of figures Prendergast observed while in Paris and St. Malo; the remainder of the book includes numerous drawings related to *The End Men*. That the theatrical sketches follow the ones made in France suggests they were made after Prendergast's return and relocation in New York.

3. Wilfred Granville, *The Theater Dictionary* (New York: Philosophical Library, 1952), p. 67.

Maurice Prendergast
91. *Long Beach*, 1920-23

Watercolor over graphite, with touches of pen and black ink on thick, rough-textured, cream wove paper
15½ x 22½ in. (394 x 570 mm)
Signed lower center in brown ink: Prendergast
Hayden Collection. Charles Henry Hayden Fund.
50.562

In the last decade of his life, Prendergast returned frequently to the settings and subjects of his younger days: the beaches of the Massachusetts North Shore. In the late teens and early twenties, he spent several summers in Annisquam with his old friends Oliver and Esther Williams and in Gloucester with William and Edith Glackens. Many of the oils and watercolors produced during these visits are arcadian idylls, featuring large-scale, generalized figures moving dreamily through a verdant landscape. Others, like *Long Beach*, depict more quotidian pleasures, and as such more closely parallel (in theme, if not in style) the work of the 1890s.

There is a Long Beach in Rockport; however, Prendergast's subject was more likely the stretch of sand now called Niles Beach, located on the harbor side of Gloucester's Eastern Point. It was for the most part a middle-class resort, the site of decorous promenades in the 1890s and of exuberant bathing parties in the teens and twenties. As Gloucester's historian, Joseph Garland, described it:

> Here the Beachcroft [a large hotel at the northern end of Long Beach] was the center of activity, the road before it cluttered and clomped and dust-puffed with driving parties and cyclists, and the beach itself well occupied by bathers, sunners, showoffs, baby carriages, romping and shouting children, the athletically inclined and the determined walkers. If the light afternoon easterly was floating off the Point in little flutters of cat's paws over the water, a few gaff-rigged sloops would be taking advantage of it.[1]

Many elements familiar from Prendergast's earlier work appear here: his organization of the composition into horizontal registers, his idiosyncratic but effective shorthand for defining figures. But his technique is now far more direct: his palette is brighter, his strokes larger and looser than in the work of the 1890s. He no longer constructs his pictures from layers of wash, but allows

Fig. 1. Sheets from sketchbook, 1920–23. Pencil on paper, and watercolor on paper. Williams College Museum of Art. Gift of Mrs. Charles Prendergast in honor of John W. Chandler, President of Williams College, 1973–85, 85.11.1.

colors to bleed into one another, to go their own way. He is more apt to draw with the brush, defining contours with distinct, bold, squiggly strokes – the shoreline, for example – and he leaves lots of sparkling reserves, finding new enjoyment (and effectiveness) in his textured paper. This directness, which characterized the approach to watercolor of many twentieth-century artists (among them, Arthur G. Dove and Georgia O'Keeffe), is the key feature of Prendergast's investigation of a new modern vocabulary.

It should be noted that Prendergast's directness here is not unrehearsed. A sketchbook (Williams College Museum of Art, Williamstown, Massachusetts) depicting various sites on Cape Ann includes several studies relating to *Long Beach* (fig. 1). The first, a rapid pencil sketch, records the same view but from a higher vantage point so that the rocks in the foreground obscure the right half of the pier. The second sketch, in scribbly pencil and very liquid watercolor, represents a refinement of the composition, and includes all the elements and the same point of view as *Long Beach*. Other sketches show the same stretch of beach as viewed from the pier. In these, Prendergast practiced the series of parallel arcs he would use in the final version to denote the curving shore line and the waves lapping up against the beach. In the end, Prendergast may not have been entirely comfortable with how abstract and generalized his picture had become, for in some areas – the boat at left, the body of the woman in gray sitting near the steps of the pier, the scarf worn by the woman in blue at lower right – he felt the need to reinforce contours with pen and ink. Again there are parallels with modernist watercolors, for Dove and others would also use pen line to give definition to areas of flat color.[2]

Prendergast's critics recognized the change in his style, but found his struggles with modernism tentative compared with those of other painters of the period. The critic for *Art News*, reviewing a 1930 show in which *Long Beach* appeared, felt that his paintings "begin to date a bit, to take on a somewhat faded look beside the high-keyed work that is being thrown upon the market in ever-increasing quantities." He was nonetheless receptive to the convivial mood of Prendergast's

pictures, which he found more cosmopolitan than their conventional subject might suggest: "But the unending enjoyment that Prendergast had in nature adorned with humanity on pleasure bent is felt down the whole line of paintings and affords an interesting glimpse of a New England temperament tinged with a typically Parisian preference for life *en fête*."[3]

CT

1. Joseph E. Garland, *Eastern Point* (Peterborough, New Hampshire: Noone House, 1971), p. 172.

2. Prendergast may have known Dove, for he stayed at Dove's house during one of the summers (1922 or 1923) when he was at work on these pictures. (Nancy Mowll Mathews, *Maurice Prendergast* [Williamstown, Massachusetts: Williams College Museum of Art, 1990], p. 37.) However, during that time, Dove was living on his boat with Helen Torr ("Reds"), while his estranged wife Florence ran a hotel in Westport, and it is not clear whether the two artists met. (Barbara Haskell, *Arthur Dove* [San Francisco: San Francisco Museum of Art, 1974], p. 36.)

3. "Exhibitions in New York. Maurice Prendergast, Kraushaar Galleries," *Art News* 29 (November 8, 1930), p. 10.

John Marin

Born Rutherford, New Jersey, 1870;
died Cape Split, Maine, 1953

John Marin is one of several twentieth-century American painters known principally as a watercolorist, and for whom stylistic developments in watercolor paved the way for advances in other media. Born in 1870, he trained at the Pennsylvania Academy of the Fine Arts under Thomas P. Anshutz and Hugh Breckenridge, and also at the Art Students League in New York. He spent most of five years in Europe (1905-10) making Whistler-inspired pastels and etchings, and returned to the United States a modern painter with an extraordinary facility in watercolor. In 1909, the photographer Edward Steichen introduced him to Alfred Stieglitz, who from then on would be his champion, opening almost every season at his gallery with a Marin watercolor show. Although for most of his career Marin found a ready market for his work and an enthusiastic critical following, he remained somewhat detached from the turbulent New York art scene. He preferred to work in the winters in his modest home in Cliffside, New Jersey, and in the summers in the Berkshires, the Adirondacks, New Mexico (1929, 1930), and most famously, in Stonington and later in Cape Split, Maine.

Marin was extremely prolific, working with great energy (and sometimes, reportedly, with both hands) both out of doors and in his studio. During his sixty-six years of activity as a painter, he produced more than three thousand watercolors and oils. He participated in most of the important contemporary art exhibitions of his long career: the Armory Show (1913), the Forum Exhibition of Modern American Painters (1916), the Brooklyn Museum's survey of contemporary American watercolors (1921), and many others. At the same time he was a regular, and acclaimed, participant in the annual watercolor exhibitions at the Pennsylvania Academy of the Fine Arts and other mainstream institutions, an indication of his broad appeal.

At the height of his career Marin was the subject of major museum retrospectives (such as the show organized by the Museum of Modern Art in 1936) and thoughtful biographies (such as MacKinley Helm's *John Marin* of 1948). In subsequent years, he received numerous awards and honors from both the popular press and the art community: in 1948 a *Look* magazine poll proclaimed him America's "Artist No. 1," and he was the featured artist at the 25th Venice Biennale (1950). Because of the generosity of such patrons of the avant-garde as Duncan Phillips, Ferdinand Howald, and Philip Goodwin, by the early 1930s Marin's work already had begun to enter museum collections. In 1948, Georgia O'Keeffe divided Stieglitz's enormous group of Marins among the Philadelphia Museum of Art, Fisk University, the Art Institute of Chicago, the National Gallery of Art, and the Metropolitan Museum of Art, ensuring the artist a significant presence in major public collections across the country. The recent gift of Norma and John Marin, Jr., to the National Gallery of Art has made that institution the largest repository of the artist's work.

John Marin
92. *Clouds and Mountains at Kufstein*, 1910
Watercolor on moderately thick, rough-textured, off white wove paper
15½ x 18⅝ in. (393 x 472 mm)
Signed and dated lower left in blue watercolor:
Marin 10
Hayden Collection. Charles Henry Hayden Fund.
61.1139

In the summer of 1910, Marin spent six weeks in the Austrian Tyrol, based in the small Alpine town of Kufstein, on the German border. He produced more than thirty watercolors of the Tyrol, some painted on the spot and others, like the present picture, most likely done from memory. These formed the subject of his second solo exhibition at Alfred Stieglitz's 291 Gallery, held in February of 1911, some four months after the conclusion of his five-year sojourn in Europe. In tribute to their lyrical beauty, the reviewer of the show for *Camera Work* (quite possibly Stieglitz himself) described the Tyrolean watercolors as "a breath of fresh air or a field of flowers to one who had just left the classroom after working out an arduous problem of trigonometry."[1] And in fact Stieglitz admired the Tyrolean works so much that he kept several for his own collection, *Clouds and Mountains at Kufstein* among them.[2]

The Tyrolean watercolors mark a break with the muted tonal manner in which Marin had been working during most of his time in Europe. In acknowledgment of their Whistlerean softness, an early and enthusiastic reviewer referred to these watercolors as "color stains."[3] Yet in them Marin's colors are brighter, his harmonies brasher than before. Using the blues and violets beloved of such traditional watercolorists as Dodge Macknight (cats. 67, 68) who were his contemporaries, he pairs the cool tones with their coloristic opposites — bold yellows and oranges, applied in opaque staccato strokes and in broad, emphatic sweeps — to energize the image. In these watercolors, he abandons the picturesque architectural views that had been his principal subject matter while in Europe, and adopts a more sublime vision. For the first time, in the Tyrolean watercolors, the drama of nature becomes Marin's subject.

In *Clouds and Mountains at Kufstein*, majestic peaks emerge from clouds of fog and mist that hover over the tiny village. The extremely elevated perspective further diminishes the elfin scale of Kufstein, whose famous castle and rococo church with its onion dome are visible as dots of opaque color at the very bottom of the sheet. In this, one of the most abstract of the Tyrolean watercolors, mountains and clouds can barely be distinguished from one another (anticipating Marin's deliberate confounding of landscape forms in his later works, as reflected in such titles as "Movement – Sea or Mountain as You Will").[4] Marrying the decorative and the descriptive, Marin's billowing shapes drift across the surface of the sheet, creating a lyrical pattern even as they suggest a spectacular panorama.

CT

1. *Camera Work* 36 (July 1911), p. 29.

2. After Stieglitz's death in 1946, the watercolor was acquired by the Downtown Gallery, from whom the Museum bought it in 1961.

3. James Huneker, *New York Sun*, reprinted in *Camera Work* 36 (July 1911), p. 47.

4. As Marin noted at the end of his career, "I'm calling my pictures this year 'Movement in Paint' and not movements of boat, sea or sky, because in these new paintings - although I use objects - I am representing paint first of all and not the motif," Cleve Gray, ed., *John Marin by John Marin* (New York: Holt, Rinehart and Winston, 1970), p. 96.

John Marin

93. *Crotch Island, Maine, The Cove*, 1924

Watercolor, black crayon, and a pointed tool (brush handle?) on thick, rough-textured, white wove paper, partially affixed to cardboard to which silver leaf has been applied

14⅜ x 17¼ in. (366 x 451 mm)

Signed and dated lower right in blue watercolor and black crayon: Marin '24

Signed and dated on verso in graphite: Crotch Island Maine / 1924. / The Cove

Signed on reverse of original silver mat in graphite: Crotch Island Maine / The Cove – 1924

Hayden Collection. Charles Henry Hayden Fund. 61.1140

Crotch Island is a small island off Deer Isle, Maine, which in the early twentieth century was the site of a flourishing granite quarrying industry.[1] Marin painted about half a dozen views of the island during the decade (1919-1928) when he was summering and painting at the nearby fishing village of Stonington.[2] One of the earliest of these, *Crotch Island Quarry, Off Deer Isle, Maine*, is quite specific, showing clearly the buildings and some of the machinery associated with the quarrying operation (fig. 1).[3] The others, including *Crotch Island Maine, The Cove*, are far more abstract, and focus on the island's primeval terrain.

The rather blurred and indistinct foreground of this watercolor no doubt alludes to the stonecutting industry on Crotch Island. The vertical strokes of black watercolor and black crayon may have been suggested by the cranes or derricks used to hoist the blocks of granite onto waiting barges. The area outlined in deep blue, with squares of pale, reddish-brown wash suggestive of the sheer rock face, may well be a quarry pit, and the hulking brown forms could represent the shadows or silhouettes cast by winches or other quarrying machinery. Yet Marin's intent was not descriptive, but evocative, and by means of a dazzling variety of techniques transformed a place of crude machinery and rough labor into a handsome, decorative design.

The imposition of arbitrary, abstract structures on natural views was an essential part of Marin's Stonington vocabulary in the early 1920s (see fig. 2). He used long dry strokes to frame the picture

Fig. 1. *Crotch Island Quarry, Off Deer Isle, Maine*, 1920. Mixed media on paper. Kennedy Galleries, Inc., New York.

Fig. 2. *Maine Islands*, 1922. Watercolor on paper. The Phillips Collection, Washington, D.C.

on two sides (and further underscored its decorative quality by floating the watercolor on a silver mat). Strokes of dark wash, reinforced with black crayon (and occasionally with an incised line, made, perhaps, with the end of the brush) rise like a screen of columns through which the cove is seen. Despite this emphasis on surface, Marin was careful to create a readable space, and augmented the naturalism of his image with an atmospheric palette (dark greens, browns, and blues to conjure up a cold, foggy day) and with the liberal use of dry-brush strokes, leaving reserves of white paper

that evoke sunlight dancing across the surface of the water. In the foreground, Marin made extensive use of blotting to lift up and spread his color, thus softening his already transparent washes – a handsome effect that enhances the mystery and ambiguity of that area. Rather than specific forms carefully detailed, the foreground contains only shadows, negative spaces, and indistinct shapes. It is the middle distance that, in violation of the conventions of perspective, is more carefully detailed and fully realized.

Crotch Island, Maine, The Cove was one of twenty-seven watercolors – depicting the White Mountains, New York City, and the Maine Coast – that Marin showed in the historic exhibition "Alfred Stieglitz Presents Seven Americans."[4] He was identified as "the keenest experimenter" of the group,[5] and was especially lauded for his Maine subjects: "in some of these his always explosive force expresses itself with an admirable restraint."[6] *Crotch Island* was shown by Stieglitz and then by Edith Halpert of the Downtown Gallery, whose "Marin Room" was for many years a feature of her promotion of modern American art. The Museum of Fine Arts bought the watercolor from the Downtown Gallery in 1961.

CT

1. The quarries were especially prosperous during the "granite boom" that lasted from about 1885 to about 1925. They supplied stone for the Brooklyn and George Washington Bridges, for the Museum of Fine Arts, for Rockefeller Center, and for the John F. Kennedy Memorial at Arlington National Cemetery, after which stonecutting was discontinued at Crotch Island. However, occasional building projects requiring Deer Isle granite – such as the construction of the West Wing of the Museum of Fine Arts in 1979-1980, in which the stone façade was designed to match that of the original building – have led to a modest revival of the industry. Information from the Deer Isle-Stonington Chamber of Commerce brochure; see also Hank and Jan Taft, *A Cruising Guide to the Maine Coast* (Camden, Maine: International Maine Publishing Company, 1988), pp. 245-247.

2. These include, in addition to the watercolors mentioned in the text, *From Crotch Island, Maine* (1922, estate of the artist), *Blue Sea, Crotch Island* (1923, Addison Gallery of American Art, Phillips Academy, An-

dover, Massachusetts), *Boulders and Trees, Crotch Island, Maine* (1923, estate of the artist), and *Crotch Island Granite Quarry* (n.d., National Gallery of Art, Washington, D.C.). Ruth Fine and Charles Ritchie graciously supplied the information about the National Gallery's Marins.

3. Although Marin's image is relatively straightforward, his technique is quite eccentric, incorporating not only watercolor and graphite, but also various cut-out elements pasted and sewn to the sheet.

4. That exhibition, held at the Anderson Galleries March 9-28, 1925, included 159 works by Charles Demuth, Arthur Dove, Marsden Hartley, Georgia O'Keeffe, Paul Strand, Stieglitz, and Marin. *Crotch Island, Maine, The Cove* was no. 69.

5. Deough Fulton, "Cabbages and Kings," *International Studio* 81 (May 1925), p. 147.

6. H. C. [Helen Comstock], "Stieglitz Group in Anniversary Show," *Art News* 23 (March 14, 1925), p. 5.

John Marin
94. *New Mexico*, 1930
Watercolor and black crayon on very thick, rough-textured, off-white wove paper; partial J WHATMAN watermark
15⅛ x 20⅜ in. (397 x 518 mm)
Signed and dated lower left in gray wash: Marin 30
Abraham Shuman Fund (by exchange). 67.31

Marin spent two summers in New Mexico as the guest of Mabel Dodge Luhan. He was part of a free-floating group of artists and writers living at Luhan's ranch near Taos, many of whom – Georgia O'Keeffe and Rebecca Strand, among others – he had known in New York. As was his custom, however, he remained apart from the petty jealousies, tantrums, and squabbles of the group;[1] during his visits there he was remarkably productive. He painted nearly one hundred watercolors in two summers. The best of these were featured the following seasons in solo exhibitions at Alfred Stieglitz's gallery, An American Place.

New Mexico appeared in the second of these shows, in the fall of 1931.[2] As in many of Marin's watercolors of the Southwest, topographical concerns are more apparent here than in his relatively abstract landscapes painted on the East Coast in the 1920s, as though Marin was deliberately mas-

tering a new vocabulary of landmarks. His subject is the segment of the Sangre de Cristo Range that runs north of Taos (fig. 1).[3] The truncated profile of Wheeler Mountain (elevation 13,161 feet) at right and the folded foothills beneath it have not been reduced to geometrical planes dancing across the sheet, but remain recognizable and dominant. The distance from Taos Canyon is as measured and calculable (for Marin) as in a nineteenth-century landscape. To paint this new terrain, Marin introduced a new palette as well. For the deep greens, blues, and yellows of many of the Maine landscapes of the 1920s, he substituted a rich terracotta and azure. The white of the paper plays an active role, perhaps in tribute to the brilliant light and vast spaces of the New Mexico desert.

Marin struggled to contain that vastness, noting that "My picture must not make one feel that it bursts its boundaries. . . . I can have things that clash. I can have a jolly good fight going on. There is always a fight going on where there are living things. But I must be able to control this fight at will with a blessed equilibrium."[4] As a result, *New Mexico* is more formally balanced than many of Marin's earlier watercolors. The flat-topped mountains rising suddenly from the valley floor – the "elemental big forms" Marin said an artist must seek – suggest a simple, horizontally divided composition that he employed repeatedly in these New Mexico landscapes.[5] To enclose his panorama, he used an internal frame whose motifs evoke the ornamental designs on Pueblo jewelry and pottery: a terracotta zigzag above the clouds, and a decorative stepped design at the bottom of the sheet, punctuated with dots of turquoise (perhaps applied directly from the tube).

New Mexico is both decorative and primeval, tranquil and monumental and, when shown at An American Place in 1931, moved reviewers to operatic prose. One critic found in these 1930s watercolors an "almost scriptural solemnity and grandeur," a spiritual quality Marin sought to achieve. "The way Marin's mountains and valleys and skies seem to move into place out of the strangely august patterns that hem in his designs makes one conscious of that 'In the beginning' as recorded in the first chapter of John. They have a

Fig. 1. View of Wheeler Mountain, near Taos, New Mexico, 1991. Photograph courtesy of Jonathan Fairbanks.

cosmic force, an extraterrestrial patterning that has no other accounting for."[6]

CT

1. As described by Marsden Hartley, who had worked there in the late teens, "Taos was another spelling for Chaos." Hartley to Rebecca Strand, quoted in Barbara Haskell, *Marsden Hartley* (New York: Whitney Museum of American Art, 1980), p. 142. For one of the most recent of many accounts of life at Luhan's compound, see Benita Eisler, *O'Keeffe and Stieglitz: An American Romance* (New York: Doubleday, 1991), pp. 380-403.

2. Stieglitz customarily opened his season with an exhibition of Marin's watercolors. This show, which ran from October 11 to November 27, 1931, featured thirty New Mexico watercolors and fourteen oils of Maine.

3. I am grateful to Jonathan Fairbanks, who identified the site of Marin's watercolor.

4. John Marin, "John Marin by Himself," *Creative Art* 3 (October 1928), reprinted in *The Selected Writings of John Marin*, ed. Dorothy Norman (New York: Pellegrini and Cudahy, 1949), p. 126.

5. Ibid., p. 127.

6. Ralph Flint, "Recent Work by Marin Seen at An American Place," *Art News* 30 (October 17, 1931), pp. 3, 5. Flint's enthusiastic review was a front-page story in *Art News*.

Abraham Walkowitz

Born Tyumen, Siberia, 1878;
died New York City, 1965

Abraham Walkowitz was principally a graphic artist, and his most adventurous work was done in watercolor or charcoal. His favorite subjects were the skyscrapers of New York City and the celebrated dancer Isadora Duncan, of whom he produced thousands of studies in a fluid, exuberant manner inspired by Rodin. Walkowitz's work on paper drew on many influences: Kandinsky, Marin, Rodin, and Cézanne; Fauve color; the exciting motion studies of the Futurists. He was one of the first American artists to produce (in the mid-teens) totally non-objective compositions. As a young artist he was well regarded by critics and fellow artists – Oscar Bluemner, writing in *Camera Work* in 1913, called him "master of his pictorial means" and noted that "with him the bare enclosed spaces live" – but later Walkowitz's reputation declined, perhaps a reflection of the repetitive nature of his work and of his difficult personality.

Walkowitz emigrated to the United States in 1889. He first studied art at Cooper Union in New York, and then beginning about 1898, at the National Academy of Design. Although he would later denigrate this training, the conventional figure studies he produced throughout his career reflect his academic beginnings. He would furthermore always admire his first mentor, Walter Shirlaw, from whom he studied etching in 1899. By 1900, Walkowitz was teaching at the Educational Alliance (an East Side community house) with Jo Davidson and Henry McBride; he taught there until 1906, when he traveled to Europe.

In Paris, he studied at the Académie Julian, and soon embraced the avant-garde: his friends were Max Weber and Walter Pach; he visited Gertrude and Leo Stein, met Rodin, and saw the Cezanne watercolor exhibition in June of 1907. It was during this trip that he first saw Isadora Duncan dance. He returned to New York late in the summer of 1907. He had his first solo show the next year at the Haas Gallery, which attracted the attention of Arthur B. Davies, who later bought two of his works. Through Marsden Hartley he met Alfred Stieglitz, who would support him enthusiastically for the next several years: Walkowitz had four shows at 291 between 1912 and 1917; was featured in a 1914 issue of *Camera Work* and designed the cover for the May 1915 issue of *291*,

Stieglitz's new magazine; and he visited Stieglitz at his summer home at Lake George on several occasions.

Walkowitz was involved with progressive art in New York through the teens. He exhibited at the Armory Show of 1913, and at the 1916 Forum Exhibition of Modern American Painters. In 1917, he helped found the Society of Independent Artists, and was elected a director the next year. In 1920, he joined the Société Anonyme, an organization of European and American modernists to whose stylistic diversity Walkowitz's eclectic enthusiasms were well suited. However, by the 1920s, the experimental phase of Walkowitz's career was essentially over, and from that point he dedicated himself to rather conventional figurative compositions, generally in oil, with emphatic social messages.

In the mid-1940s, Walkowitz's eyesight began to fail, ending his career. A studio fire in 1948 destroyed much of his work and many personal papers; however, before that time he had donated many of his works to important collections of American art, among them the Museum of Modern Art, the Brooklyn Museum, the New York Public Library, and the Newark Museum.

Abraham Walkowitz
95. *Times Square Abstraction No. 2*, about 1914
Watercolor on moderately thick, dark cream wove paper
19¼ x 15 in. (489 x 381 mm)
Signed and dated lower right: A. WALKOWITZ [in black paint], 1914 [in blue pen]
Gift of Louis Schapiro. 40.626

Walkowitz's images of New York City are almost as well known as his drawings of Isadora Duncan. He exhibited them at 291 and at the Forum Exhibition, he distributed them liberally to museums, and in 1948, after his artistic career was over, he supervised the publication of *Improvisations of New York: A Symphony in Lines*, which contains reproductions of several hundred of his New York images, some full-page, some arranged collage-fashion, twenty to a page. Novelist Carl van Vechten's introduction to that volume remains the most succinct analysis of Walkowitz's involvement with the New York theme:

> Having glorified the American dancer, Isadora Duncan, in over 5000 drawings, that indomitable artist, Walkowitz, has now determined, apparently, to perform a like aesthetic service for the city of New York. In his sketches for this tortured, terrifyingly aspiring and ambitious metropolis, the artist has borrowed an idea from Gertrude Stein and employs repetition for emphasis. None of these pictures is exactly like its predecessor, but each one of them carries the intention one step further. Towers shoot upward in endless carefully arranged projections, now as flames, now as rhomboids, now as stalagmites, now as phallic obelisks, growing out of the sewers below and overshadowing the grovelling populace. . . . The emotion in these drawings, indeed, is inherent in the city itself.[1]

Walkowitz began to draw and paint New York in the early teens, or about the time that Marin, Stella, and Weber, and, in Europe, Delaunay, Boccioni, and Severini, among others, were embracing the theme of the modern city. *Times Square Abstraction #2* in particular owes a debt to Marin's lively 1912 watercolors of New York (fig. 1).[2] Like Marin and the others, Walkowitz's interpretations of New York grew progressively abstract, but unlike them, he rarely applied his energetic vision to specific buildings. Rather, his skyscrapers

Fig. 1. John Marin, *St. Paul's, Lower Manhattan*, 1912. Watercolor on paper. Delaware Art Museum, Wilmington. Gift of John L. McHugh.

Fig. 2. *Times Square Abstraction #1*, about 1914. Watercolor on paper. Museum of Fine Arts, Boston. Gift of Louis Schapiro.

are generic; his interest was in representing the dynamism and cacophony of the city, not its landmarks.[3] Here, the buildings seem ephemeral. The central skyscraper is composed of a series of pulsating squiggles that evoke flashing lights, not towers of stone and steel. It is flanked by buildings shown only as attenuated silhouettes that have been rendered flowingly, in pale even washes, so that they rise like columns of smoke from a jumble of comma-like strokes swirling around their bases.

This watercolor was the gift of Louis Schapiro, a Brookline, Massachusetts, resident who was a friend and adviser of Walkowitz's. It came into the collection with *Times Square #1* (fig. 2), a watercolor of the same size and a similar palette, but far more abstract than the present picture. Their pairing may have occurred retrospectively, as did the date on this watercolor, for it is reproduced in the 1925 volume *One Hundred Drawings by A. Walkowitz* with no date and bearing the title *The City*.[4] Walkowitz is known to have put dates on many of his pictures long after he painted them,[5] but even if it is not exact, the date inscribed here is consistent with other pictures of New York produced at this time.

CT

1. Carl van Vechten, "Comments," *Improvisations of New York: A Symphony in Lines by A. Walkowitz* (Girard, Kansas: Haldeman-Julius Publications, 1948), n.p.

2. Sheldon Reich, "Abraham Walkowitz: Pioneer of American Modernism," *American Art Journal* 3 (spring 1971), p. 81.

3. Martica Sawin. "Abraham Walkowitz, Artist," *Arts Magazine* 38 (March 1964), p. 44. Sawin quotes Walkowitz's statement of 1913: "I do not avoid objectivity or seek subjectivity, but try to find an equivalent for whatever is the effect of my relation to a thing . . . I try to record the sensation in visual form."

4. *One Hundred Drawings by A. Walkowitz* (New York: B. W. Huebsch, Inc., 1925), plate 53.

5. The chronology of Walkowitz's pictures is problematic, for he dated some of his pictures incorrectly, long after they were painted, and most remain undated. He often employed several styles at the same time, and seems not to have kept any systematic record of his oeuvre. See William Innes Homer, *Alfred Stieglitz and the American Avant-Garde* (Boston: New York Graphic Society, 1977), p. 283, n. 48.

Charles Demuth

Born Lancaster, Pennsylvania, 1883;
died Lancaster, Pennsylvania, 1935

Charles Demuth's biography is marked by contradiction. He spent half his life "in the Province," the cozy Pennsylvania German town of Lancaster, his birthplace, and the other half in the haunts of the bohemian elite: Paris, Greenwich Village, Provincetown. He was a cosmopolite who loved puttering in his mother's garden, and a patron of New York's seamy nightlife whose principal artistic subject was floral still lifes. Although trained as a painter in oils at the Pennsylvania Academy of the Fine Arts (1905-1911) – and much of his surviving student work is in that medium – he soon gravitated to watercolor. And although his acknowledged masterpiece is a large oil, *My Egypt* (1927, Whitney Museum of American Art, New York) and his "poster portraits" in tempera and oil have excited much critical interest, it is on his modestly scaled, delicate watercolors that his reputation rests.

Demuth traveled to Europe several times during his student years. The most significant trip came in 1912-14, when he attended the academies Julian, Moderne, and Colarossi in Paris. He met Gertrude and Leo Stein during this period, and traveled to Berlin with Marsden Hartley. Upon returning to the United States, he divided his time between Lancaster and New York, and summered at watering holes popular with artists and writers: Provincetown (where he met Eugene O'Neill), and Gloucester. Between 1914 and 1919, he produced many figurative watercolors in a sensuous, liquid style, including several series of illustrations for stories by Emile Zola, Henry James, Franz Wedekind, and Edgar Allan Poe. Beginning in 1914, the prescient dealer Charles Daniel gave him a solo show almost annually, and he enjoyed generally favorable notices in the press and the patronage of leading collectors of modern art, among them Ferdinand Howald and Albert Barnes. Among his closest friends in those years were Alfred Stieglitz and the artists the photographer championed, especially Hartley and Georgia O'Keeffe; surprisingly, Demuth didn't exhibit with Stieglitz until 1925, when several of the poster portraits depicting members of the Stieglitz circle were shown in the exhibition, "Alfred Stieglitz Presents: Seven Americans."

Demuth's health was always fragile. He suffered from lameness, the result of a childhood injury; in his late thirties he was diagnosed with diabetes, to which he nearly succumbed in 1921. Thereafter his sprees in New York were followed by increasingly long periods of recuperation in Lancaster. Nevertheless, the early and mid-twenties were an extremely productive period for Demuth. He worked in watercolor, tempera, and oil, painting many of his celebrated floral still lifes, as well as architectural and industrial images all exhibiting his elegant interpretation of cubism. Although his illness diminished his energies, in the years before his death in 1935, Demuth produced a group of oil paintings of buildings in Lancaster, a number of figurative watercolors, many of them overtly erotic, and some of his best-known still lifes.

Charles Demuth
96. *Illustration No. 8 for Zola's* Nana
    (Chapter XIII), 1915-16
Watercolor over graphite on thin, dark cream laid paper; watermark: Geniune Irish linen.
7⅞ x 11¾ in. (199 x 297 mm), irregular
Inscribed verso, in graphite, upper left: Painted by Charles Demuth, 1916, willed to Robert E. Locher
Hayden Collection. Charles Henry Hayden Fund. 58.30

This is the eighth of twelve watercolors Demuth made in 1915 and 1916 to illustrate Emile Zola's 1880 novel, *Nana*. Nine of them were acquired shortly after they were made by Demuth's patron, Albert Barnes; one was bought by Abby Aldrich Rockefeller and given to the Museum of Modern Art in 1935. The present picture, "Scene after Georges Stabs Himself with a Scissors (second version)," and illustration no. 6, "Nana before the Mirror" (New York art market) remained with the artist until his death in 1935; these are the most disturbing and violent images in the series, and whether they were the artist's favorites or whether they were simply too frank to find a buyer is not clear. Although their libertine, *fin-de-siècle* spirit would not have shocked Demuth's Greenwich Village circle, their unconventional style and sexual explicitness may have caused Demuth's dealer, Charles Daniel, to hold them in reserve, and to show them only to his most sophisticated clients. Nonetheless, they were not made solely for private viewing, as has been suggested,[1] but were exhibited by Daniel along with some of Demuth's early industrial pictures in December 1920, and were well received in the press. Henry McBride, in a typically tongue-in-cheek review for the *New York Herald*, cautions clergymen to shun the display at Daniel's[2] – guaranteeing, as was his intention, a brisk attendance – while Forbes Watson, writing in *Arts and Decoration*, recommended them to viewers who enjoy "a whimsical imagination."[3]

The episode in which the courtesan Nana's young lover Georges, in despair at her infidelity, stabs himself with a scissors, occurs near the end of the novel, and marks the beginning of the collapse of Nana's world and the destruction of all the men around her.[4] It is the only scene for

Fig. 1. *Scene after Georges Stabs Himself with the Scissors, Illustration No. 8 For Zola's* Nana (first version), 1915-1916. Watercolor and graphite on paper. Photograph © copyright 1992 The Barnes Foundation, Merion, Pennsylvania.

which Demuth made two drawings. In the first version (fig. 1), a rather matronly looking Nana stares ahead as her servant, Zoë, scrubs at the blood on the floor. In the Museum's version, Nana reclines voluptuously in her armchair, her skirt hiked up, her face shown in profile with the classical elegance and hauteur of a Nadelman head. Her black-gloved hand, gracefully arched like the neck of a swan, dangles the bloody scissors before Count Muffat, her principal lover. In her boredom, Demuth's Nana seems even more corrupt than Zola's, her detachment even more chilling than her hysterical protests of innocence in the novel.[5] The agitated surface of the watercolor expresses the tension of Demuth's theme: there is vigorous blotting and scraping out, and the artist has pooled colors in the hollows and wrinkles of the smooth paper, generating a surface that is as distressed as the image is distressing. The loosely drawn figures owe a debt to the languid watercolors of Rodin.[6] They also find perhaps an even closer parallel in the sexually charged watercolors of Egon Schiele.

CT

1. Reviewing the Demuth retrospective held at the Museum of Modern Art in 1950, the critic Henry McBride wrote of the Nana illustrations, "the artist himself must have looked at them as essentially private entertainments" ("Demuth: Phantoms from Literature," *Art News* 49 [March 1950], p. 21.). And indeed when they first were shown, at the Daniel Gallery in 1917, they were kept separate, as McBride suggested: "There are some watercolors of Mr. Demuth's that have not been hung upon the walls. The subjects were suggested by a reading of Zola's 'Nana.' They are kept hidden in a portfolio, and are only shown to museum directors and proved lovers of modern art upon presentation of their visiting cards. They are quite advanced in style." (McBride, *New York Sun*, as quoted in Emily Farnham, *Charles Demuth: Behind a Laughing Mask* [Norman, Oklahoma: University of Oklahoma Press, 1971], p. 116.) However, in addition to the 1920 show at Daniel's, when the illustrations were hung in a second room in the gallery, some of the works in the series were displayed at the Grafton Galleries in London, and possibly again in New York in 1929. See Barbara Haskell, *Charles Demuth* (New York: Whitney Museum of American Art, 1987), p. 111, notes 4 and 5.

2. Henry McBride, "News and Reviews of Art: Charles Demuth Displays His Beautiful Landscapes at Daniels," *New York Herald*, Sunday, December 5, 1920, sec. 3, p. 9.

3. Forbes Watson, "At the Galleries," *Arts & Decoration* 14 (January 1921), p. 215.

4. See Chapter 13 (edition translated by George Holden, London: Penguin Books, 1972).

5. "When she saw him [the Comte Muffat] she relieved her feelings in a flood of words, telling him the whole dreadful story, repeating the same details a score of times. . . . Above all else she was intent on proving her own innocence." Ibid., p. 425.

6. Stieglitz showed Rodin drawings and watercolors at 291 in 1908 and 1910.

Charles Demuth
97. *The Purple Pup*, about 1918

Watercolor over graphite on thin, cream laid paper; watermark: CLOVER LINEN / GOLDSMITH BROS.
8¹⁄₁₆ x 10⁷⁄₁₆ in. (206 x 265 mm)
Signed lower left in graphite: C Demuth-
Charles Henry Hayden Fund. 62.324

By about 1918, when *The Purple Pup* was painted, Greenwich Village was becoming domesticated. A number of "tearooms" – as many as twenty-five by the close of the war – had sprung up to compete for the patronage of the avant-garde with the Village's many smoky Italian restaurants, raucous saloons, and seamy nightclubs. These tearooms sported self-consciously arty names ("The Samovar," "The Mad Hatter," "The Dutch Oven"); their programs featured amateur entertainments (such as ukelele serenades) and handicrafts (batik hangings); and their handwritten menus promoted such resolutely healthful fare as near-beer, loganberry juice, and bran-nut muffins.[1] The Purple Pup, a meeting ground for local radicals and moneyed uptowners eager to observe rakish Village life, opened in 1917 at 38 Washington Square West, a few blocks from Demuth's sometime residence at the Hotel Brevoort (Fifth Avenue at 8th Street). It was one of several fashionable underground haunts Demuth portrayed in watercolor in 1918 and 1919.[2] Depictions of café society had become increasingly common since Manet's and Degas's paintings of the 1870s (or, perhaps more relevant to the risqué flavor of some of Demuth's watercolors, since Toulouse-Lautrec's *fin-de-siècle* nightclub scenes), and the apparent spontaneity and off-hand manner of these watercolors make them seem all the more like eye-witness accounts.

The Purple Pup is carefully crafted in the energetic pencil-and-watercolor technique Demuth had developed from about 1915 in a number of paintings of vaudeville and circus performers and, more importantly, in a series of watercolors illustrating stories by Henry James, Franz Wedekind, and Emile Zola (see cat. 96). The underpinnings of *The Purple Pup* are a scribbled network of spiky pencil lines that do not always contain the color areas or even function descriptively. Washes are quite transparent in some areas and nearly opaque

in others. Demuth made extensive use of blotting – even using his fingertip, as is evident in the temple of the waiter – to create a soft, blunt texture. Elsewhere (such as the head of the blond man, seen in profile at right, who is possibly Demuth's friend, the novelist Carl van Vechten)[3] silhouettes are so sharp as to seem cut out. Demuth's tendency to use the white of his paper to articulate such details as sherbet cups, cigarettes, shirt collars, and some of the more caricatured faces, is especially pronounced in this watercolor. And just as his unsteady line conjures up the cacophonous conversation and intoxicating atmosphere of this popular tearoom, so the blank areas create a jumpy surface pattern that seems to compress the space of the picture, making the packed tables of The Purple Pup seem all the more crowded and desirable.

CT

1. See Caroline F. Ware, *Greenwich Village 1920-1930: A Comment on American Civilization in the Post-War Years* (Boston: Houghton Mifflin, 1935), p. 53, and Steven Watson, *Strange Bedfellows: The First American Avant-Garde* (New York: Abbeville Press, 1991), p. 226.

2. These include *The Drinkers (Chez Ritz)*, 1915; *The Nut (Pre-Volsted Days)*, 1916 (both Columbus [Ohio] Museum of Art); and especially *At the Golden Swan* (1919, collection of Irwin Goldstein, M.D.), and *Cabaret Interior with Carl van Vechten* (about 1918, private collection).

3. Demuth frequently included witty portraits of his friends in these watering-hole pictures. *At the Golden Swan* (a boisterous Irish bar also known as "The Hell Hole") includes representations of the artist, who sits with his back to the viewer at lower left; Marcel Duchamp; and fellow painter Edward Fisk. In *Cabaret Interior*, Carl van Vechten is presumably the figure at left. Whereas it has been suggested that *The Purple Pup* also contains portraits of Demuth (supposedly the man standing at right) and Duchamp (at center, with red nose), these rather beefy, wavy-haired characters are markedly different from the lithe figures with slicked hair and sculpted profiles that are shown patronizing the Golden Swan. Based on a general similarity to the figure at the left in *Cabaret Interior*, and to photographs from the period (see Watson, *Strange Bedfellows*, p. 51) the blond man seen in profile at right in *The Purple Pup* may also be Carl van Vechten, but this identification remains conjectural.

Charles Demuth
98. *Sailboats and Roofs*, about 1918
Watercolor over graphite on moderately thick, moderately textured cream wove paper
14 x 10 in. (346 x 253 mm)
Anonymous gift. 67.1163

Demuth spent part of the winter of 1917 in Bermuda, and the succeeding summers in Gloucester and Provincetown, respectively.[1] These holidays inspired him to experiment with new subject matter – architecture, landscapes, marine views – that supplemented the narrative, figurative watercolors for which he was already known. He also adopted a crisp style marked by taut pencil contours and carefully limited areas of color that contrasts with the more fluid manner of his figurative work. Between 1917 and 1920 Demuth produced at least fifteen pictures (most in watercolor, a few in tempera) of seaside buildings and ocean views. These are generally credited with embodying "the origins of the Precisionist paintings that some scholars identify as his greatest achievement."[2]

The vertical slice of space in *Sailboat and Roofs*, in which blocky shapes are piled up and seem to slide forward even as they recede into the distance, is of course the legacy of cubism, which had been in the air among the New York avant-garde since the Armory Show. Equally radical is the simulation of texture in paint (here Demuth's blotting technique cleverly evokes the salt-mottled rooftops; incised lines suggest the grid patterns of shingles). But like his friend Marsden Hartley, who was his frequent traveling companion in those years, Demuth had a penchant for romantic vistas. *Sailboats and Roofs*, which depicts the view from a high window over several blocks of slate-topped roofs to the water, is an evocative image, full of salt air and thoughts of the sea. In its emotional appeal it may owe a debt to Hartley's *A Bermuda Window in a Semi-Tropic Character* (fig. 1), executed during the period Hartley and Demuth spent together in Bermuda. The mood of Demuth's watercolor, created by the pale fragile washes barely covering the white paper, and the rendering of the sailboats as simple triangles of blank paper with the merest aura of yellow wash

Fig. 1. Marsden Hartley, *A Bermuda Window in a Semi-tropic Character*, 1917. Oil on board. The Fine Arts Museums of San Francisco. Memorial Gift from Dr. T. Edward and Tullah Hanley, Bradford, Pennsylvania.

at their bases, reflects this tender sensibility.

The heavier paper and larger format of the architectural watercolors suggest that Demuth intended them for a more public forum than his illustrations. However, the two subjects were exhibited side by side at Charles Daniel's gallery in the late teens. *Sailboats and Roofs* probably was shown at Demuth's fifth exhibition at Daniel's, in November and December of 1918, one of a group of watercolors (or "drawings," as they were called in the catalogue) displayed under the laconic title of "New England Houses." These works were well received. Although some reviewers found them excitingly modern,[3] for others, their attraction was almost sentimental, their mottled surfaces and faceted planes seen as more poetically evocative than avant-garde.[4]

CT

1. Demuth first visited Provincetown in 1914. On this and subsequent visits (in 1915, 1916, 1918, and 1920),

he continued his association with the avant-garde writers, artists, and other personalities who summered there, becoming acquainted with Eugene O'Neill and even participating in some of the productions of the Provincetown Players. See Barbara Haskell, *Charles Demuth* (New York: Whitney Museum of American Art, 1987), p. 55.

2. Haskell, *Charles Demuth*, p. 121.

3. See, for example, "Cubism has Share in Demuth Exhibit," *The New York Sun*, December 1, 1918, p. 11.

4. "The artist has managed . . . to combine style with truth to nature. To an extraordinary degree he has let nature do his work for him, setting himself down before the angle of a frame building in New Hampshire or Massachusetts and copying it literally, the texture of the material of which it is built, the color bestowed upon it by age and weather, the shapes of doorways and windows, whatever contributes to its character as a building. . . . But belonging to the younger generation of artists . . . he breaks off his pictorial sentences long before he reaches the end of them. . . . He leaves an opening for the imagination to enter and complete his picture. He lets his public do for him whatever nature has left undone." "Exhibition of Paintings in Great Variety. Art at Home and Abroad." *New York Times*, Sunday, December 1, 1918, sec. 7, p. 11.

Charles Demuth
99. *In the Province (Roofs)*, 1920

Opaque watercolor over graphite on very thick cardboard ("Beaver Board," a multilayered building material)
23¾ x 19⅞ in. (602 x 504 mm)
Signed and dated lower left in graphite: C. Demuth 1920 / Lancaster Pa.
Inscribed verso, left center in graphite: Roofs / In the Province #1 / C. Demuth / Lancaster Pa / 1920-
Anonymous gift in memory of Nathaniel Saltonstall.
68.790

Like his contemporary, Charles Sheeler, Demuth was attracted to vernacular architecture rather than monuments, and frequently chose unexpected vantage points from which to portray those buildings. Although the specific site depicted in *In the Province* has not been identified – and in fact the view may be a composite[1] – it has been assumed that the structures shown here reflect the back alleys and rooftops of Lancaster, Pennsylvania, and are of the type that were visible from Demuth's family home at 118 East King Street.[2]

In the Province is one of at least three Lancaster pictures painted in 1919-20 that bear the same title (see fig. 1).[3] Viewed in sequence, they demonstrate Demuth's increasing interest in using opaque media and vibrant color (with posterlike shades of red, black, and white predominating), and working in a larger scale. However, in composition and spirit, this *In the Province* is closer to two other Lancaster pictures that were among Demuth's first essays in oil: the ironically titled *Modern Conveniences* (fig. 2), which likewise shows the backs of ordinary Lancaster houses, and the enigmatically titled *Nospmas M. Egiap Nospmas M.* (1921, Munson-Williams-Proctor Institute, Utica).

Unlike the other paintings called *In the Province*, where heroic spires dominate the composition,[4] in this image Demuth eschews a single dramatic focus. Roofs and gables succeed each other closely, but in seemingly random order. The view ascends from just above street level to a band of pale gray rooftops that merge with an overcast sky. Although most of the architecture is domestic, Demuth has also included blank facades of industrial buildings. At the center is a flourish of the

Fig. 1. *In the Province #7*, 1920. Watercolor and pencil on paper. Courtesy Amon Carter Museum, Fort Worth, Texas.

Fig. 2. *Modern Conveniences*, 1921. Oil on canvas. Columbus Museum of Art. Gift of Ferdinand Howald.

smoke that reappears in such paintings as *Incense of a New Church* (1921, Columbus [Ohio] Museum of Art) and at far right is a billboard or sign with cropped letters ("F or P" and "E" or "B") – a device that Demuth would use again in *Nospmas M. Egiap Nospmas M.* and other works of the early 1920s.

The juxtaposition of domestic and industrial forms is a leitmotif of Demuth's architectural pictures, and stems from his own experience, for townhouses and factories existing at close quarters is characteristic of Lancaster. But whereas the other pictures in the series feature soaring towers and rays of light that connote optimism and civic pride, this image is more complex, less buoyant and comforting. The black windows that punctuate the surface, the steps and boards that zigzag, and the dentiling that ascends busily along the rooflines define a visual environment as stimulating as that of Demuth's other place of residence, New York (whose architecture, interestingly, he did not paint). At the same time, the claustrophobic space generates a sense of restriction and limitation that also mark life in the province.

CT

1. Betsy Fahlman, *Pennsylvania Modern: Charles Demuth of Lancaster*, (Philadelphia: Philadelphia Museum of Art, 1983), p. 44.

2. Betsy Fahlman, "Charles Demuth's Paintings of Lancaster Architecture: New Discoveries and Observations," *Arts Magazine* 61 (March 1987), pp. 24-25.

3. The others are: *In the Province* (also called *In the Province #7*), 1919, Amon Carter Museum, Fort Worth, Texas; and *In the Province* (*Lancaster*) (also called *In the Province #2*), 1920, Philadelphia Museum of Art.

4. The spires have been identified as those of the P. Lorillard Company tobacco buildings (in the Philadelphia picture) and St. John's German Reformed Church (in the Amon Carter picture). See Falhman, *Pennsylvania Modern: Charles Demuth of Lancaster*, pp. 39, 41, and S. Lane Faison, Jr., "Fact and Art in Charles Demuth," *Magazine of Art* 43 (April 1950), p. 124.

Charles Demuth
100. *Eggplants and Pears*, 1925
Opaque and transparent watercolor over graphite on moderately thick, slightly textured, off-white wove paper; partial watermark: 1924 UNBLEACHED ARNOLD
14 x 20 in. (354 x 507 mm)
Signed and dated center left in graphite:
C. Demuth- / 1925-
Inscribed center right in graphite: Lancaster Pa.
Bequest of John T. Spaulding. 48.765

Perhaps the most stringently organized of Demuth's kitchen garden still lifes, *Eggplants and Pears* features two glossy eggplants and two green pears arranged in a cruciform shape on a table top. The example of Cézanne was extremely important for Demuth's still lifes of the period, in which forms float on the sheet, while the cloth backdrop appears to melt into the surrounding space. But the seemingly casual, additive arrangement of forms that is typical of many of Demuth's compositions of the mid-twenties gives way here to an architectonic sense of stability and mass. The soft folds of the cloth become taut creases and the tabletop's sharp edge defines a horizon line from which the central eggplant rises like a tower.

Demuth clearly enjoyed the parallel shapes from which he constructed this composition: the bulbous eggplants with their shaggy stems loom over the smaller, meeker pears. The color scheme is equally clever, based on secondary hues of purple and yellow, with greens knitting the eggplants and pears together in the kind of perfect symbiosis that caused one critic to find Demuth "more reliable than Chevreul."[1] Despite the austerity of the composition, however, Demuth gave his produce character, an anthropomorphic quality that he acknowledged (while at the same time requesting that his handsome images *not* be over-analyzed). Of another eggplant watercolor completed a few years earlier he wrote to Alfred Stieglitz: "I'm so glad you want the eggplant (*Eggplant and Peppers*, 1922; collection of Fisk University, Nashville, Tennessee). I kept it here, it turned into a heart – maybe mine. Anyway, I hope no one will discover "Art" or "Painting" engraved on it."[2]

CT

1. "Chevreul [one of the major color theorists of the nineteenth century] was not so much interested in those faint plum colored tones on the carrots or the carroty rust on the plums." Henry McBride, "Demuth," *New York Sun*, April 10, 1926, quoted in Daniel Catton Rich, ed., *The Flow of Art: Essays of Henry McBride* (New York: Atheneum Publishers, 1975), p. 218.

2. Demuth to Stieglitz, January 29, 1923. Stieglitz Papers, Collection of American Literature, The Beinecke Rare Book and Manuscript Library, Yale University, New Haven, Connecticut.

Charles Demuth
101. *Youth and Old Age*, 1925

Transparent and opaque watercolor over graphite on
moderately thick, moderately textured, cream wove
paper; fragmentary Whatman watermark:
(. . . MAN 1919 ENGLAND)
18 x 12 in. (458 x 304 mm)
Signed and dated center right in graphite:
Aug - C. Demuth 1925 - Lancaster, Pa
Inscribed in graphite: Youth and Old Age [lower cen-
ter], Black Eyed Susans [upper left]
Frederick Brown Fund. 40.231

When Demuth painted *Youth and Old Age*, he was
emerging from a near-fatal bout with diabetes.
Preoccupied with his fragile health, he wrote to
his friends, "My old age has started – at least,
middle period. 'It's great fun.' "[1] Despite the self-
mockery of such statements, and the melancholy
implications of Demuth's inscription, there is
nothing in the picture itself – no drooping blossoms or fallen petals – to suggest that he made the
watercolor during a period of depression or serious concern about his mortality. On the contrary,
Demuth chose to depict sturdy flowers at the
height of their bloom. Zinnias were known as
"youth and old age" in Lancaster County, according to Richard Weyand, the first cataloguer of
Demuth's work,[2] and were popular in family gardens like the one Demuth tended with his mother.
Black-eyed Susans, common field flowers, are also
abundant in Pennsylvania in August, the month
inscribed on the picture. In most of the watercolors of the '20s, Demuth's preferred subjects were
not hothouse flowers, but ordinary ones such as
these, seemingly artlessly arranged in tribute to
their natural beauty. Yet in this pyramidal composition, he combined a carefully balanced, nearly
symmetrical structure with a liquid line and the
elegantly diaphanous washes that mark his best
work.

In a posthumous tribute to Demuth, the critic
Henry McBride noted that "the proper place for a
Demuth flower, I sometimes think, is in the hands
of an educated gardener – one who knows what a
flower is and what an artist is."[3] Shortly after
Youth and Old Age was painted, it was acquired,
not by a gardener but by an artist who was herself
a specialist in floral still lifes. Sarah Choate Sears,

Marguerite (Thompson) Zorach

Born Santa Rosa, California, 1887;
died Brooklyn, New York, 1968

an accomplished photographer and pastellist and an enthusiastic patron of the arts, bought *Youth and Old Age* from the Montross Gallery, possibly from a group exhibition of American watercolors held there in 1926.[4] It joined a collection rich in modern French paintings and works by John Singer Sargent and Mary Cassatt, but also marked by adventurous purchases of pictures by John Marin, Arthur B. Davies, and Maurice Prendergast. Along with two watercolors acquired by the Fogg Art Museum in 1925,[5] *Youth and Old Age* was one of the few paintings by Demuth to enter a Boston collection in the artist's lifetime.

CT

1. Demuth to Alfred Stieglitz, July 30, 1923, quoted in Emily Farnham, *Charles Demuth: Behind a Laughing Mask* (Norman, Oklahoma: University of Oklahoma Press, 1971), p. 139. In fact, this theme begins even earlier. About 1919, Demuth wrote to Eugene O'Neill, "You see, dearies, I'm back in the province in the garden of my own chateau, – where I'll be for the remaining days of the season. The quiet and yellow velvet [?] old age, which I always predicted for myself, has started." Stieglitz Papers, Collection of American Literature, The Beinecke Rare Book and Manuscript Library, Yale University, New Haven, Connecticut.

2. Richard Weyand to Charles C. Cunningham, September 10, 1940. Object files, Department of Prints, Drawings and Photographs, Museum of Fine Arts, Boston. According to Alice M. Coats (*Flowers and their Histories*, [New York: McGraw-Hill Book Company, 1956], p. 272), the zinnia "is sometimes called Youth and Age; a name for which I can find no explanation." See also Liberty Hyde Bailey and Ethel Zoë Bailey, compilers, *Hortus Third: A Concise Dictionary of Plants Cultivated in the United States and Canada* (Revised ed.; New York: Macmillan Publishing Company, 1976), p. 1184, which lists "Youth-and-old-age" as a vernacular name for *Zinnia elegans*.

3. Henry McBride, "Charles Demuth, Artist," *Magazine of Art* 31 (Jan. 1938), p. 21.

4. The critic for *Art News*, enthusiastic about the group show at Montross (which also included work by Burchfield, Prendergast, Marin, and others), expressed special admiration for Demuth's contribution. "One single watercolor, a flower still life, dated 1925, but it seems to us the finest and happiest we have ever seen." "Exhibitions in New York: Water Colors. Montross Galleries, to April 24," *The Art News* 24 (April 17, 1926), p. 7.

5. *Lily* (1923) and *Fruit and Sunflowers* (about 1924). See *American Art at Harvard* (Cambridge, Massachusetts: Fogg Art Museum, Harvard University, 1972), nos. 135 and 136.

Marguerite Zorach was an accomplished watercolorist and textile artist. Her marriage to William Zorach was a true creative partnership: they shared a facility in several media; they often collaborated on projects and, especially in the late teens, they developed very similar painting styles. If his reputation has eclipsed hers it may not be due to superior talent, but rather to the greater status accorded sculpture, his preferred medium.

Marguerite Thompson grew up in Fresno, California. She intended to study at Stanford University, but had barely enrolled when a windfall from an aunt enabled her to go to Europe in 1908. Over the next three years, she traveled through Belgium, Italy, Switzerland, Germany, and most importantly, France. By 1911, she was in Paris, where she studied painting with John Duncan Fergusson and Jacques-Emile Blanche at La Palette, an informal art school. There she also met her future husband, William Zorach, and the two of them began working in a rather decorative style, inspired by both the expressive colors of Fauvism and the emblematic forms of the Symboliste movement. In the winter of 1911-12, she traveled through the Middle East, India, and the Orient, finally returning to California in April of 1912. She had her first solo show in Los Angeles that year.

Marguerite Thompson married William Zorach late in 1912. They settled in New York, and thereafter alternated winters in the city with summers in upstate New York or New England. She exhibited an oil in the Armory Show (1913) and in subsequent years displayed her paintings, drawings, and watercolors almost annually, although she and William often would mount shows of their art in their own studio, since they lacked regular gallery representation. About the time of the Armory Show she began to work in wool, noting "when I returned from Paris full of enthusiasm over the world of lively color the fauves had discovered for me, paint seemed dull and inadequate. The wealth of beautiful and brilliant colors available in woolen yarns so fascinated me that I tried to paint my pictures in wool" (Zorach papers, quoted in Roberta K. Tarbell, *William and Marguerite Zorach: The Maine Years* [Rockland, Maine: William A. Farnsworth Library and Art Museum, 1979], p. 20). Thereafter, crewel, tapestry, and batik would be her favorite media, and her work in wool supported the family for many years. She often made watercolors in preparation for a tapestry, and her work in watercolor generally is marked by the same light palette, rhythmic exuberance, and stylized forms that characterize her work in wool. In both her textiles and her paintings, Zorach drew on her daily life for subject matter; however, some of her themes stem from literature and have a clear symbolic content. At the end of her career, Zorach devoted more energy to painting: her last solo shows (at the Kraushaar Galleries) were of paintings.

Marguerite Zorach
102. *Sheep Island, Maine*, 1919
Watercolor over graphite on moderately thick, slightly textured, off-white wove paper; watermark: ARNOLD FIBRE
12½ x 15¾ in. (317 x 400 mm)
Signed lower right in black wash: M. ZORACH
Curator's Discretionary Fund. 1980.13

Zorach frequently based her paintings on family events and on places that had rich personal associations. She described the emotions associated with this watercolor in a letter to a former owner:

> It was painted in Stonington, Maine in 1919. We spent a wonderful summer there – living in a tiny house above the sea, on a cove. The cove was full of fierce rocks and out beyond were islands. Sheep's Island was the nearest and our favorite – a beautiful barren island of granite rocks and patches of green grass – there were outcroppings of a strange green stone that we always wanted to go back and collect pieces of after Bill began to do sculpture in stone. The island was used to pasture sheep – there was grass enough for a small flock and they were safe from dogs – and too far out for them to swim to shore. Each winter they were brought back.[1]

Among the Zorachs' neighbors in Stonington in 1919 was John Marin; like the watercolors he painted that summer, hers exhibits a bright, ebullient palette and a patternistic approach to the hills, jagged rocks, and inlets that form the local terrain. Also like Marin's, her handling of the watercolor medium is relaxed and free. Working on dampened paper, she applied her color in broad, blocky areas over a skein of pencil lines. There are no crisp contours; rather, passages of color are allowed to flow into one another, creating the effect of a shaggy patchwork. At lower left blotting has been used to suggest a tidal pool. Although there are reminiscences of Cézanne and the cubists in the compressed, tilted-up space of this watercolor, Zorach's deliberate spatial distortions and her penchant for rhythmic, stylized forms is equally indebted to the decorative vitality of American folk art, then avidly collected by many of her artist-friends.[2] And the outlined sheep, transparent against the green hillside just left of center, are typical of Zorach's gentle wit.

CT

1. Marguerite Zorach to William Bender, April 20, 1964. Curatorial files, Department of Prints, Drawings, and Photographs, Museum of Fine Arts, Boston.

2. Many of Zorach's hooked rugs deliberately emulate traditional forms. See Roberta K. Tarbell, *William and Marguerite Zorach: The Maine Years* (Rockland Maine: William A. Farnsworth Library and Art Museum, 1979), pp. 16-17.

M. ZORACH

Marguerite Zorach
103. *Adam and Eve*, 1920

Watercolor over graphite on moderately thick, cream wove paper; partial watermark: HAN [probably part of "HAND MADE"]
13⅞ x 9¾ in. (342 x 238 mm)
Signed and dated lower left: M. ZORACH / -1920-
Jesse H. Wilkinson Fund. 1992.63

William Zorach described his and Marguerite's travels through California in 1920 as a trip to "the garden of Eden, God's paradise,"[1] and Yosemite (the source for this watercolor), inspired both of them to produce highly imaginative works. In *Adam and Eve*, Marguerite's palette is that of the forest primeval, and she populated her Eden with the fauna of northern California: the blue jay, the deer, and the grizzly bear.

The all-over, decorative quality of this watercolor is central to Zorach's aesthetic, and appears in her tapestries of this period, as well as in the mural she painted some years later on the walls of Robinhood, the Zorach house in Maine.[2] Further affinities with her textile work are apparent in the tilted-up composition, and in the forms piled on top of one another, with shared contours and interwoven edges. The stylized figures and the composition, densely packed with rhythmically repeating shapes, also recall Persian miniatures, to which Zorach was undoubtedly exposed during her travels in India and the Middle East.[3]

Zorach's affectionately painted animals are the most charming feature of this watercolor, and they occur in many of her works in all media. Youthful male and female nudes in sylvan landscapes – an aspect of her connection with the Symboliste aesthetic – are also recurring motifs. The figures of Adam and Eve, tucked in behind fanciful vegetation, are reminiscent of the graceful contours of Derain's and Matisse's nudes, which Zorach admired during her student days in France. But her figures are appropriately innocent and shy (their faces are featureless; their bodies are defined by reserved paper or the palest of neutral washes), and as such are quite distinct from the elegant sensuousness of the French. Zorach has represented Adam and Eve before the Fall. The very density of the picture, the warmth of the color, and the

William Zorach

Born Euberick, Lithuania, 1889;
died Bath, Maine, 1966

soft, moist luminosity of her delicately applied washes, are all evocative of genesis.

CT

1. William Zorach, *Art is My Life* (Cleveland: The World Publishing Company, 1967), p. 60. For Zorach's full statement, see cat. 104.

2. The murals are reproduced in Roberta K. Tarbell, *William and Marguerite Zorach: The Maine Years* (Rockland, Maine: William A. Farnsworth Library and Art Museum, 1979), p. 26.

3. I thank Clifford S. Ackley for this suggestion.

Although William Zorach abandoned oil painting mid-career to devote himself to sculpture, he painted in watercolor all his life. His sculpture is massive and figural; in watercolor, he indulged his love of nature, for most of his works on paper are landscapes, and are lyrical, brightly colored, and delightfully pastoral in spirit.

Zorach came to this country in 1891 and spent most of his childhood in Cleveland. His interest in art surfaced early: at sixteen, he was apprenticed to a lithographer by day and studied at Cleveland Art School at night. Subsequently he trained at the National Academy of Design and the Art Students League in New York.

In 1910, Zorach went to Paris, where he worked at La Palette, an informal art school. There he met his future wife, Marguerite Thompson. While in Paris, he exhibited at the Salon d'Automne, and became thoroughly versed in the strongly colored, expressionist style that many of his fellow Americans, among them Stuart Davis and Thomas Hart Benton, also adopted. Whereas most of them would soon diverge from this manner, Zorach remained more or less faithful to it for the rest of his painting career.

Upon returning to New York in 1912, Zorach married Thompson and the two developed parallel artistic careers, participating in many of the major contemporary art shows of their era – the Armory Show, the Forum Exhibition – and living in impoverished but artistically rich circumstances. Summers were spent in the country, generally in dilapidated houses provided by friends or patrons; winters were spent working in New York at the periphery of the avant-garde artistic community – the Zorachs knew and admired Alfred Stieglitz, for example, but he did not show their work. In 1922 Zorach turned to sculpture, which proved a more successful medium for him: in 1924, he had his first solo exhibition of sculpture at Kraushaar Galleries; his solo show at the Downtown Gallery in 1931 firmly established his reputation and resulted in the first museum acquisition of his work, and in many public commissions. For the next several decades, Zorach would teach sculpture at the Art Students League in New York, and would have frequent exhibitions of his sculpture, and occasional shows of his watercolors. Watercolor

continued to be an important and appreciated medium for him for the remainder of his career: In 1931, he won the Art Institute of Chicago's prestigious Logan Prize for his sculpture; the following year he won it again, this time for his work in watercolor.

William Zorach
104. *Yosemite Falls*, 1920
Watercolor over graphite on moderately thick, white wove paper
18⁹⁄₁₆ x 13⅝ in. (472 x 346 mm)
Signed lower right in brown ink: - William Zorach -
Inscribed lower left in brown ink: Yosemite Falls 1920
Gift of Claire W. and Richard P. Morse. 1992.64

William Zorach's trip to Yosemite in the summer of 1920 was both a personal and an artistic adventure. He spent five months exploring and hiking there, frequently in the company of photographer Ansel Adams, who noted that "Bill sketched madly whenever we stopped for a breath."[1] That summer was Zorach's most productive period as a painter; he himself described the experience as transporting: "[It] carried me beyond myself. . . . I spent five months in the Yosemite Valley sketching, drawing, painting, and doing watercolors. Every now and then in life we have an experience that moves us so deeply, that holds us with such sheer, transcendent beauty, that it takes us completely out of this world. It is this feeling that only an artist can convey in his art. It is a journey into infinity. . . . This was the garden of Eden, God's paradise. I sketched and painted in ecstasy."[2]

Zorach produced hundreds of drawings and numerous watercolors at Yosemite. When he returned to New York in October, the creative exuberance continued.[3] He generated a series of oil paintings of Yosemite that combine recognizable natural forms and wholly abstract passages.

The subject of this watercolor, the majestic Yosemite Falls, became well known through photographs by such nineteenth-century artists as Carleton Watkins, and subsequently through Adams's luminous photographs. Zorach achieves a like sense of drama through expressive color and a deliberately naive drawing style. While readily legible, his natural forms are so simplified that

Yosemite Falls. 920   William Zorach

Joseph Stella

Born Muro Lucano, Italy, 1877;
died New York City, 1946

they seem primordial – a kind of stylization that resonates with the contemporary Art Deco style. In Zorach's vision, rock and spray are equally fluid: the rush of water and mist are rendered in shimmering, pale gray tones; stone and earth are translated into cascading salmon washes; sea greens and lemony hues define the pine trees, their stick-figure skeletons painted in a deeper green. Zorach's joyous reaction to Yosemite is clear in the spontaneous energy of this watercolor, as is the sense of wonder, the sense of being in Eden, that he so eloquently described.

CT

1. Ansel Adams with Mary Street Alinder, *Ansel Adams An Autobiography* (Boston: A New York Graphic Society Book; Little, Brown and Company, 1985), p. 61. Adams describes a terrifying climb the two made that July, during which Zorach slipped, lost a whole portfolio of sketches over the edge of a cliff, and nearly slid over the precipice himself.

2. William Zorach, *Art is My Life* (Cleveland: The World Publishing Company, 1967), p. 60.

3. He brought home the exalted sense of physical conquest as well. In a telling transposition of his wilderness experience to a more familiar urban environment, Zorach remarked that he'd been doing so much hiking "I'm sure I could climb the Woolworth Building . . . without an effort." William Zorach to Dr. John Weichsel, June 17, 1920 (Weichsel Papers, Archives of American Art, quoted in Donelson F. Hoopes, *William Zorach, Paintings, Watercolors and Drawings, 1911-1922* [Brooklyn: The Brooklyn Museum, 1968], p. 13).

Joseph Stella was one of the most original draftsmen of the twentieth century. Watercolor was only one of many media he used – he also worked in graphite, charcoal, pastel, colored pencil, crayon, collage, and the old-fashioned medium of silverpoint, often combining several media in one image. His themes were equally varied, and included portraiture, figure studies, landscapes, urban views, abstract compositions, and especially small-scale flower pieces. Stella frequently turned to watercolor for preparatory sketches; he also used it for a series of paintings of skyscrapers and other city buildings done in the late teens and early 1920s, and for several of the tropical images he produced toward the end of his career.

Born in the picturesque mountain village of Muro Lucano, near Naples, Stella followed his older brother to the United States in 1896 and, like him, was directed to a career in medicine. Unsuited for that profession, he returned to his childhood love of art, studying briefly at the Art Students League and then with William Merritt Chase at the New York School of Art. His first mature subjects were the poor and immigrant populations of the Lower East Side. In 1907, the radical periodical *The Survey* hired him to record a mining disaster in West Virginia. The next year, he produced a series of powerful illustrations of the industrial city of Pittsburgh, also for *The Survey*. A trip to Italy in 1909 – the first of many return visits – reinforced his interest in traditional techniques; a trip to Paris in 1911-12 exposed him to avant-garde painting and drawing, particularly that of the Futurists. Stella's two seemingly contradictory allegiances – to old-master traditions and to radical contemporary art – would remain constant throughout his career.

Beginning about 1913, Stella produced a group of major works – among them *Brooklyn Bridge* and *Battle of Lights, Coney Island* (both Yale University Art Gallery, New Haven), and *Tree of My Life* (collection of Mr. and Mrs. Barney A. Ebsworth Foundation and Windsor, Inc.) – that established him as one of the leading modern painters in America. While he was creating these complex, large-scale canvases, he was also making hundreds of small-scale works on paper. Their subjects are generally recognizable, but they also reveal a

highly imaginative, personal symbolism. He returned to Naples several times in the 1920s, and visited North Africa and Barbados over the next two decades. The tropical fantasies that resulted are among his most passionate and original works.

Stella's paintings were exhibited frequently during his lifetime, especially under the auspices of the Société Anonyme, the modern art organization founded by Marcel Duchamp, Man Ray, and Katharine Dreier in 1920. Dreier became one of Stella's most loyal patrons; their association lasted until his death in 1946.

Joseph Stella
105. *Cactus and Tropical Foliage*, about 1919-22
Watercolor over graphite on moderately thick, moderately textured, cream wove paper; watermark: ANC^NE MANUF^RE CANSON & MONTGOLFIER VIDALON LES ANNONAY
18¼ x 24⅛ in. (464 x 614 mm)
Signed center right in graphite: Joseph Stella
Sophie M. Friedman Fund. 1984.412

Cactus and Tropical Foliage was probably painted at about the time Stella began working on his monumental canvas, *Tree of My Life* (1919, collection of Mr. and Mrs. Barney A. Ebsworth Foundation and Windsor, Inc.), an ambitious, allegorical composition necessitating many preliminary drawings of its components, some of which – such as the prickly pear cactus – also occur here. That project enabled Stella to indulge in his love of flower painting, a subject that, although embraced by many modernists (Charles Demuth and Charles Sheeler among them), was disdained in the academies, as Stella discovered to his annoyance. (He grumbled that, although there was a prohibition against painting flowers, "there were no rules forbidding the pupils to paint vegetables or dead fish. This rule came into vogue for the simple reason flowers were pretty and old maids were in the habit of painting them.")[1] Stella found the subject essential to his aesthetic well-being ("My devout wish – to begin and end each day with the study of a flower"[2]), and he painted and drew them singly and in elaborate combinations, as here. The floral subjects demonstrate the astonishing range of styles in which Stella worked. Some of his flowers

Fig. 1. *Tropical Still Life*, about 1919. Watercolor, silver paint, crayon on paper. The Jan Perry Mayer Collection.

are lush, darkly lyrical, and quite stylized; others exhibit a cool, spare elegance and precision – though even among the latter group, botanical accuracy was not Stella's intention. Rather, these drawings were a source of sensual gratification and a spiritual outlet for him.

The composition of *Cactus and Tropical Foliage* seems to have developed organically. The shapes crowd one another, fanning out across the surface of the paper. There is little penetration of space, and the use of the white paper as background as well as for parts of the blossoms further flattens the image. At left, the leaves spill over the edge of the sheet, while at right stems and blossoms are left unfinished. The concentration of forms in one corner is unusual for Stella, who favored frontal, centralized, hieratic compositions. This arrangement seems far more natural – except, of course, that cacti and these exotic, tropical blossoms are unlikely to exist together in nature.

Another version of this composition (fig. 1), in which silver paint and crayon are added to the watercolor washes, shows the same prickly pears and flowers, even more densely arranged than in the Museum's watercolor. In both works, Stella's imaginative boldness is paralleled by audacious handling: the drawing is emphatic, the color is strong, the closely packed leaves and foliage seem aggressively sensual. While forms are realistically rendered, the washes that escape their penciled

contours enhance the abstract, decorative qualities of the image, and the contrast between richly painted areas and drawn but uncolored forms makes the watercolor seem all the more voluptuous.

CT

1. Joseph Stella, in an interview published in the *New York Sun*, May 25, 1913, quoted in Irma B. Jaffe, *Joseph Stella* (New York: Fordham University Press, 1970 [rev. ed., 1988]), pp. 11-12.

2. Stella, quoted in ibid., p. xiv.

Stuart Davis

Born Philadelphia, Pennsylvania, 1892; died New York City, 1964

Stuart Davis was associated with progressive art and politics from the outset of his career. His mother, Helen Stuart Foulke, was a sculptor. His father, Edward W. Davis, was art director of the *Philadelphia Press*, and the employer of John Sloan, William Glackens, Everett Shinn, and George Luks, whose novel style of urban realism the young Davis would soon appropriate. In 1909, he began to study in New York with Robert Henri, and for some years followed Henri's practice of painting the grittier aspects of city life. Though Davis would soon abandon his teacher's raw, bravura style for a more sophisticated manner influenced, in part, by Cubism, the urban imagery Henri recommended would remain a constant presence in his art.

In 1913, Davis joined the art staff of the radical periodical *The Masses*. That same year, he sent five watercolors to the Armory Show, marking his first significant public exhibition. The Armory Show also introduced him to avant-garde European art; as a result, he became impatient with his own Ashcan school style and resolved to become a "modern" artist. Though it would be fifteen years before he could travel to Europe, the impact of French modernism was dramatic. Whereas his Armory Show watercolors (mostly of music-hall scenes) were naturalistic and were rendered with a relaxed line and thin, spontaneously applied washes of color, he soon began to experiment (in both watercolor and oil) with abstracted forms, thickly textured paint, carefully worked out multiple perspectives, and collage; he also began using words and letters in his work. His line was jaunty, his color bold. Behind the obvious humor and energy of his art was a disciplined creative process involving numerous sketches and theoretical deliberations.

For the early years of Davis's career, his exhibitions would feature watercolors more often than oils – his first solo show, in 1917, was of watercolors and drawings; watercolors also figured prominently in his retrospectives at the Whitney Studio Club in 1926 and 1929. During this period, as Davis's oils became denser, his watercolors also became more opaque. While the lively group of watercolors Davis produced during a trip to Cuba in the winter of 1919-20 are skillful examples of the transparent wash technique, by the late twenties gouache and tempera had for the most part replaced transparent pigments in his works on paper. Thereafter, he would use gouache primarily for preparatory studies for larger work in oil.

Davis had his first show with Edith Halpert (who would be his dealer for the balance of his career) at the Downtown Gallery in 1927. On the strength of its success he went to Paris for a year. In the 1930s, working for the WPA Federal Art Project, Davis painted a number of murals, including *Men without Women* (1932, Radio City Music Hall, New York) and *Swing Landscape* (1938, Indiana University Art Museum, Bloomington) whose jazzy complexity were without precedent in the genre. Davis's paintings from the last two decades of his career are almost pure abstractions, with few recognizable images or navigable space. His alternation between abstraction and realism meant that his art never lost currency; he was active and producing vigorous work up until his death in 1964.

Stuart Davis
106. *Myopic Vista*, 1925

Transparent and opaque watercolor over graphite on moderately thick, slightly textured, dark cream wove paper
15³⁄₁₆ x 18 in. (386 x 458 mm)
Signed and dated upper left in graphite: Stuart Davis 1925
Gift of the William H. Lane Foundation. 1990.393

Myopic Vista was painted in Gloucester, where Davis had been spending summers since 1914. Although abstract, the watercolor was based on Gloucester landmarks, accurately observed. It includes the fish pier, the town hall with its rounded tower, the spire of the First Baptist Church, and, at far right, the steeple of St. Ann's Roman Catholic Church, as viewed across Gloucester's Inner Harbor from Smith's Cove in East Gloucester.[1] A photograph made in 1911 from the same vantage point (fig. 1) shows most of the features of Davis's landscape, including several – the Baptist Church, the circular brick gas tanks, and even the fruit trees in the foreground – that have long since disappeared.[2] The spot where Davis chose to work was just a few steps away from the "red cottage" that Davis had shared with John and Dolly Sloan in the teens, as though Davis were heeding Sloan's admonition, "Don't walk miles looking for a subject. Look down the road and use your imagination."[3] Davis had recorded this attractive vista from nearby Rocky Neck a few years earlier, in the oil, *Morning Walk (Harbor View)* (1919, collection of Earl Davis). *Gloucester Harbor* (1924, Butler Institute of American Art, Youngstown, Ohio), a watercolor contemporary with *Myopic Vista*, also focuses on the juxtaposition of the city hall tower and the church spire, a feature of many modernist views of Gloucester.[4]

This watercolor and a related subject, *Boat Landing* (1926, Museum of Fine Arts, Boston) were part of a group of pictures that were acquired from Davis's 1929 exhibition of watercolors at the Whitney Studio Galleries by Juliana Force, its prescient director, for what would become the Whitney Museum.[5] It complements another early Force/Whitney acquisition, *Early American Landscape* (fig. 2), which is also a

Fig. 1. *View of Gloucester.* Photograph, from Joseph E. Garland, *The Gloucester Guide, A Stroll through Place and Time* (Rockport, Massachusetts: Protean Press, 1990), p. 85.

Fig. 2. *Early American Landscape*, 1925. Oil on canvas. Collection of the Whitney Museum of American Art, New York.

Gloucester subject, but without the landmarks that punctuate the watercolor's skyline. These pictures of the mid-twenties mark the end of a period of naturalism for Davis – however schematized his forms in *Myopic Vista*, the view is topographically accurate – before he plunged into the abstraction of the Eggbeater series. They also illustrate his penchant for decorative patterning, which here is especially apparent in the blue and orange confetti in the sky. The wedge-like shapes painted in opaque pigment over the pale green wash in the

sea evoke both the lapping waves and the fishing nets ("seine") spread over the water.

In both *Myopic Vista* and *Early American Landscape* the waterfront view is framed by the twisted fruit trees.[6] The three-dimensional quality of these trees contrasts markedly with the flatness of the townscape (in *Myopic Vista*, the tree takes on an almost anthropomorphic muscularity; in *Early American Landscape*, the denuded trees are given a glossy, burnished texture, and so appear as slender bronze sculptures resting on gray slab pedestals). Their mass converts a conventionally picturesque view of Gloucester into a theatrical backdrop. In *Myopic Vista*, the tree also serves as a sentry against the blank spaces at left. Like the punning textural patterns, such negative spaces (for example, the lozenge shape formed by the intersecting tree branches) reflect the lessons Davis was eagerly absorbing from Picasso and Braque even before he got to Paris. At the same time, such devices reflect his continuing concern with abstract, compressed, and conceptual spatial relationships (hence the "myopic" of his title), and with the tensions between the traditional and the modern that he found so energizing: in this lively image, he combined government, religion, industry, nature, and the airy, empty spaces of the imagination.

CT

1. I am grateful to James O'Gorman and Karen Quinn for helping me locate Davis's view.

2. The First Baptist Church, at Pleasant and Middle Streets, was torn down in 1966. A parking lot is on the site now; across the street is the Cape Ann Historical Association, whose curator, Britt Crews, generously provided the information about the church. Davis depicted the gas tanks in a 1916 oil (*Brick Gas Tank*, private collection). For the fruit trees, see below.

3. John Sloan, *Gist of Art* (New York: American artists group, inc., 1939), p. 146.

4. See, for example, John Sloan's *Sunflowers, Rocky Neck* (1914, collection of Alfred Mayor and Martha M. Smith).

5. The Whitney Museum, which owned nine Davises by 1931, deaccessioned these pictures in the early 1950s. They were subsequently acquired by William H. Lane. The Lane Foundation presented the Davises to the Museum in 1990.

6. Davis used these tree forms – sometimes depicted naturalistically, sometimes greatly simplified and abstracted – in several later works. See, for example, *Town Square* (1925-26, Newark [New Jersey] Museum); *Trees and El* (1931, Henry Art Gallery, University of Washington, Seattle); and *Cigarette Papers* (1933, private collection).

Charles Burchfield

Born Ashtabula Harbor, Ohio, 1893;
died West Seneca, New York, 1967

The bare facts of Charles Burchfield's life do not suggest the highly imaginative nature of his art. From the age of fifteen, he kept journals in which he described his intense feelings toward his surroundings and recorded the artistic problems he set himself. In his landscapes the artist set down the patterns of nature's sounds and movements, painting the song of the katydid and the seasonal winds. He interpreted the small-town architecture of Ohio and upstate New York, filling it with melancholy and imbuing doors and windows with such anthropomorphic features as expressive mouths and shifty eyes. Although Burchfield was never formally associated with the avant-garde, his bold and decorative deformations of natural and man-made forms and the interpretive nature of his art parallel the work of the more abstract modernist Arthur Dove (see cats. 119-122).

Burchfield preferred painting in watercolors to oils, which he found unsatisfactory, and most of his more than 1500 known works are watercolors. On many of his sheets he handled the materials as if they were oil paints, using flat, stiff brushes and opaque pigments. With their large size and serious intent, many of Burchfield's watercolors achieve the presence of oils.

Burchfield's father died when he was a boy and as a youth Burchfield worked after school and in the summers to help the family. He was nonetheless able to graduate from the Cleveland School of Art in 1916. There he was introduced to the turn-of-the-century fantasy illustrations of Arthur Rackham, Edmond Dulac, and Ivan Bilibin, to Japanese prints, Chinese calligraphy, and the flat patterns of modern poster design, all of which influenced his early work. He said that Henry G. Keller, who worked in watercolor, was his most influential teacher. Burchfield received a scholarship to the National Academy of Design, and went to New York City in the fall of 1916 to enroll in classes there. He was displeased with its programs (especially figure drawing), and after two months returned to Salem, Ohio, and took a full-time accounting job. He painted in every spare moment. During his brief stay in New York he made contact with a bookstore that sold his work for several years before it began to be handled by art dealers. Burchfield's first major one-man show, at the

Kevorkian Gallery in New York, was held in 1920 and others followed with regularity.

In 1921 the artist moved to Buffalo, where he held a position in the design department of the Birge Wallpaper Company until 1929. Only then, with the encouragement of the New York dealer Frank K.M. Rehn, did the artist resign his job and devote himself to painting. The Museum of Modern Art gave Burchfield a one-man exhibition in 1930 and from then on his work became increasingly popular. It was exhibited and published with frequency, and was acquired by innumerable collectors and institutions. Burchfield occasionally taught an art course and also published articles on art and artists. He was awarded numerous prizes and honorary degrees, including one from Harvard University in 1948. He was made a full member of the National Academy of Design in 1954.

Charles Burchfield
107. *Sunlight*, 1916
Watercolor over graphite on moderately thick, cream wove paper
14 x 9¹⁵⁄₁₆ in. (355 x 253 mm)
Signed and dated lower left in black chalk: Chas Burchfield 1916. On verso in graphite: "Sunlight"/ $10.00 / June 20, 1916
Abraham Shuman Fund. 1970.390

Sunlight was painted in June 1916, shortly after Burchfield graduated from the Cleveland School of Art and returned to Salem, Ohio.[1] Like many other pictures produced during that month, *Sunlight* records a view near the artist's home, the rooftop and chimney of a bungalow next door.[2] This paean to brilliant summer sun uses zigzagged outlines and spotted patterns to describe trees that seem to shimmer in the heat and vibrate to the song of the cicada. Burchfield set down on paper some of the elements that would reappear in his work throughout his life: a familiar subject, rhythmic patterns, and visualized sounds.

The style and execution of *Sunlight* is characteristic of many works from 1916, reflecting the flat decorative aspects of poster design and the calligraphic line of Chinese painting, both of which the artist admired during his school years.[3] The weight of the graphite line is important and the underdrawing plays a role of its own, in harmony with the flat areas of color. The watercolor pigments used here are neither transparent nor opaque, but something in between. The artist has recorded that at this time he was working with prescribed colors such as yellow for sunlit leaves, blue or blue-green for shadows, and an execution "in flat pattern with little or no evidence of a third dimension."[4] The vivid reds and yellows in this picture appear less frequently in later work, but the quieter tones of blue, blue-green, and tan would remain typical, as would Burchfield's use of a smooth paper. In a few years the sunny temperament revealed here would give way to a gloomier and more fantastic interpretation of small-town houses and industrial scenes.

SWR

1. Paintings from June 1916 are listed in Joseph S. Trovato, *Charles Burchfield: Catalogue of Paintings in Public and Private Collections* (Utica, New York: Museum of Art, Munson-Williams-Proctor Institute, 1970), nos. 96-132. This is probably no. 100, formerly with Bernard Danenberg Galleries. It was purchased by the Museum in 1970 from Adelson Galleries, Boston.

2. This information was supplied by Karl Ludwig. Curatorial files, Department of Prints, Drawings, and Photographs, Museum of Fine Arts, Boston.

3. See John I.H. Baur, *The Inlander: Life and Work of Charles Burchfield, 1893-1967* (Newark, Delaware: University of Delaware Press, 1982), p. 27.

4. Charles Burchfield, *Charles Burchfield: His Golden Year: A Retrospective Exhibition* (Tucson, Arizona: University of Arizona Press, 1965), p. 16.

Charles Burchfield
108. *Spring Patterns*, 1917
Opaque watercolor over charcoal on moderately thick, dark cream wove paper
17½ x 21 in. (455 x 542 mm)
Signed and dated lower right in graphite: C. Burchfield 1917
Sophie M. Friedman Fund. 1971.8

Spring Patterns may have been painted at Turkeyfoot Lake, Barberton, Ohio, where Burchfield worked in the summer of 1917.[1] However, it was not the specific topography that interested Burchfield, but rather the abstract, ornamental patterns he perceived in nature. While the wind-rippled surface of a lake is the overt subject of *Spring Patterns*, the implied content is solitude or isolation. The viewer is invited to regard and admire, but is prevented from imaginatively entering the picture space by the strong sense of surface pattern and lack of solid foreground.

Burchfield later explained the change in his technique between 1916 and 1917, writing: "I virtually abandoned the pointed brush for the sable 'bright' oil brush, which allowed a more robust, firm stroke, similar indeed to the oil on canvas technique. This led directly into what I call the '1917 manner'."[2] *Spring Patterns* illustrates this new "manner" to perfection. Using flat brushes, Burchfield painted stroke over stroke, virtually covering the smooth surface of the paper and handling the relatively opaque paints as if they were oils. As if for an oil painting on canvas, the underdrawing for the watercolor was executed in charcoal, whose grainy particles were subsequently worked into the paint. Opaque white provided the highlights in the foreground. The cool tonality, limited to black, white, and greens, contrasts with the bright warm colors of *Sunlight* (cat. 107), and heralds Burchfield's later, more subdued palette.

Burchfield organized the composition on a rectilinear grid of four horizontal bands and four vertical sections. The distant water is handled decoratively, with repetitive strokes forming a herringbone design. This gives way in the foreground to broader, less regular brushstrokes, more suggestive of ripples. Light falling between the clumps of trees on the distant shore creates three narrow bands of reflections on the water. In its non-naturalistic qualities, both of design and coloration, and in its simplicity and abstraction, *Spring Patterns* is even more modern than *Sunlight*. Its somber mood anticipates much of the artist's mature work.

SWR

1. Burchfield made several paintings there, one of which is entitled *Reflections* (Joseph S. Trovato, *Charles Burchfield: Catalogue of Paintings in Public and Private Collections* [Utica, New York: Museum of Art, Munson-Williams-Proctor Institute, 1970], no. 366). Burchfield's journal entry for July 17, 1917, also refers to a lake, identified as Lake Westville, five miles west of Salem (*Charles Burchfield's Journals: The Poetry of Place*, J. Benjamin Townsend, ed. [Albany: State University of New York Press, 1993, p. 111.]) Despite its title, *Spring Patterns* may have been painted during the summer; see *In May* (cat. 110), actually executed in June, but titled by Burchfield to reflect the look of spring.

2. *Charles Burchfield, His Golden Year: A Retrospective Exhibition* (Tucson, Arizona: University of Arizona Press, 1965), pp. 17-18.

Charles Burchfield
109. *Winter Bouquet*, 1933
Transparent and opaque watercolor over graphite and charcoal on moderately thick, cream wove paper, affixed overall to thick gray cardboard
35¾ x 27⅛ in. (910 x 688 mm)
Signed and dated lower right in black wash: monogram CEB/1933
Ellen K. Gardner Fund. 34.43

In this large and imposing watercolor Burchfield combines two themes he rarely painted – still life and interior.[1] The familiar setting of the artist's studio in Gardenville, New York (fig. 1) provides the background for *Winter Bouquet*. Bottles and jars are arranged on the workbench, bins of stacked art work line the wall, and mounted high up is a stuffed crow whose lifelike pose cannot help but recall Edgar Allen Poe's talking raven. Attention is focused on an arrangement of dried wildflowers, in which the deep brick red and dense forms of sumac enliven the quiet hues and lacy textures of milkweed, thistles, goldenrod, and Queen Anne's lace.

In a letter discussing this painting Burchfield wrote:

The 'Winter Bouquet' was painted in my studio at Gardenville in November, 1933. . . . The impulse to paint such a subject came about gradually. I had amused myself all fall in gathering various dead flowers and seed-pods, in order to have a bouquet for my studio through the winter; in fact I have always thought that many of our flowers and weeds are just as beautiful dead as when growing. I decided to express this idea in painting. The bouquet, while beautiful in itself, did not seem sufficient to express the whole idea, and I conceived the idea of putting in a background suggestive of November and the impending doom of winter . . . the stuffed crow up above, black and sinister, from behind which comes the fading light of an autumnal dusk; in the half-light, when ordinary objects assume a new significance, the bouquet seemed to take on a life that it had never had in the summer; the silken milkweed down seemed to possess a sort of phosphorescent glow. All this I tried to get into the picture.[2]

Burchfield painted with broad, flat brushes and opaque paints, gathering up particles of the charcoal underdrawing as he painted. The mottled,

Fig. 1. Thomas Hollyman, *Burchfield in his Studio, Gardenville, New York*, 1955. Photograph. © Thomas Hollyman.

textured look of the paper and the somber, muted colors contribute to the full, rich appearance of the picture. In aspects of its technique, as well as its large size, it resembles an oil painting. As a measure of Burchfield's stature at this time, the picture was purchased directly from the artist by the Museum within months of its creation. Considered a major work by the artist, it has since been included in a number of important watercolor exhibitions.

SWR

1. Other floral still lifes in interiors include *Flower Pot in Window* (1919, collection of Mr. Bengt E. R. Julin), also with a snowy view outside the window; and *Pussy Willows* (1936, Munson-Williams-Proctor Institute, Utica, New York).

2. Burchfield to C.C. Cunningham, Department of Paintings, February 20, 1934. Curatorial files, Department of Prints, Drawings, and Photographs, Museum of Fine Arts, Boston.

Charles Burchfield
110. *In May*, 1939
Watercolor with touches of black crayon on thick, cream wove paper
24½ x 19½ in. (632 x 504 mm)
Signed and dated lower right in black crayon: monogram CEB 1939
Hayden Collection. Charles Henry Hayden Fund. 39.762

Such a view down a rolling country road is fairly frequent in Burchfield's work. This site is not far from the artist's home near Buffalo, however, Burchfield had painted similar views in his early days in Ohio.[1] In his journal for June 8 and 9, 1939, the artist wrote:

> To country southwest of Cowlesville, but cannot find a subject all morning.
> Park along the Williston-Marilla Rd to eat lunch. I thoroughly enjoyed the hour. The fields still have a "May" look about them due probably to the very late cold season. The scattering clouds make rapidly moving shadows that steal silently across the earth – here, where I am all is in shadow; down the road appears a ragged patch of sunshine which comes closer and closer until all at once the buttercup filled meadow before me burst into glorious golden light.
> After lunch to Three Rod Road to a favorite hill just north of Williston Corners. Here I determine to make a sketch – a view of the hot white road stretching southwards. In spite of the dry weather, the country-side still has the raw yellow-green quality of mid-May. My subject grows in interest as I progress.
> It is very hot in spite of the wind; the sunlight is reflected up from the dry white road in a blinding glare. Fleets of white clouds come and go. Soft violet shadows pursue each other along the road toward me. On the right-hand side of the road is a patch of wild-roses, in full bloom. The hot wind brings their odor to me. All afternoon a blue-bird came and perched at regular intervals on a dead apple-tree, singing his haunting spring song (incongruous in this strange blistering heat, which in itself belied the fresh green earth.)
> June 9 – Out again to Three-Rod road to paint on the foreground. Finish in an hour or so. . . . The very quality of the landscape suggesting May, determined me to call it "In May" even tho it was painted in June.[2]

Burchfield's words show his sensitivity not only to the sights but to the sounds and smells that accompanied his execution of this watercolor. His pleasure in the out-of-doors is borne out by the vernal colors and spirited mood of this painting. Like *Winter Bouquet* (cat. 109), this large watercolor has the look of an oil painting. The paint is not applied very thickly, yet the red-brown, and the greens and grays of the palette are cloudy and retain the marks of the flat brushes favored by the artist.

In May at first seems to represent quintessential American farm country: a rutted dirt road viewed straight on, arched trees in the middle distance, and, far away, hills accented with trees and a cloud-capped sky. Despite its seeming naturalism, the artist constructed the space so as to draw the viewer swiftly in and over the undulating road, almost as if he were a soaring bird. The darks and lights of the windows of three farm houses make anthropomorphic faces in the characteristic manner of Burchfield, although their expressions are more restrained than those found in earlier works.[3] Indeed, this picture can be viewed as a transitional work, situated between the reportorial pictures of the 1930s and the return to nature fantasies in the 1940s.

SWR

1. For an early version of this composition see *Mysterious Bird* (1917, Wilmington [Delaware] Society of the Fine Arts).

2. Quoted by the artist in a letter dated January 13, 1940, to W. G. Constable, Curator of Paintings. Curatorial files, Department of Prints, Drawings, and Photographs, Museum of Fine Arts, Boston.

3. See, for example, *Black Houses* (1918, Mr. and Mrs. Barney A. Ebsworth Collection).

Edward Hopper

Born Nyack, New York, 1882;
died New York City, 1967

Although Hopper is now best known for his oil paintings, he first came to prominence in New York as a watercolorist. In 1923, the Brooklyn Museum exhibited six of his works in its second watercolor biennial, and purchased *The Mansard Roof* (see Carol Troyen, "A War Waged on Paper: Watercolor and Modern Art in America," this volume, fig. 21) for $100. This was Hopper's only sale in ten years, and the first to a major museum. The following year, he exhibited eleven watercolors at the Frank K.M. Rehn Gallery, and the show sold out; his 1927 show at the gallery, which included twelve watercolors, was equally successful. Hopper began working seriously in watercolor only in 1923 (though he had used it earlier for his commercial work); the impetus to use the medium may have come from his future wife Jo Nivison. For the next two decades Hopper was a prolific watercolorist, using the medium for many of his best-known themes – Victorian architecture, boats, lighthouses. Although in his early years almost all of Hopper's non-commercial work was done *en plein air*, by the 1920s he produced his oils in his New York studio, while he turned to watercolor for outdoor work done on his summer holidays. Nonetheless, Hopper always regarded watercolor as a vehicle for important statements, and rarely used it simply to produce studies for his oils.

Hopper's watercolor style was deliberately non-virtuosic. Although he was a skilled technician, he was not given to flashy effects or the creation of elaborately textured surfaces. Nor did he capitalize on the accidental effects of watercolor. Rather, he was attracted to the medium because of its portability, and because it enabled him to record the clear, hard, structure-revealing light of New England, where most of his watercolors were painted.

Hopper enrolled in the Correspondence School of Illustration in New York City in 1899, immediately after graduating from Nyack High School. The next year, he transferred to the New York School of Art, where he studied with Robert Henri. Over the next few years, he made three trips to Europe. He spent most of his time in Paris, where he was influenced by Impressionist painting but, unlike many other young American artists then in Europe, he seems not to have pursued the avant-garde (the salons of Gertrude Stein, the painting of Picasso and Matisse). Upon his return, he supported himself as an illustrator while participating in several group shows, among them the Armory Show, in which he exhibited one painting.

In December of 1913 Hopper moved his studio to 3 Washington Square North, which would be his home for the rest of his life. About 1915, he took up etching. He had his first solo paintings show at the Whitney Studio Club in 1920 (he was thirty-seven); it failed to attract the attention of either critics or patrons. However, his subsequent success as a watercolorist gave a tremendous boost to his career, enabling him to marry, to give up illustration, and, beginning with *House by the Railroad* (1925, Museum of Modern Art, New York) to produce a masterful series of oil paintings. By the twenties, the pattern of Hopper's life was established: he spent winters in his Greenwich Village studio and summers in New England (first Gloucester, then, after building a house in South Truro in 1934, on Cape Cod). Hopper's 1933 retrospective at the Museum of Modern Art was one of the first exhibitions that institution dedicated to the work of a living American artist. The Whitney Museum mounted Hopper shows in 1950, again in 1964 (three years before his death), and in 1980; the last of these gave special recognition to his work in watercolor.

Edward Hopper
111. *Deck of a Beam Trawler*, 1923
Watercolor over graphite on moderately thick, slightly textured, cream wove paper
11¾ x 18 in. (298 x 457 mm)
Signed and dated lower left in gray wash: Edward Hopper / Gloucester 1923
Bequest of John T. Spaulding. 48.715

Although he would later turn his attention to more glamorous pleasure boats, between 1923 and 1926 Hopper painted at least ten watercolors of the hard-working beam trawler.[1] Beam trawlers, introduced to the American fishing industry at about the turn of the century, represented a great technological advance over dory trawling,[2] and were much in evidence in Gloucester and in Rockland, Maine, the summers Hopper was working there.

These watercolors, among the first Hopper painted outside of his commercial work, reveal him at his most adventurous, and most abstract. Unlike the pictures of Victorian houses he produced at the same time, which generally are anchored by a massive shape, these watercolors have no central motif. With one exception (fig. 1), the boats are severely cropped, and are shown docked and unoccupied, sometimes (as here) at an ambiguous angle to the pier. Parts critical to the ship's function, such as the winches and the inverted U-shaped "gallows frames," used to haul up the nets (both in brick red here, a singing color

Fig. 1. *Trawler and Telegraph Pole*, 1926. Watercolor on paper. The Art Museum, Princeton, New Jersey. Laura P. Hall Memorial Collection.

accent deliberately inserted to contrast with the prevailing cool tones), are difficult to identify at first. *Deck of a Beam Trawler* is perhaps the most daring of these pictures, for the boat's deck is pitched at an oblique angle, condensing its already jumbled contents. Many of the objects in this area and at the tower at right are defined only by their shadows, or by the slightest pencil outlines – a visual shorthand Hopper mastered as an illustrator. The watercolor's two dominant verticals, normally the stabilizing structures of a composition, here suggest the queasy rocking of the ship, for the gray tower inclines to the right while the yellow mast leans left – a device Hopper would use frequently to produce a vaguely disorienting effect.

Deck of a Beam Trawler was one of six works Hopper submitted to the Brooklyn Museum's 1923 watercolor biennial, where they attracted the attention of the Museum's curators and more than one critic. His work was called "exhilarating," and a tribute to "what can be done with the homeliest subject if only one possesses the seeing eye."[3] The next year, *Deck of a Beam Trawler* was included in Hopper's solo exhibition at the Frank K.M. Rehn Gallery in New York, his second such exhibition and the first in four years. That show, of eleven watercolors, sold out; works were acquired by such thoughtful collectors as Stephen C. Clark and the painter George Bellows. The respected Boston collector John T. Spaulding bought four, including *Deck of a Beam Trawler*. Critics again applauded, sounding the theme that would echo though reviews of Hopper's work from then onward: "Edward Hopper . . . seems to be opposed to the 'charm,' but to use to the full his ability to fascinate. His subjects, all from Gloucester, are often ugly; his paintings have beauty."[4]

CT

1. In addition to the Museum's, these include: *Two Trawlers* (1923-24, Whitney Museum of American Art, New York); *Beam Trawler Teale* (1926, Munson-Williams-Proctor Institute, Utica, New York); *Bow of the Beam Trawler Osprey* (1926, Saint Louis Art Museum); *Trawler and Telegraph Pole* (1926, The Art Museum, Princeton University, Princeton, New Jersey); *Deck of the Beam Trawler Widgeon* (1926, Metropolitan Museum of Art, New York), as well as three privately owned watercolors and one recently on the art market.

2. William H. Bunting, compiler and annotator, *Portrait of a Port: Boston, 1852-1914* (Cambridge, Massachusetts: The Belknap Press of Harvard University Press, 1971), pp. 212-213.

3. Royal Cortissoz, "A Fine Collection at the Brooklyn Museum," *New York Tribune*, 25 November, 1923, p. 8; Helen Appleton Read, "Brooklyn Museum Emphasizes New Talent in Initial Exhibition," *Brooklyn Daily Eagle*, 18 November 1923, p. 2B.

4. "Hopper's Water Colors," *Art News* 23 (October 18, 1924), p. 2.

Edward Hopper
112. *Anderson's House*, 1926
Watercolor over graphite on moderately thick, slightly textured, cream wove paper
13¹⁵⁄₁₆ x 19¹⁵⁄₁₆ in. (354 x 508 mm)
Signed lower left in black wash: Edward Hopper / Gloucester
Bequest of John T. Spaulding. 48.720

Hopper painted a group of watercolors of clapboard buildings in Gloucester in the fall of 1926. He later noted that he was attracted to these subjects because of their clear structures, strong shadows, and emphatic geometries: "At Gloucester when everyone else would be painting ships and the waterfront I'd just go around looking at houses. It is a solid looking town. The roofs are very bold, the cornices are bolder. The dormers cast very positive shadows. The sea captain influence I guess – the boldness of ships."[1] Critics marveled at his ability to wring beauty out of such awkward, out-of-fashion subjects:

[Hopper is] forcefully eloquent upon the hitherto concealed beauty of some supposedly hideous buildings built during the Garfield administration. The dwellings, in fact, are hideous, and people of sensibility were quite justified in shuddering when they passed these relics of a dark era in American history upon the streets of Gloucester, although now that an artist has shown how to extract beauty from them there will no doubt be a temptation to view them with affection.[2]

Anderson's House and the other house portraits Hopper painted that autumn do not, in fact, evoke nostalgia, even now when Victorian architecture is admired. Nor do they seem to exhibit disconcertingly human personalities, as do Burchfield's watercolors of similar houses (fig. 1) painted at about the same time. A recent photograph of this house[3] demonstrates how faithful Hopper was to the building's appearance. Yet his vision is not neutral; rather, with its mute façade and deep shadows, the house is ambiguous and, like Burchfield's, vaguely unsettling.

Although Hopper always handled watercolor confidently, his technique here is as plain as the building he painted. His dealer noted that he avoided "clever brushwork or 'washes'," [4] and indeed there is little evidence of scraping out or

Fig. 1. Charles Burchfield (1893-1967), *Sulphurous Evening*, 1922-29. Watercolor. The Saint Louis Art Museum. Purchase, Eliza McMillan Fund.

painting wet-on-wet or other bravura techniques. Rather Hopper constructed this picture by meticulously applying layer upon layer of thin wash, sometimes – for example, on the side of the house – in conjunction with wiping out of color to produce a granular effect. Sometimes his thin regular strokes – so unlike the broad, seamless washes of classical watercolor technique – create harmonies within the picture. This is especially apparent in the sky, where the narrow stripes of wash parallel the clapboards in the house and animate an otherwise monotonous area. But on the whole, the result is rather consciously inelegant. Instead, the attraction of this watercolor stems from Hopper's ability to evoke clear New England light, the kind of light that emphasizes structure; from his interesting color sense, apparent in his audacious use of orange in the chimneys at left, for example, against the otherwise cool tones of the picture; and from what his friend Burchfield called "the extreme simplicity" of the image, "verging, in many instances, on starkness."[5]

Anderson's House was one of twelve watercolors shown, along with four oils and a group of etchings, in February 1927 at the Frank K.M. Rehn Gallery in New York. It was Hopper's second show with the dealer who for many years would be his representative and supporter. Hopper was forty-five, and until recently had been unable to

sell his work. But this show was well received, and three oils and nine of the watercolors sold, testifying to Hopper's sudden popularity.

CT

1. Hopper to William Johnson, unpublished interview, 30 October 1956, p. 17, quoted in Gail Levin, *Edward Hopper: The Art and the Artist* (New York, Whitney Museum of American Art, 1980), p. 44.

2. Henry McBride, "Hopper's Watercolors," *The New York Sun*, 25 October, 1924, in Daniel Catton Rich, ed., *The Flow of Art: Essays and Criticisms of Henry McBride* (New York: Atheneum Publishers, 1975), p. 202.

3. Reproduced in Gail Levin, *Hopper's Places* (New York: Alfred A. Knopf, 1985), p. 58.

4. Frank Rehn, quoted in Garnett McCoy, "Charles Burchfield and Edward Hopper. Some Documentary Notes," *Archives of American Art Journal* 7 (July-October 1967), p. 12.

5. Charles Burchfield, "Hopper: Career of silent poetry," *Art News* 49 (March 1950), p. 16.

Edward Hopper
113. *House of the Fog Horn, No. 2*, 1927
Watercolor over graphite on moderately thick, slightly textured, cream wove paper
13⅞ x 19¹⁵⁄₁₆ in. (352 x 506 mm)
Signed lower right in blue ink: Edward Hopper / Two Lights, Me
Bequest of John T. Spaulding. 48.722

Buoyed by recent successes at the Frank K.M. Rehn Gallery (1924, 1927), at the Art Institute of Chicago's fourth annual International Water Color Exhibition (1924), and at Boston's St. Botolph Club (1926), Hopper purchased his first automobile in 1927.[1] His new mobility enabled him to make a number of excursions in New England that summer, including a trip to Two Lights, Cape Elizabeth, Maine (just south of Portland), where he found many subjects for his brush. He painted several views of the picturesque Two Lights lighthouse in both oil and watercolor,[2] and executed two watercolors of a group of smaller buildings in the lighthouse complex, returning in 1929 to paint a third version of *The House of the Fog Horn* (figs. 1, 2).

The Museum's watercolor is the second in the series, and is the simplest and most emotionally resonant of the three. It shows the side of the foghorn house, two smaller buildings at the right and a strip of ocean in the far distance at left. Even though they were part of an active Coast Guard station when Hopper was there,[3] the two small pavilions that are the focus of the composition are portrayed as stark and empty: the single visible door is closed, the single window darkened. Hopper's emphasis on the buildings' low, blocky regular shapes gives them a powerful presence, and the lack of any architectural detail (especially notable compared to the other two watercolors of the site) and the structures' apparent isolation in the landscape make them seem all the more desolate. But while Hopper characterizes the buildings as stolid, unchanging fixtures in the landscape, his radiant light and deep shadows give the scene a just-observed quality. He makes much of the shadows in this picture. Some of these, such as the blue square on the near building, have no identifiable source, while others, such as the long blue shadow

Fig. 1. *House of the Fog Horn, No. 1*, 1927. Watercolor on paper. The Metropolitan Museum of Art. Bequest of Elizabeth Amis Cameron Blanchard, 1956.

Fig. 2. *House of the Fog Horn, No. 3*, 1929. Watercolor on paper. Yale University Art Gallery. Gift of George Hopper Fitch, B. A. 1932.

in the foreground, seem to be cast by something just outside the picture, countering the scene's sense of immutablity with one of immanence.

Hopper's technique here is deliberate yet unassuming. The artist carefully applied numerous layers of thin wash over graphite underdrawing (leaving nothing to chance, Hopper even sketched in the contours of his wispy white clouds). The cool, blue-green palette shared by all three watercolors is enlivened here by touches of brick red in the foreground, where there is also evidence of a deft use of sponging. Hopper created a rock embedded in the ground by carefully lifting up a small area of brown wash, and then gave it bulk by adding a stroke of blue, to suggest shadow, alongside.

House of the Fog Horn, No. 2 was one of nine watercolors the Boston collector and Hopper enthusiast John T. Spaulding bought from Frank Rehn in the 1920s. Among them were two other views Hopper painted at Cape Elizabeth that summer, *Hill and Houses* and *Lighthouse and Buildings, Portland Head*, both now in the collection of the Museum of Fine Arts.

CT

1. Gail Levin, *Hopper's Places* (New York: Alfred A. Knopf, 1985), p. 29.

2. Many of these are reproduced in Gail Levin, *Edward Hopper: The Art and the Artist* (New York: Whitney Museum of American Art, 1980), for example, *Light at Two Lights* (about 1927, watercolor on paper, Whitney Museum of American Art, New York) *Light at Two Lights* (1927, watercolor on paper, Blount Collection, Montgomery, Alabama), and *Lighthouse Hill* (1927, oil on canvas, Dallas Museum of Fine Arts).

3. Levin, *Hopper's Places*, p. 29. For a photograph of the foghorn buildings as they looked recently, see p. 30.

Edward Hopper
114. *First Branch of the White River, Vermont*, 1938
Watercolor over graphite on very thick, rough textured, cream wove paper; watermark: HAND MADE J. WHATMAN 1936 ENGLAND
21¾ x 26⅞ in. (553 x 683 mm)
Signed lower right in blue-green watercolor: EDWARD HOPPER
William Emerson Fund. 39.43

Hopper had greater ambitions for this watercolor than for other works in this exhibition. Considerably larger than they, *First Branch of the White River* was not painted on the relatively thin paper of a watercolor block, but on a heavier paper, which Hopper took some pains to prepare.[1] The watercolor was purchased by the Museum of Fine Arts a few months after Hopper completed it, and in 1945 was one of only nine works by the artist chosen for the landmark exhibition "American Watercolor and Winslow Homer."[2]

In a letter to W.G. Constable, then curator of paintings at the Museum of Fine Arts, Hopper described the occasion on which the picture was painted, noting in his laconic, droll way, that he considered the scene beautiful but not in any way exceptional:

> There is not much to tell about the doing of it. It was painted in Vermont last autumn, while I was staying at the farm of Robert Slater, at South Royalton, near the junction of the First Branch with the White River. I sat in a steep mountain pasture of Slater's looking down on this little stream, so very steep a hill that I had to prop up the front legs of my stool to keep from sliding down. Aside from that and the curiosity of the cows, the occasion was not momentous.[3]

First Branch of the White River was made on Hopper's second visit to South Royalton. During this and the preceding September he produced a small group of watercolors of local scenery whose subjects were unusual in his oeuvre. Hopper painted relatively few pure landscapes, perhaps because the foliage and other amorphous shapes in nature were not an obvious subject for an artist so deeply concerned with structure, and in fact the trees, hills, and riverbank in this watercolor are strongly sculptural. The acid palette of *First Branch of the*

Reginald Marsh

Born Paris, France, 1898;
died New York City, 1954

White River, audacious for its inclusion of so many shades of green, first appears in Hopper's South Truro, Massachusetts, landscapes of the early and mid-1930s, as do the hazy sunshine and long shadows of late afternoon. The palette also connects these pictures with the work of American scene painters (with whom Hopper was sometimes associated, to his discomfort) as does the mannered perspective of *First Branch of the White River*. The viewer looks down on the curve of the river and up again at the rolling hills in the distance; the terrain swells and falls like ocean waves. With its untraveled road and still, empty river, the landscape seems like a stage set, suggesting imminent arrival, or sudden departure.

CT

1. Hopper's choice and use of materials here suggest he intended a statement comparable in importance to that of his oils. His paper has a pronounced diagonal twill pattern, very much like a canvas weave. To prepare it, Hopper dampened the sheet and stretched it to affix it to a stretcher. Interestingly, he did not exploit either the dampened surface – by painting wet-on-wet, for example – or the unusual texture of the paper, by using dry-brush. Rather, the watercolor was painted with Hopper's characteristically meticulous technique: he applied layer after layer of thin wash, eschewing textural variety, but instead almost staining the paper with color which, on such a thick, toothy sheet, resulted in a scrubbed effect.

2. Lloyd Goodrich, *American Watercolor and Winslow Homer* (Minneapolis: Walker Art Center, 1945), p. 107. The show surveyed Hopper's career as a watercolorist from 1926 to 1943.

3. Edward Hopper to W.G. Constable, 26 January, 1939. Curatorial files, Department of Prints, Drawings, and Photographs, Museum of Fine Arts, Boston.

Reginald Marsh's characteristic subjects were bathers at Coney Island, burlesque queens, taxi dancers, and denizens of the Bowery – people associated with the earthier side of urban life, living apart from the ordinary nine-to-five world. His preferred media were watercolor, pen and ink, and tempera. His observations on New York between the wars, though often sharply satirical, were couched in a style that paid deliberate homage to old-master painting (he especially admired Rubens, and the "Marsh girl," the blond, curvaceous woman found in many of his pictures, was frequently Rubenesque in stature).

Marsh was born in Paris to American parents, both of whom were artists. His aesthetic interests surfaced in childhood, and were developed at The Lawrenceville School in New Jersey and later, at Yale. He studied art history at Yale, and provided humorous drawings for the school magazine. After graduating in 1920, Marsh sought jobs as an illustrator in New York City, and worked for the *Daily News* and *The New Yorker*. In the early 1920s, Frank Crowninshield, editor of *Vanity Fair*, sent Marsh to make sketches of Coney Island. The beaches, sideshows, and boardwalk delighted him, and he drew, painted, and photographed them repeatedly for the next thirty years. Also in the early 1920s Marsh began to study painting at the Art Students League with Kenneth Hayes Miller, an inspirational teacher who encouraged both his developing interest in old-master painting and his continued fascination with tawdry urban subjects.

Throughout his career, Marsh experimented with a variety of media. Like many twentieth-century American painters, he achieved his greatest success in watercolor (and the allied medium of tempera), and sought to make these media, traditionally considered minor, his vehicle for major statements. He worked in black and white in the early twenties, subsequently taking up watercolor. At about the same time, he began making prints. Marsh did not paint in oils until 1923, and was never fully comfortable with the medium. By 1929 he had set aside oil painting in favor of tempera; in the course of the next decade he also began to use watercolor for ambitious, large-scale pictures. About 1940 he worked (with indifferent results) under the French painter Jacques Maroger, who

claimed to have uncovered the secret of old-master painting. More successful were the large drawings in Chinese ink that Marsh began to produce at about the same time. In these he returned to the monochromatic palette of his illustrator days, his satiric images becoming more dreamlike and visionary.

Reginald Marsh
115. *Steel Structures*, 1934
Watercolor over graphite on moderately thick, moderately rough, cream wove paper
14 x 20 in. (355 x 507 mm)
Signed lower right, in black ink: Reginald Marsh '34
Seth K. Sweetser Fund. 39.583

Drawings preserved from Marsh's childhood reveal an early interest in trains, bridges, and industrial structures. His return to those themes as an adult preceded the beginning of the Depression by only a year or two, and some of his views of railroad yards show roughly dressed figures dwarfed by the mammoth engines.[1] On the whole, however, the drawings, watercolors, and prints detailing these subjects are unpopulated, although – as in *Steel Structures* – many are painted from a perspective that emphasizes their heroic bulk and height, and the implied diminution of the human observer.

Steel Structures was bought by the Museum of Fine Arts from its 1939 exhibition, "Ten American Watercolor Painters," an exhibition that also included work by Charles Burchfield, Edward Hopper, Adolf Dehn, Arthur G. Dove, and John Marin. In a letter to W.G. Constable, the Museum's curator of paintings, Marsh expressed uncertainty about the exact location of the bridge: "it is [either] of a 'lift' bridge over the Hackensack River outside Jersey City, otherwise it may be of a bridge in Chicago." He nonetheless remembered the day, and his method, vividly: "I painted it in from one to two hours on Whatman paper wet in wet in Winsor Newton transparent watercolors – probably 85 degrees F. in the sun, with a long walk to get to the place."[2]

The watercolor, however, does not reflect the heat. Marsh painted it almost as a grisaille, restricting his palette to cool blues, blacks, and

Oscar Bluemner

Born Prenzlau, Germany, 1867;
died South Braintree, Massachusetts, 1938

grays. Some grayed-down ocher, used principally for the pilings along the bottom of the picture, is the only chromatic accent. And although he described his technique as "wet in wet," Marsh has also drawn much of the watercolor with his brush. His lively graphic style of bold lines and slashing strokes, made with drybrush as well as with more fluid strokes, is especially apparent in the bridge's massive towers. The virtuosic swirl of smoke at right is reminiscent of oriental ink paintings and, along with the emphasis on line and the near-monochrome palette, anticipates Marsh's Chinese ink drawings of the next decade.

CT

1. See, for example *Railroad Yard* (1929, collection of Rita and Daniel Fraad). Marsh credited other painters with his renewed interest in trains: "Begin to tire of dandyism in taste. I'll never forget a locomotive in *The Dial* by E. E. Cummings. . . . Seeing a Burchfield watercolor – the same magazine starts me doing locomotives." Marsh, quoted in Lloyd Goodrich, *Reginald Marsh* (New York: Harry N. Abrams, Inc., 1972), p. 26.

2. Marsh to W. G. Constable, June 3, 1939. Curatorial files, Department of Prints, Drawings, and Photographs, Museum of Fine Arts, Boston.

Trained as an architect at Berlin's Königliche Technische Hochschule, Bluemner came to the United States in 1892. He settled first in Chicago, where he was attracted by the promise of work on the World's Columbian Exposition, but ultimately was disappointed by the conservative nature of the fair's building projects. He moved to New York City in 1901, continuing to work as an architect. In 1912, a dispute over credit for the design of the Bronx Borough Courthouse was resolved in his favor. The settlement enabled him to give up his foundering architectural practice and return to Europe. There he pursued his interest in modern painting, kindled by avant-garde exhibitions in New York, especially the Cézanne watercolor show at Alfred Stieglitz's gallery, 291.

Although Bluemner did not begin to paint in oils until about 1911, he had worked in watercolor as an architecture student, and by about 1900 was using the medium for landscape studies produced during rambles in rural New Jersey and Long Island. He made his artistic debut at the 1913 Armory Show, submitting three watercolors and two oils; he would use those media (as well as egg tempera and, in later years, casein) for major pictures for the rest of his life. He also used watercolor for preliminary sketches, often as an intermediate step between a charcoal or pen and ink sketch and a final painting. In his earlier watercolors, Bluemner used transparent washes for the most part. However, he applied them in layer after layer to produce a dense, resonant effect, all the more emotionally charged for being in brilliant color. By the end of his career, he often incorporated gouache, casein, and other media into his works on paper. Bluemner was also deeply absorbed by the science of painting, and made elaborate studies of materials and of color theories, exploring not only optical relationships but also the symbolic and expressive meanings of colors.

Although he never achieved the prominence of many of the artists in Stieglitz's circle, Bluemner was associated with 291 from the beginning of his painting career. Stieglitz gave him his first American solo show in 1915, and included him in the Forum Exhibition the following year. Bluemner wrote for Stieglitz's *Camera Work* and provided the introduction for the catalogue of Georgia

O'Keeffe's 1927 Intimate Gallery show. Through the 1920s, Bluemner was associated with some of the most progressive art dealers in New York, showing with Stephan Bourgeois, N.E. Montross, and, in 1928, with Stieglitz at the Intimate Gallery. From 1924, J.B. Neumann was his principal dealer.

The death of Bluemner's wife in 1926 marked a tragic turning point in his career. He moved to South Braintree, Massachusetts, where, in that artistic isolation, his work became even more mystical and self-referential. He painted landscapes almost exclusively; his vibrant color and elemental forms – sun, moon, a single tree – were invested with deeply personal meanings. Bluemner found few buyers for his work, and the last twelve years of his life, spent in South Braintree, were marked by extreme poverty, illness, and loss of vision. In the midst of planning his first museum exhibition (which opened at the University of Minnesota Art Gallery in 1939) he took his own life.

Oscar Bluemner
116. *Van Cortlandt Park*, 1936
Opaque watercolor on thick, slightly textured, cream wove paper
13⅝ x 19⅝ in. (346 x 498 mm)
Signed lower center in blue watercolor: O Bluemner - 36; signed at left in red watercolor, then painted out: Os. Bluemner - 11[?]; signed verso in black ink: Oscar Bluemner
Gift of the Massachusetts WPA Program. 60.1426

Bluemner worked for two New Deal art projects during the Depression. In 1934, under the auspices of the Public Works of Art Project, he produced three paintings, unusual for their large size and for their social commentary – they showed factory buildings, a laundry, and a flophouse; all of these have been lost. In January of 1936 he joined the Works Progress Administration's Federal Art Project, and returning to more characteristic subject matter, he produced a number of small landscapes in watercolor and gouache,[1] including *Van Cortlandt Park*. The work done during this period is marked by a return to the tighter, more precise painting style Bluemner had employed in the teens. In fact, it has been suggested that he delib-

erately modified his style in these pictures, making it less intense and less abstract, in the hope that it would then be more acceptable to the government and the public.[2] Unfortunately, his efforts had the opposite effect: the director of the Massachusetts Federal Arts Project, the painter and critic Harley Perkins, expressed disappointment that the work Bluemner produced was relatively "unmodern."[3]

Less mystical and evocative than Bluemner's watercolors of the previous decade, *Van Cortlandt Park* is hardly less adventurous in its palette. Bluemner, who had steeped himself in optical and psychological theories of color, employed his trademark primary and secondary hues in carefully worked-out pairings: yellow bushes against soft violet hills, a vivid blue for a passing train against the yellow bushes, a green railing in the foreground matched with a railing in the middle distance that he rendered in a brilliant red-orange. The red-orange was Bluemner's favorite; he styled himself the "Vermillionaire" in acknowledgement of its importance to him. Although the colors in this picture don't seem to carry the symbolic meanings Bluemner assigned them in other, less descriptive pictures, the pairing of the green (feminine in Bluemner's vocabulary) and red (masculine, passionate, active) railings does generate an emotional contrast that goes beyond structural function.[4]

Although he lived in South Braintree during this period, Bluemner painted many of his WPA watercolors during visits to New York. *Fort Washington* (1936, Museum of Fine Arts, Boston), *Hudson River* (n.d., location unknown), and *Van Cortlandt Park* were all painted in the northern reaches of the city. Van Cortlandt Park, in the Bronx, bordered on the west by the fashionable Riverdale section, is characterized by the kind of civilized wilds that Bluemner had preferred since his sketching trips through New Jersey in the teens. He found such settings no less evocative for being familiar: "I prefer the intimate landscape of our common surroundings, where town and country mingle. For we are in the habit to carry into them our feelings of pain and pleasure, our moods."[5]

CT

1. Jeffrey Hayes, *Oscar Bluemner* (Cambridge, England: Cambridge University Press, 1991), pp. 162-163 and 207, n. 99.

2. Edith A. Tonelli, "The Avant-Garde in Boston: The Experiment of the WPA Federal Art Project," *Archives of American Art Journal* 20 (no. 1, 1980), p. 22.

3. Oscar Bluemner to Edward Bruce, December 2, 1936. Edward Bruce Papers, Archives of American Art, quoted in ibid.

4. *Oscar Bluemner: American Colorist* (Cambridge, Massachusetts: Fogg Art Museum, 1967), n.p.

5. Bluemner, Guggenheim Fellowship application, July 1932, Bluemner Papers, Archives of American Art (roll N 737: 533) quoted in ibid.

Peter Blume

Born Smorgon, Russia, 1906;
died New Milford, Connecticut, 1992

Peter Blume is best known for his oil paintings of the 1930s and 1940s with their commentaries on the ironies, inequities, and disjunctions of modern life and their style that borders on the surreal. In one of the best known of these, *The Eternal City* (oil on gessoed panel, 1934-37, Museum of Modern Art, New York) Rome's classical past and fascist present coexist as if in a nightmare, dominated by the enormous green head of Benito Mussolini emerging as a jack-in-the-box. While its individual components are depicted with realistic clarity, they are out-of-scale with each other and irrationally related. During the same decades the artist painted a few watercolors that serenely and realistically depict regional American scenes. A skilled and meticulous draftsman, Blume was scrupulous in his attention to technique in a number of media, often incorporating the materials and methods of the old masters.

Peter Blume's father was a Russian revolutionary who brought his family to Brooklyn in 1911. After attending public school, during which time he took evening art classes, Blume held various jobs including one in a lithographic shop. During the early twenties he attended art classes at The Educational Alliance, aimed at providing facilities for aspiring immigrants. Among his fellow students were the Soyer brothers – Isaac, Moses, and Raphael – and Chaim Gross. When he was in his teens Blume spent some weeks painting watercolors in Woodstock, New York. He also studied sculpture at the Beaux-Arts Institute in the interest of improving his painting. In 1925 his paintings were accepted by the Daniel Gallery, where they were shown with the work of such recognized avant-garde painters as Charles Demuth (see cats. 96-101) and Charles Sheeler. Blume painted floral, figural, and architectural subject matter in a modernist, Cubist-derived style termed Precisionism, often with a touch of whimsical humor in his unexpected juxtapositions. For the rest of the 1920s Blume painted both in rural settings and in New York City, where he encountered new intellectual and life experiences such as surrealist poetry and Greenwich Village bohemianism.

Blume's first one-man show at the Daniel Gallery in 1930 featured as its centerpiece the oil on canvas, *Parade* (1930, Museum of Modern

Art, New York), in which he combined unrelated fragments of observed reality – the New York docks and a suit of medieval armor – and rendered them three-dimensionally in space with startling clarity. Subsequent paintings, with their virtuosic old master technique and disturbing dreamlike imagery simultaneously awed and shocked the public. The unique qualities of Blume's work were recognized by such champions of the avant-garde as Alfred Barr, director of the Museum of Modern Art. A high point in Blume's career was reached in 1943 when that museum acquired *The Eternal City*; less controversial major paintings had already been purchased by the Whitney Museum of American Art (*Light of the World*, 1932) and The Metropolitan Museum (*South of Scranton*, 1934).

Blume received Guggenheim fellowships that permitted him to work in Italy in 1932-33 and 1936, and he was twice artist-in-residence at the American Academy in Rome (1956-57 and 1961-62). These sojourns helped him to continue his studies of original Renaissance paintings, which contributed so much to his individualistic style of painting – perhaps best termed magic realism – a style that he continued to practice at his studio in Sherman, Connecticut until his death in 1992.

Peter Blume
117. *Lilies*, 1938

Opaque watercolor over graphite on very thick, slightly textured paper, affixed overall to thick cardboard
15 x 22 in. (383 x 560 mm)
S gned and dated lower left: PETER BLUME / 1938
Hayden Collection. Charles Henry Hayden Fund.
41.264

Blume submitted *Lilies* to the prestigious Carnegie International Exhibition for 1938.[1] Three years later, when the Museum of Fine Arts acquired the painting, the artist wrote:

> The "lilies" is one of three gouaches I did in recent years immediately following the long vigil over "The Eternal City." I have always been pleased with the "Lilies" the way one is when something occasionally

issues forth painlessly. It represents in a general way the view from my studio window looking towards the Sherman (my town) church, in the early spring. A color reproduction of the painting hangs within the church itself. The townsfolk like it.[2]

Peter Blume always loved flowers and he and his wife maintained gardens at their home in rural Connecticut. Throughout his career he made keenly observed, botanically accurate pencil studies of plants and he often included a vase of blossoms or a colorful field of flowers in his complex allegorical paintings.

In its precise drawing, clearly articulated forms, and meticulous execution *Lilies* recalls works by Flemish and Italian artists of the fifteenth century. The floral still life is a detail that often appears in Flemish paintings, whereas the thoughtful composition recalls the clarity and order of Piero della Francesca. The matte surface and refined handling of pigment is to be found in tempera paintings by Sandro Botticelli. Blume painted the wooden elements of the window frame and sill with no evident signs of brushwork; he drew in the thin branches and blades of grass with the finest of brushes.[3] The cool, restricted palette – a range of subtle grays and yellows – brings to mind the stony hues of paintings by Andrea Mantegna. This relationship is reinforced by the similarity between Blume's crisp sculptural handling of the blossoms and leaves and Mantegna's sharp geometric drapery folds.

Blume's first biographer, Charles Buckley, noted that Blume's "way as a painter was through a precisely calculated relationship of fragments of reality and memory,"[4] and most of his works of the late 1920s and 1930s are based on surprising, often troubling, combinations of objects drawn from Blume's experiences and his imagination. In contrast, *Lilies* seems quite plausible on the surface; it depicts a vase of flowers on a window sill, with a grassy field and New England church beyond. But it is tempting to read more into this apparently simple image. Its stylistic connections with old master paintings (and their religious subjects), as well as the fact that literary content is generally present in Blume's paintings, suggest hidden meaning. The choice of a species of lily associated both with the Virgin and with Easter,

in combination with a church tower, allude to a subtle religious content in this image.

SWR

1. He may have chosen this non-controversial image in reaction to the poor reception of *The Eternal City*, when first exhibited in New York in 1937. See Frank Anderson Trapp, *Peter Blume* (New York: Rizzoli, 1987), p. 65.

2. Blume to W. G. Constable, curator of paintings, Museum of Fine Arts, Boston, headed "Gaylordsville, Connecticut 16 May 1941." Curatorial files, Department of Prints, Drawings, and Photographs. A related gouache is *Sherman Church* (1937, collection of Arthur Peck).

3. Blume's letter cited in note 2 contains a passage on the technique: "My method of painting the picture is I believe 'straight' gouache. The pigment is for the most part mixed with white (titanium) and applied opaquely with thin glazes of pure color here and there." Blume handled gouache (opaque watercolor) as if it were tempera; in the late thirties and early forties magic realists and realists, including Andrew Wyeth (see cats. 126, 127), were reviving true egg tempera.

4. Charles Buckley, *Paintings and Drawings, Peter Blume in Retrospect, 1925-1964* (Manchester, New Hampshire: The Currier Gallery of Art), p.130.

Milton Avery

Born Sand Bank (later Altmar), New York, 1885;
died New York City, 1965

Watercolor played a liberating role in Milton Avery's art. He used it almost annually for scenes painted on holidays, and regarded it as a relaxing, playful medium. Avery's watercolors tended to be more experimental in theme than his oils from the same period, and they often became the bases for canvases painted at a later date in the studio. The thin pigments and loose brushwork of the watercolors also affected his handling of oil pigments. Avery's first independent watercolors (1927-28) were figural: a lively series, loosely executed, depicting beach goers and vaudeville performers, painted unconventionally with pale, opaque pigments on dark construction paper. At about the same time he began to make views of sea and land during summers he spent in New England throughout the 1930s and he continued this practice later on trips to places farther away.

Milton Clark Avery was born into a working-class family (his father was a tanner) that moved to the area of East Hartford, Connecticut, in 1898. He went to work in 1901 at the age of sixteen, and for more than twenty years held factory and clerical jobs, taking art classes in his free time at the Connecticut League of Art Students, Hartford, and the School of the Art Society of Hartford. His figure drawings demonstrate a thorough grounding in academic practice. His *plein-air* landscape paintings from the early 1920s show the heavy impasto of Ernest Lawson and the pastel colors of John Henry Twachtman, both of whom were active in Connecticut in the 1890s.

In the early twenties Avery painted for several summer vacations in Gloucester, Massachusetts, where he met Sally Michel, a young painter. In 1926 they married and settled in New York City. Sally Avery worked as a freelance illustrator and made it possible for Avery to paint full time. He was exposed to a wide range of painting styles in the city, and his work soon came to incorporate a well-integrated understanding of Picasso's figural distortions and above all, Matisse's saturated color. Winters were spent in his urban studio, making oils of friends and family or genre figure subjects; summers were spent in the country, painting watercolors out-of-doors. Avery's watercolors were regularly featured by his various dealers, beginning with a one-man show at the Frank K.M.

Rehn Gallery in 1928. He won a prize for a watercolor, *White Horse*, exhibited in Chicago in 1930. The Phillips Collection, which was the first museum to acquire one of Avery's oils in 1929, also gave the artist his first one-man watercolor exhibition in 1944. After the war the Averys traveled more extensively and held several residencies at artists' colonies. Avery was also a printmaker and made many drypoints, woodcuts, and monotypes.

By the 1940s Avery had completely broken with academic practices, but his art never became non-representational as did that of his good friends Adolf Gottlieb, Barnett Newman, and Mark Rothko, and his shapes, though simplified and flattened, always remained linked to natural forms.

Milton Avery
118. *River in the Hills*, 1940
Watercolor on thick, rough, cream wove paper; watermark: HAND MADE J WHATMAN 1934 ENGLAND
30¾ x 22¼ in. (782 x 565 mm)
Signed lower right in graphite: Milton Avery
On verso: unfinished version of same subject; inscribed in green marker (in Avery's hand): "River in the Hills" / by Milton Avery / wc. / 22 x 30 / circa / 1941. Image and inscription crossed out in black crayon.
Hayden Collection. Charles Henry Hayden Fund.
1971.147

Between 1935 and 1940 Avery, his wife Sally, and their daughter March (born in 1932) spent five summers in southern Vermont. During these holidays Avery painted numerous watercolors of the renowned green and hilly terrain. These works, which are apparently casual, were important to the artist's development. *River in the Hills* was painted during the last visit to Rawsonville near the Green Mountains, on a tributary of the West River. It is consistent in its stylistic vocabulary with a watercolor probably painted in 1935, *Spring in Vermont* (collection of Sally M. Avery).[1]

Barbara Haskell relates an amusing and revealing story about that first Vermont summer:

> It rained continuously for the first three weeks; when it stopped, everything was the same brilliant green. Avery hated it and wanted to leave because he felt it impossible to paint a landscape that had so little color variation. Fortunately, a few sunny days and shoots of new vegetation sufficed to change his mind and Vermont eventually became an important source of fresh imagery. Perhaps the necessity of confronting each day a landscape dominated by one color furthered Avery's sense of the subtlety and power of a single hue.[2]

The chalky coloration and gray sky of *River in the Hills* imply that it was painted on a drizzly day. Avery swiftly set down a landscape consisting of a row of trees that partly screens the bend of a mountain stream flowing between two conical hills. These elements are subtly deployed across the sheet in a limited number of hues – grayed-down blues, greens, and browns, and a touch of black. The bold formal patterns reinforce the integrity and flatness of the paper surface. In each part of the composition the paint was applied

Arthur G. Dove

Born Canandaigua, New York, 1880;
died Huntington, New York, 1946

differently. For example, a rhythmic pattern of brushstrokes suggests the character of the trees: upthrusting diagonals for the foliage at the right, horizontal zigzags for the evergreen. In spite of the generalized, two-dimensional shapes, Avery managed to suggest atmospheric distance through subtle variations in the color and density of the paint, the visible overlays of strokes, and the white of the paper that emerges here and there.[3]

SWR

1. An oil painting of similar theme and date is *Pink Field* (1935, collection of Lady Kleinwort).

2. Barbara Haskell, *Milton Avery* (New York: Whitney Museum of American Art, 1982), p. 60.

3. For a different and more illusionistic treatment of space see Edward Hopper's virtually contemporaneous view of a similar site in Vermont, cat. 114.

Around 1910 Arthur G. Dove began to paint in an abstract, non-illusionistic style, basing his organic designs on the natural or industrial landscape. He worked in this style quite consistently for most of his career. He was the first American artist to exhibit abstract work publicly, at Alfred Stieglitz's gallery in 1912. Stieglitz remained Dove's representative for the rest of his life, showing him in association with such other American modernists as Georgia O'Keeffe, Marsden Hartley, Charles Demuth (see cats. 96-101), and John Marin (see cats. 92-94). Dove was always comfortable working on paper; his first career, and one he returned to periodically, was magazine illustration. Beginning about 1930 he often made preparatory studies in watercolor for his oil paintings; he also sent watercolors to the gallery for sale as independent works of art, although they seldom appeared in exhibition listings. Late in life, Dove worked more frequently in the smaller scale of watercolor. After his death Edith Halpert of the Downtown Gallery promoted Dove's watercolors by featuring them in exhibitions in 1949 and 1954.

Dove was raised in Geneva, New York, the son of a building contractor and property owner. He graduated in 1903 from Cornell University, where he took many art courses, and immediately moved to New York City. There he made a good living as an illustrator for high quality, popular magazines. Dove spent a year in France (1908-09), where at first he painted rural landscapes in an impressionist style. He was befriended by Alfred Maurer, an artist who showed at Stieglitz's 291, and who probably introduced him to avant-garde art.

Soon Dove was painting bold still lifes in the colorful Fauve manner, one of which, *The Lobster* (1908, Amon Carter Museum, Fort Worth, Texas), was shown at the Paris 1909 Salon d'Automne and in New York at a 1910 group exhibition at 291. Dove subsequently gave up illustration, moved his wife and son to Westport, Connecticut, and devoted himself to painting. His first one-man show with Stieglitz (1912) presented ten abstract pastels; most critics were at a loss to explain them. Although Dove did not exhibit at the 1913 Armory Show, he did submit sixteen paintings to the Anderson Galleries' 1916 Forum Exhibition of Modern American Painters, and to

other early exhibitions that included American modernists. Dove's abstractions appealed to a very limited number of collectors; primary among these was Duncan Phillips, whose monthly stipend was often Dove's only source of income.

More than once during the First World War and the Depression Dove returned to illustration or resorted to farming for a living. From 1924 to 1933 Dove and artist Helen Torr (later his second wife) lived on a modest sailboat – sometimes their only studio space – moored near Huntington, Long Island. From 1938 until his death, his combined studio and dwelling was a small former post office overlooking a pond in nearby Centerport.

Arthur Dove
119. *Untitled*, 1942-1944
Transparent and opaque watercolor and black ink on very thick, rough, cream wove paper
3 x 4 in. (76 x 102 mm)
Gift of Mr. and Mrs. William C. Dove. 1988.180

120. *Untitled*, 1942-1944
Opaque watercolor on very thick, rough, cream wove paper
3 x 4 in. (76 x 102 mm)
Inscribed on verso: 331 (pen and black ink); 14 (in graphite)
Gift of Mr. and Mrs. William C. Dove. 1988.181

121. *Untitled*, 1942-1944
Transparent and opaque watercolor on thin, smooth, cream wove cardboard
2 15/16 x 3 7/8 in. (75 x 100 mm)
Inscribed on verso: 333 (in pen and black ink); 25 (in graphite)
Gift of Mr. and Mrs. William C. Dove. 1988.192

122. *Untitled*, 1943
Opaque watercolor on very thick, rough, cream wove paper
2 15/16 x 4 in. (75 x 102 mm)
Dated on verso in graphite: 6-14-43 and undecipherable notes
Gift of Mr. and Mrs. William C. Dove. 1988.193

These four diverse compositions by Arthur Dove are representative of the thirty-five small works given to the Museum in 1988 by his son, William Dove. Dove made hundreds of such miniature studies on paper in the early 1940s when poor health frequently confined him to his home in Centerport, Long Island. In some of them he used oil paint, in others he experimented with tempera and wax emulsion;[1] often he used transparent and opaque watercolors sometimes combined with pen and ink. In these small studies the artist worked in much the same way he did when painting in a larger scale on canvas. The colors were restricted and carefully related. He paid close attention to paint application, brushing on the pigments either thickly or thinly, and leaving the marks of the brush to enliven the surface. William Dove has explained that the studies were projected and enlarged to help the artist decide if he wanted to paint them full-sized on canvas:

> There must have been three or four hundred of these sketches all done within the period of 1942-44, or thereabouts. Many of them are dated. Sometimes he'd do more than two in the same day. Sometimes they are very particular things. Some of them very obviously exploring the medium. . . . They are visually something worth looking at; it's amazing how complete he made them. Of course, there are many of them that he made into paintings that look exactly like them. Sometimes the large paintings varied a bit; he had evidently changed his viewpoint by the time he got to paint. The small studies are all about 3 x 4"; that was the size that fitted the magic lantern.[2]

Only one of the Museum's group is known to have been expanded in this way. Its composition of mountainous shapes closely replicated in *Runaway* (1946, collection of Harold Giese).

The four watercolors included here are retrospective and relate in general style and referential subject matter to completed oil paintings of the late twenties and thirties, rather than the non-representational paintings of the forties. A richly brushed composition (cat. 122), recalls the industrial architecture that recurs in Dove's works, such as in *Tanks* (1938, Museum of Fine Arts, Boston). Rhythmic, repeated blue shapes (cat. 119) suggest sailboat races, a common sight on Long Island

Sound, and recall works such as *Clouds and Water* (1930, The Metropolitan Museum of Art, New York). Dove outlined contours in this watercolor as he had done in that painting and in other works from the thirties. More difficult to pin down are the pyramidal elements of cat. 120, although the foreground shapes suggest a landscape, and a like bilateral symmetry is found in *The Moon* (1941, Regis Collection, Minneapolis, Minnesota). Here, the use of bright turquoise and the way the pigments were dragged over the rough paper, leaving white "holidays," point in the direction of John Marin's southwestern watercolors, such as *New Mexico* (cat. 94). Another image (cat. 121) seems to relate to Dove paintings of the sun or moon over the water such as *Harbor in Light* (1929, private collection). It demonstrates Dove's totally different handling of the medium – painting quite wet on a very smooth paper. The look of wetness remains in the record of the brushstroke, and in the pooling and bleeding of the paints. This image recalls Georgia O'Keeffe's broadly brushed, economically stated landscape watercolors dating from the teens. Dove admired the work of both Marin and O'Keeffe, who were also part of Stieglitz's group of artists.

Each of these tiny but fully expressed works reveals Dove's rich imagination, and underscores his resourcefulness at producing new images. Like Emil Nolde, who was prevented from working on a large scale during the Second World War and so turned to watercolor, Dove also created a multitude of "unpainted pictures," among them these small gems.[3]

SWR

1. Many of the studies at the Pennsylvania Academy of the Fine Arts were executed using a waxy binder. For Dove's experiments with materials during this period see Anne Cohen DePietro, "Beyond Abstraction, The Late Work of Arthur Dove," in Anne Cohen DePietro et al., *Arthur Dove & Helen Torr: The Huntington Years* (Huntington, New York: The Heckscher Museum, 1989), p. 46.

2. Quoted in Anne Cohen DePietro, "A Form Finding a Form, An Interview with William C. Dove," in ibid., p. 78. The practice was not entirely new to the artist; since the early thirties he had been using watercolors or

drawings as models for oil paintings, and employed a pantograph to enlarge and transfer the design to canvas. See Ann Lee Morgan, *Arthur Dove, Life and Work, With a Catalogue Raisonné* (Newark, Delaware: University of Delaware Press, 1984), p. 54.

3. Nolde was forbidden by the Nazi government to paint in what it considered his "degenerate" style. Although he lived in a remote part of Germany, between 1938 and 1945 he worked almost exclusively in watercolor, whose materials were easier to hide.

119

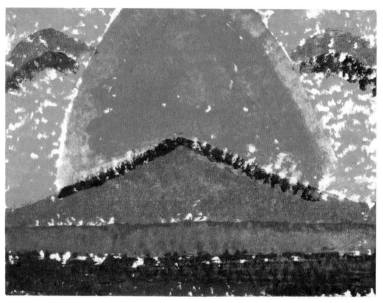

120

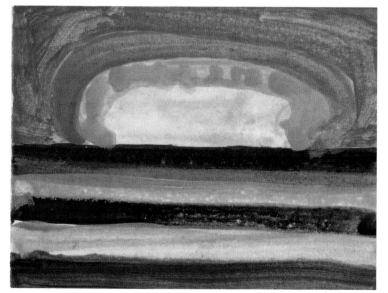

121

122

James Fitzgerald

Born Boston, Massachusetts, 1899;
died Aranmore Island, Ireland, 1971

James Fitzgerald's finest paintings interpret the sea and mountains in a bold, simplified style. He worked mainly in watercolor, and exhibited extensively in the medium between 1930 and 1947. The adventurous artist went to sea, fished, and panned for gold; he also acted, played the violin, and studied philosophy.

Born into a large Boston Irish family, Fitzgerald was encouraged by his mother to draw. After completing high school and serving with the U.S. Marines during the First World War, he attended the Massachusetts School of Art where he studied painting with Ernest Major, graduating in 1923. He spent the following year at the School of the Museum of Fine Arts, where Philip Hale taught drawing. Fitzgerald received a traditional Boston art education, one that emphasized academic drawing and a high degree of finish. He had a lifelong love of the sea and between 1925 and 1928 he painted in Boston and Rockport, Massachusetts, and Monhegan, Maine. In 1928 he worked his way on a ship to the West Coast, settling on the Monterey Peninsula, where he built a home and studio in 1930. There he associated with such local artists as Paul Dougherty and with the group of men linked to "Cannery Row," immortalized by John Steinbeck (whose portrait Fitzgerald drew).

Between 1930 and 1942 Fitzgerald exhibited watercolors regularly with the California Water Color Society in Los Angeles and the Santa Cruz Art League, and was represented by commercial galleries in Monterey and Los Angeles. He also sent watercolors to exhibitions in Brooklyn, New York, and London. He painted a mural under the WPA 1936-37. An interest in eastern philosophy and calligraphy led him to draw with old Chinese ink, a practice that he kept up throughout his life, making multiple, large, broadly brushed studies for his watercolors and oils.

In 1943 Fitzgerald moved to Monhegan Island. He was occasionally shown in New England museum exhibitions and was represented by commercial galleries in New York and Boston until 1954; the last exhibition to which he submitted work was that of the Boston Society of Watercolor Painters in 1947. He spent summers on Monhegan Island, where he bought Rockwell Kent's former studio in 1952, sometimes selling paintings there. For a number of years Fitzgerald spent part of the autumn painting Mount Katahdin and vicinity, and worked as a gilder in New York during the winter to earn money. Toward the end of his life he was captivated by the rugged islands off the west coast of Ireland, which he visited several times between 1965 and his death in 1971.

James Fitzgerald
123. *Home by Moonlight*, probably mid-1940s
Transparent and opaque watercolor over graphite on moderately thick, rough, white wove paper
20 x 25 1/4 in. (507 x 640 mm)
Signed lower right in pen and black ink: James Fitzgerald
Gift of Mr. and Mrs. Edgar Hubert. 1982.368

Home by Moonlight represents a farmer returning at night from plowing his fields with a team of oxen. Fitzgerald repeatedly painted and drew scenes of plowing, and is said to have enjoyed watching the plow horses as a child at his grandparents' farm in Milton, Massachusetts.[1] This scene is thought to have been painted in Vermont, which Fitzgerald visited in the thirties; he also painted there during the winter of 1944 and perhaps again later in the forties.[2] Like most of his works, this watercolor is undated; however it is less conventional and more modern than his California work from the 1930s, which still exhibits Fitzgerald's traditional Boston training. *Home by Moonlight* is also cooler in its palette than the golden-toned western works. With its arbitrarily flattened forms, recognizable but simplified, it seems to belong to the 1940s, and can be likened to works from that period by Milton Avery (see cat. 118).

Painted in broad areas of limited color, the black silhouettes of farmer and mountains (varied somewhat by dripping paint that implies surface texture) and the gray oxen and earth are relieved somewhat by the blue sky, white clouds, and yellow moon. The forms appear to be bleached of color by the moon's cool light, which casts strong shadows. The simple, powerful forms of the design and the strong surface patterns remain vigorous and vital without becoming decorative.

SWR

1. Calvin Hennig, *James Fitzgerald* (Rockland, Maine: William A. Farnsworth Library and Art Museum, 1984), p. 15.

2. The pamphlet for the 1945 Vose Galleries, Boston, exhibition of Fitzgerald's work states that the artist had painted in Jamaica, Vermont, during the past winter.

Jacob Lawrence

Born Atlantic City, New Jersey, 1917

James Fitzgerald

124. *Waterfall, Baxter State Park, Maine*, probably
1950s

Watercolor over graphite on very thick, rough, white
wove paper
30½ x 22½ in. (778 x 563 mm)
Inscribed lower right in graphite: AB; on verso: 595 /
Waterfall V
Gift of Edgar and Anne Hubert. 1991.406

The large scale, bold brushstrokes, and massive
forms of this image demonstrate the power of
Fitzgerald's watercolors. *Waterfall* was probably
created at his studio on Monhegan Island, Maine,
during the years when he was regularly visiting
Baxter State Park to paint Mount Katahdin.
Fitzgerald's forceful execution matches the forces
of nature depicted: the waterfall crashing continu-
ously on enormous, rounded boulders and the
upward thrust of the pointed firs. The gestural
qualities recall not only Asian calligraphy but also
Abstract Expressionism and thus place this picture squarely in the mainstream of American art
of the 1950s. Despite his apparent isolation on
Monhegan, Fitzgerald worked during the winters
in New York City, and kept abreast of artistic
developments there.

The artist tended to prepare his paintings by
making full compositional drawings on large
sheets of paper, using charcoal, chalk, or brush
and Chinese ink. Here he worked out the composition in two preliminary watercolors. Neither *Waterfall* nor the studies are dated, but a sequence of
execution can be proposed.[1] The first study (collection of Anne and Edgar Hubert) is virtually the
same size, but it is relatively naturalistic and it is
rendered with more depth, cooler colors, and more
drawing. The second (private collection) is a
smaller, sketchier study closer to the final version
in which Fitzgerald introduced the autumnal,
rusty red into the trees, flattened out the upper
part of the waterfall, and defined the elements of
the composition with rapid, wet brushstrokes
rather than with the drawn line.

This third version of *Waterfall* is less about
three-dimensional mass than about rhythmic flat
shapes. Heavy black strokes outline the restrained
neutral colors that are accented by strong blue,

green, and rust. The intensity and sheen of some
of the black brushstrokes suggest that they may
have been executed in Chinese ink. In his culminating gestures, Fitzgerald scraped into the wet
pigments with broad tipped instruments (one of
which may have been a bamboo pen) to define the
slender trunks of the birches and the streaks of
light in the rushing water.

SWR

1. Anne Hubert has suggested the chronology of the
three versions. She and her husband, Edgar Hubert, are
the executors of Fitzgerald's artistic estate, and have
had an unparalleled opportunity to study the many related works it contains. A number of other studies and
finished works were included in the Portland (Maine)
Museum of Art's 1992 exhibition, "By Land and Sea:
The Quest of James Fitzgerald."

Like Ben Shahn and José Clemente Orozco (whom
he especially admires), Lawrence combines a commitment to historical themes and topics of social
concern with equally telling subjects drawn from
his own experience. His best-known works were
produced in series, and honor a major figure, such
as Toussaint L'Ouverture, Harriet Tubman, or
Frederick Douglass or, as in the John Brown
Series, document important episodes in African-
American history. He has also dedicated major
narrative cycles to themes of the present and
recent past such as the Migration of the Negro
(1940-41), the Hospital Series (drawn from his
own brief stay in a psychiatic hospital in 1950) and
the Harlem Series of the early forties, reflecting
daily life in his working-class neighborhood.
Lawrence paints almost exclusively in tempera,
casein, and gouache. Although his works are modest in scale, their intense color, sharp contrasts,
and energetic stylization make their social message all the more powerful.

Lawrence spent his childhood in Easton and
Philadelphia and moved with his family to New
York at the age of thirteen. His first mentor was
the painter Charles Alston, who taught Lawrence
at the Harlem Art Workshop in the early thirties.
Within a few years Lawrence's talent was recognized and he began to win art school scholarships,
prizes, and fellowships. In 1938, he had his first solo
show, at the Harlem YMCA; in 1939 his Toussaint
L'Ouverture series was exhibited at the Baltimore
Museum, and in 1941 (the year of his marriage to
the painter Gwendolyn Knight), Edith Halpert, the
director of the prestigious Downtown Gallery, gave
him a show and added him to her roster of artists.

Throughout the 1940s (and despite service in
the Coast Guard during World War II), Lawrence
was extremely productive as a painter. His work
was included in major group shows, among them
the Metropolitan Museum of Art's "Artists for
Victory" exhibition in 1942, and the Art Institute
of Chicago's annual watercolor exhibition in 1948.
Since the 1940s, Lawrence has also been active as
a teacher, having served on the faculty or as artist
in residence at Black Mountain College and Pratt
Institute, among others. In 1970, he joined the
faculty of the University of Washington in Seattle,
where he now resides.

Jacob Lawrence
125. *Café Comedian*, 1957
Opaque watercolor (probably casein) over graphite on moderately thick, cream wove paper
23 x 29 in. (584 x 737 mm)
Signed lower right in black wash: Jacob Lawrence 1957
Gift of Mr. and Mrs. William H. Lane and Museum Purchase. 1990.378

In the 1950s, Lawrence returned to some of his celebrated subjects of the early 1940s, but in a more complex and decorative style. *Café Comedian* is a recapitulation of some of the more ebullient images from the Harlem Series of 1942-43, and indicates his continuing interest in urban nightlife.[1] It is, in Lawrence's words, "one of my many impressions of growing up in New York's Harlem community and visiting the many bars, pool halls, night clubs and the great Apollo Theatre – a vaudeville house in Harlem. It is a theme as I saw it of life in Harlem – tenements, workers, store front churches, produce stalls and people at work and play among other subjects. It was a great community. . . colorful, exciting, energetic and creative."[2] Lawrence was no longer living in Harlem when he painted this picture, and the interior of this nightclub, with its odd wall decorations, its flattened spaces, and its jumpy irregularities of scale, has a fantastic quality that makes it seem like a memory. At the same time, *Café Comedian* has a contemporary look: the costumes of the patrons, the strident colors of the decor, and the jazz quartet itself reflect the styles and tastes of the 1950s.

Lawrence painted *Café Comedian* in casein, his preferred material in those years. Casein is an old-fashioned, milk-based medium, one that provides the matte finish of gouache or tempera, but has the additional virtue of insolubility.[3] Lawrence was clearly drawn to its flat, chalky surface and its capacity for textural variety. In some passages – such as the black and white area under the bar – he thinned it down and layered it like gouache; in others – such as the costumes of the figures – he took advantage of its opacity; and in still others – for example, the dark wooden counter and the reflections on it – he manipulated it like oil to yield a brushy surface. Lawrence's use of visual puns is

equally deft. Details like the tumblers on the bar with their disappearing contours, or the drumstick that dissolves into the wall pattern behind, or the gestures of the musicians that echo the thrusts and curves of their instruments, were inspired by both the witty vocabulary of cubism and the syncopated energy of jazz. But these playful aspects are counterposed by the automaton-like stance of the comedian and the dolorous expressions and weary postures of the patrons, especially the men.

Café Comedian was included in the Whitney Annual of 1958, marking the artist's first appearance in that forum in some years. William Lane purchased it shortly thereafter and it was shown extensively in the 1960s and seventies in William H. Lane Foundation exhibitions.[4] It was acquired by the Museum of Fine Arts in 1990.

CT

1. See, for example, *And Harlem Society looks on* (1942-43, Portland [Oregon] Art Museum) from the Harlem Series, and for a later exploration of the theme, *Village Quartet* (1954, private collection).

2. Jacob Lawrence to author, May 28, 1992.

3. Ralph Mayer, *A Dictionary of Art Terms and Techniques* (New York: Thomas Y. Crowell, 1969), pp. 65-66.

4. For a complete exhibition history, see Theodore E. Stebbins, Jr., and Carol Troyen, *The Lane Collection, 20th-Century Paintings in the American Tradition* (Boston: Museum of Fine Arts, 1983), p. 175.

Andrew Wyeth has produced a limited number of paintings in the demanding medium of egg tempera, but the majority of his finished works over the past fifty years have been watercolors. At the age of twenty his talents were publicly recognized when his first one-man exhibition of watercolors sold out. It was held at the Macbeth Gallery in New York, an important center for American realist art, where The Eight had first exhibited and where interest in Martin Johnson Heade and Fitz Hugh Lane would shortly be revived. Wyeth's watercolors were predominantly images of the Maine seacoast, painted in a wet, loose manner, which he continued to employ into the early 1940s.

Wyeth soon made a conscious effort to tighten up his style, disciplining himself by drawing rigorously from the human figure as well as from manmade and natural objects. He also turned to tempera, a medium that permits great control in the delineation of forms. In the early 1950s Wyeth began to employ a different watercolor technique, which he termed drybrush. This involved the use of passages of drier pigments over underlying washes and permitted a combination of precision and suggestion that has marked all his subsequent work. Wyeth's realistic style and narrative content has enormous popular appeal, and has influenced several generations of younger artists (including his son Jamie) to use watercolor and to work in a similar fashion.

The youngest of five children and frail, Wyeth received his art instruction at home under the sensitive tutelage of his father, the famous illustrator N.C. Wyeth. As a boy Wyeth was encouraged to draw on his own, which he did with lively abandon and innate skill, and only gradually did his father introduce him to the disciplines of academic drawing – at first still-lifes and later casts and live models. Wyeth also learned by studying works of art. Winslow Homer's watercolors were particularly important, for their technique and for their realistic, yet evocative images, often depicting the Maine coast that Wyeth also painted. After the initial success of his 1937 watercolor show in New York, Wyeth was included in a prominent exhibition held at the Museum of Modern Art in 1943, *American Realists and Magic Realists*.

Throughout his career Wyeth has worked at

home, depicting the lands, possessions, and faces of neighbors and family. He spends winters in rural Chadds Ford, Pennsylvania, and summers in Cushing, on the coast of Maine. Intimately involved with his subjects, Wyeth can endow an inanimate object as well as a person with emotional overtones. The works of Andrew Wyeth – published and reproduced with frequency – are among the best known and most popular of any living American artist.

Andrew Wyeth
126. *Mr. River's Garden*, 1942
Watercolor over graphite on moderately thick, rough, white wove paper; watermark: cᴬm water colour paper england 1940
17¾ x 29⅝ in. (450 x 752 mm)
Signed lower right in pen and black ink: Andrew Wyeth
Hayden Collection. Charles Henry Hayden Fund. 43.1

Painted in August 1942, *Mr. River's Garden* depicts a neighbor's vegetable garden in the town of Cushing, Maine, located on the St. George's River on Muscongus Bay.[1] Although the owner of the garden is present, it is only his rather anonymous back that is glimpsed behind the screen of vegetables. The clump of half-grown stalks of corn is the centerpiece, drawn and painted with botanical accuracy. The ground level point of view recalls Albrecht Dürer's watercolor, *The Large Piece of Turf* (1503, Albertina, Vienna), a work that Wyeth knew intimately through a fine color reproduction.[2] As with most of Wyeth's paintings, a personal experience lies beneath the subject's universal appeal. Of *Mr. River's Garden* the artist wrote, "The real reason for me painting this picture was the memory of an experience I had as a small boy at my grandfather's home in Needham, Mass. My grandfather always picked his corn early in the morning and I remember so clearly walking behind him with the fresh green leaves of the corn brushing in my face."[3]

Wyeth created *Mr. River's Garden* during a period in which he was deliberately altering his painting style. He wished to temper the dashing washes and spontaneous effects of painting wet on wet that had characterized his watercolors of the thirties – in which he paid homage to the work of Winslow Homer – feeling them to be too messy and flashy.[4] For discipline, he turned to the slow, demanding medium of egg tempera. In his watercolors he began to use fine brushes and drier paints (drybrush), that could achieve the surface texture and matte finish of tempera, as well as maintain some of the dash of Homer. Wyeth continued to use broad watercolor washes for initial studies and as the bases for finished watercolors. *Mr. River's Garden* is a transitional work that re-

tains ties with the earlier watercolors, and yet shows steps in the new stylistic direction.

On a large sheet of relatively rough watercolor paper, the artist began to work in a conventional manner, loosely sketching the composition in graphite and laying in broad washes for the setting. The somewhat drier washes of the brownish fields permit the tiny white concavities of the untouched paper to reveal themselves and suggest the texture of mown hay. Against the pale sky the dark evergreen trees are silhouetted; brisk strokes of a stiff-bristled brush suggest the bundles of sharply pointed needles. In the underdrawing for the corn plants Wyeth made long, curving lines to capture the shape and direction of the leaves waving in the wind. Not all of the lines were incorporated into leaves and painted over, and some pencil lines remain, trailing across the sky. One of the few instances of wet on wet can be seen in the broadest leaf, totally successful in defining the concavity. Wyeth made modest use of scraping to lighten the tip or define the edge of a leaf and to depict the tall grass at the lower right. Narrow brushes delineated blades of grass and hay. These finer, isolated strokes indicate the direction in which Wyeth was moving at the time, culminating in the layers of fine brushstrokes characteristic of the temperas and drybrush watercolors for which he would soon become famous.[5]

The theme of corn or corn shocks appears more than once in Wyeth's oeuvre. Two slightly later paintings, *Winter Corn* (drybrush) and *Seed Corn* (tempera), both dated 1948 (private collections), depict dry, brown stalks and ears of corn, rather than the exuberant, green plants of this Maine farm garden.[6] While it has justifiably been said that Wyeth's art becomes more sober and introspective after the death of his father in 1945, it is dangerous to read too much symbolism into the corn pictures. Nonetheless, it is tempting to suggest that Wyeth was conscious of N.C. Wyeth's many romantic illustrations of the past when he said: "I can think of nothing more exciting than just sitting in a cornfield on a windy day and listening to the dry rustle. And when I walk through rows of blowing corn, I'm reminded of the way a king must have felt walking down the long line of knights on horseback with banners blowing."[7]

SWR

1. The title, "Mr. River's Garden," was first published by Doll & Richards in December 1942 ("Third Exhibition of Water Colors by Andrew Wyeth") and has been maintained in subsequent literature. It may be the fault of a misplaced apostrophe, for the name was more likely to have been "Rivers."

2. N. C. Wyeth gave a set of facsimiles of Dürer's watercolors to Andrew when he was thirteen. See *Two Worlds of Andrew Wyeth: Kuerners and Olsons* (New York: The Metropolitan Museum of Art, 1976), p. 17.

3. Wyeth to W.G. Constable, curator of paintings, Museum of Fine Arts, Boston, January 13, 1943. Curatorial files, Department of Prints, Drawings, and Photographs.

4. Wanda M. Corn, *The Art of Andrew Wyeth* (San Francisco: The Fine Arts Museums of San Francisco, 1973), p. 130.

5. While Wyeth exhibited a tempera, *Winter Field* (1942) in the Museum of Modern Art's 1943 exhibition, "American Realists and Magic Realists," the beginning of his enormous public success can be dated to that museum's purchase in 1949 of *Christina's World* (1948).

6. Both paintings are illustrated in *Andrew Wyeth* (Boston: Museum of Fine Arts, 1970), pp. 62 and 169.

7. Wyeth to an unidentified friend, quoted in Richard Meryman, *Andrew Wyeth* (Boston: Houghton Mifflin Company, 1968), p. 37.

Andrew Wyeth
127. *Memorial Day*, 1946
Watercolor over graphite on moderately thick, rough, white wove paper
14 x 20 in. (356 x 510 mm)
Signed lower left in black ink: Andrew Wyeth
Verso: unfinished watercolor study of barn, windmill, trees, crossed out with broad brushstrokes of dark watercolor
Charles Henry Hayden and Abraham Shuman Funds. 46.1455

The site of this evocative image is an old building near Wyeth's home in Chadds Ford, Pennsylvania. The octagonal stone structure was originally built by the Quakers as a schoolhouse, but its last official use was by a black woman preacher and her congregation, and it was locally referred to as "Mother Archie's Church." The building's unusual shape and state of disrepair appealed to Wyeth who depicted its exterior and interior numerous times.[1] He often included the distinctive, broken chandelier, a remnant of the building's more elegant past. The building still occasionally housed an event. On June 4, 1946, a memorial service was held there for black soldiers who had served in the war. When Wyeth stepped in on the following day he found a faded American flag fastened to the wall for the occasion, and a young black man seated on the long bench. "The mood of it made me do this painting."[2]

The success of *Memorial Day* is largely due to its understatement. In the words of the poet David McCord on Wyeth, "I come again and again to the tentative washes. They rightly omit so much."[3] This watercolor shows Wyeth well on his way to the reductive style that marks his later watercolors and drawings. Over a very sketchy graphite drawing, he washed in the somber greenish-gray walls and ceiling, drawing their cracks with a fine pointed brush. Some washes, for example, those below the flag, are wet and pooled, but more often a drier brush was dragged across the paper, suggesting the texture of rough plaster. The artist let the flow of paint take over the descriptive function, and then used small touches to correct or strengthen the forms. These can be brushstrokes (on the vertical beam at right, and elsewhere) or scraped highlights (on the side of the boy's face and shoulder, on the uprights of chair and bench). A few accents of color enhance the almost monochromatic image: deep red tints the boy's shirt, the flag, chair, and bench; wetly painted greens with scratched highlights suggest the dense summer foliage outside the window. The bright outdoor light is reflected on the uppermost part of the window embrasure. This is essentially the only part of the sheet where the white paper is left untouched, an indication of the artist's mastery of light.

SWR

1. A large painting of the interior is *Mother Archie's Church* (tempera, 1945, Addison Gallery of Art, Andover, Massachusetts). A nocturnal, exterior view of the building is *Night Lamp* (tempera, 1950, private collection), and another view is *The Corner* (dry brush, 1953, Wilmington [Delaware] Society of the Fine Arts). *Tillie Taggert* (watercolor, 1948, Museum of Fine Arts, Boston) was also painted in the building..

2. Wyeth to W. G. Constable, curator of paintings, Museum of Fine Arts, Boston, December 28, 1946, explaining the circumstances of the picture's creation. Curatorial files, Department of Prints, Drawings, and Photographs.

3. *Andrew Wyeth* (Boston: Museum of Fine Arts, 1970), p. 25.

INDEX OF ARTISTS